C.   D.

E.   F.

irginis nunc Meſkita. D.Colles viniferi. E.Baſsa Budenſis.
acinus perpetrandum paratum: Dellij vulgo appellantur:
lege plura in deſcriptionibus Turcicis Ioannis Lewenclauij.
us Anno 1 6 1 7.

PUBLICATIONS
OF THE
MILMAN PARRY COLLECTION

GENERAL EDITOR

ALBERT B. LORD

MANAGING EDITOR

DAVID E. BYNUM

TEXTS AND TRANSLATION SERIES
Number One

Avdo Međedović at Bijelo Polje in 1935

Serbo-Croatian Heroic Songs

Collected by Milman Parry

VOLUME THREE

The Wedding of Smailagić Meho
Avdo Međedović

Translated with introduction,
notes, and commentary
by Albert B. Lord

With a translation
of conversations concerning
The Singer's Life and Times
by David E. Bynum

Harvard University Press
Cambridge, Massachusetts   1974

TO AVDO THE SINGER

Acknowledgments

The translation of Avdo Međedović's "Smailagić Meho" was begun many years ago by Milman Parry. The few pages which he was able to do before his death have been utilized in the present translation. Avdo is not easy to translate. There are not a few obscure passages as well as what in ancient Greek one would have labeled as *hapax legomena.* I sought long for the solution of such difficult passages. I fear that some of them still remain, and I have signalled them in the notes. Publication could not be delayed any longer.

In other respects too Avdo's song has presented special problems. Its unusual length is due in part, but not—I must stress—by any means entirely, to the singer's development of two main catalogues. The list of letters written by the pasha inviting the leaders of Bosnia to Meho's wedding and the description of the contingents as they arrive at the place of assembly have been printed in smaller type than the rest of the translation. In this way we have tried to show dramatically the fullness of these parts of the song. The reader is urged, however, not to slight them. because they contain vital information about some of the leaders and the roles they will play in the ensuing action of the tale.

A number of friends have helped with various aspects of this book and to them across the years and time I give my warmest thanks. Miloš Velimirović was with me in the field in Yugoslavia in 1950 and 1951 and assisted in recording the newer texts from Avdo. Later, when he was at Harvard, he transcribed those texts from the wires, together with other texts collected in those years. I benefited greatly from his help with the initial and early stages of the text and hereby express my deepest appreciation.

There were long stretches of the manuscript which the late Milenko S. Filipović generously read and on which he made many valuable suggestions about translation and interpretation. I shall always be grateful for his friendship and help. I owe much also to David E. Bynum's expert knowledge of the text and of South Slavic epic. He assisted me in a number of thorny passages. I am especially appreciative of the care that he has taken in planning, designing, and managing this volume, as Curator of the Parry Collection and Managing Editor of its publications.

No one has read this translation and all related materials in more drafts than my wife, Mary Louise Carlson Lord, whose diligence in correcting and polishing and whose tact in encouraging me to persevere are responsible for the fact that the work was finally completed in publishable form. It is impossible for me to express adequately in words the depth of my gratitude to her.

Albert B. Lord

The publication of this volume was financed entirely with gifts and grants given to the Milman Parry Collection for this purpose by the American Council of Learned Societies, the American Academy of Arts and Sciences, and Harvard's own Friends of Oral Literature.

Mr. James R. Cherry (Harvard Class of 1927), a distinguished and understanding Friend, made the first personal gift establishing the fund for this volume. The American Council of Learned Societies, which earlier gave the principal support to Parry's expedition of 1934–35, now gave its help again to publishing some results of that expedition. Finally, a nonrecurring source available to the American Academy of Arts and Sciences enabled it to complete the fund, together with Professor Samuel P. Bayard (A.M. Harvard, 1936) and Mrs. Mary Bayard, who have long been faithful and kind Friends of both Oral Literature and the present editors.

The editors also thankfully acknowledge their debt to Mr. Frederick Burkhardt, President of the ACLS, and to Mr. John Voss, Executive Officer of the American Academy of Arts and Sciences, for their swift and skillful help in this project.

Cambridge, Massachusetts   Albert B. Lord
June 1974   David E. Bynum

Contents

ILLUSTRATIONS

A Note
ON SERBO-CROATIAN NAMES
AND PRONUNCIATION

Whether Moslem or Christian, Serbo-Croatian personal names commonly consist of a family name, often a patronymic ending in -ić, and a given name. The family name is called *prezime*, or "forename," because it is frequently given first, followed by the *ime*, or "(given) name."

Two-syllable familiar or appellative forms of given names are very common. Thus the hero Mehmed is often called Meho, the heroine Fatima is often Fata, and Hasan is Haso; Ibrahim, Ibro; Sulejman, Suljo.

A few ostensibly "family" names are epithetical rather than patronymic, especially those ending in *-ja* or *-ica* or the vocatives thereof: *-je*, *-jo*; *-ice*, *-ico*. The names Trhlje and Hrnjica are examples. But such family or clan names may also function as given names or familiar appellatives; thus Hrnjica is understood to be Hrnjica Mujo unless it is explicitly combined with some other given name, e.g., Hrnjica Halil, who is Hrnjica Mujo's brother. Similarly, Grdan is Grdan Osmanaga unless it is explicitly predicated on some other given name, e.g., Grdan Omeraga.

The English reader must also understand the use of Turkish titles with personal names. Titles may either precede names or be suffixed to them. "Aga" (= *agha*) and "bey" (= *beg*) are usually suffixed and may in this position alter the form of the name itself, e.g., Smail, Smailaga; Mustafa, but Mustajbeg. "Pasha" (= *paša*) also usually follows a given name, but we treat it as a separate word, e.g., Ibrahim Pasha or Hasan Pasha Tiro. Since a vizier is normally a pasha (which is like saying that a field marshal is normally a general), the title *vizier* is not used with the name, but is usually accompanied by an adjective indicating the seat of his vizierate (*budimski vezir* = the Vizier of [or in] Buda; *travnički vezir* = the Vizier of Travnik; *bosanski vezir* = the Vizier of Bosnia). Vizier is an administrative title, whereas pasha is a military rank.

A few personal names, proper nouns, and numerous place-names have two forms, one "correct" and the other as found in actual usage. Thus Smail is sometimes Smajil, gusle is sometimes gusli, Osijek is Osjek or even Otsjek, and Nikšić is consistently Ni'šic. The Hungarian city Buda (the western half of Budapest) is regularly Budim in Serbo-Croatian; Mohács is Muhač, and the Turkish metropolis Istanbul is Stambol. Similarly, Kanidža is Kaniža, Sjenica is Senica, and the Macedonian town Skopje is Skoplje in Serbo-Croatian.

The accent in Serbo-Croatian names is never on the last syllable. It usually occurs on the antepenultimate syllable of words of three syllables or more, except that the case-ending does not count; thus, Králjević, Králjevića; Jovánović, Jovánovića; Međédović, Međédovića.

The five vowels of Serbo-Croatian are given a "continental" pronunciation. The consonants are generally pronounced as in English with the following exceptions:

c	*ts*
ć	palatalized *t*; like *ch* in English "*ch*eap" when pronounced softly
č	Eng. hard *ch* as in "*ch*urch"
đ	*dj*, a palatalized *d*; Eng. *j* as in "*J*im"
dž	*dg* as in "ju*dg*e"
g	hard *g*, as in "*g*o"
h	*ch* as in Scottish "Lo*ch*"
j	Eng. consonantal *y* as in "*y*ou"
lj	palatalized *l*, Eng. soft *l* as in "bri*ll*iant"
nj	palatalized *n*; Eng. soft *n* as in "la*n*yard"
r	trilled, as in Scottish "braw." It is sometimes vocalic.
š	*sh*, as in Eng. "*sh*all"
ž	Eng. *z* as in "a*z*ure"

In reading Serbo-Croatian every letter is pronounced; there are no silent letters.

Introduction
BY ALBERT B. LORD

Avdo Međedović

The song presented in translation in this volume (see volume IV for the Serbo-Croatian text) is one of the two longest ever collected from Slavic oral epic tradition.[1] Yet it is not only their length that makes these songs extraordinary; their excellence as heroic-romantic sung story and the seriousness of their intent as depictions of a glorious past raise them above the usual performances in the tradition to which they belong. Their significance goes well beyond Slavdom. From the songs themselves and from the study of the way in which they were composed we can learn much about the processes of composition and transmission of oral epic poetry in many tongues and of many times.

The song of "The Wedding of Smailagić Meho," Parry Text No. 6840, published here, was dictated by Avdo Međedović of the village Obrov not far from Bijelo Polje in eastern Montenegro, from July 5 to July 12, 1935. The scribe was Nikola Vujnović of the village of Burmazi in the district of Stolac Hercegovina, who was Milman Parry's assistant from 1933 to 1935 in the field.[2]

1. The other, also by Avdo Međedović, is "Osmanbeg Delibegović and Pavičević Luka," Parry Text Nos. 12389 and 12441. This was sung for recording on July 17–20 and August 1–3, 1935, and contains 13,331 lines.

2. Much of what follows was first published in my article, "Avdo Međedović, Guslar," *Journal of the American Folklore Society*, 69 (July–Sept. 1956), 320–330. For a description of the Milman Parry Collection, see the General Introduction to *Serbocroatian Heroic Songs*, collected by Milman Parry, edited and translated by Albert Bates Lord, vol. I: *Novi Pazar: English Translations* (Cambridge, Mass., Harvard University Press, and Belgrade, the Serbian Academy of Sciences, 1954).

Avdo was Moslem, as is clear from his given name, Abdullah; but by blood he was Slavic. In centuries past his family had been Orthodox and had come from central Montenegro; they were related to the Rovčani and came from Nikšić.[3] Avdo knew neither when nor why they had become Moslems. During the first half of his life Avdo was a Turkish subject; for up to the First World War Bijelo Polje belonged to the Sandžak of Novi Pazar in the Turkish Empire. Here Avdo was born, and here he lived and died. His father and grandfather were butchers in the town, and in his mid teens Avdo began to learn their trade. After some two years of apprenticeship he went into the army as "a still beardless youth," and when he returned seven years later his father did not recognize him.

In the army he spent three years in Kriva Palanka on the Bulgarian border. For another year he fought with Šemsi Pasha in Albania, and then after six months in Kumanovo near Skopje in Macedonia, he was sent to a school for noncommissioned officers in Salonika, where, according to his own account, he "rotted for a year and emerged a sergeant." He then passed another year in Kriva Palanka drilling others in the tactics he had learned under "Alamani" officers in Salonika, after which he was on guard duty for six months at a post on the Bulgarian frontier "under the skies, high in the mountains." When he returned to headquarters his discharge came.

It is characteristic of Avdo that the only time that he was disciplined in the army was when he struck an "Anatolian" with the butt of his rifle for cursing the faith (*din*). Ordinarily a peaceful man, he was stirred deeply by the religious laxity of the Anatolian Turks, whom he called "unbelievers." He was himself devout and conservative, a person of lofty principles, yet unostentatious. All this is reflected in his poems.

Although Avdo learned to speak and understand Turkish in the army, he was never able to read or write any language. In those days there were only Turkish language schools, and his father had never sent him to them. During his lifetime he saw the growth of literacy in younger generations and shared both the feeling of inferiority and the pride of accomplishment of those illiterates who had led successful lives. It was "stupid" he thought, in retrospect, that he had never learned to read and write; and yet, in spite of that, he had been a good tradesman because he was honest. He had the respect and confidence of his fellow

3. This sketch of Avdo's life is based on Nikola's conversations with him. The conversations themselves are translated by David E. Bynum in this volume.

merchants. One of the greatest shocks of his life had come when the son to whom he had given over his business and all his capital, that Avdo himself might retire peacefully to the farm, had squandered everything in riotous living. There was bitter disillusionment in his voice as he told of it. He had been brought up to honor and obey his father and to believe that "as a man sows, so shall he reap." Having been a good son, he felt that he deserved to have a good son.

In Avdo's song, "The Wedding of Smailagić Meho," there is a deep personal ring in the words of young Mehmed when asked whether the old men are better than the young. "Opinions are divided," he says, "but mine shall ever be that the old men are better than the young." His questioner replies: "Bravo, my dear son! If God grants, you will be an honor to us." Avdo was singing of a past age, the ideals of which were his own, tried and not found wanting in the acid of his own experience.

After serving in the army Avdo returned to his trade with his father, but later he was called up again as a border guard, this time on the Montenegrin frontier, where he stayed for a year and a half. He was wounded in the Balkan wars; his right arm was broken by a bullet. With some epic exaggeration he told of how the doctor in Bijelo Polje could not stop the blood for four days and finally had to put him on a horse and send him with two soldiers to Senica. Here the doctor did not dare even to inspect his wound but sent him on to Novi Pazar. Four doctors looked him over, saw the danger, and sent him to Mitrovica, where twelve doctors consulted together about his case and then sent him posthaste by train to Salonika. There he lay in the hospital forty-five days. One bullet was extracted, but another remained in his arm for the rest of his life.

Two years after returning from the army he was married, when, according to his reckoning, he was twenty-nine years old. At this time he acquired the little farm in Obrov. His friends had praised a girl in that village to him, and he married her, as the custom was, without ever setting eyes on her. He lived through the terror of the First World War and somehow managed to keep his butcher shop. His descriptions of the lot of the Moslem in Bijelo Polje during the few months immediately following the downfall of Turkey are graphic. Until the new law and government were set up, for a period of about three months the Moslems were robbed and killed by their former Christian subjects, the *raja*. Avdo was among those who survived; his family had never been rich, they had never been "agas."

He watched the world around him torn to shreds once more by the

Second World War. During these later years of his life he had the satisfaction which as father and patriarch he felt was his right. His two sons
stayed by him and cared for him. He had daughters-in-law to help his
wife and a grandson to dandle on his knee. He was a quiet family man
in a disturbed and brutal world. The high moral tone of his songs is gen-
uine. His pride in tales of the glories of the Turkish Empire in the days
of Sulejman, when it was at its height and when "Bosnia was its lock
and its golden key," was poignantly sincere without ever being militant
or chauvinistic. That empire was dead, and Avdo knew it, because he
had been there to hear its death rattle. But it had once been great in
spite of the corruption of the imperial nobility surrounding the sultan.
To Avdo its greatness was in the moral fiber and loyal dedication of the
Bosnian heroes of the past even more than in the strength of their arms.
These characteristics of Avdo's poems, as well as a truly amazing sensitivity to the feelings of other human beings, spring from within the
singer himself. He was not merely "preserving the traditional"; Avdo
was the tradition.

Milman Parry of Harvard University's department of Classics collected epic songs from Avdo during the months of July and August,
1935.[4] Avdo had a repertory of fifty-eight epics; Parry recorded nine of
these on phonograph discs, and Nikola Vujnović, Parry's assistant, wrote
down four others from Avdo's dictation. They are:

Recorded

"The Death of Mustajbeg of the Lika" (Parry Text No. 6807, Record Nos. 5146–5180, June 28, 1935, 2,436 lines)

"Hrnjica Mujo Avenges the Death of Mustajbeg of the Lika" (Text
No. 6810, Rec. Nos. 5181–5278, June 29–30, 1935, 6,290 lines)

"The Wedding of Vlahinjić Alija" (Text No. 12375, Rec. Nos.
5459–5552, July 14–15, 1935, 6,042 lines; there is also a dictated version of this song from Avdo, Text No. 6841, July 16,
24, 25, 1935, 5,883 lines)

---

4. For an account of the purposes of Milman Parry in making his collection
and of the rigorous field techniques that he employed see the introduction to vol. I
of this series, and my book, *The Singer of Tales* (Cambridge, Mass., Harvard University Press, 1960). For Milman Parry's work as a whole see *The Making of Homeric
Verse: The Collected Papers of Milman Parry*, edited by his son, Adam Parry (London, Oxford University Press, 1971).

"The Heroism of Ðerđelez Alija" (Text No. 12379, Rec. Nos. 5595–5635, July 15–16, 1935, 2,624 lines)

"Osmanbeg Delibegović and Pavičević Luka" (Texts Nos. 12389 and 12441, Rec. Nos. 5712–5817, 6471–6561, July 17–20, August 1–3, 1935, 13,331 lines)

"Sultan Selim Captures Kandija" (Text No. 12447, Rec. Nos. 6677–6763, August 4, 5, 8, 1935, 5,919 lines)

"The Illness of Emperor Dušan in Prizren" (Text No. 12463, Rec. Nos. 6848–6857, August 8, 1935, 645 lines)

"The Captivity of Kara Omeraga" (Text No. 12465, Rec. Nos. 6888–6906, August 9, 1935, 1,302 lines)

"Bećiragić Meho" (Text No. 12471, Rec. Nos. 7015–7108, August 10–11, 1935, 6,313 lines)

Dictated

"The Arrival of the Vizier in Travnik" (Text No. 6802, June 29–30, July 1, 3, 4, 5, 1935, 7,621 lines)

"The Wedding of Meho, Son of Smail" (Text No. 6840, July 5–12, 1935, 12,323 lines)

"Gavran Harambaša and Sirdar Mujo" (Text No. 12427, July 26, 1935, 4,088 lines)

"The Captivity of Tale of Orašac in Ozim" (Text No. 12428, July 30, 1935, 3,738 lines, unfinished)

The mere bulk of these epic songs is astonishing: 637 record sides, or 319 twelve-inch phonograph discs recorded on both sides; 44,902 lines sung on discs, and 33,653 lines written from dictation. His longest song on records contains 13,331 lines and fills 199 record sides, or 100 twelve-inch dics recorded on both sides. If one reckons five minutes of singing on one side of a record, then this song represents over 16 hours of singing time. The total singing time for all the recorded material listed above is approximately 53 hours.

To these songs must be added the conversations with Avdo which were recorded on discs. These conversations cover 180 twelve-inch records recorded on both sides. In other words, the total recorded songs and conversations from this single singer fill 499 discs on both sides, or nearly one-seventh of the 3,584 twelve-inch records in the entire Parry Collection. The conversations contain the story of Avdo's life, a lengthy discussion of the singers from whom he learned his songs, and a running commentary, from questions prepared beforehand by Parry, to two of his texts, "The Arrival of the Vizier in Travnik" and "The Wedding of Meho, Son of Smail."

It was my privilege to return to Bijelo Polje in 1950 and 1951, where I had been with Parry as a student in 1935, and to find Avdo still ready, in spite of poor health, to sing and recite epic songs. At that time I recorded on wire the following texts, partly sung, partly recited:

> "Osmanbeg Delibegović and Pavičević Luka" (Lord Text No. 33, May 23, 24, 26, 1950, 6,119 lines)
> "The Wedding of Meho, Son of Smail" (Lord Text No. 35, May 23, 1950, 8,488 lines)
> "Bećiragić Meho" (Lord Text No. 202, August 16, 1951, 3,561 lines)

These additional 18,168 lines bring the total lines of epic from Avdo Međedović to 96,723.

These statistics alone are an indication of the value which Milman Parry placed on Avdo as a singer and tell at a glance one of the reasons for this high regard. Avdo could sing songs of about the length of Homer's *Odyssey*. An illiterate butcher in a small town of the central Balkans was equaling Homer's feat, at least in regard to length of song. Parry had actually seen and heard two long epics produced in a tradition of oral epic.

On July 5, 1935, Avdo completed dictating the song of "The Arrival of the Vizier in Travnik," Parry Text No. 6802 (he had dictated lines 6852 to 7621 of that song that day), and began "The Wedding of Smailagić Meho." That day, July 5, he dictated lines 1 to 1460 of "Smailagić Meho." In short, on July 5, 1935, Avdo dictated 2,230 lines, ending one song and beginning another. Every day for the next week he continued the dictating of "Smailagić Meho." The following table shows the number of lines he dictated each day:

July 5	Text 6802, lines	6852–7621	770 lines	
	6840	1–1460	1,460	2,230 lines
July 6		1461–2191		731
July 7		2192–4674		2,483
July 8		4675–6288		1,614
July 9		6289–8199		1,911
July 10		8200–10118		1,919
July 11		10119–12068		1,950

July 12	12069–12323	255	
Text 6841, lines 1–1290	1,290	1,545

On July 12 he finished dictating "Smailagić Meho" and started the dictation of "The Wedding of Vlahinjić Alija," Text No. 6841. He had begun the dictation of Text 6802 on June 27, and, with the exception of July 2, when he seems to have had a vacation, he had been dictating something every day. In addition to dictating Text 6802 every day except July 2, Avdo on June 28 sang the complete song of "The Death of Mustajbeg," Text No. 6807 (2,393 lines) and on June 29 he sang lines 1 to 2596 of "Mujo Hrnjica Avenges the Death of Mustajbeg of the Lika," Text 6810, which he completed on the following day, June 30, singing lines 2597–6291, the end of the song. In sum, when Avdo began the dictation of "Smailagić Meho" on July 5 he had been singing and dictating for an entire week before that, having composed 8,684 verses in song as well as the 7,621 verses of "The Arrival of the Vizier in Travnik" for the scribe to write down, a total of 16,305 lines.[5] He was in top form. At the conclusion of the writing of "Smailagić Meho" Nikola made a note:

> Ovo je najdulja pjesma što su do danas pisane. Ja sam pisao 5 dana punih i nešto više.
> Pri koncu ove pjesme, reče mi Avdo da ima još duljih pjesama.
> U Bijelom polju Jula 12, 1935
> Nikola Ivanov Vujnović

> This is the longest song that has been written down to the present day. I wrote five full days and a little more. At the end of this song, Avdo told me that there are still longer songs.
> In Bijelo Polje July 12, 1935
> Nikola Ivanov Vujnović

We all recognized this as an historic moment. It was only the beginning, but it was a brilliant one.

Avdo's singing of this or any other song was always longer than anyone else's performance, because he belonged in a tradition of singers who habitually "ornamented" their songs by richness of description,

---

5. From these statistics alone it is clear why Avdo's songs attracted the attention of Milman Parry, for in those years (the thirties) as well as before and since, the length of the Homeric songs presented a problem for those who felt that they were traditional songs by a traditional singer.

and because he had himself always had a fondness for this "ornamentation." His technique, and that of his fellows, was expansion from within by the addition of detail and fullness of narrative. Catalogues are extended and also amplified by description of men and horses; journeys are described in detail; assemblies abound in speeches.

Avdo had culled his "ornaments," as he himself called them, from all the singers whom he heard. But he did not stop there. He admitted that he thought up some of them himself; and this is true. He told me once that he "saw in his mind every piece of trapping which he put on a horse." He visualized the scene or the action, and from that mental image he formed a verbal reflection in his song. Avdo's songs are living proof that the best of oral epic singers are original poets working within the tradition in the traditional manner. These texts provide priceless evidence for the theorists in comparative epic studies.

Avdo belonged to a tradition which had been in the hands of fine singers for many generations. Without such a rich tradition behind and around him he could not have had the materials of song. He learned his art from skilled men — first, and most lasting importance, from his father. Avdo's father had been deeply influenced by a singer of his generation whose reputation seems to have been prodigious, Ćor Huso Husein of Kolašin. We know something of this singer not only from Avdo, who heard about him from his father, but also from other singers in Bijelo Polje and Novi Pazar, who learned songs from Ćor Huso.[6] From the material in the Parry Collection we shall some day be able to reconstruct part of his repertory, at least, and probably also his handling of specific themes. His most distinctive characteristic as a singer was his ability to "ornament" a song. Of this we are told by all who knew him. Avdo was a worthy student of the Ćor Huso school.

With Avdo the song, the story itself and the telling of it, was paramount. He had exceptional powers of endurance, but his voice was not especially good. He was hoarse, and the goiter on the left side of his neck could not have helped. Nor was his playing of the gusle in any way of virtuoso quality. He told Parry that he learned the songs first and then the musical accompaniment. His singing ran ahead of his fingers on the instrument; thoughts and words rushed to his mind for expression, and there were times when he simply ran the bow slowly back and forth over the strings while he poured forth the tale in what seemed to be

6. For more about Ćor Huso see vol. I of this series.

prose of lightning-like rapidity but was actually verse. He was not a musician, but a poet and singer of tales.

Parry in 1935 made trial of Avdo's ability to learn a song which he had never heard before. Among the singers from whom Parry collected while Avdo was dictating or resting was Mumin Vlahovljak of Plevlje. Parry arranged for Avdo to be present and listening while Mumin sang "Bećiragić Meho," a song which Parry had adroitly determined was unknown to Avdo. Mumin was a good singer and his song was a fine one, running to 2,294 lines. When it was over, Parry turned to Avdo and asked him if he could now sing the same song, perhaps even sing it better than Mumin, who accepted the contest good-naturedly and sat by in his turn to listen. Avdo, indeed, addressed himself in his song to his "colleague" (*kolega*) Muminaga. And the pupil's version of the tale reached to 6,313 lines, nearly three times the length of his "original," on the first singing!

Avdo in 1935, when he was already over sixty years of age, maintained that he had been at the height of his powers when he was in his forties. We have seen a glimpse of the quality of this talented singer in his sixties and can only guess at his excellence twenty years earlier. We should do well not to minimize the extraordinary feat which he performed when he was in his eighties. For at least ten years he had sung very little. He was weak and ill in 1950 and 1951, and, alas, the circumstances of collecting were far from ideal. I had very little time, and working with a singer like Avdo requires leisure. Yet, even under adverse conditions, he sang and recited two long songs totaling over 14,000 lines in about a week's time! When he finished the song of "Osmanbeg Delibegović and Pavičević Luka," he apologized that it was shorter; he had cut down some of the description of the army. He was indeed unwell, and we took him to the doctor. Six thousand lines is still a sizable song. And the 8,000 and more lines of his "Smailagić Meho" in 1950 was a prodigious undertaking which few, if any, younger men could have accomplished.

On May 21, 1939, in Cambridge, Massachusetts, Nikola Vujnović completed his review of his transcription from the records of the words of Avdo's song "Sultan Selim Captures Kandija." He wrote this note at the bottom of the page: "Onda kad ne bude Avda među živima, neće se naći niko ko bi bio ovakav za pjevanje"—"When Avdo is no longer among the living, there will be no one like him in singing."

Avdo Međedović died sometime during 1955 at the approximate age of eighty-five. It may well be that he was the last of the truly great epic singers of the Balkan Slavic tradition of oral narrative song. He has left behind him, however, songs which will be remembered in days to come.

Avdo's Originality

The version of the song of "The Wedding of Smailagić Meho" dictated by Šemić and published in 1886 (see Appendix A) depicts treachery to the sultan on the part of the vizier in Buda in the middle part of the sixteenth century, a treachery which involves collaboration between the vizier and the Christian leaders of neighboring countries against the Moslems who are loyal to the sultan. The Bosnian Moslems are shown to be champions of both the sultan and the Moslem faith. Such is the background for Meho's story, which itself shares the double aspect of the historical circumstances as presented, namely, the story of his succession as a faithful follower of the sultan, and the story of his marriage to the daughter of another of the faithful. *Deo et imperio* is the burden of the song in the Šemić tradition, and the version of Međedović fifty years later emphasizes the same two themes.

In his introductory lines Avdo states the ethos of his song, and what he does with it is in keeping with that statement.

> It is a song of the olden times, of the deeds of the great men of old and the heroes on both sides in the time when Sulejman the Magnificent held empire. Then was the empire of the Turks at its highest. Three hundred and sixty provinces it had, and Bosnia was its lock, its lock it was and its golden keys, and a place of all good trust against the foe.

This quotation underlines the song's bias in favor of Bosnia and the Turkish Empire. It is nostaglic for the days of magnificence that Avdo will re-create so vividly in his version of the story.

And magnificence is the keynote of Avdo's expansion of Šemić's

song. Magnificence characterizes the leaders of the northern marches of
the Turkish Empire as well as the courtiers of the sultan in Istanbul,
and, of course, it is most characteristic of young Mehmed himself.

In the opening assembly we are immediately struck by the length
and detail of Avdo's description. The songbook, in contrast, lists the
assembly in ten lines (16–25):

> Thirty-four agas of Kaniža are drinking wine. At their head is the
> leader Cifra Hasanaga and next to him his nephew little Mehmed-
> aga. Next to Mehmed was Nožinagić Ibro and next to Ibro Pločić
> Oručaga and the remaining agas. All the court of Hasanpasha was
> there and before them was the pasha's captain.

Avdo augments the gathering both in numbers and in importance. There
are thirty beys and twenty-four agas. At the head of the gathering is,
not the alaybey Cifra Hasanaga, but Hasan Pasha Tiro himself with his
fifty men of war. Cifrić Hasanaga and his nephew Mehmed thus find
their proper place in the entourage of the pasha. This is an important
gathering. There are no empty names in Avdo's song as there are in
Šemić's; for not only are Nožinagić Ibro and Pločić Oručaga in Šemić's
text unknown persons, but they also play no role in the song and are
never again mentioned. In Avdo's song the persons named are all important in the story. In Avdo's version, indeed, Šemić's gathering has
come alive with pageantry, with important figures, with warriors and
standard-bearers and fortress commanders. Hasan Pasha's court is there,
and so is Hasan Pasha himself and his honor guard, not merely a representative captain. Avdo has taken time to expand because his expansion
is meaningful.

In Avdo's "Smailagić Meho," after the listing of persons present in
the gathering come fourteen lines that increase the stature of the men
listed. They are rich and unworried. They have plenty of everything.
They are not oppressed by demands from their superiors. One of the
most important points in Avdo's mind is that the leaders of Bosnia have
the indulgence of the sultan and his permission to act on their own.
These men have accomplished much, as their boasting indicates, and
they are quivering with excitement because of their own excellence.
They are glorious in deed as well as in outward appearance.

Against the magnificence of the description of the gathering the
person of Mehmed flashes with white Venetian velvet and pearl and the
gold of embroidery and-breastplate. The mention of the breastplate

leads directly to the special relationship of Mehmed and his family to
the sultan; for the breastplate has been sent by the sultan to Mehmed's
father Smail for him and for his true son.

> For that house had held the command for full forty-seven years,
> by the charter of Sulejman the Magnificent, by his imperial
> charter and appointment. Than that lord there was none older,
> either pasha or vizier, in Bosnia's seventy cities, nor was there any
> of nobler descent than the alaybey, Hadji Smail, or his brother
> Hasanaga. Both these old men have only one heir, Meho (may God
> protect him!).

When we know of this special relationship between the holder of power
in Istanbul and our hero Mehmed, we do not find it surprising that the
pasha in Kanidža, Hasan Pasha Tiro, is concerned about the young son
of the alaybey. Avdo has raised the scene in its entirety from that of a
local older alaybey Cifrić Hasanaga and his young nephew Mehmed to
the involvement of a pasha and his whole elaborate court in the fate of
the scion of the oldest house, bar none, in Bosnia, a house which traces
its dignity to the sultan himself. Avdo has made the dimensions of his
song "epic" through these descriptions. They are purposeful in the song,
not "merely ornamental." They are missing entirely from the Šemić
text.

Among the most striking differences between the published song
and Avdo's is that in the former Meho is sent to Buda to become the
new buljukbaša, not the new alaybey. When Avdo was asked about this
difference, he defended his change by saying that to obtain the position
of buljukbaša one would not have had to go to Buda, nor even to Hasan
Pasha Tiro; Mustajbeg himself could have bestowed that. "A buljukbaša
commanded a hundred men, but this rank was for thirty thousand.
Would that be an alaybey or a buljukbaša?" In other words, Avdo had
made the song not only much more meaningful, more magnificent in its
scope, but also more accurate!

In contrast to the self-satisfaction with accomplishment, position,
and possessions exhibited by all the other members of the gathering in
Kanidža, it is ironic that Meho is more glorious in appearance than any
other, richer than the rich, more favored of the sultan than anyone else,
yet inferior in accomplishment. Avdo's description and expansion
heighten that irony. Meho *has* more of everything than anyone else, but
he has *done* nothing. He is not merely the untried hero, he is the hero

who has not been given the chance to try himself. The others are free to *do*, but Meho has been inhibited by his elders. One thinks immediately of Telemachus.

It is a particular nicety of Avdo's song that Hasan Pasha Tiro himself notices Mehmed's silence and, from a delicacy of feeling that was one of Avdo's own personal qualities, calls, not the boy himself, but his uncle, in order that the uncle may inquire, after due pause, the reasons for the young man's dejection. Here is displayed a fine awareness of human sensitivity. At the same time the action of the pasha exhibits Avdo's feeling for protocol and the singer's skill in involving Mehmed not only with his uncle but also with the chief man, the highest ranking official in the assembly. It all increases Mehmed's stature. The additions are not made simply to lengthen the song by useless description.

Meho's threatened revolt is recounted dramatically by Avdo, as usual with great fullness. The enormity of this threat is made clear from the reaction of Hasan Pasha Tiro in his thoughts, though not in speech, and by the extraordinary tale of Meho's birth and upbringing. Both the pasha's concern and the sultan's deep involvement with Meho stress the significance of our hero. They are thoroughly consistent with the picture of Meho and the importance of his family as painted by Avdo from the very beginning of the poem. They are pure Avdo.

The central piece in the assembly is Cifrić Hasanaga's reply to his nephew Meho. He relates the previous history of Meho's family and tells the boy of his inheritance. The most remarkable part of Meho's uncle's speech is the marvelous tale of Meho's birth and upbringing. Like so many other heroes Meho was born after years of his father's and uncle's childlessness. Even the sultan sent a note of rejoicing at the news. When Meho was twelve, gifts came to him from the sultan: a horse with wondrous trappings, a glorious sword, rich clothing. Such gifts remind us inevitably of the magic horses of Achilles, his Pelian spear, the shield and armor made by Hephaestus, the special horse and armor and weapons of all heroes of legend and fairy tale. They are the gifts of a supreme power to a specially chosen hero, honoring both, and blessed by the gods. With the sword blessed in Mecca the religious element in the poem comes to the fore as it does again a few minutes later when Cifrić Hasanaga tells of his brother Smail's pilgrimage to the Kaaba. Meho and his house are champions of the sultan and of the Moslem faith. Against this background of political and religious perfection Meho's threatened rebellion stands out as infamous, and, as will soon be revealed in the

the Old Babylonian Epic of Creation the revolt of Tiamat is narrated by
the poet (Tablet I, lines 128–161); Ea hears of it and reports it to his
grandfather Anshar in the same words as those used by the poet in the
narration (Tablet II, lines 15–48); Anshar calls an assembly of the gods
by sending his vizier Gaga to Lahmu and Lahamu, and his instructions
repeat the same report (Tablet III, lines 19–52), which is then, of course,
repeated by Gaga to Lahmu and Lahamu (Tablet III, lines 77–110). In
"Smailagić Meho" the repetition is not so mechanical and stylized as in
the Old Babylonian text. In this way the repetition in Avdo is more
realistic.

Cifrić Hasanaga, too, has great sensibility, for he refrains from telling old Smail of the threatened rebellion of young Meho. He says to
Smail, indeed, that he will not say more of what Meho had told him.
Instead he launches into the repetition of his reply, which is Hasan's
story par excellence. It is fitting that the history of the alaybeyship be
given by the reigning alaybey himself.

The words of Smail which follow Hasan's speech are striking and
in a way amusing. He cannot give permission for Meho to go to Buda
and to receive the alaybeyship until he has seen whether the special
clothes and the Persian sword suit the young man. In the 1925 text
Smail gives permission and then sends the boy to change, telling him to
come back so that he may see him. This is done very briefly (lines 114–
130): Meho says to his father: " 'Give me your permission and your
blessing.' 'I will, my son, since the men of Kaniža are in agreement. Put
on your clothes [no mention has been made, of course, of any special
clothes] and then come before your father.' Straightway Meho went
into the small room, put on his clothes, and came before his father in
full regalia." This is a full translation of lines 114–123. When one com-
pares what Avdo has done with the scene, one sees once again some of
his Homeric qualities. In Avdo's song Smail's instructions about the
clothes are preceded by advice about the grave responsibility and difficulty of the alaybeyship, about the character of the men whom Meho
will lead and the qualities needed in a leader. Smail thinks that Meho
may be too young, still not mature enough for the task. At any rate, he,
Smail, will expect that Meho will always be just; if he hears otherwise
from anyone, he will kill his own son. In this last remark by Smail Avdo
is preparing for the scene when Meho returns from Buda and recounts
the incident with the maiden in the coach, teasing old Smail by saying
that he had not saved the girl from being carried away. Smail becomes

so angered at this alleged, or confessed, breach of the heroic code of justice that he draws his sword and nearly kills Meho, but Osman intervenes and tells Smail the truth. Just as there is a connecting line from Meho's threatened revolt to the vizier's actual treachery, so there is a line from Smail's advice to Meho to his desire to kill Meho when he thinks that advice has been flaunted. Related to this second line is Hasan's diplomatic omission of Meho's threatened revolt from his account of the assembly to Smail. Avdo has demonstrated hereby that the oral poet may indeed make references early in a song that prepare for or at least have a bearing on later incidents.

The second scene of this section of "Smailagić Meho" adds another dimension to the family picture. This scene is between Meho and his mother; it depicts his investiture, his dressing in those magnificent special clothes sent him by the sultan on his twelfth birthday. When Meho's mother, at sight of her son, asks why he looks ill, we might expect some further repetition or explanation of what had happened in the tavern, some word as to why he must put on the clothes that had been kept for him for so long. Yet all that he says is that for some reason his father wants to see him in these new clothes. This is clearly not the moment to explain to a woman, even his mother, what this is all about. She herself, however, has a ready explanation, a woman's explanation; Meho is going courting. There is nothing like this, of course, in Šemić; here again it is Avdo himself describing the mores of his epic world.

The third scene, the appearing of Meho before his father, a kind of epiphany, is the climax of this section. It is predictable that Smail finds his son more than acceptable. After he has gazed with satisfaction at Meho, the old man calls for Osman the standard-bearer. A figure who is shadowy in Šemić comes to full life and clear outline, with a past as well as a present, in Avdo's song. In Šemić we first see Osman coming back with Meho from the assembly. He appears a second time when he and Meho are about to depart. Osman joins Meho when he is ready, they embrace one another, and go together hand in hand down the steps into the courtyard to mount their horses. After Meho's mother has brought them their rifles and given them her blessing, Meho says a single-line farewell, and then Osman addresses Meho's mother with a farewell speech in which he says that he fears neither wolves nor bandits; wolves are old acquaintances, and bandits flee from the hand that cuts down heroes with the sword and the good horse beneath a hero. Finally Osman says he will not return without Meho. All this is very stereotyped.

In Avdo's version the case is very different. When Smail has approved of his son, he calls for Osman to come from the guardhouse, where standard-bearers, and especially *the* standard-bearer, are stationed. When Osman appears before Smail, Smail reviews the great services of Osman to himself and to his brother and lays upon him the continuation in the service of the new alaybey. He is to accompany Meho to Buda. Meho is still young and foolish and needs Osman's advice and guidance. Osman replies in a speech reminiscent of Eumaeus in the *Odyssey*, telling how he had left his own family to serve the house of Smail and how devoted he was to it. Here again is the leisure of telling, the fullness and the spirit of epic. Now we *know* Osman. He is not a reference, he is not a stereotype to be taken for granted. He is a human being with a past, a present, and a commitment for the future.

The ensuing section of the departure deals with a character of whom we have indeed heard before, but whom we meet for the first time, namely, the chestnut horse. The description of the harnessing of the horse is the most elaborate I know in South Slavic oral epic, and can be matched, to my knowledge, only in Asiatic Turkish or Asiatic epic in general. The gray stallion of Osman, which we shall meet shortly, is not described, but the tribute it pays to Meho's chestnut horse is dramatic; it rears at the sight of the mighty chestnut, and the squires that hold it are lifted a meter or more into the air.

The departure scene itself is bright with color and filled with the prancing of horses and flashing of arms. The two who are to journey stand resplendent before the two old men who give them their blessing, and Smail delivers his son formally into Osman's care: "Standard-bearer, my golden wing, take care not to delay, for I give my son into your keeping" (lines 2109–2111). The horses are brought to the mounting stone, and the heroes mount. Osman goes first and Meho rides behind him. The steeds seem to fly across the open plain, the foam from their mouths falling onto their flanks and then to the ground; one would say that ewes were lambing. From their nostrils flames flash and scorch the mesh on their foreheads; clouds of smoke precede them, as if Venetian rifles were being fired. Thus the two heroes on their wondrous horses set forth on Meho's initiatory journey, and the first part of this extraordinary song comes to a close.

An interlude follows, but it is not without significance. The two stops on the way to Buda are not original with Avdo. They are mentioned in Šemić, the first at Jasika with Knez Vukašin, the second at Veselice with Toroman Vuk. In both cases Šemić says that the heroes

were well received, and in the first instance he added that Knez Vukasin
stood all night holding a candle and pouring brandy for them. Šemić
then tells how Meho and Osman rose at dawn, drank wine, and prepared
for the journey. The knjeginja brought them their rifles, and the knez
prepared their horses and brought them to the mounting block. Meho
came forth and the knjeginja held his stirrup, gave him his rifle, and
opened the courtyard gate. Meho gave the woman a coin, and she said:
"Good-bye, blood-brother. If God grant, when you return, you will stay
the night with us again." In Šemić these two overnight stops cover only
36 lines, but in Avdo's song they take up a total of 744 lines. I have
demonstrated elsewhere, in an article entitled "An Example of Homeric
Qualities of Repetition in Međedović's 'Smailagić Meho' " (published in
a festschrift for the late Dr. Alois Schmaus of Munich), the variety in
the two parts of the journey, between the two stops, in Avdo's song.
Each is very distinct from the other, although both are much elaborated.

I have written elsewhere also ("Composition by Theme in Homer
and Southslavic Epos," *Transactions of the American Philological Association*, 82 [1951], 71–80) some time ago of the parallel between the
journey of Meho and Osman to Buda with its two overnight stops and
Telemachus' journey to Pylos and Sparta. Telemachus, too, has a companion on his trip: Mentor (Athena) on the first lap from Ithaca to
Pylos, and Peisistratus, Nestor's son, on the second stage from Pylos to
Sparta. I do not know what force led Avdo in his song to emphasize
daughters in one episode and sons in the other, but the latter at least
cannot but call to mind the scene of Nestor and his sons at Pylos,
the feasting to which Telemachus and Mentor are invited there, to say
nothing of the sweet sleep Telemachus enjoys in Nestor's palace at the
point at which Peisistratos takes over from Mentor (Athena) the role of
companion. The twin daughters in the first episode in "Smailagić Meho"
and the references to their weddings when Meho gives them gifts are less
strikingly paralleled by the double wedding in progress in Menelaus's
palace when Telemachus and Peisistratos arrive; Menelaus and Helen
celebrate the wedding of son and daughter and mention is made of
Helen's only child Hermione. Avdo has, however, made much more of
the two overnight stops than simply two well-demarcated stages in a
journey. Strangely enough, they are elaborated in ways that are also
reminiscent of Telemachus' journey in the *Odyssey*. It is almost un-
canny that, even as Telemachus learns valuable information on his trip

to the mainland, so also Meho and Osman are advised of something that neither they nor the listener had known previously, namely, the treachery of the Vizier of Buda. In the first episode they are warned by their Christian estate manager that they should beware of the vizier. This bit of information contrasts with Smail's earlier statements that the vizier is their good friend, and it paves the way for the disclosure by Fatima in the next section of the song of the deception and treason of the vizier. The two episodes on the trip to Buda are not simple ornamentation, but, *Odyssey*-like, they play a role in the development of the song.

Finally, by enlarging the description of the entertainment of Meho and Osman by the two Christian estate managers Avdo has demonstrated the ideal relationship between the Turkish lords like Meho and his family and their Christian subjects. Their loyalty contrasts with the treachery of the vizier, and their astuteness in knowing of that treachery is contrasted, ironically enough, with old Smail's faith in the sultan's representative in Buda. Avdo's originality, first in inserting the warning into the song, and second in placing it here and in the mouths of the Christian subjects, has added much both artistically and ideologically to the value of the poem.

Now the complications of the story begin. To some extent, as we have seen, they have been prepared for by Avdo; and I do mean by Avdo, because the hints and ironies do not come from the songbook text but are additions by our singer. Even back in Kanidža Meho's mother had thought her son might be going to seek a wife. There are many songs which begin with a hero telling his mother to prepare him for a journey, because he is setting out to find her a helpmeet. We shall soon see, indeed, that this is the opening of a song which becomes fused with "Smailagić Meho" in Avdo's repertory. In addition, Meho's father had intimated that the sultan had but recently taken Buda and that things were even then not entirely settled in the city. There was still unrest. The central part of the section of the song that we now begin, relating Meho's first meeting with Fatima, is the story told by her to Meho of how the new vizier had been welcomed in Buda, but how he had soon executed and exiled many of the chief men, including her father, how she had been sought in marriage by the vizier, and how now, after having refused him, she was being sent to General Peter—the same General Peter to whom Meho himself had threatened to desert. Meho had come upon a coach being driven from Buda with a guard.

Someone in the coach was wailing, and when the captain of the guard refused to tell Meho what was wrong and who was in the coach, Meho had killed him and Osman had subdued the remainder of the guards. Fatima then told the story of the vizier's treachery.

This section and the ensuing scenes in Buda (though to a slightly less degree) form the romantic kernel of this otherwise elaborated heroic epic. Actually the romantic element is not so strong, I believe, as it may seem to be at first blush. Meho has saved a maiden in distress, to be sure, but this is heroic and done with a sense of justice, as stressed by Smail, and Meho attacked the captain of the guard only after he had insulted the young hero and Osman had approved of retaliation. True, when Meho first sees Fatima, after he has lifted with his spear the curtain of the coach, he is stunned by her beauty in a properly romantic way. And he takes her up behind him on his horse as they return to Buda, again in a properly romantic way. But the scenes in Buda are designed to show the wealth of her father and mother rather than to disclose any romantic attachment. And, finally, Meho's refusal to spend the night with Fatima, as her mother suggests (if that be romantic), because it would be contrary to their laws and his father would be very angry with him, scarcely reflects a hero daring all for the favors of his beloved. Avdo is more interested in right conduct, law, justice, and the glory of the empire than he is in romantic love.

Fatima's speech forms a link between "Smailagić Meho" and another song in Avdo's repertory, "The Wedding of Zajim Alibeg" (No. 57 in Avdo's repertory). In Šemić's "Smailagić Meho," where Fatima's speech awkwardly precedes the battle with the guard, we are told that Fatima's father had been exiled by the vizier, but we are not told to what place he had been exiled, nor is there any mention of his return. Since Avdo denied in conversation that he had invented either Bagdad or the return, but rather insisted that they were in the published book he had had read to him, the question arose where Avdo had found this new material.

In conversation texts 12,450 and 12,457 Nikola and Parry probed this question with Avdo. Parry's attention was drawn to song number 42 in Avdo's repertory, which bears the title "The Tyranny of the Traitorous Vizier in Buda When He Exiled Five Hundred Agas to Bagdad and Caused Many to Be Cast into the Sea." Avdo told Nikola at the time of dictating his repertory list that he had learned the song from Ahmet Cikotić of Trpezi, Rožaje. Later (in conversation 12,450) Avdo denied having heard it from Ahmet or that, indeed, he had learned any songs from him. He admitted, however, that there was another tyranny of the Vizier of Buda in "The Wedding of Zajim Alibeg" (No. 57 in Avdo's repertory), which he had learned from his father. After further conversation it became clear that numbers 44 and 57 were the same song, and that, as Avdo himself suggested, he may have learned it from his relative by marriage Abid, not Ahmet, Cikotić. Since titles for songs do not exist in pure tradition, Avdo looked at the same song from two different aspects and thus described it differently twice in his repertory. This teaches us something about the nature of both titles and songs, as they exist in a singer's mind.

In "The Wedding of Zajim Alibeg" the vizier exiles Hasan Pasha to Bagdad and demands his daughter Zlata in marriage. Avdo said that his song began with the rising of Zajim Alibeg in his house in Buda two hours before dawn. He had only an aged mother, and she prepared coffee for him. He told her that he had been wrong in letting her serve him so long. He would take his standard-bearer Omer and his forty guardsmen who served at his gate and go throughout Buda, from garden to garden, beginning with the court of the vizier. Wherever he found in a kolo of maidens a girl who suited him, he would take her and not ask permission from anyone. He would bring her home to help his old mother, so that she would not have to cook wheatcakes for him. So Zajim went from kolo to kolo until he came to a house all adorned in black. He gave his stallion to Omer, and he himself entered. There he found the wife of Hasan Pasha combing her only daughter's hair. She wore a black dress, black gloves, and black stockings. When Zajim entered the mother hid her daughter in another room and greeted the stranger, who asked her what her trouble was.

At this point Avdo's telling of the beginning of the song "The Wedding of Zajim Alibeg" breaks off. But from another part of the recorded conversations we discover that presumably Zajim became betrothed to Zlata, whom the vizier was demanding from her mother, because the vizier said that he would gather an army and destroy the Zajimovi when he heard that Zajim had sought Zlata in marriage in spite of him. But the vizier's advisers told him they had a better plan. They suggested that he invite Zajim Alibeg to his court, receive him well, and tell Zajim that, although he (the vizier) had told Zlata she should marry either the vizier or the black earth, he did not really mind that she had been betrothed to Zajim. Zajim was, however, to take an army of forty thousand men from Buda with another forty from Bosnia and cross the Danube. He should go to India to capture Anđa, the sister of two generals, as a bride for the vizier. She was nicknamed "Devilish Anđa." This is all we know of the contents of this song of Avdo's, but we assume that Zajim survived the journey intended to be his last, because he lived to beget a daugther Fatima, our heroine, and to be himself, like his father-in-law, exiled to Bagdad. Avdo does say later in the conversations that it was not the same vizier who exiled both Hasan Pasha and Zajim Alibeg.

Avdo had heard the song of Zajim Alibeg's wedding, he said, about forty years ago (i.e., forty years before 1935). The first and only printed version of this song with which I am acquainted is "Mustaj beg Delibegović i budimski vezir," No. XIX in volume I of Kosta Hörmann's collection, which he got from Foča. This was first published in 1888.

At one point in the conversations, when Avdo was informed that the songbook that Milman Parry had and about which Nikola was talking was printed in Latin script, he remarked that it was published by a certain aid society in Sarajevo. Nikola asked how he knew that, and Avdo said that "a catalogue had come from that society the year before and that they were offering in one cover seventy-six heroic songs for the Moslem youth, to give them courage for circumcision, to urge them to worship during Ramazan, and for the young people to read and look at during the days of Bajram. Bound it was twelve "banki" [120 dinars], unbound a hundred dinars." Someone read it to him, and it had thirty-six of his songs in it, so he had not wanted to buy it. A few young men in Bijelo Polje had wanted to buy it and give it to him and read it to him but not to any other singer. Some gave money and some did not, so the affair rested. Nikola asked him if he had learned the song of the battle of Osek from it, but Avdo replied that in Austrian times there had been a bookstore full of books in Latin script—it had nothing in Cyrillic—up until a year before the plundering, and he learned that song from one of those books. An Austrian gendarme had read it to him in the village!

The preceding account, taken from the conversations, is somewhat confused, but I gather from the above evidence that Avdo at least knew of Hörmann's collection and probably had some of the songs in it read to him a number of years before, exactly when is difficult to say. That it is Hörmann's collection of which Avdo is speaking is clear from the number of songs he mentions as being in the book he saw, namely, seventy-six. Hörmann's collection has seventy-five songs, thirty in the first volume and thirty-six in the second. "The Battle at Osijek" is No. XVII in the first volume and "Mustajbeg Delibegović and the Vizier of Buda" is No. XIX in the same volume. The latter is a multiform of parts of "Smailagić Meho."

When "The Wedding of Meho, Son of Smail" was read to Avdo, he had long been acquainted, I believe, with this multiform of an important section of the story, especially the exiling of the father of the bride, her being sought by the vizier but won by the hero, the treachery of the vizier in offering the girl to a Christian ally (a general in Vienna), and the battle at the bridge over the Danube. Avdo did not, however, get the return of the exile from the Hörmann multiform, because in it Mehmedbeg, father of Zlata, died in exile. While Avdo had not heard, so far as he remembered, at least, the song of "Smailagić Meho" before it came to him from the songbook some four or five years earlier, in 1927, 1928, or 1929, he had heard, and sometimes he sang, a multiform of part of it. In addition to adapting, probably quite unconsciously, one multiform to another—the usual mode of transmission and re-creation within a tradition—Avdo also added some original elements, one of which, to the best of my present knowledge, was the return of the exiled father of the bride. The reading of the songbook to Avdo was pretty much the same as his hearing it from another singer. If one remembers that in an oral tradition one is dealing constantly with multiforms and parts of multiforms rather than with rigidly distinct songs, then the "Smailagić Meho" of Avdo is an excellent illustration of the processes of tradition in the hands of an extraordinarily gifted singer.

We see the magnificence of Buda and of the possessions of Zajim Alibeg through Meho's eyes as he rides with Fatima behind him on his horse along the streets and through the squares of the city. He stands amazed before the stunning portal of her father's palace, and he enters the courtyard in time to save her mother from self-destruction. Such was her grief at the loss of her daughter. With the mother's permission Meho and Osman, after having obtained the writs necessary for Meho's new command from the vizier, go to the judge and force him to issue a marriage license so that Fatima may marry Meho. Then they return to Fatima's house.

I cannot comment in detail on the whole of this song in what is essentially an edition of it with translation. But there are a few more highlights that I should like to emphasize for the sake of those who are unfamiliar with the tradition to which it belongs, and one or two comparisons with other traditions that seem to me to be significant and may suggest other lines of approach as well. For example, the moral and heroic ethos reflected in much of the song reminds one of the heroic idea of face or glory. When Meho returns to Fatima's house after having become the new alaybey and after having received the marriage license, Fatima's mother makes two actually improper suggestions to him. First that he take Fatima back with him to Kanidža and forgo the gathering of wedding guests and coming to bring her with due ceremony to Kanidža. Second, she suggests that, since the future is very dangerous, he enjoy Fatima before returning to Kanidža. Meho rejects both of these proposals with some sense of shock. He says that even if he himself were to want to do the first of these, his father would not allow it, and it would mean that men would ever reproach him for being afraid to come with wedding guests for his bride. He could never live down the shame of it. As for the second suggestion, his argument is sensible and also considerate. It would be wrong to change Fatima's maiden status and then leave her a widow. He considers both proposals as unthinkable according to both the heroic code of his society and that of human decency, which recognizes the realities of social and familial structure. Once again this is a characteristic of Avdo himself not only as traditional singer but also as a human being.

So the story moves on. After due expressions of pleasure and concern on the part of the ladies, the questions of date and number of wedding guests are discussed and, laden with gifts, Meho and Osman return to Kanidža. They report what happened, and Smail sends out invitations to the wedding guests, thus summoning in effect a mighty army to march against Buda and the vizier. The song, which has not by any means been lacking in this respect before, now reaches the peak of spectacle, where both sound and sight collaborate in proclaiming the glory and prestige of the house of Smailaga and of the Bosnian Border, all under the benign munificence of the sultan. The mountain rumbles, contingents arrive in successive waves of bright colors and shining arms, of prancing horses in full array, horses of many breeds and hues. I have made a separate study of Avdo's catalogues in this and several other poems, qua catalogue. Here I should like to comment briefly on the catalogues, not as ornament but as having real meaning in the song.

Avdo has built up the song from opening scenes of local and

limited relevance to scenes whose scope includes the sultan and the whole empire of the Turks. An army of a few names, as in Šemić, with scanty description is out of the question. Avdo has made of this something really big, or rather he has realized, as no other singers have, that the song is about the treachery of the vizier in Buda. That is not an insignificant matter. Avdo has tried to realize the potentiality of his subject. This is not a local hero stealing sheep or even a bride. This is the ignominious action, dangerous to the whole empire, of the most powerful official on the northern edge of Turkish territory. A small and perfunctory catalogue of forces just would not do for the size and implications of the action involved.

Here Hasan Pasha Tiro is joined by no less than three other pashas, Ibrahim of Travnik, Fetibegović of Banja Luka, Sehidija of Sarajevo, all seats of administrative and military power in the pashalik of Bosnia. The lordly houses of Hercegovina are represented, those from Mostar, Nevesinje, and Trebinje, including, of course, the famous Ljubovići of Nevesinje, heroes of many a song themselves. The Border is fully present, and many of the outlying parts of Bosnia and the Lika are there too, such as Brčko and Gradašac in the north and Livno and Vrljika in the south. To those who know the area and its history this is an impressive and inclusive array of the mighty men of this northern and western bastion of the Turkish Empire. After all, they are to proceed against the powerful vizier in Buda whose prerogatives stem directly from the sultan himself, but the Bosnians are marching without the sultan's permission. Moreover, the vizier also commands the force of Janissaries in Buda under their own pasha, and he is allied with a powerful Christian general. This is no local raid. A catalogue of less extent would be inappropriate for the magnitude of the action involved. The wedding of young Mehmed, son of Smail, the new alaybey, has become a military venture against the strongest forces of the northern frontier.

It is a grave error, one arguing an ignorance of the entire background of the song and attributing that same ignorance to the singer and his audience, to look on these catalogues of letters, arrivals, and order of departure merely as padding to lengthen the song. They are an indication of the seriousness of the situation of the vizier's treachery, of the might needed to save not only Bosnia but actually the entire empire from the Christian north, and of Avdo's awareness of the significance and import of his subject. Meho, our initiatory hero, is almost forgotten until the final battle is ended and he appears leading General Peter captive. When the Bosnians return to Buda after the battle on the plain, and the treacherous vizier and General Peter are executed, the personal tale of Meho's wedding and the story of wider public import have reached a final climax; the villains of both have been defeated and eliminated.

The elaboration of the magnificence of the armies of Bosnia has made one of the key figures of the Border and his retinue even more of a contrast than he normally is. Tale of the Lika, in rags, riding an old nag, is a special kind of traditional character in the songs. He belongs to the circle of Mustajbeg of the Lika, whence he also comes, and of the Hrnjičići of Kladuša, Mujo, and Halil. Avdo's awareness of the contrast that Tale made with the four pashas, who cannot understand why the men of the Border would wait for such a one's arrival, is demonstrated in his attempt to avoid too much contact between them by sending Tale to be hosted by Smailaga's wife rather than entertained with the pashas. The first of these two elements, the pashas' amazement at the Borderers' insistence on waiting for Tale, is itself traditional. Other singers have faced up to the problem of introducing outside figures of importance, such as the pashas, into the intimate group of Mustajbeg of the Lika and his entourage. The second element, the hosting of Tale by Smailaga's wife, is not found elsewhere, to the best of my knowledge, and represents, I believe, a further unconscious attempt on the part of Avdo himself to reconcile this traditional figure with historical reality. It is to be noted that once the armies set out and Tale makes a reckoning of them, further remarks about his appearance are lacking, and he emerges as the real tactician and strategist of the campaign.

Actually there are, I think, two levels being worked on here. The pashas are illustrious outsiders. With them and with a comparatively complete coverage of Bosnia Avdo has raised his song to a significance beyond the border raid, to a higher historical level. But the traditional structure of the Borderers remains, together with their own traditional roles in the epic. Two groups of them stand out in this song as belonging to a different level from the historical one of the pashas. The first is made up of Cifrić Hasanaga and his brother Smailaga, the latter's son Mehmed, and perhaps Hasan Pasha Tiro; in short, the Kanidža group. They are peculiar to this song and occur, if at all, only incidentally in any other songs. They are the local names given to the actors in the age-old story of succession, initiation, marriage, a mythic pattern, if you will, for such is Meho's tale. The second group consists of the circle of

Mustajbeg of the Lika mentioned above, but especially Mujo, Halil, and Tale. Whereas the pashas and the other men of the song, exclusive of the figures in these two groups, are on the historical-geographical level of the song, the members of these two groups are on a more mythical level. Yet Avdo, inheritor of an ancient tradition, is oriented as well toward a present and past that are urgently historical and urgently religious. So the song is a fascinating example of the wedding of myth and history, of past splendor and present defeat. But the mythical level is subordinate to the historical. Avdo did not view his songs as myth but as history and as having nevertheless both a religious and a moral value.

Let me pursue a bit further the mythic character of the group around Mustajbeg of the Lika, with a particular view to understanding Tale, whose idiosyncracies led us to these deliberations. Unlike the Kanidža group, which is peculiar to this song of Smailagić Meho, the Lika-Kladuša group is found in many songs, and both singly and as a group its members have songs of their own. One has only to mention the first three songs that Parry collected from Avdo as cases in point. Behind the pseudohistorical roles played by Mujo, Halil, and Tale in those songs and others, we find that these men have attributes that proclaim that they play other parts as well. For they are Moslem Bosnian manifestations of traditional figures. Mujo and Halil, for example, are the ubiquitous two brothers; their counterparts in Christian Balkan Slavic narrative are Marko Kraljević and his brother Andrija. Mujo is famous for his white horse, and Marko for his Šarac, a piebald, multi-colored steed. Halil, like Andrija, is younger than his brother Mujo, and he is much better delineated in tradition than is Andrija, who is far overshadowed by his brother Marko. There are many songs about Mujo and Halil, and about Tale as well, in volume I of this series, and I urge those who wish to understand the Balkan Slavic Moslem tradition to note in those songs the difference in tone between them and this and other songs of Avdo Međedović, even in the treatment of Mujo and Halil. Avdo's attitude toward those two heroes is historical rather than traditional; we do not see them, even in the songs of the death of Mustajbeg and of Mujo's vengeance for that death, as the marvelous, almost magic, figures for whom a mysterious stranger once captured wondrous horses. They are to Avdo living historical heroes, not wonder-working mythical actors. Avdo does not seem to have been as interested as some other singers in the supernatural elements in the tradition.

Mustajbeg may be the ranking official leader of the Border, and

Mujo Hrnjica, with or without his winged white horse, may be commander designate of the army, but in reality, except in one decision
which proved fatal for part of the army and was against his advice, it is
Tale who directs almost all the action from the moment of his arrival at
Kanidža. The Lika-Kladuša group takes over the leading role in the song
from the Kanidža group; for the initiatory pattern of the song shifts to,
or perhaps better, becomes mingled with the pattern of a military expedition of considerable magnitude, far beyond that of which an alaybey is capable, and that pattern belongs in Moslem Bosnian tradition to
the Mustajbeg group. They are specialists, and the greatest specialist of
them all is Tale. Tale has knowledge, wisdom, and judgment, and he is
inspired. Allah listens to his prayers. He is a kind of holy man himself,
yet he has his own hodža with him, who has the scriptures in one hand
and a bottle in the other. Here would seem to be knowledge beyond the
orthodox clerical power, a magic like that of fools and soothsayers, for
Tale looks most like a mendicant fool. These traditional trappings of
Tale are so distinctive that they cannot be ignored. He, therefore, stands
out even more in the brilliant surroundings in Avdo's song than in
others. He is a traditional figure difficult to reconcile with the historical
atmosphere in Međedović's "Smailagić Meho."

It is not by chance that Milman Parry chose this song to begin his
translations of Serbo-Croatian heroic song. The reader cannot but be
struck, as I have indicated on several occasions above, by its correspondence with the Telemachus part of the *Odyssey*, and, in the return
of the exiled Zajim Alibeg, perhaps with Odysseus himself. The joining
together of two multiforms in Avdo's song might suggest the same
process in the formation of the *Odyssey*. Moreover, the theme of treachery and the destruction of the rear guard, as well as the importance in
the song of the catalogues and of military tactics, must also remind us
of the Old French *Chanson de Roland*. Nikola Banašević long ago
pointed out the similarities between the Kosovo Cycle and some of the
songs of Marko Kraljević and the *chanson de geste* tradition ("Le cycle
de Kosovo et les chansons de geste," *Revue des Études slaves*, 6 (1926),
224–243; *Ciklus Marka Kraljevića i odjeci francusko-talijanski viteške
književnosti, Knjige skopskog naučnog društva*, vol. III, Skoplje, 1935).
The comparison of some of the military action of "Smailagić
Meho" with the *Song of Roland* is intriguing. On Tale's instructions a

rear guard was left at the bridge on the far side of the plain from the city of Buda so that General Peter might not cut off the return of the wedding guests at that point. The rear guard was under the command of Grdić Husein and his brother Osman. All perish except Husein, who survives to tell of the battle. In Šemić, incidentally, both Grdići perish, and a sole survivor, a standard-bearer, comes on foot across the plain to the main body of the wedding guests before the principal battle and reports the fighting at the bridge. There is no treachery in the assigning of Grdić Husein and his brother to the rear guard. They were specialists who had been brought for that purpose. So in this respect the rear-guard drama differs from that in the *Song of Roland*. Yet there is treachery in the attack of General Peter, as there is in that of the paynim soldiers in the ambush at Roncevalles. Moreover, there is unwitting, or at least, unthinking treachery on the part of Mujo Hrnjica, who keeps the Bosnians an extra-long time in Buda because he is enjoying the vizier's hospitality. He is warned by Tale that delaying will give the vizier time to bring General Peter to the bridge; he is warned of deceit on the part of the vizier and of the dire consequences that will result from delay. But Mujo refuses to listen, and by this action he betrays the rear guard and causes its destruction. With this ignoring of Tale's warning, however, the parallel with *Roland* ends, although two additional scenes in "Smailagić Meho" bring the Old French epic to mind. Before speaking of them, I should like to point out that there is an even closer parallel to *Roland* in Avdo's song of "The Death of Mustajbeg."

After the wedding guests leave Buda and set out across the plain, they notice a cloud of mist in the direction of the bridge. There is consternation as to what it may be, and finally it is revealed that it is a cloud of dust and smoke from a battle. This scene is perhaps reminiscent of the gradual realization on the part of Charlemagne and the Frankish forces that it is the horn of Roland, the oliphant, that has been heard, announcing that Roland and the rear guard are in deep trouble.

Before I leave the comparison with the *Song of Roland*, I should like to add one more parallel. In the main battle with Peter's forces volunteers are sought for a suicide attack on the bridge. One by one the volunteers make their appearance, after a long interval of waiting for a response. In *Roland* the parallel scene begins in *laisse* 69 when Marsile's nephew takes his uncle's glove first and then calls for twelve lords to ride against the twelve peers of France. One by one they come forth, each with a boast.

These and other parallels are suggestive. A comparative study of the *chansons de geste* and the Moslem epic tradition in the Balkans would be particularly rewarding. For the Moslem epic tradition even more than the Christian holds ancient patterns and significant details akin to those in the Homeric poems and other ancient Near Eastern epics; in medieval times it seems closest to the richest of recorded traditional songs in Europe, the *chansons de geste*. Avdo Međedović's "Smailagić Meho" is an excellent starting point not only for a thorough investigation of processes of composition and transmission in the work of a highly gifted singer, but also for an exploration on all levels, including historical background, of the oral epic traditions in the Balkans and in southern France and Spain.

Translations

Conversations

TRANSLATED BY DAVID E. BYNUM

The Singer's Life and Times
Avdo's Repertory
The Singer Talks about His Songs
Hivzo Džafić Talks about the Songbook

The Singer's Life and Times
Parry Text *12436*
Bijelo Polje
July 31, 1935

Nikola: So now, old fellow, tell me, what is your name? *Avdo:* Avdo Međedović. *N:* How old are you? *A:* Sixty and something more, I don't know exactly. *N:* Can you write? *A:* No. *N:* Do you know how to read? *A:* No. *N:* Why didn't you learn? *A:* Well, it was just stupidity, I suppose, and the fact that my father didn't send me to either the Moslem or civil school. *N:* Still, even if your father didn't send you to school, you could have learned anyway, when you were fifteen or twenty, say, or even when you were thirty. *A:* Well, you see, at the time when I might have learned the only books were Turkish, and that was difficult to learn once I had gotten older.

N: Where are you from? *A:* I'm from Bijelo Polje. That's the district, Bijelo Polje, and Rasovo is the commune. Nowadays they call it Obrov, the village of Obrov. *N:* What kind of place is it? *A:* Balkan. Mountainsides. Where I live, it's all just the side of a mountain, one big mountain. *N:* What do you mean when you say "balkan"? *A:* Mountains. In Turkish it's *balkan*. I spent a long time in the army and now a lot of my words are Turkish; it's terrible. *Balkan* means mountains in Turkish, rocky ones. *N:* Is there any tillable land, or is it all rock? *A:* Some of both. *N:* Are there any fields? *A:* Do you mean where I live? *N:* Yes. *A:* Not much. *N:* Well, do you have any land to work? *A:* We do, yes. Some more, some less, but no one has more than a poor plot, two or three days' plowing each. *N:* Do you sow grain? *A:* We do. *N:* Then how much grain would you be able to raise? *A:* How much? Oh, five or six meters or so. *N:* How much is a meter, how many kilos would that be? *A:* Five or six quintals.

N: Well now, how is it, living up there? *A:* So-so; until winter comes one works here and there, takes care of things. Then when winter sets in and you can't work, at least you have something to eat. So it goes. *N:* What do you mean you can't work? Surely one can work any time, summer or winter? *A:* Of course we could, if there were only something to do. *N:* How do you mean, isn't there anything? *A:* Well, what is there? This whole region is mountains; no railroad, no kind of factory. And winter work? In winter we have deep snow here, and bitter cold so that you can't even go out, your hands get frostbitten; its hard enough just to go from one place to another. *N:* Well then, how do you manage to live here if it's such a bad place as you say? *A:* It's just that it's the place where I was born, I suppose; one's native ground always seems best to him.

N: Do you have fruit trees hereabout? Pears or apples? *A:* You mean where I live now? *N:* Yes. *A:* No, there aren't any where I live now, but down here toward my old village, where my family came from, they have plums and cherries. *N:* Where was your family's old village? *A:* Down this way, toward the town. But now I live over on the other side of the peak. The village multiplied, and there got to be a lot of families and not much land to go around, so we moved over there and started building terraces. I'm entirely on terraces now. *N:* What do you mean, terraces? *A:* You collect branches and deadwood, embed it, and build up earth that way. *N:* Do you have a family: *A:* Yes. *N:* How many are there? *A:* I have a wife and five children.

N: What do you do now for a living? *A:* For the past two years I've done what I've been telling you about. I work here and there during the summer and squeeze what I can out of my own little bit of land, and then in the winter I sit still. I get in a little wood to keep the children warm, and have nothing else to do. I'd like to work, even though I am old. I'd rather die of work than sit around idle, but you see, these are bad times and there's nothing to do. *N:* You say you've been working at home the last two years. What did you do before that? *A:* Oh, things were splendid then. I inherited something from my father and grandfather, and I made a go of it. We had a shop here in town, a butchershop. We were butchers. *N:* Aha! And then what happened? *A:* Then I had a son, and it seemed to me that he was a very fine person, well-mannered and orderly. He grew up. I thought then that I'd soon be able to retire, stay home, and let him run things. I had good credit, too. The merchants trusted me, gave me credit, even without any witnesses. They used to loan me money and trust me even without I-owe-you's. I figured too that I'd brought that son into the world and that he was a credit to me, but it didn't turn out that way. I was silly, and turned things over to him, set him up in business. There are plenty like him, his age and all, and they do well. I thought he'd take after them, and I could enjoy myself a little in my old age. No, sir; he turned out to be just a bum and a good-for-nothing. *N:* I see. *A:* He took to drinking and playing cards, and then fell in with bad women. That went on for a whole year. Everyone at home knew about it, but not a one of them told me what he was up to, that's how little we seem to care about one another. Not even my own brothers or the merchants around town would tell me. I was at home the whole time, working along, so I wouldn't have to burden him with hard farm work. When the corn got ripe I was doing all the digging and bringing in the firewood so that he could carry on the business in town. When the year was up, it came time to borrow some money, and I suddenly found that I had no credit. What little capital we had, he had eaten up. "What's this?" I thought. People in general started avoiding me, just like the merchants. "Don't take it so seriously, Avdo, he's still just a maverick and hasn't got any sense yet." So I put up with it for awhile, and contented myself with admonishments. He rebelled, though. He stayed on with me another two years, and then went off into the world. The army caught up with him there, and I haven't heard from him since. That's how I lost my credit. He just spent all my capital. That's how things are now.

    N: But why did you just give everything to him at once that way? Why didn't you keep watch over the accounts? *A:* It's true, I'm not very good about accounts. I thought that the boy had his heart in the right place, since I didn't deserve such treatment from him, sir. I took care of my father and honored him. Our book says, "Do, and others shall do for you." I figured I'd done well for my father, so that I could expect the same from him. But somehow the page got turned, I guess, so it all just goes backwards. *N:* So it seems. How are things now, with him gone? *A:* At least I don't have that turmoil going on inside myself any longer. But what does it matter; it's as though I had never had him, and so I don't have him now, either. It doesn't matter any more.

N: You say that you had a butcher shop. Now how in God's name could you have had a butcher's shop, when that requires a literate man, to keep the accounts. How was it you could keep the accounts not knowing how to read and write? *A:* Well, in fact, as God would have it, no one ever made any distinction between me and those who could read and write; everyone liked me. Even officials traded with me, and I served them well. I was always respectful toward a superior. They didn't care in the least about my literacy. I got along that way very well. I'm sure I'd do as well now, even though I am illiterate, if only I had some capital, any at all. I might not get on as well as the big fish, but I'd manage well enough. *N:* Did you have a place to live here in the town? *A:* No, only the mutton shop. During Turkish times, the shops all belonged to the commune. They were state property, just like the butcher shops you see here now. You rented them by the month. You paid a state tax on them, too. What was left you'd take along home to make ends meet, as God granted; by heaven, I didn't do badly, either. *N:* I see. Did you work as a boy, were you here in town then? *A:* I started working two years before I joined the army. I worked for two years, and then the army took me. Seven years I was in the army, and when I came back the merchants here set me up in business again right off. They were a lively lot, good capitalists.

N: Whom did you work for first? *A:* You mean to learn the trade? *N:* Yes. *A:* My father took me into his shop. *N:* How old were you when you came down to the town to work? *A:* I was eighteen; that was before I joined the army. *N:* Oh ho! You were already an old man then, weren't you? *A:* Ha! But not really. I mean, I didn't work when I was just a boy. *N:* How did it go, when you first came down to the town? *A:* I started helping my father, working along with him, gradually getting into it. Then later my father began to get old, and I took on more and more. That's why I trusted my own son as I did. *N:* How many years did you spend working with your father that way? *A:* A whole decade. Two years before the army and five years after, that's seven.

Then another three years, when the old man felt like it. Sometimes he'd
come around, sometimes not. Altogether I worked ten years with him.

N: Where were you stationed while you were in the army? A:
Three years and three months in Kriva Palanka, in Macedonia, on the
Bulgarian border. I spent a year with Šemsi Pasha campaigning in
Albania. That makes four. From Albania we returned to Skoplje, and
then six months in Kumanovo. Then in Kumanovo they decreed that
no one could become a sergeant or even a corporal without a year of
school in Salonika. We cast dice for it. I had the bad luck to win the
throw, and so I rotted there for a year. I came out of it a sergeant. That
makes five years. Then I spent another year in Kriva Palanka, drilling
my company the way they had taught us to. That makes six. Finally,
after six years and six months they sent me to Rujan, over toward the
Bulgarian border, to a garrison right up under the sky. It was on top a
huge, high mountain. I spent six months there. Then I was posted back
to my regiment for two months, where I got my discharge. So I was in
the army seven years and two months. Then I worked here in the butcher shop. When they later formed frontier corps here, they found my
documents and made me a sergeant again, and I was stationed a year
and a half on the Montenegrin frontier. I was wounded in the Balkan
War. N: Where were you wounded? A: On the border, at Bjelasnica, on
the other side of the mountains, over toward Kolašin. N: Where did
they hit you, Avdo? A: They got me here, sir, on the left side. It ripped
through to the skin there, then went right into my arm and shattered it.
The bullet stayed right inside, and my arm just hung down, like this.
There was a doctor here, so they brought me to him, but he couldn't do
a thing with it; couldn't even stop the blood running for four days. So
they put me on a horse, gave me two soldiers from the regiment, and we
traveled night and day to Sjenica. In Sjenica a doctor examined me, but
didn't dare even look me in the face afterwards. He sent me on to Novi
Pazar, where four doctors examined me together. They saw the danger,
and hustled me off to Mitrovica. In Mitrovica I had a committee of
twelve doctors. They shipped me by train to Salonika, where I was laid
up for forty-five days. Finally they operated on my arm. The enemy
took Greece and the Balkans, and invaded Macedonia. The fighting
caught me in Salonika with an open wound in my arm a good seven
inches long. The doctor got one bullet out, and the other is still stuck
here in my bone. N: Can you use that arm? A: Well, you see, I can't
raise it any higher than this, but when I hold it down beside me this

way, I can manage, thank God. *N:* Well, but actually it wasn't such a big wound you had in your arm, was it? Why couldn't they cure it before you got to Salonika? *A:* The whole arm swelled up like a stovepipe, like a big stovepipe on a baker's oven. It just ran with pus, so the doctors couldn't see anything when they examined it. Three or four times they used electricity, electric current on me, but they couldn't make up their minds whether to cut the arm off or pull out the bullet. So I just lay around for forty-five days.

    N: How long were you in the army then, altogether? *A:* Including the time with the frontier corps? *N:* Yes. *A:* Almost nine years, nine years less one month. *N:* Did you draw pay when you were on duty? *A:* With the frontier corps? *N:* Yes. *A:* I did. Not bad, either. *N:* How much was it, Avdo? *A:* Two liras, a silver *mecidiye*, and a quarter. That was a sergeant's pay. Two liras, that's two hundred and fifty piasters; a *mecidiye*, that's twenty-three; a quarter is six: two hundred and eighty piasters. That would be in today's money about three or four thousand dinars. *N:* Monthly? *A:* That's right. *N:* Did you pay for your own provisions, or draw them from the imperial stores? *A:* We paid for our own keep. They paid us, and then we would buy figs, flour, and the like. *N:* Could you save up anything that way? *A:* Quite a lot, in fact. Living was cheap. Figs and flour cost very little. Tobacco three piasters for two and a quarter pounds; coffee cost eight piasters, or ten for the best grade. Sugar two, two and a half. I saved out a lot of money. *N:* How was it that you became a sergeant? *A:* In the school, the academy, in Salonika. *N:* Was it because you went to the school, or were you promoted for bravery? *A:* No, it was only because of the academy, for learning all about military discipline. I passed the examination and so became a sergeant. *N:* Was it hard work, Avdo? *A:* God spare me ever having to do it again! *N:* Why so? *A:* The only time we ever got off was Thursdays, to wash our clothes and clean our rifles. Fridays we'd maybe be able to stroll in the square for a couple of hours, if they'd let you off. That's all the rest we ever got, except for six hours sleep out of every twenty-four; everything else was just work. And even that wasn't six hours of sound sleep. You'd sleep two hours, then they'd rouse you out to do this or that for the next two. There would be instruction in the middle of the night, or you'd be put on guard duty even where there wasn't any need for it, or they'd keep you on parade from dawn to noon. Then at noon you'd sit down and brush each other off and spit-and-polish, and light up a single cigarette for five of you. Next the bugle would blast again and we'd go off to class for half an hour. From there we'd go on various duties until two hours before dark. Two hours before dark we drew up in parade with the band and paid our respects to the Emperor. Dinner was just at dark, and then more classes. That's what we did winter and summer. There were days in Salonika, as I've heard there are in Hercegovina and Podgorica, when such a wind blew that it could kill a man. It used to catch us out on maneuvers below Jedikula or on Karaburum on the other side of Salonika. It was such a cold wind, believe me, that it just made the blood run out from under our fingernails. No, I wouldn't care to go there again, not even if they'd give me a commission for it. *N:* Why was it necessary for you to train so much? *A:* The Germans were in charge of the place. The high command was German, and their regimen was a hard one for us. *N:* Were you always training that way, the whole time you were in the army? *A:* They trained me for that one year, and I came out a sergeant. Then I trained our whole company the same way they had taught me.

  N: Did you learn Turkish? *A:* Everything was done in Turkish. *N:* So you know how to speak Turkish, do you? *A:* I speak it well. *N:* Where did you learn it? *A:* Using it constantly in the army. *N:* I see. *A:* It was either learn or take a beating every day. *N:* What do you mean? *A:* They'd sock you one. *N:* Oh! Who would hit you that way? *A:* The corporal, sergeant, lieutenant, captain—whoever got to you first. *N:* You mean to say beatings were possible then? *A:* We had some good ones. *N:* Wasn't there anyone to put a stop to it? *A:* Sure there was. *N:* Would they penalize a man for it afterwards? *A:* Well, there was a kind of sentence to a term in eternity . . . *N:* How long? *A:* You'd give it to him with a rifle. Shoot him dead. There was no other way to stop it. If you were to hit back at a corporal, they'd immediately separate the two of you, and then you would just have to take it. Blows were a common thing; everyone got his share, great and small alike. The only way to ambush him and finish him off with a rifle. That's the only way around it we knew of. *N:* Did you ever come to blows with anyone? *A:* No, I didn't. I was a quiet man and respected a superior. During the seven years I served, I was never struck more than twice. *N:* Only twice? *A:* Only twice. *N:* And who was it hit you, Avdo? *A:* Oh, the corporal. *N:* Did he really lay into you? *A:* It wasn't for laziness. I got into a quarrel with a comrade and hit him with a shoe, right here. Then the corporal busted me one, and I told him "thanks." *N:* You say that you were a peaceable man? If that's so, why did you hit him with the shoe?

A: He was swearing at me in a way that wasn't right. He was an Anatolian and he said, "Fuck your faith!" It's going too far to say a hard thing like that. *N:* Was he a Turk? *A:* Oh, yes. He was a Turk, too. *N:* Then how could he say such a thing? *A:* That's why I don't like them. All their talk about Asia, Asia and Turkey, but they're just a pack of infidels. They behave like the young people these days who say laughingly: "God forgive me," or "by God," or "by the sun." They talk the same way: "By me faith" . . . They will even curse your wife that way, even your sister, and the faith. They make clowns of themselves; they will say such things and kiss you at the same time. That's why I don't like them. I couldn't put up with it any longer, and so I hit him with a shoe. Then the corporal cuffed me twice. *N:* And your just took it? *A:* I just took it. I was at fault. It made the blood run, but I can take a couple of cuffs. It was better than had he reported me to the commander. Had he reported me, I'd have had to do a turn in the guardhouse and would have come out with a red mark down against me. *N:* What kind of red mark? *A:* I'm telling you about it. *N:* I see. *A:* I wouldn't let that happen.

　　N: Was it difficult for you to learn Turkish? *A:* It sure was. Some of them had an awful time with it; tried for seven years and never did learn it correctly. God gave me a good mind, so that whatever I saw someone else do, I watched him closely and learned how, so that they didn't have to give me much of a peppering. I saw how things would be best. I served the corporal and the sergeant well, and they responded by giving me a good name and teaching me gently. Not roughly, but: "This is how it should be, Abdulah, this way." So I got along nicely, I'm glad to say. *N:* You didn't draw pay then, did you, when you were in the regular army? *A:* Only one *mecidiye* each month; twenty-three piasters monthly. *N:* Oho! *A:* We rarely got even that. Five or six months would pass, and not even a penny. *N:* Did the old man ever send you anything from here? *A:* Yes, he did. *N:* How was life in the army in those days, Avdo? *A:* As far as food was concerned, no one ever had it so good, nor will again. That's how good the food was. But we weren't so well supplied with clothing. *N:* So only the food was good, eh? *A:* That emperor had plenty of food, but I didn't notice that he had anything else. I asked lots of soldiers, from all over: English, French . . . I met them in Salonika, sailors, from the navy. They came to our exercises. There were eighteen thousand lads in that academy. Big wigs came to the exercises, too; generals, ministers of internal affairs, English, French, German.

Everything was investigated. I asked those soldiers about food. Only in Turkey was there such food, nowhere else. *N:* What did you usually have to eat? *A:* Well, you see, there wasn't a lot of bread, only a kilo a day. But when we got up in the morning, there was stew, with cheese and rice in it, and a lot of fat; good stew. We slurped that up, then we went to drill—that was in the company, the battalion; I'm not talking about the academy now. *N:* That's what I'm asking you about, when you were in the regular army. *A:* After the drilling, we came in and found a whole tureen full of the same stew, and another full to the brim with beans and meat. A tureen this big for every ten men. There would be ten kilos of beans and meat in the tureen for each man. Then we would eat some stew, but not so much bread. Good meat and beans, good and fatty; you'd eat your fill, and there would be something left over. Then we'd got off again, sit around awhile, then go to drill. Then dusk came. Again a tureen of beans, and another of stew. A piece of bread, about one hundred and fifty drams [= 375 grams]. You'd eat up a liter and a half, and a liter and a half would remain. Just before Friday, there'd be halva. For lunch there was stewed fruit, either of plums or grapes. That's sweet. *N:* Yes. *A:* And a whole tureen full of beans. Pilaf and the stewed fruit for supper. We'd begin a new month, and some of the boys would eat up a whole kilo of bread a day. By the end of the month there wouldn't be even a quarter-kilo left. That was real eating. Ten or twelve boys to a table, just as in a house. There was more than anyone could eat. There was enough left over before Friday and Monday from ten men's table to feed three of the poor households around there. We used to go down to the river to do KP, with an officer in command. We'd pour out the pilaf beside the river and it would lie there in white heaps like sheep, there was so much of it left over that we couldn't eat. It was very pleasant being satisfied that way. That's the kind of food they gave us out there on the frontier. They'd dispense it from the stores, and then we'd do with it as we saw fit. We just couldn't eat it all. We had so much sugar that we could have made halva every Friday, even every day. We really enjoyed it; so much white flour, so much butter, so much pepper and paprika, garlic, my good sir, coffee, rice for pilaf, everything you could imagine. But by God, we weren't so well off with clothes.

    N: Were you all Bosnians in your company? *A:* Not at all. Four hundred of us all went off together from Senica, all Bosnians. Senica, we call that the Sandžak. We left from Senica and Bijelo Polje. All the

Bosnians were put together in one camp; all the others were Albanians and Turks. We call those Anatolians Turks. *N:* Aha! *A:* The ones who speak Turkish. Afterwards they divided us up into companies.

    N: Tell me, now, about when you returned here and when you married. *A:* I went off to the army when I was like you, a child without moustaches. When I came back I had these moustaches. I arrived in front of my house and called out. My father was there and came outside. He asked, "Who is it?" *N:* He didn't recognize you? *A:* Certainly didn't. Then I was at home for not quite two years. The time came and I got married. I was twenty when I went off to the army, twenty-seven when I came back. I don't know exactly . . . a year and a half, two years . . . I married when I was about twenty-nine. *N:* Did you have a big celebration? *A:* Not bad. Ten or twelve wedding guests, all relatives. There were some ten or twelve lads up there in the mountains who had their own horses, all handsome animals. So they were able to come to my wedding, many thanks to them! *N:* Did you know the girl before you married her? *A:* No. I didn't. I took her . . . the village, you see . . . I don't know how to explain it to you even in this language. A tithe was sold. The court sold a tithe. Now a man has credit, let's say. He applies to the court and they sell him, for instance, Obrov, against his credit. His job is then to go around and collect ten kilos of grain from each man; so they were selling this tithe. I bought the village tithe for nineteen liras, since I hadn't drawn pay there (in the army). They gave me a receipt saying that I was to collect ten liras. But it took a long time. It was terribly hard to collect. So when you've collected the tithe, you deposit it against that other tithe, and pay it off that way. That's how I got that village. While I was going around collecting in the village, they began to praise this girl to me. Well, it was just fate, and even though I hadn't seen her, I took her. *N:* But how could you do such a thing, when you hadn't even seen the girl? *A:* In my time we weren't in the habit of seeing the girls, nor did the girls get a look at the boys. The father and mother just gave the girl to whomever they liked. The girl wouldn't say "I won't" nor would a lad say "I won't have one from there." *N:* You mean to say they wouldn't do that ever? *A:* They wouldn't here in the Sandžak. All this picking and choosing and looking each other over came into fashion a year before the liberation . . . four, not quite five years before the Balkan powers tried to get in here. *N:* Well, did you ever ask her, "How was it you married me, when you hadn't ever seen me?" Or did she ever ask you that? *A:* Really, I never did. I took care of all that in advance, when they started telling me how nice certain of the women were. Every woman who isn't trying to avoid it, let's say if my name is Avdo, she'll call me Avdaga. *N:* Aha! Why is that, Avdo? *A:* Well, you see, a woman wants to honor a man. A woman won't treat him just any old way, but let him be honored. So they praised this girl to me. I showed them all my documents, that I'd come out of the army a nobody, as though I were a foreigner. "I haven't even started work yet," I told them. "I'm not ready to marry." I was weak with fever, I still had a terrible fever. Caught it in Salonika. By God, I really wasn't ready to marry. Afterwards she said, "Well, he's a Međedović, and in good repute. I'll take him, whether he has anything or not" . . . So that's how it was. *N:* Are all the people in your village Međedovićes? *A:* Yes, they are. *N:* There are no other families? *A:* There are now, since the Balkans have come in here, three or four houses; although they aren't from Serbia. They've bought themselves some land here. *N:* Where are they from? *A:* They're wanderers, from Montenegro, Vasojevići. *N:* All from Montenegro? *A:* Yes. *N:* Is it true that the Međedovićes were butchers here a hundred years ago? *A:* Yes. *N:* Were they all? *A:* Some of them were; some worked the land, too. Down there in front of those two springs, where you cross the bridge, there's a pocket valley. It's called Burdelj. You'll see it sometime. That's where we had our business. Down in this direction was the Turkish court and the magistrate, the administration, just where it's all in ruins now, where you come out in front of that café, where there's that place like a small park. *N:* Yes. Are there still any Međedovićes who keep butchershops? *A:* Two or three lads do, here in the neighborhood. *N:* Are they all from the same clan? *A:* Yes, they are. *N:* Were your ancestors originally settled here? *A:* It's possible that they have lived here for as much as two hundred years, but the family is originally from Nišić. *N:* From Nikšić? *A:* That's right. Hajro here is probably of our blood, the Feriz' blood, and all the Rovčani are my relatives, the Bulatovićes from Rovce. The people in my present village on the terraces are from Rovce. *N:* In that case the family was once orthodox, wasn't it? *A:* Yes, that's right. *N:* Then why was it turkicized? *A:* Who knows? May have been for spite or for love; I don't know why they did it. *N:* Were any of them ever beys or agas? *A:* You mean my people in Obrov? *N:* Yes. *A:* As far back as I know of, they never were. As for being agas . . . I don't think one can be an aga for having only one or two fields. *N:* Well, how wealthy must one be to be an aga? *A:* I reckon five or six kmets, maybe ten, and so on up to a hundred. After that he'd be considered a rich man, would become known to the Emperor, and he'd be sent a writ of privilege with the Emperor's seal on it. That's how he'd get to be an aga.

N: So then you stayed in the village and made your living with the butchershop? How much of your life did you spend in that way? *A:* If you put it all together, from the time I was thirty continuously until two years ago, until 1933. *N:* So at the end of the Balkan War, and the World War, you were here? *A:* At the end of the Balkan War I was lying wounded in Salonika. At the end of the World War I was here. *N:* What was it like here at the end of the World War? *A:* By God, it was hard for us then. We had a hard time with the Germans. *N:* Why? *A:* Well, people thought and acted in a headlong way and didn't have any regard for honest work. Suppose you'd set out from one commune to another to sell something. Whatever they happened to find in your hands, they'd take it away from you and say you were trading on the black market. One couldn't sell anything for a profit. For instance, I was a butcher, but I didn't dare sell even a goat to anyone except the company. I could have gotten five hundred crowns for a head of cattle, but they took it away from me for twenty-five. I could sell a sheep for a hundred crowns, but they took it for five. Suppose I had gone to Šahovići or to Rasovo and bought a nice pair of calves. Were a corporal with a couple of soldiers to meet me, he would ask: "Do you have a declaration?" "I'm a butcher here, sir, down below." "I don't care about the butcher story, is there a declaration!" He would simply take the calves. We didn't get on at all well . . . They assessed our grain while it was still standing on the field. Take now, for instance, how do we know in advance what God will give us? But they assessed it while it was still standing. They said: "How many in your family?" "I have six." "Okay, six for you." When they had it all figured out, they'd make you cart it up there where that school is, that was their warehouse. You'd cart the grain away, and then have a look at home to see what was left. Not even enough for supper, but that's what they left us for a whole year's supply. That's the kind of thing we had to put up with. Yes, we had an awful time with the Germans during the war. *N:* Did they take everything away from you, even the sheep and goats? *A:* Everything was like that in those times. You weren't free to do anything. *N:* How were things when the war ended? *A:* When they were defeated and the war ended, and then afterwards when this new government came in, we suffered from the Christian peasants and from the disorders that went on before the court was set up. *N:* How did you suffer? *A:* There was a lot of raiding. There was a band of robbers and looters, and drumhead justice. If they met someone they'd just kill him on the spot and take whatever he had. *N:* The Albanian border runs through here, doesn't it? Did they raid you? *A:* Who, the Albanians? *N:* Yes. *A:* No, not them. It wasn't the Albanians, it was the Christians who were after us. When the Germans pulled out there was suddenly no government. We didn't have any court of justice here for as much as a month. Meanwhile the Montenegrins took up arms. They no sooner came to power than they lit out after the Germans to take part in the victory. We Turks didn't get into the fighting, since we were loyal to those in power. The commandant here made us a speech. There was a commandant from Osijek in Srem. He was quite a man. "Turks, we are going to advance a fortnight's march from here, and we'll be taking our officers here with us. So you take three hundred rifles and mount your own patrols. Watch out for yourselves, because the new government won't come into authority for some time." So the question was, whom would we choose? There was a Vasojević here, the schoolteacher and inspector, he was supposed to be our savior and authority. So he formed a band and plundered right and left. For three months no one could be sure of his house or his family. In this whole district of Senica, or Bijelo Polje, you couldn't so much as hear a cock crow, that's how bare they left the land. They plundered and pillaged everything; the shops, the market, houses; they carried off the bedclothes, chickens, eggs, even the husks out of the manger. The men who escaped them fled in all directions. They didn't bother a man's family once they had stripped them naked. One bad thing we can't say of them: they didn't strike at night. They didn't carry off girls or molest the women, either. But whatever else they found, they carried it off— they'd even take the head off your shoulders. That went on until the new government took over. Then the pillaging stopped, but the people were left with nothing. For a while then some of us thought we would speak out. As far as Senica is concerned, it's three hours from Senica to here, somewhat less to Plevlje. The Serbs in the town of Senica were good to the Turks, and so were the Vasojevići in Berane. The Turks there weren't robbed of even so much as a bottle of medicine. Not only that; the Vasojevići didn't allow others to go into their region. They said: "These Turks are under our protection, so stay out of here!" But we in the district of Bijelo Polje suffered as no one has since Murat came to Kosovo. We didn't think there would be a scrap of clothing left in any of our houses, or that a cock would ever crow again, nor a cow moo, nor a sheep baa. That's how little we had left.

N: Did they kill anyone? A: You aren't serious? Haven't I told you about such incidents? We would have to go to Senica together for me to show you how many graves there are where they cut down four and five men at a time. You can see them all along the way from Bare to Trešnjevica to the top of Ugrinac to Senica. People would set out with an escort. "Come with me and let me show you the way, so you won't be molested. There are bad men where you are going." Then they would set on them, ten at a time, with knives and axes. There was a lot of it, and all done by the Christians. N: Were any of the beys done in at that time? A: Well, there was Hilmibeg, poor fellow, this boy's father. And two or three other beys from the shops here. There were five of them, and he was the sixth. They got the Kurtagići too, agas from Caruk, seven brothers and the father. Eight of the Darmani, too; they were also from Caruk. Some of my relatives from Trešnjevica, four from one house, three from another. I'll tell you of others, too, sir. Two fellows were coming from Senica. When they got to Pećarska, they cut them both down and lopped off their noses. In the midst of the bad feeling afterwards, some merchants set off from here to Novi Pazar to get some goods for their shops, so they could open up again. The market was a shambles and there was still no order. Some sort of secret patrol met them on the way and was supposedly going to protect them when they got to Pećarska. What they actually did was cut down five or six of them. They got at them through the government, too. They'd come for a man saying, "Come along, they want you at the police station." Every kind of horrible thing happened. The Christians were mostly responsible for it. N: Why do you suppose they did it, Avdo? A: How would I know why? N: I don't think they had any right to do such things, do you? A: I couldn't say that they did. There might have been something eating them,—maybe someone had done something to them once, so that it was passed down from generation to generation even though the younger ones might not otherwise have cared about it. When the new government came into power the authorities called them before the commune: "Come to your senses, we aren't trying to avenge Kosovo! What is it you think you are doing? These acts of yours will be heard of near and far, and you'll get yourselves into trouble with the state. This mustn't go on!" To be sure, the court didn't make reparations to us, but until the court began to function we suffered terribly from the peasants.

N: Tell me now; you are a good singer, how did you learn to play the gusle and sing? How old were you when you began, Avdo? A: Fifteen. I sang from the time I was fifteen. N: So you began when you were a child? A: Well yes, as a child. I was telling the professor about it. Take my son for instance, he's going on fifteen, but he doesn't know enough to sing even a word. I ask him: "How is it you can't sing? I sang for my father when I was your age." My father taught me, on the sly at first, and encouraged me to keep trying, and so I learned little by little. When I finally began to sing in public, he didn't once try to stop me. N: Did you have your own gusle? A: I used my father's at first. N: So it was from him you learned to sing? A: First from him, and then later, when I went to work, from whomever I chanced to hear. Whenever I heard of a good singer, I'd just keep asking around until finally I'd get a chance to listen to him. I had an older brother. He worked at home with my father while I just did whatever I could find to do around the place. N: Did your father sing much at home? A: He was seventy when he died. He told me how he began when he was twelve, and I'm not sure now whether it was one or two years later that he began to sing to the gusle. N: Did he often sing at home? A: They wouldn't let him stay in the place without singing. There are thirty or forty houses on our terraces. By God, Nikola, in those days people had great faith in us, even the merchants were honest folk. Trade was good and lively here in our own shops and outside, too. You could get your hands on some money or anything else you wanted and really make a decent living. They'd come from all around to hear him sing. I don't think there was another singer like him in the whole village. N: He was pretty good, was he? A: He sure was. And they liked his songs, too. They'd get together and spend the whole night listening to him. Winter nights and the house full of happy, contented people. "Come on, for God's sake, sing us a song!" N: Was it hard for you? A: What do you mean? N: Was it hard for you learning to sing? A: Well, yes, it was hard learning to sing right. I always wanted to put a song together and get it straight so that it would be good to listen to. I tried to sing so that it wouldn't . . . so that no one would be confused. I had a great desire to do that, and that was hard, but there wasn't anything else hard about it. Actually I started singing first. I still don't know how to play the gusle as I should; my song gets ahead of the playing. I started singing before I learned to play, and it's been that way ever since. N: Let's stop now and have something to eat, then we can go on with this afterwards . . . A: All right. God save you!

Riverfront view of Bijelo Polje on the Lim in 1935

Avdo's Repertory
Parry Text 6801
Bijelo Polje
June 27, 1935

Avdo dictated this list of his songs to Milman Parry's assistant, Nikola Vujnović, in Bijelo Polje on June 27, 1935. The list itself is Text 6801 in the Parry Collection.

Nikola asked Avdo to tell him from whom he had learned each of the songs; Avdo's answers are in the parentheses after the titles. The numbers of the texts in the Parry Collection are given in the margin before the title of each song that was later recorded or dictated (italic numbers indicate recorded songs).

The information which Avdo gave on this occasion about the sources of his songs should be compared with what he said a month later, on July 31 and August 1 (Texts *12436* and *12443*), since there are a number of discrepancies.

1. Sultan Selim Captures Bagdad
   (from Kasum Rebronja of Goduša, Bijelo Polje).
2. The Battle of Kosovo
   (from Sado Hadžović of Kolašin).
3. Sultan Bajazit Seeks Milica the Daughter of Jug Bogdan to Wife, at the Time When He Was at Edrena with Steven
   (from Hamid Nikšić-Ferizović of Nikšić).
4. The Battle of Temišvar
   (from Sado Hadžović of Kolašin).
5. Hajdar Alajbeg Leads a Wedding Band to Istanbul
   (from a songbook).
6. Ðerđelez Alija and Vuk Jajčanin
   (from his father, Husein Međedović).
7. Ðerđelez Alija and Sibinjanin Janko
   (from a songbook).
8. The Sickness of Ðerđelez and the Courting of His Wife by Hasanaga Čengić
   (from a songbook).
9. The Battle of Osjek
   (from a songbook).

25. Halil Rescues Mujo's Sister Ajkuna from Captivity in Oblić
    (from Sado Hadžović).
26. Husein Nakić's Betrothal to a Maid of Janok Whom Ibro Amaj-
    lić Rescued When the Ban Gave Her to Todor of Zadar
    (from Nezir Kaljić).
12427 27. Mujo and Halil Capture the Bandit Chieftain Kostreš
    (from Nezir Kaljić).
28. The Bosnians Defeat Pinjo of Vienna When He Attacks the
    Sultan and Lays Siege to Osik
    (from Avdaga Šahović of Bijelo Polje).
29. The Wedding of Maksim Crnojević
    (from Rade Đurđić of Jezera, Montenegro).
30. King Vukašin and Duke Momčilo
    (from Rade Đurđić).
31. Mujo and Halil and Seven of the Bey's Ensigns Go to Vienna
    to Rescue Mejruša Kozlić
    (from his father).
32. The Captivity of Alija Alagić and Rizvan Begzadić in Zadar
    (from his father).
12465 33. Šarac Mahmutaga Espouses the Wife of Kara Omeraga While
    Her Husband Is in Prison in Lenger
    (from his father).
34. Serdar Ograšić Raises the Army of Bosnia against Serdar Diklić,
    Who Slays Him
    (from Sado Hadžović).
6840 35. The Wedding of Hadji Smailaga's Son Meho
    (from a songbook).
36. Mehmed Bosnić Rescues Hadji Kapetan's Fatima from Aršag
    (from Hamid Ferizović).
6841, 37. The Wedding of Alija Vlahinjić and the Daughter of Alajbeg
12375   of Klis After Thirty Agas of Udbina Had Sued for Her Hand
    (from Islam Radoglavac of Bistrica, Bijelo Polje).
38. Halil Hrnjica Rescues Ramo of Glamoč's Fatima from Captivity
    in Sinje
    (from Rešo Alihadžić of the district of Sjenica).
39. The Men of Zadar Kidnap Mustajbeg of the Lika While He Is
    Sitting at Ease before His Castle, and Mujo Rescues Him after
    a Duel with the Ban of Zadar
    (from Nezir Kaljić).

53. The Captivity of the Imperial Queen in Koltok and Her Rescue
by the Hrnjica Brothers after Eight Years
(from Orle Kaljić).

12447 54. The Captivity of Sultan Selim's Two Daughters in Crete and
the Twenty-Seven Years' War to Conquer Crete and Liberate
Them
(from his father).

55. The Wedding of Ahmet Lalić to Hajkuna Babahmetović of
Udbina and Her Drowning in the River Vrbas with Ahmet's
Brother
(from his father).

56. Mujo Hrnjica's Raid on the Grazing Lands of Captain Šimun
at Požursko
(from his father).

57. The Wedding of Zajim Alibeg in Buda
(from his father).

58. The Commissioning of Alija Bojičić
(from his father).

The Singer Talks about His Songs
Parry Text 12436
Bijelo Polje
July 31, 1935

N: Now I'll ask you about your songs. *A:* All right. *N:* From whom did you hear the one about how Sultan Selim captured Bagdad? *A:* From that fellow Kasum Rebronja. *N:* Where did this Kasum Rebronja come from? *A:* From Goduša, from the district of Lozna. *N:* Is that a long way from here? *A:* It's five hours away. *N:* Where did you hear him sing? *A:* I heard him here in Bijelo Polje, in a café. *N:* What was he doing here? *A:* He came here one day on some business at the court, and they got him to sing for them while he was here: "Come on now, give us a song!" He used to sing here in town. *N:* Did you listen to him often? *A:* Only this one song. I didn't listen to him very much . . . *N:* And you heard the song only from him? *A:* I never heard anyone else sing it. *N:* I've heard that it was Ćor Husein's most important song. *A:* The one about Bagdad? *N:* Yes. *A:* What difference does it make whether it was Husein's song or not, when the singer who heard it from him wasn't a good one. *N:* You mean he isn't a good singer? *A:* Kasum? *N:* Yes. *A:* No, I don't think he is, but then, you see, other people seem to like him. *N:* When was it, Avdo? *A:* What? *N:* When you heard him sing. *A:* That was two years ago. *N:* How old was he, then? *A:* He was two years younger then than he is now. There isn't much difference between then and now. *N:* Come on, you know what I mean, how old do you think he was, roughly? . . . *A:* Now he looks to be about eighty, but I really don't know. *N:* Isn't he the one who came to see us here? *A:* Yes, that's him, that's the one. *N:* Why didn't he come back any more, Avdo? *A:* Well, I don't know. I suppose I could boast a little. Once we were all visiting Iljaz Sijarić at Šipovica. Radovan Božović was there, the director of the commune of Korita, and the treasurer, Ragib Hajdarović. There are nine houses of the Sijarići, and several of his relatives were there, too. And then this group with Kasum arrived; they were collecting the commune's budget. They found me staying with Iljaz Sijarić. He's my nephew, Osman's son. I had just lost my voice. They had been making me sing all night long for five nights running, and I had completely lost my voice. That's when Kasum and the others arrived: "Oho, come on and sing for us!" Radovan insisted: "Absolutely,

Međedović, you must sing for us now!" I said: "By God, I just can't any more." So I didn't sing that night. Kasum sang, fooled around for a while, and someone named Mihailo Božović, Radovan's brother. Then another time, about a year later, they found me there again. "Well, do you think you can do it now?" They were just the same people, Radovan Božović and Ragib Hajdarović, and Kasum, and the Sijarići, the whole lot of them. You see, I often visit that nephew. "Do you think you can do it now?" Radovan said: "I haven't heard a real singer; with you here, now's my chance. I keep hearing these young singers, and I don't like them." "I could sing some, but let's let Kasum sing for us." That's what I said. "No, no, you sing." "No, I won't; I want him to. In official company like this, wherever the chief Montenegrin officials gather, it must be Kasum who sings. Besides, I'd like to hear him, I've never heard him sing. Will you do it, Kasum?" It was an hour and a half after dark Turkish time when Kasum started singing the song about Zaim Alibeg and how he told his mother: "You're too old to knead my bread any more. I shall mount my white steed,

> And take with me forty footmen.
> Tomorrow will dawn our blessed Friday
> When I shall take Budim's vizier
> To the court of old Pasha Tiro.
> Wheresoever I may find a maiden in her pleasure garden,
> Will she but consent to me,
> So shall I wed her and bring her home,
> For you, mother, shall not knead me bread again."

That's a very good song, too. But do you know what he said, sir? He said that it wasn't Zaim Alibeg but Čengić Alibeg who did that. Yet there aren't any Čengići in Budim. What's more, the way I sing it, it's a very long song. But he sang the whole song between 1:30 and 2:30 Turkish time, and even then he paused three times! The way he was doing it, I didn't even want to hear him finish it. You'd think it wasn't even the same song. Then he offered to let me sing. "By God, I can't do it. I don't know anything about this song, brother." Then he started singing another song, an even shorter one, just fooling around and making a lot of racket. Finally it began to get on my nerves, and I told him: "Kasum, you're not singing it right just to spite me." Then I took the *gusli*. I sang about the death of Mustajbeg of the Lika. I started at three o'clock Turkish time and sang straight through 'til seven o'clock, and didn't stop once. Radovan was sitting on a chair about as far from me as your bed over there. While I was singing he kept moving closer and closer until he ended up sitting right in front of me. Kasum had been sitting behind me, and he came around in front of me and said: "Avdo, by God and the holy faith, from now on I'll never again sing in any place where you are." So it's possible he noticed me here when he came to see you, and maybe that's why he didn't come back again. I really don't know. Or maybe he saw that the professor wanted some real work out of him. When he starts singing, he gets off no more than two or three lines and then says: "I'm tired." If those aren't the reasons, then I don't know what kept him from coming back. You know how the professor makes a sign to me when I'm singing: "Go on, sing a little more!" Kasum would just say: "I'm too tired." He sings like a weasel, only five or six lines loud enough to record; he can manage to do that much, but that's about all.

N: Avdo, you say that when two singers sing the same song, if they don't . . . A: Kasum said that, Kasum said it, I didn't. N: That's right, he said it, Kasum said that if two singers don't sing the same song alike, then it isn't a true story. . . . he said that if they don't sing it alike, then it can't possibly be true history. A: Well, maybe one of them isn't right, because one of the two may not know the song exactly, and the other may know it better. Whichever is the better is the true one. N: But how can you tell which is the better? A: If you've got two singers, why, you can tell from the first third of the song which is better. If a singer is any good, he won't borrow things from one song and put them in another. And if some other singer makes the same song come out differently, then you have to say that he just doesn't know it as well as the first man. He may know some other songs, and he'll take some lines from them. That's how I judge it. N: I don't suppose Kasum really likes singing very much? A: Oh, you think he doesn't? N: He'd get a good laugh out of that, wouldn't he? A: Well, I'm sure he'd like to sing if he could, but he just doesn't know enough. N: So he sings what little he does know? A: He does what he can.

N: I've heard he's rather wealthy? A: You could say that. At least he has a lot of livestock. He has some seventy sheep, and ten cattle; he's got an old nag, too. He does pretty well growing grain. He has three or four sons and a couple of nephews who live with him. They're a regular commune up there in the mountains. Yet when you see him around here you'd say he's just a poor beggar. You know, you saw him that day he came here. Actually, I wouldn't want to trade places with him, but he brags a lot about how well off he is. But I've never gone up there to visit him, I've never even taken dinner with him. My nephew Iljaz told me how many cattle he has; I don't know anything about him firsthand. *N:* Does he sing around in the cafés? Is he ever asked to sing somewhere here in town for the month of Ramazan? *A:* Of course not. *N:* They don't ask him? *A:* Certainly not. *N:* But why not, Avdo? *A:* How should I know why not? Maybe . . . You see, Nikola, here in Bijelo Polje and the district around there are maybe twenty people who like to listen to Kasum, but for every twenty of them there are a hundred and twenty who don't. So the coffeeshop owners don't ask him to sing, nor has he ever come into town for that reason. Now he might just happen to be here on some market day in Ramazan and be delayed by some business or other so that he'd have to spend the night here and he might end up in a café: "Come on now, Kasum, sing for us, in God's name." Then he might sing them two or three songs in an hour's time before going off somewhere for the night. I guess that's why: either he can't sing well enough and doesn't come around, or people just don't like his singing; in any case not a single café owner ever invites him. *N:* Do you know whether he ever made a living by singing? *A:* Never. *N:* Never at all? *A:* Not that I ever heard of. Nor have I, for that matter, and I've been around a few years myself, you know. *N:* You say you've heard Kasum sing only that one time? *A:* Only that once at Iljaz Sijarić's place when he sang those two songs I've told you about, sawing away at 'em. Then as I told you I decided to show him how and rattled off that song without stopping. I had heard the song from him, too. And do you know what else I heard from him? The one about Bagdad. People kept asking me: "By God, how does that one about Bagdad go? The one about Bagdad is a fine song." I said: "Who sings it?" "Kasum and that fellow Mustafa sing it." Has Mustafa sung here for you? *N:* Which Mustafa? *A:* The one from Trhlje. *N:* I suppose he shortened it, too? *A:* Eh, then I asked Kasum: "Who did you hear this song from, Kasum?" He said: "From Mustafa. And I've sung it exactly as Mustafa sang it to me. Better than that I can't do." But I could see that somehow he wasn't doing it well.

Prof. Parry: So Kasum said that he had gotten it from Mustafa? *A:* That's what he told me . . . *N:* Which Mustafa? *A:* Biguljica, that chap Čelebić.

N: There's another song here now that you told me about, "The Battle of Kosovo" . . . From whom did you learn it? *A:* Mostly from Sado Hadžović. *N:* Did you ever hear it from anyone else? *A:* Yes, but I liked it best the way Sado sang it. *N:* I see. Where was he from? *A:* From Vraneš, under Grab. The place is called Grab, it's a good six hours from here. *N:* In which direction? East or north? *A:* To the north . . . *N:* Where did you hear him sing, Avdo? *A:* Here in town. Where you cross the bridge there used to be a coffeehouse that's closed now, on the downstream side. It used to belong to Doctor Martinović, only now it's gone out of business. But it used to be the main coffeehouse in town, and there used to be singing there. The courthouse was right across from it, on the upstream side, by those two fountains. *N:* Did you hear him sing very often, Avdo? *A:* A number of times. Once I had heard of his singing that song, I went around to hear him as soon as I could.

N: How old was he when you heard him sing? *A:* He was my age. *N:* How long ago was it? *A:* Thirty or forty years ago. *N:* Oho! What did he look like? *A:* He was a man with moustaches, a rather dark complexion, bushy eyebrows, that sort of thing, an ordinary kind of man, roughly my height. *N:* What sort of clothes did he wear? *A:* He wore embroidered white leggings with a lot of white fastenings on them, and black Montenegrin pants from here to here, such as they used to wear. You don't see them around here anymore, except maybe on some Montenegrin. He had a double-breasted jacket too, and a fancy open vest of the kind they make in Scutari. Then he had a skullcap like this, with a turban wrapped around it. *N:* Was he a good singer, Avdo? *A:* Yes, I have to admit that he was a good songst . . . singer, because he really was. *N:* Did he make a living by the gusle? *A:* No, he didn't. Neither he nor anyone else tried to earn a living from the gusle in those days, except at the residences of beys and agas. *N:* Did he go to sing at beys' houses? *A:* Yes, he did . . . If he were to come to market and if they happened to notice that he was here, they'd send a man to watch him all day so that he wouldn't slip off and go home but would stay and sing for them at the residence. *N:* Who was it that would keep watch on him like that? *A:* Osmanaga Kučević and Fehimbeg Kajabegović. They were Efendi Dervović's men. There used to be a whole family of Dervovići here: Hadji Hamdija, Hadji Halil, Hadji Ibro, Hadji . . . All of them tried to ambush Sado that way. He was a wonderful singer. *N:* Well, would they pay him something when he did stay? *A:* Yes, they'd make him a gift, but he wouldn't ask them for anything. When they had all gotten together in the room, then you'd hear the quarters start to fall, and the dollars . . . *N:* Was he a working man? What was his business? *A:* He was just a laborer, but he had his own commune; he had nephews and brothers. He didn't actually have to work very much. You see, he was really a wealthy man, although he was just a laborer.

    N: Did he sing long or short songs, Avdo? *A:* He sang his songs as long as he could possibly make them, and decorated them beautifully . . . *N:* Did you ever hear a better singer than he? *A:* Well now, it's true that I've heard Avdaga Šahović, but not very much, only one or two songs. I didn't study one of his songs at all, but I learned the other one from him. Avdaga sang with a fuller voice and Sado was quieter, but I think that's better, he was easier to understand, and so far as I'm concerned I've never heard anyone sing more enjoyably than Sado. *N:* Where was Sado from by birth? *A:* He was from here too, a Kolašiner from the Hasanbegović, Hodžić and Hadžović families. They were all founded by three brothers, all from Kolašin. *N:* But how can you say that he was born here when he's really a Kolašiner? How can that be, for God's sake? If he was born here, then he must be a native of Bijelo Polje! *A:* But that's not the way we do it. We call everything between here and the river Lim Kolašin. *N:* Aha! *A:* We still call it that. And the part up there where it borders on it, that's upper Kolašin. *N:* So which Kolašin was he from, upper or lower? *A:* Oh, I don't know that. Even if his old man sent him down from up above, we consider him born here.

    N: Now how about Sultan Bajazit, when he sought the daughter of Jug Bogdan? *A:* I heard that song from Hamid Ni'šić-Ferizović, Hajro's brother. *N:* Aha! Where was he from? *A:* He was from Ni'šić, obviously. When Ni'šić was captured, he packed up and emigrated and came to live in my village of Obrov. His house is still there. Both his house and Hajro's have since been sold to a Serb . . . So I heard him sing right in my own village. *N:* Did you hear him often? *A:* Yes, I did. He came and sang in my father's house many times. *N:* Was he a good singer? *A:* Yes, he was. *N:* How old was he when you used to listen to him, Avdo? *A:* Oh, he was a good sixty-five. *N:* And you? *A:* I was no more than fifteen or sixteen at the time, still a boy. But I'd already begun to sing then myself . . . *N:* Now tell me, how did this Kolašiner from Nikšić earn a living? *A:* Well, about as you'd expect of an immigrant. They were hard-working people. They worked as diggers in the quarry. There were three brothers, Hadžo, Hajro, and Hamid. They had formed a commune and lived on their wages. They were honorable immigrant folk and they got along very well. They didn't go in for a lot of heavy eating and drinking. I think that's because they weren't like the rest of us with property and a position in the world to keep up. *N:* Where did this Nikšićer sing mostly? *A:* Everywhere; sometimes at the agas', sometimes at the beys', then later for the more prominent Serbs after the Balkan War when King Nikola came to power and we became his subjects, he sang then, too. I even heard him sing once at the church, when there was a council. He used to sing over by the town park, and in coffeehouses. They'd ask him to sing wherever he turned up, because he was a good singer. *N:* And you say he sang for the beys? *A:* Of course he did. *N:* And they would invite him to their houses? *A:* That's right. *N:* And did he sing in the hans, too? *A:* Yes, but I don't know that he ever sang in the hans for money. He might just happen to be there, and they'd say: "Pass that gusle over to Hamid!" *N:* Did the beys ever go to the hans when he sang there? *A:* They used to sit around the hans like everyone else. The beys around here never did any work. Living was easy in those days. No one . . . well take for example, maybe you've already noticed those people outside, those two peasants. One of them was out there in front of the house until just a little while ago, standing right by the door; he looks like any ordinary peasant. His former property is just down there, but now he can hardly call his soul his own and does homage to others. All of them have fallen on hard times the same way. But in the old days they used to get some grain and other things in tribute, and they'd give someone two or three cows to take care of for them in return for the calves, or they'd hire out two or three oxen for ploughing. From that they would make enough to keep them in tobacco and coffee and a little meat now and then. Each had his own fig trees and patch of grain. That's how they used to live. Living used to be carefree hereabouts; we didn't have all these taxes to pay. The emperor didn't impose any great tax, and people didn't worry so much about their business.

N: You said something about the "prominent Serbs"? Who were they? *A:* They came in when the Balkans became independent and when Montenegro got power. People like Mile Dožić, like the Medenica family and the Vojsijići from Montenegro, and let's see who else . . . the

Vasojevići. *N:* But why would they come to listen to Turkish songs?
A: After all, they lived here too. And he didn't sing Turkish songs to
them. He sang about Derviš Pasha's attack on Ni'šić and about the attacks on the Montenegrins by the raiding bands of Ni'šić, he sang songs
like that about the fighting around Mount Krnovo for them. But before
that, in Turkish times, when I used to go around the hans, he sang such
songs as the one about Bajazit, and Bosnian songs like the one about
Paul the Croat. I once heard Šećo sing the second half of that song. But
Šećo didn't know it as well as he did. But then I didn't hear him sing all
of it. *N:* Did he earn a living that way, supporting himself by this gusle?
A: Absolutely not, brother! He didn't get anything from it, they didn't
even give him anything as a gift, unless somewhere in a coffeeshop they
were to beg him: "For God's sake, please do it" and he would insist:
"I can't." Then a few people might take out maybe three piasters apiece
and give them to him. But he didn't earn his living that way at all, he
had his work for that, the work he did with his brothers. *N:* Were his
songs long or short? *A:* Well, he might have decorated them better. Sado
decorated a song better than he did. But he had a fine voice, good and
clear, so that you could understand whatever he said.

N: Now how about the song: "The Battle of Temišvar"? From
whom did you hear it? *A:* I got it out of a songbook. *N:* What do you
mean "out of a songbook," when you can't even read or write? *A:* No,
I swear to you, there was a boy here who had four years of grammar
school, I've forgotten who he was . . . seems to me he was one of Šoro's
children from that quarter of town. He was the one who had the songbook. He read it to me several times and I liked it, so I learned it.
N: Did he read it to you very often? *A:* Yes, several times. *N:* Had you
ever heard the song sung anywhere before that? *A:* Several people had
told me the story before, but I hadn't ever bothered to learn it from
anyone because I didn't like it very well. *N:* Did you find it easier to
learn from a songbook or from the gusle? *A:* I know for a fact that the
songbook was in Latin characters, but there was some Cyrillic mixed in,
so that the song was shorter than it should have been. Had it been entirely in Latin type, it could have been a good song. But I would have
liked it best if I head heard it from a good singer. *N:* What do you mean
it could have been a good song if it had been in Latin characters? What
do you mean by that? *A:* Take for example "The Siege of Osjek" . . .
against Šestokrilović. It's in Latin characters. I heard it from a song-

book, one of the lads here read it to me several times, and I learned it
that way. Then afterwards I sang it one night in a coffeeshop, and a
lieutenent from Lauž was there in the shop, though I didn't know it.
The place was packed solid with people of all kinds, a huge crowd all
crammed into one little café. When I finished the song, the waiter
brought me a cup of tea and a dime. I asked him: "Who ordered this?"
He said: "The lieutenant over there wishes to honor you with the tea."
And sure enough, there he was sitting up by the chimney. "And the
dime is so you can buy tobacco." I said: "Give him my thanks." He
called to me from where he sat: "Old fellow, are you literate?" All this
happened only year before last. "No, I'm not." "So you don't read the
newspapers?" "No." "Bravo! I'm here all the way from Lauž, and here's
the songbook with this song in it. The way I read it, you haven't made
a single mistake." Then we looked in the book and saw that it was written in Latin type . . . Latin characters, the kind the Germans sell all the
way down here. Cyrillic is what they print in Montenegro, and they
either shorten the songs or tell them topsy-turvy. But all the songs I've
heard from singers and then later heard read from songbooks in Latin
characters, when I've compared them with the songs as I know them,
I've never found that they conceal any details, such as an attack on
them by the Turks or theirs on the Turks. They don't do what the
Montenegrins do and make the one side better than the other every
time. Because I've noticed that theirs always make one side more noble
than the other . . .

N: Now about the song of Hajdar Alajbeg, when he led the wedding band to Istanbul . . . from whom did you hear it? A: From a songbook. One of the little beys read it to me, the brother of the one I told
you about before. N: Good. How often did you listen to it? A: No more
than that one time. N: Only once? A: Only once. N: Is it a good song,
Avdo? A: It's a nice song. N: Is it a long one? A: I believe it's a thousand, over a thousand verses long. N: Is it nicely decorated? A: Beautifully decorated. It's a very nice song. N: Is there a blackamoor in
the song? A: Idriz is in it. N: Idriz the Blackamoor? A: That's right.
N: What did he do, try to stop a wedding band? A: Yes. N: Who beheaded him? A: Ðerđelez. Only he didn't cut off his head. Instead he
ripped out his beard, cut off his ears and took him to the Emperor alive.
N: Aha!

Who told you the song: "Đerđelez Alija and Vuk Jajčanin"? *A:* It's from a songbook. *N:* It too? *A:* Yes. *N:* Then who read it to you? *A:* One of the lads, and it was just a few years ago, too. But I swear, I can't remember the names of all these young people. If one of them happens to own a songbook, someone is always after him to read him the song, and they keep selling the book from one to another among themselves. *N:* I suppose it must have been a songbook about Đerđelez Alija. *A:* That's right, "Vuk Jajčanin and Đerđelez." That's the main song in it.

N: How about "Đerđelez Alija and Sibinjanin Janko"? *A:* It's also from a songbook. Šoro's boy read it to me . . . Actually, I've never either heard that song from any singer nor seen it anywhere else . . . The boy bought the book for fifteen dinars, and it had two songs in it, this one and "The Sickness of Đerđelez." *N:* Is it a long song, Avdo? *A:* "Sibinjanin Janko's Combat with Đerđelez"? . . . It's rather long. As I sing it, about a thousand verses, no more. *N:* And "The Sickness of Đerđelez Alija"? *A:* Shorter. . . . *N:* When you learn a song from a songbook, do you decorate it somewhat more when you sing it? *A:* When I see an instance where he's done a nice job of decorating, I'm in the habit of going one better. *N:* So wherever he wants to, you do too, is that it? *A:* Yes.

N: And "The Battle of Osjek"? *A:* From a songbook. *N:* It's from a songbook too? *A:* Yes. *N:* Who read it to you? *A:* A man from Korita named Lazović read it to me at Iljaz's house. *N:* Did he read it for you often? *A:* No. Only twice, on two successive days. One day he dropped in to visit his neighbor, and I happened to be there. The next day they went off together on some business or other, and came back that same night. I had liked the song, so I said: "Please read it through for me again!" That's how I heard it twice. *N:* Is it a long song? *A:* Yes, it's very long. *N:* And you think it's a pretty good one? *A:* By my faith, I do, brother. I don't know why he did such a lot of shouting about it. I have a song, for example. When someone is dear to me as he is it doesn't matter to me what the village thinks of him, it's enough for me that I like him. *N:* Is there a Ljubović in that song? *A:* Yes, Ahmetbeg is in it . . . *N:* Was he killed in it? *A:* Yes. *N:* Where? *A:* Up there at Trome-đa. General Hajvaz and he slew each other, laid each other out dead one beside the other.

N: From whom did you hear the song about when General Save prevented the marriage of Osmanbeg Šestokrilović's daughter? *A:* From Orle Kal'ić. *N:* And where did this Eagle Kaljić hail from? *A:* From Vraneš. Vraneš is in Kolašin, the village of Lijeska. *N:* In upper or lower Kolašin? *A:* Vraneš is lower Kolašin. *N:* Where did you hear him, if he came from so far away? *A:* He used to come to town like the others, and they'd chase after him the way they did the others. He was a good singer, even though he was a bit of a dandy. Just when he'd have everyone all excited so that they were really enjoying it, he'd suddenly throw down the gusle and rush out the door as though a devil possessed him. And that would be the end of it, he wouldn't come back. *N:* Why would he do that? *A:* That's the kind of person he was. *N:* High-strung? *A:* That's right. But he was still a good singer . . . and a handsome buck to look at. *N:* Did you listen to him often? *A:* Brother, I sure did! *N:* Did you learn many songs from him? *A:* I didn't get all his songs from end to end, but I did this one. This is the one I got down best, and a good song it is. *N:* How old was he when you listened to him? *A:* There wasn't actually much difference in our ages. He wasn't much older than I was, around ten or twelve years. *N:* Was that a long time ago? *A:* Oh, quite a long time ago, yes, back in Turkish times. That was even before I joined the army! . . . *N:* Did you to hear him in the coffeehouse? *A:* In the big coffeehouse on the upper side as you come down this way. It's that tall building, the tallest one on that side. It's vacant now, but it used to be the main coffeehouse, Osmanaga Kučević's. *N:* What did he look like? *A:* Who, Orle? *N:* Yes. *A:* He was a handsome lad. Blond, not one of these dark-skinned fellows, a bushy moustache, and a lover's expression on his face. Big, tall, slim fellow. *N:* What did he wear? *A:* The same as Sado Hadžović, only better; he was good-looking. *N:* The same kind of Montenegrin clothes? *A:* That's the only kind he ever did wear. The whole of Kolašin wore Montenegrin clothes up until the end of the Turkish empire. They even wore them right here in town. *N:* Did he earn his living as a singer? *A:* Good God, no! He was Feizaga Kaljić's son, his pride would never permit that. *N:* How can someone named Orle Kaljić be a Moslem? How is that possible? *A:* Of course it's possible. The Moslems in these parts have all sorts of names: Šoro, Orle, Rogo, Hrnjo, Mujo. Any name you could think of you could find among the people of Kolašin. There were probably three or four brothers in the family, and one day his mother or his father said: "Look at him run! He's just like an eagle!" "Yes, just like an eagle!" And so the nickname stuck. His real name was Osman. . . . *N:* So Orle was his nickname, but he was really Osman? *A:* Orle was his common name . . . *N:* Did he ever sing for the beys? *A:* Sure he did. Wherever the chief people were, Orle would sing for them. *N:* What do you mean by "the chief people"? *A:* The beys and agas. You have to understand, he was the son of one of the chief agas. Those aristocrats kept pretty much to their own kind. He didn't esteem just anybody enough to sing for him, nor did just anyone dare say to him: "Let's have a song!" *N:* Did they ever invite him home to sing for them? *A:* To be sure! Amiraga for example, Osmanaga's son. He was his sworn-brother and closest friend, the brother of Began, Smailaga. He kept company with such men as the Ni'šići, the Dervovići, and Kajabegovići. There was Hamzibeg Kajabegović . . . hey! What a blade he was! He and Orle would get together and go around the wineshops and coffeehouses raising the devil, or ride their horses through the market scaring everyone and firing off their rifles, what a pair they were!

N: Did they pay him when he sang for them? *A:* Absolutely not! No one would have even dared to suggest it. *N:* Why not? *A:* He simply wouldn't have accepted it. Eh! He wouldn't stoop so low. *N:* I see. He behaved as though he were above all that. *A:* Well, he really *was* above it, that's all there is to it. *N:* And he was a good singer? *A:* He was a good singer. *N:* How could someone like that, an aga or a bey, how could he be a good singer? How is that possible? *A:* It's perfectly possible. He was a real aga, and his father before him, and they used to invite him to sing, and they owned serfs, too, and . . . Would you like me to tell you something else about them? Every last one of them is gone now. They've all emigrated to Asia. Some of them were killed, and all that were left went to Asia. There isn't a one of them here anymore. But the time was when this whole region from upper Kolašin to the district beyond the Tara, during the reign of the king and the prince and even after the prince, the whole of Montenegro honored them and trembled at the thought of them. *N:* The Kaljići? *A:* On my faith! That's no exaggeration. If people showed up along the Tara and the border there, you could always count on Orle and Feizaga, Feizaga especially would always get into it. They were good people and famous fighters, that's all there is to it.

N: Did he sing long songs? *A:* This song about how Šestokrilović's daughter was prevented from marrying is a long one. She's the one who nuzzled up to Hadji Smail. *N:* How do you mean, nuzzled him? *A:* She made advances, the way a mare does when it goes after a stallion. *N:* Aha! Did he sing shorter songs too? *A:* I guess he did. As I was telling you, I used to come in in the middle of his songs, and sometimes he no sooner began that than he'd throw down the gusle and go off. But I learned this one from him whole. *N:* How could you have learned it whole, when all you ever heard him sing was one piece at a time? *A:* It wasn't that he only sang one piece at a time, it was only now and then that he had these fits. It didn't always happen. *N:* Aha! You say he was about your age? *A:* No, there was a ten-year difference, ten years more than me. . . . I began to learn songs when I was about fifteen, so he must have been twenty-five. That must have been it, because I remember when I was twenty-five it was the best time of my life. I could sing a song for five hours straight without stopping.

N: Since you were so nearly the same age and all, how is it you didn't learn the songs from the same people he was learning from? *A:* His father was a good singer, but I never had any occasion to meet his father. I had to learn where I could.

N: The song "The Death of Mustajbeg of the Lika," whom did you hear it from? *A:* It must have been from Hasan Ni'šić. *N:* Where was Hasan from? *A:* He was chased out of Ni'šić and lived here as an immigrant. *N:* So he was a newcomer, was he? *A:* Yes, a newcomer. *N:* Where was it you heard him sing? *A:* At the han on the other side of the bridge, over where the hotel is. That's where he sang mostly. The men of Nikšić used to get together there all the time. That was the main han, and the Nikšićers would gather there to talk, with a few Bijelo Polje people mixed in. *N:* I suppose he used to sing for that crowd at Ramazan? *A:* Yes, indeed, during Ramazan when those men congregated. *N: N:* Did he sing all during Ramazan, the way you did in the han here, for example? *A:* You mean continuously? No. *N:* I mean did he sing all through Ramazan? *A:* No, no. *N:* You say he didn't eh? *A:* No, only some nights. *N:* Did you hear him sing often? *A:* Well, now and then. *N:* How many times did you hear him sing this song that you say you got from him which you had me write down here? *A:* Oh, I suppose I heard it two or three times. But you know, Nikola, he couldn't sing many songs. Maybe ten, or at most twelve. *N:* That's all he knew? *A:* Yeah, and not many of his were

Bosnian songs either, more the Montenegrin kind, like the one about Jašar Babić and that sort. People used to tell me how good a singer he was, but I never cared much for that kind of song—. *N:* How could he get away with singing the same song over and over all the time? *A:* That never made any difference. Take me, for example, I know fifty or sixty songs. I might happen to sing only this or that song in the coffee-house where I sing during a particular Ramazan, and some other—the others I know—another time. But nobody ever got bored with my songs on that account, because they liked them you see, and it didn't make any difference whether I sang this one or that. *N:* Was he an old singer? *A:* Yes, he was sixty when I learned that song from him. *N:* And how old were you? *A:* I was—, well, God help me, I was not much more than a full-grown lad—, I suppose about twenty. *N:* I see. What did he look like, this old fellow? *A:* He wore the same kind of clothes I told you about earlier, elegant: the usual sort of waistcoat with long sleeves, and a silken turban wrapped 'round his head. Trousers and Montenegrin leggings. *N:* How did he make his living? Was he just an ordinary working man? What was he? *A:* No. He had a couple of houses in the town, mostly let for rent. He was involved with tobacco, too. He used to buy it around here, and carry it over Kamena Gora or by way of Brenčani, just like in the song that fellow was singing the other day. He used to take it to Plevlja and Taslidža were it was contraband, and sell it there. He made something of a profit that way, and got along well enough. *N:* I see.

Did he ever sing for the beys? *A:* Whenever they went down there where he was, but they didn't send for him to sing for them in their own homes. *N:* . . . Did he go around singing at the other hans? *A:* As I said, mostly at the han where the Nikšićers went, but not much of anywhere else. *N:* Did they usually give him something when he sang? *A:* I never noticed. *N:* Nothing at all? *A:* Not that I saw. *N:* Did they at least honor him with coffee? *A:* Oh yes, there was always coffee, of course. Coffee, and tobacco in boxes sold by weight. It cost only—, three dinars, two bits for a kilo and a quarter. Local tobacco was a hundred mills, three bits for the better quality. Skoplje shop cost twelve bits—, "Vardar"-brand tobacco. *N:* And you say he never earned his living with the gusle? *A:* No, brother, he didn't, not that I saw. Now whether the Nikšićers down there, his own people, ever gave him anything on account of his being "their man," that I wouldn't know. But as for my seeing them give him anything—I never did.

N: Would you say he was one of the better singers, or just average,

or a poor one? How do you rank him? *A:* I consider him a good one.
N: He was a good one, was he? *A:* That's right. *N:* Did he decorate a
song well? *A:* It could have been better. *N:* Better, you say? *A:* Could
have been. *N:* But then how can you call him a "good singer?" *A:* He
said everything clearly and kept it going, so you can't hold it against
him for not being able to decorate very much. His song would go
straight along, smoothly and cleanly, so no one could say of it: "There's
a bit of the lie in this one!" *N:* I see. *A:* So I think he was a good singer.
N: What you mean is that he sang only what was true? *A:* More or less.
For my part, I never got into that war, nor any since it. *N:* How do you
mean? You were wounded, weren't you? *A:* Oh, that was the Balkan
one, that war, not the, not—.

    N: Now when Sirdar Mujo avenged the Bey of the Lika, from
whom did you hear that song? *A:* That was from him, too. *N:* From the
same one? *A:* That's right. *N:* And where did you hear it? *A:* Right here
in the han. *N:* Did you hear it often? *A:* Two or three times, maybe
four. *N:* God, but that's a long song! *A:* Long, you say? *N:* Yeah. *A:*
Yes, it is rather long, by God.

The Singer Talks about His Songs
Parry Text *12443*
Bijelo Polje
August 1, 1935

[Disk No. 6582] *Nikola:* How about the song when Hrnjica and Halil—
Hrnjica Halil and the bey's seven ensigns—when they went to Vienna to
rescue Mejruša Kozlić, from whom did you hear it? *Avdo:* From Sado
Hadžović. *N:* I suppose it's a fine song too? *A:* It's not one of the long
ones, I guess not more than a thousand or twelve hundred lines, but it's
a nice one. *N:* How many times did you hear it? *A:* Oh, I heard that
one, two, or three times. *N:* Didn't you sometimes hear it from others
besides Sado? *A:* Never did. *N:* Only from him? *A:* Yes, just from him.
No one else. If I ever did hear anyone else sing it, I didn't pay any attention. Wouldn't be any reason to—no one else would sing it the way
Sado did. *N:* I see. Good. Now what about "The Captivity of Ali Alagić
and Rizvan Begzadić in Zadar"? *A:* Seems to me I heard it from Hasan

Ni'šić or maybe the son-in-law—one of the Ljucas, must have been Pašo. One of those two, anyway; I don't remember which—*N:* But how do you sing it? *A:* You mean Ali Alagić? *N:* Yes. *A:*

Procmiljela do dva pobratima—

N: Yes, I know that's how it begins. *A:* What, then? *N:* You say you heard it from the both of them? *A:* That's right. *N:* But then you'd have to learn it according to the particular manner of one or the other, wouldn't you? *A:* I learned it the way I heard it first from the first of them. Then afterwards when I heard it again from the other man I wasn't learning it anymore. But it doesn't matter, there wasn't any difference between them that I could tell. *N:* They sang it just the same? *A:* They sang it exactly alike. *N:* You mean everything exactly alike? *A:* Everything. Not more than ten words' difference in the whole thing. *N:* But I'll bet the decoration of the song was different, now wasn't it— the things that they dressed up in the song? *A:* That's just what I mean —it wasn't. *N:* Nothing different at all? *A:* Nothing, so help me, no more, no less. *N:* Is it at least possible that you do it a bit more amply than they did? *A:* Well, maybe I decorate it better. *N:* Is it a long song? *A:* Well, yes, it is. *N:* Like "The Captivity of Tale"? *A:* Not that long. Tale's Captivity is a long one. *N:* Eight years long, if I remember rightly —*A:* No, I mean the song is a long one. *N:* Eh, eh.

N: Now how about Kara Omeraga, when he was a prisoner in Lender? *A:* Didn't I hear that one from my father? *N:* From your father? *A:* I think so. *N:* Is it a big song? *A:* No, it's short. *N:* I see. Is that the one where he kills Šarac Mahmutaga on the day of his return, for wooing his wife while he was away? *A:* That's the one.

N: And Sirdar Ograšić, when he raised up Bosnia against Sirdar Diklić, from whom did you hear that? *A:* I think it was from Avdaga Šahović. *N:* Good. *Parry:* I believe you said something to me earlier about that song being rather tragic? *A:* Yes, it is—all about how he called up the men of Bosnia, and the big battle that followed, and how Diklić won it. He was his mother's only son, you see, and he not yet even twenty years old. His family was impoverished. At one time it had five hundred rents, and warehouses, and stores—all that went for dowries, and only the mother was left. And when all the property was gone, Mujo took him in. That's why it's a sad song, on account of the property all being lost in dowries, and the lady his mother going through all that trouble in her later years, so it's a sad song for that reason, you see. But then Mujo avenged him. And an awful lot of the men of the Krajina were slain. The battle lasted some four or five days—

N: How about "The Wedding of Smajilagić Meho"? A: Let's see— did I tell you about how I heard it from a songbook? N: From a song-book? A: Yes. N: I believe you did. Who read it to you? A: Hivzo Džafić. There was a lad here in the slaughterhouse, who got it from somewhere. It was about this size. P: (Words too faint). N: (Response to Parry) Yes, yes, in the songbook. (To Avdo): How many times did he read it to you? A: Five or six times. N: Did you ever hear anyone sing it to the gusle? A: No. N: Are you sure you never heard it sung by any-one at all? [Record No. 6583] —yes. A: No, I didn't.

N: All right, Avdo. Was it a big book or a little one? A: I think there were about a hundred and forty printed pages in it. N: A hundred and forty pages? A: Yes. N: Was the format big or little? A: It was pretty big. Long and wide, like this. N: Aha! A: I haven't seen any song-books that large since then—it was almost as big as the gentleman's over there [meaning Parry's] —. N: Those books over there? A: Aye, those. It was thick like them. N: And Bosnić?—. P: Does he mean to say that he never, *never* heard the song sung to the gusle? N: Are you sure you never heard it sung to the gusle—never heard anyone at all sing it with the gusle? A: I'd never heard it from a living soul until the day he read it to me. N: Not even once? A: No.

N: I'm still amazed that you could learn it from a book just by someone reading it to you. A: But you see, he—he's no scholar, he just pecks away at it little by little, a word at a time. And actually I like it best that way, when it's read slowly—. N: Did you decorate everything in the song just the way it is in the songbook? A: No, I did more of that. N: More, you say? A: Yes, more, by at least twice. N: Aha! At least twice as much? A: That's how I do it. Do you want me to lie to you, or tell you the truth? N: The truth, just tell me the truth! A: Aye! N: Yes, we've got to get at the truth. A: Well then, mate, as I've told you before, when some other good singer takes five hours to sing a tale, I need ten. I don't know whether that's good or bad, but that's how it is. I'll sooner die than lie to you. N: Right, that's the way it has to be. A: Aye. N: That's it, Avdo. P: Okay, Avdo, that's good.

N: Now, what about "When Mehmed Bosnić Rescued Fatima from"—uh, from Aršan? A: I heard that from Hasan Nikšić. N: From Hasan Ni'šić? A: Yes. N: Okay. P: (Words too faint). N: And "The

Wedding of Ali Vlahinjić and Zlata, Daughter of the Alaybey of Klis"?
A: I think I heard it from Sado Hadžović. *N:* All right. And "The Captivity of Ramo of Glamoč's Fatima in Senj"? The one about how Halil
Hrnjica rescued her? *A:* In Senj, you say? *N:* Yes. *A:* Ramo of Glamoč's
Fatima? *N:* Right. *A:* I heard it too from—er, either Hamid or Hasan,
mate. By god, I'll confuse you if I'm not careful. I honestly don't remember which of the two it was. *N:* You told me here that it was from
Rešo Alihadžić. *A:* Do you mean this one or the one before? *N:* Oh, no,
no! It's my mistake, my mistake. You said Nezir Kaljić. *A:* Right.
N: That's it. *A:* I learned all of them that I know from those six or eight
singers whom I've told you about already. I sometimes get them confused myself.

N: When the men of Zadar kidnapped the Bey of the Lika as he
sat at table before his house—whom did you hear it from? *A:* From a
songbook. *N:* From a songbook? *A:* Yes. *N:* Who read it to you? *A:* The
young bey here, Zajimović's son. *N:* Is he the one who's the waiter
here? *A:* Beg pardon? *N:* Was that the fellow who's the waiter here,
Džemo? *A:* No, no. He was just a young lad in the second year of
school. *N:* So it was someone else, then. When did he read it to you?
A: Last year. *N:* Just a year ago? *A:* That's right.

N: When did he read you the one about Hadji Smajilaga's son?
A: That was three years ago. *N:* Three years? *A:* Yes. *N:* How many
times did he read it? *A:* Five or six. I had a butchershop then, and his
shop was just next door, where the slaughterhouse is. It was his book.
When the meat gave out, I used to go round and say: "Hivzo, read me
some of that song now, will you?" So he'd start in reading it bit by bit
as long as he could, and I'd be studying it all the while. I liked it awfully, and I could tell it was a good song.

Hivzo Džafić Talks about the Songbook
Parry Text *12474*
Bijelo Polje
August 10, 1935

Nikola: Hivzo, where did you buy the songbook that you used to read Avdo Međedović that song? *Hivzo:* From Mihail Milanović, the bookseller in Sarajevo. *N:* Just when was that? When did you buy it? *H:* It was during—actually, I should say that I bought the whole lot for him from a student. But judging from the inscription on it, it was from Mihail Milanović, the bookstore in Sarajevo. That was back in Austrian times, when the government was—*N:* Austrian? *H:* That's right. That's when it was printed.

N: Now tell me, what size was the songbook? *H:* It wasn't one of the little ones. *N:* But was the format small? *H:* Yes, it had a small shape. *N:* Do you remember how many pages it had? *H:* Forty. *N:* Forty pages? *H:* Forty pages. *N:* And was it all one song inside? *H:* No. *N:* Not? *H:* No, there was a—a supplement at the end. *N:* Can you remember what it was about? *H:* It was the "Nine Atlagići." *Parry:* Was that a long song? *N:* Was it long? *H:* No, it was a small one. It was a small part of the book, scarcely three pages. *N:* Only three pages? *H:* That's right. *N:* And what did it say on the cover of the book? *H:* It said "Cifra Hasanaga." *N:* Nothing more than that? *H:* That's all. Just "Cifra Hasanaga." *N:* What kind of cover did it have, hard or soft? *H:* Soft. Thin. *N:* Ordinary paper? *H:* That's right. *N:* How much did you pay for it? *H:* I don't rightly know. It was part of a lot, and I paid a lump sum for the whole lot. There were some ten books besides—but it wasn't any big amount. *N:* You mean you bought a number of books all at the same time? *H:* That's right. *N:* I see. So then you read the song to Avdo, is that it? *H:* Yes. *N:* Now just how did it all happen? *H:* Actually, you see, I've already pretty well—forgotten. I remember only that, uh—Smail—, uh—, Cifra Hasanaga and Hadji Smailaga, they were brothers. *N:* That's right. *H:* And they had—uh, that is, he had a son, Mehmed. *N:* Right. *H:* So there you have it so to speak, those two were brothers, see, both of them brothers, and, and he was the son, and the nephew of the other one. *N:* Okay. All that's easy for us to find out. But how did you happen to read Avdo that songbook? *H:* Oh, I just read it to him once over, that's all. *N:* Only once? *H:* Really, that's all, on my honor!

Only once. *N:* But how was it that Avdo happened to be there to hear you read it? *H:* I told him about it. I told him I'd gotten hold of such and such a book. I said, "I've gotten a book called, uh–'Cifra Hasanaga' and, uh–the one about what happened at Osjek." *N:* I see. *H:* Those two. That's what that book was about inside, that and the other one about Osjek, the business at Osjek, Osmanbeg's, uh–the Death of Bey Ljubović–I remember that he was in it. *N:* Yes. *H:* But I don't recall the rest. Read it to him right in the shop. Read it through just once.

N: What sort of shop was it you used to keep down here? *H:* Slaughterer, butcher. *N:* Butcher? *H:* Yes, I'm a butcher. He was a butcher too, and we were right next door to each other. *N:* Aha! So that's how you got together, is it? *H:* Yep. *N:* How many days did it take you to read it to him? *H:* Well now, you have to understand that I taught myself to read, so I can't read fast. *N:* Yes, yes. *H:* So for that reason I read it to him slowly, when there was a lull in the business, so to speak, and we weren't working. A half a day at a time, I suppose I was at it three days or so. *N:* Three days? *H:* Yes, about three days, because remember I can't read fast. My brains just get worn out from reading.

N: Was the printing Cyrillic or Latin characters? *H:* Latin. *N:* Latin characters all the way through? *H:* Uh huh. *N:* Did you read through the song in advance? *H:* Yes, I read it all to him one thing after another, uh–just the way it went in the book. *N:* And you never repeated anything? *H:* No, by God, nothing at all. *N:* Do you know how to read well enough not to make mistakes? *H:* Oh, you know how it is,–pretty well. *N:* Which is harder for you to read, Cyrillic or Latin characters? *H:* They're both about the same to me, I can make out either one. *N:* So it's all the same to you then? *H:* Makes no difference.

N: Did Avdo up and sing the song as soon as you'd finished reading it to him? *H:* Yes, actually, he did. Ramazan came on right afterwards, and he sang it in the coffeehouse. *N:* I see. Did you happen to hear him when he sang it? *H:* Yes, I heard him personally. Aye, that's just when he sang it, and it took him a long time, too. *N:* Did he sing it just the way it was in the poem, or did he sing longer than that? *H:* No, no, ah– so to speak, he, uh–, he sang it all exactly as it is in the book, but what I mean to say is that it got to be quite long by the time he was through with it because you see, it uh–, it doesn't take as much time to read it as it does to sing it. *N:* Of course. But do you suppose there was possibly some difference, that he maybe added something here or there?

H: Oh, I couldn't judge that at all. *N:* So there wasn't anything added?
H: On my word of honor, I didn't notice anything to criticize. *N:* Did
Avdo pay you anything for reading to him? *H:* Ha, ha—good God, no!
What do you mean, pay?! A man doesn't pay for a thing like that. Why,
if I had fifty books, I'd do the same thing with every one of them, and
gladly. Every book I've ever gotten my hands on, I've told him all about
it. I'd say to him, "I've got so and so and such and such a book—." But
not for money. Once I, uh—, I got hold of "Mujo and Halil"; I've forgotten whose it was now—. But he'd never do any such thing as offer
money for it. *N:* I see. Of course not. *H:* He just wouldn't do such a
rude thing. *N:* Did you read him the song about the Seven Atlagići?
H: No, I didn't read him that one. *N:* You didn't read that to him?
H: No, but there wasn't anything there to read, there wasn't anything
to it.

   N: What other songs did you read to him? *H:* Didn't actually read
any others to him—I did start to tell him another one that I knew, the
one about the Death of Bey Ljubović at Osjek. *N:* I see. *H:* I know that
one. *N:* How do you think Avdo got to know it? *H:* I don't know.
N: Do you suppose he learned it from the songbook, or from another
singer? *H:* I really don't have any idea. *N:* You don't know the answer
to that? *H:* No, I don't. Except that it's the same way in the book as it
is when he sings it. If I were to take the book, and open it up like this
while he was dictating, I'd see exactly the same thing there with my
eyes as he'd said. *N:* And it's the same way with the song of Smailagić
Meho, is it? *H:* No, no. I mean the song about the Death of Bey Ljubović. *N:* Ah, the Death of Bey Ljubović. *H:* That's right. *N:* So I presume
that song's in a songbook too? *H:* Which? *N:* Bey Ljubović's Death.
H: Sure it is. *N:* Ah, so. Which book is it in? *H:* The one about the
Death of Bey Ljubović at Osjek. "The Death of Bey Ljubović." *P:* Aha!
"The Death of Bey Ljubović"? *H:* That's it, at Osjek.

   N: What's your name? *H:* Hivzo Džafić, butcher, Bijelo Polje.
N: And what's your place of residence? *H:* That's Bijelo Polje too, in
the town. *N:* In Bijelo Polje proper? That's the right address? *H:* Yes.
N: Do you know how to sing? *H:* Nope. *N:* So you don't know how,
then? *H:* No, I don't. *N:* Okay.

Transcription dated July 1937
N. Vujnović

The Wedding of Smailagić Meho

TRANSLATED BY ALBERT B. LORD

Let the first word be: "O God, be thou our help," and the next: "It shall be as God wills."[1] If we call often upon him, then he will help us well and save us from all woe, from fierce woe and the hand of our enemy, and from every mishap and evil. Worst of all evils is poverty, worse even than wretched debt and a faithless friend. Rain will fall and the year will bear its fruits, and the debtor will free himself of his debt, but never of a bad friend, nor yet at home of a bad wife. A husband can have no greater sorrow than her. He can neither go in peace to his home, nor bring with him a friend, but as he walks along with him, he thinks ever of the troubles which will befall him through the bad and shameless mistress of his house. Blacker is his heart than the raven. Roof over your house and it will not leak. Strike your wife and she will not scold. Yet it goes hard when man and woman fight and she follows not her own good understanding.

Now to you, sirs, who are gathered here I wish to sing the measures of a song, that we may be merry. It is a song of the olden times, of the deeds of the great men of old and the heroes on both sides in the time when Sulejman the Magnificent held empire. Then was the empire of the Turks at its highest. Three hundred and sixty provinces[2] it had, and Bosnia was its lock, its lock it was and its golden keys, and a place of all good trust against the foe.

In that time the elders and nobles gathered together in Kanidža in the gay tavern, as the custom long had been. At that gathering were thirty beys, the chief men of all the city of Kanidža,[3] and four and twenty of the sultan's agas.[4] At the head of the gathering was Hasan Pasha Tiro[5] with his fifty men of war, and beside the pasha at his left side, Omer of Kanidža, the elder of the city, an old man. Beside him were the sultan's two fortress commanders, and beside them was Cifrić Hasanaga. Next to Hasanaga was his nephew Mehmed, the dear son of Hadji Smail, (50) and brother's son of Cifrić Hasan. Round about them were the sultan's captains, and beside these sat the standard-bearers. Everywhere elder was seated by elder, peer beside peer. The sultan's agas sat in order with the beys, and the standard-bearers one beside another, Hasan Pasha with his warriors at the head of the gathering, between the windows, in the middle of the circle of the beys.

Two standard-bearers served the wine, even the warriors Hasan and Husein, one the standard-bearer of Kanidža's elder, the other of the fortress commander. Beneath their arms each held a goatskin of wine, and in his right hand a great measuring cup. Ever in order did they serve their chiefs, Hasan Pasha and the great men of the realm. When they had served every man, then they thrust their hands behind their sashes and stood at homage to their lords, that their lords might find their drink the sweeter.

Now when the agas had drunk of their wine they put the wine glasses aside, for the wine had flushed their faces, and they took up the brandy cups. When wine and brandy mingle, brandy is ever a talker, and of those beys and agas of the sultan not one was a man who had to borrow. They had clothes as many as they wished, and arms, and sabers, and ready money in their pockets, and ready Arabian steeds, and for their heads imperial caps of fur with imperial plumes of gold.

So the talk began in the tavern, and the men of the Border began their boasting, who had won the most combats, either for himself or for some comrade, or for some pasha or vizier, or for his glorious sultan; or had done the most to broaden the border; who had carried off a German captive, or won a bride for a comrade; who had reared the finer horse or begotten the better son, or reared the fairer sister; who had gotten himself the better clothing, (100) or belt of arms, or sharp sword at his side. One boasts of his breastplate, another of the arms and trappings of his horse. The men of the Border began their boasting: who had wedded what maiden, or was about to wed one; which family was better than another, which hero stronger than another. They began to push back their caps of fur, to hang their golden mantles on the pegs, and to lay their sharp swords across their two thighs. Their white beards began to wave, the sable fur began to glisten on the brows of the old men, and the dark eyes of the young men reddened. Above their heads flashed the metal plumes. Each man boasts somehow of something: one boasts of his daughter, another of his sister, another of his brother's daughter. Each man made talk as was his desire.

There were more than sixty agas, and more than twenty beys of Kanidža, besides the pasha and his sixty warriors. Though you gazed long you could not tell who was the best lord among them, whether the elders were better than the young; yet the young were surely not better than the old. Great were their limbs, their clothes of gold, their heads were large, their eyes were black. The faces beneath their eyes were noble, and each man's cheeks shone like the rose of the garden on Saint George's day. Their eyes were dark, their brows were broad. On their heads were set imperial caps of fur, and in the caps were imperial plumes. Their faces were white, their plumes of gold, and on their heads the shaggy wolf's fur bristled. About their necks were collars of gold fastened beneath the throat by a clasp, and all the clasps were of 'fined gold. On every man's chest was a breastplate of silver strips, and on his shoulders a cloak of Venetian stuff: the cloaks of the old men were blue and green and those of the young men white and red. Each man's cap upon his brow was of sable and on his heroic shoulders was gold embroidery like branches, and along his arms were braided snakes whose heads met beneath his throat: one would say and swear that they were living. (150) The belts of arms about their waists were all alike, both the belts and the arms in them. The sights on their rifles were alike, even the same precious stones and the fastenings of 'fined gold. They wore breeches of finest make;[6] the cloth was dark, and the gold shone brightly. Along their legs golden branches glistened, and on their thighs were braided snakes whose heads met beneath the belt of arms. Tempered swords with hilts of 'fined gold lay across their thighs, the scabbards of hammered silver. Clustered together like a thick forest[7] beside the agas were their poisoned spears.

It was indeed easy for them to be merry: they had their own horses, their own estates; they needed to give no thought to head tax or to other tribute, nor to their daily bread at noon or at night. Each had his own tenant farmers and chests of ready money. Even a person of little understanding, were he to see them, would swear that they were courtiers of a great pasha. Leaning on supple sabers, the standard-bearers attended upon the elders, even as the nobles wait upon the sultan in council.

Were you to cast your eyes about the gathering to see which hero

was the best, one would stand out above them all, Mehmed, the young
son of Smail the alaybey.[8] What a countenance had this falcon! He was
a youth of not yet twenty years, and one would say and swear by Allah
and the Rosary[9] that the radiance from his two cheeks was as sunshine
and that from his brow like the light of the moon. The black queue
which covered his white neck was like a raven which had perched there.
He was the only child his mother had borne, and she had cared so
lovingly for his queue that she had bound his locks over his forehead,
and the thick dark locks of her son curled around his rich fez. His
mother had strung them with pearls, which completely covered the
strands. His eyes were black like a falcon's, his teeth fine as a demon's.[10]
His forehead was like a good-luck charm,[11] his eyebrows as long and
black as leeches. (200) His eyelashes were so long that they covered his
two cheeks like swallows' wings. Beard had he none, nor yet moustache.
One would say that he was a fair mountain vila.[12]

The boy's raiment was of Venetian stuff, his shirt of choice silk
embroidered with gold. There was, indeed, more gold than silken fabric.
His doublet was neither woven on a loom nor hammered, but was hand
embroidered with pure gold. All the seams of his cloak were covered
with richly embroidered gold, and there were golden branches around
his right sleeve. The young man's arm was as thick as any other fine
hero's slender waist. The youth's breeches were of white Venetian velvet, embroidered with pure gold, with braided snakes on the thighs.
The whole youth glistened like the moon. He wore two Tripolitan
sashes about his waist, and over them a belt of arms woven of Venetian
gold. In the belt were two small Venetian pistols which fire without
flint, all plated with gold. Their sights were of precious stones, and the
handles were inlaid with pearl. His Persian sword with hilt of yellow
ducats was at his left side, in its scabbard inlaid with pearls. Its blade
was of deadly steel. As the sword lay thrown across the youth's thighs
one would say a serpent was sleeping there.

A golden breastplate embraced the young hero, two-pieced, reaching to his white neck. Each half of the breastplate contained an even
half-oke[13] of gold, and on them both was the same inscription. That
breastplate had been sent by the sultan to the alaybey, Hadji Smail, and
to his true son; for that house had held the command for full forty-
seven years, by charter of Sulejman the Magnificent, by his imperial
charter and appointment. (250) Than that lord there was none older,
either pasha or vizier, in Bosnia's seventy cities, nor was there any of

nobler descent than the alaybey, Hadji Smail, or his brother Hasanaga. Both these old men have only one heir, Meho (may God protect him!). They have no other sons or daughters.

Looking about the gathering you would see that that youth with his noble face is the making of the whole assembly there in the tavern, like the seasoning which the housewife adds to the sweets in her pan or to the omelette in her skillet. When that good Turk, Hasan Pasha Tiro, than whom there is no better, looked about the circle of nobles, all the heroes were merry, gaily talking. But Mehmed, the hadji's son, was unhappy. His fair face was saddened, his black eyes downcast. He looked as though he had just buried his father or his uncle, Cifrić Hasan. His hands were thrust into his sash. He looked as if he were dying. He drank neither wine nor brandy, nor did he draw upon his pipe, or say a single word. It is not a pleasant thing even to think about, much less to look upon, to see such a fine son of such a good father, the only heir of these two elders, so downcast and unhappy.

Hasan Pasha Tiro was afraid the falcon was ill and that the house of the alaybey might be extinguished, that the wings of the whole Border might be broken and harm brought even to the sultan in Stambol. And the pasha began to be troubled. He could not bear to see the young man's sadness, nor could he ask the lad before all the beys to speak out the cause of his sorrow. So Hasan Pasha leaped to his feet and called Cifrić Hasan: "Come here with me a moment, Hasanaga, that I may have a word with you!" Hasanaga went to Hasan Pasha (300) and sat beside him. Then Hasan Pasha whispered to Hasanaga: "Hasanaga, golden plume, my heart breaks within my breast to see your brother's son, Mehmed, son of Hadji Smail. All the rest are merry. He alone is sad. Go and sit beside him. Do not question him immediately, lest he notice that I called you to me for that purpose and be angry at me."

Then Hasan obeyed the pasha and took his seat beside Meho, the son of Hadji Smail. The cups flew around, and the agas drank; for they had no cares, and no one noticed that that hero was unhappy. Since he has all he wants, why should the young man be sad?

A half hour passed. Then Cifrić Hasan leaped to his feet: "O pasha, and all you beys, have patience a moment!" They all stopped and looked at him. Cifrić Hasan knelt and then asked his brother's son Mehmed: "My Mehmed, honor of our house! Why do you sit there so sad in the company of the imperial Hasan Pasha Tiro and the fifty warriors of the sultan? Of all those assembled here, agas and beys, imperial captains, and standard-bearers, my dear son, not one is unhappy. Each boasts somehow of something: one of himself, one of his horse, another of his sword or arms. One boasts how he has broadened the border, another, my son, of taking a captive. One boasts how well he has wed, another how he shall wed. One boasts of his son, another of his daughter or his sister or his brother's daughter. All are merry, not one is sad. But you, my star, why are you so sorrowful? (350) Are you sad because we old men have lived so long, your father Smail and your uncle Hasan, because your elders weary you? Our time will very quickly come. Whoever lives must die. O Mehmed, honor of our house, is it that your money has all been spent in the streets or in the taverns, my dear son, among your comrades, or in the garden with the maidens? Or have your clothes been torn, the fine velvet and satin on your shoulders? Has someone reproached you, my son?"

When Meho, the son of Smail, heard what Cifrić Hasanaga said, he raised his falcon head, and his falcon eyes flashed. On his cheeks a rosy flush bloomed and along them flames crept, like the billowing veil of a bride. Then Mehmed thus addressed his uncle: "Uncle Hasan, it were great shame for Mehmed, the son of Smailaga, to think that his elders had become hateful to him or that they had lived too long. God knows, uncle, and the Border knows, that I serve you and my father three or four times a day: once, uncle, when you say your morning prayers, once at the midday meal, and once, uncle, when we return from council. Then I fold my arms before you on my breast and wait upon you thus for half an hour, as a newlywed waits upon her husband, or her husband's brother, or his father, even as the nobles wait upon the sultan in council."

They all said that this was true, that there was no one more obedient to his father and to his uncle, Cifrić Hasan, than was Mehmed.

"And it is shameful, Hasanaga, to ask if my money is gone, spent in the tavern with my friends, or in the garden with the maidens. I have money in abundance, thanks to God's help and to the health of the sultan (400) and to the lives of my father and my uncle. Were I to spend it on food, I could not eat it up, and were I to spend it on drink, I could not drink it up, and were I to give it to my horse instead of oats, he could not consume it all. You ask about my clothes, if they have become worn. I have so many suits of all sorts in my chests and baskets that I cannot count them or know their number. I could change all my clothes every other day for a whole year, uncle. I have clothes of all kinds, I have a good horse and good weapons. I have need of nothing more, uncle.

"But when you ask about my unhappiness, as long as I live and trace of me abides, I shall never by merry, by the health of my old father and of my uncle, Cifrić Hasan! You have heard what the beys are saying, the imperial captains and the agas, and all our slender standard-bearers, men of my own age, or somewhat older. It is quite true that there is none younger than I. Just listen, Cifrić Hasanaga, to the boasts of the Turks in the tavern. One says that he has raised a band, another that he has joined one. One boasts that he has raised an army, another that he has enlisted. One says that he has broadened the border, or won in combat, or taken a captive. But, O uncle, Cifrić Hasanaga, by the health of my father, Smailaga, and of my uncle, I have known nothing of raiding or campaigning, not to mention single combat. The broadening of borders is unknown to me. I do not even know where the border is, nor where our ancient battlegrounds are. How then could I have crossed the border to raid and take captives, and so marry off a friend? Although I am a man, there has been nothing heroic in my life. No one will say that I am a man. (450) I have nothing else to boast about. There is nothing for me to do but to take off these men's clothes and put on those of a girl—since I have neither beard nor moustache, and my pigtail is like a maiden's tresses—and embroider and spin. Let them all say that I am a woman!"

Then hear what Mehmed, son of Smail, said to his uncle: "Listen, Uncle Haso. You two have no one but God and myself. Just wait, O uncle, Cifrić Hasanaga, until our assembly is ready to be dismissed at dusky evening; for I will not break up the assembly. When we go to our courts, to the dwelling of Hadji Smail, you and I to my father's house, there to perform your ablutions, you two and I in turn beside you, and to make our vows at evening and to say our evening prayers, then you two will sit upon the couch, side by side, and I shall wait upon you as I have been taught. I will not disrupt this custom. I shall stand and serve you, uncle. I shall not sup with you, however; I cannot. Nor can I longer stand this disgrace. Everyone is boasting, but I have nothing of which to boast. I have everything, but my father will not grant that I go anywhere with the men, not even to follow them. Of leading them, there is of course no question. Uncle Haso, I shall go to the stable and prepare my long-maned chestnut horse, saddle him with the trappings as at the time of Bajram, when I send him with my father to the mosque. The clothes I have on are good enough. I shall seek nothing better. I shall take only the gun from its peg and my bone-breaking spear from the wall, mount my horse, and in the night turn from Kanidža. I shall give my horse full rein, spurring him on with the bronze stirrups. The horse is as swift as the wind in the mountains, and he will carry me wherever I wish. (500) Rest assured, Uncle Hasanaga, that I shall cross the frontier of the empire.

"I shall not stop in Austria, but will proceed through the Hungarian land to Kara Bogdan[14] and approach General Peter,[15] the strongest force in that country. He rules and passes judgment independent of all. There is no other force like him in the world; no other steed like that beneath him; nor such a saber as his in the hands of a hero; nor such a serpent for the Turks, as is Peter. He asks neither the sultan nor the emperor. Against whomever he wishes, Smail,[16] my father, he raises as much of an army as he wants of regular and of his own hosts. He has plenty, and can gather them together, to strike wherever he desires. The standing army is under his command. Food and ammunition and war cannon too are ready at hand for him.

"When I ride my chestnut steed into Bogdan, to the court of General Peter, I shall dismount—I shall be wearing my breastplate and my plumes and they will be recognized as belonging to the Turks—and enter Peter's courts. General Peter will recognize me as the dear son of Hadji Smailaga by my breastplate and plumes and by the golden clasps beneath my throat on which is the name of Mehmed, the dear son of Hadji Smail. When General Peter sees me, he will wonder why I have come there; whether perchance my father had sent me to him. My father's reputation is not a laughing matter; all the kingdoms know of him. Peter will rise quickly to his feet. He will not receive me seated; for this mighty man is of a good family. It is by such a thing that good families are recognized, and the best heroes in battle and the best leaders of armies. They ever humble themselves; whoever humbles himself, God exalts. From the doorway I shall hail him: 'Good morning!' and he will reply to me: 'Welcome, Meho!' He will offer me his hand, and I shall bend over it (550) to kiss him as my elder.—I know that my faith forbids this, but you all have forced me to it, uncle.—'What has happened with Mehmed?' Peter will think, and he will wonder: 'He is the son of the leading hero of the sultan, of the victorious Turk, Smail the Alaybey, whose fame is known in all the seven kingdoms.[17] There is no war in which he has not taken part, and wherever he has gone, victory was his. Their house has had the command under seal and decree of the sultan,

day after day for forty and seven years; first in Smail's hands and then
in Hasanaga's. That house is respected in Kanidža. Betrayal has never
been in it. What has happened to make Mehmed betray his father and
uncle?'

"Peter will put his arm around me and kiss me and ask: 'Why,
Mehmed, son of the alaybey, of the victor, Hadji Smailbeg, have you
not left your father's house before now? I have been watching you. I
ask you, what has happened to you? Is your heroic father alive, and
your uncle Hasan? Are you all well and enjoying God's peace? How are
the lords of Kanidža? How is Hasan Pasha Tiro, the imperial pasha and
wing of all Bosnia? Do you make war and raid across the border into
the land of the emperor? Do you set fire to villages and towns? Do you
capture beautiful Magyar women and marry them to Bosnians?'

"Then I shall say to General Peter: 'Peter, my father is alive, both
my father Smail and my uncle Hasan. We are well and enjoy God's
peace. Yet there is not good feeling among us. As for what you now ask
me: people go on raids—other people, that is. And other people wage
war. The captains lead the raids, but when the army fights Hasanaga
goes—he must; for he is the alaybey. But now I have quarreled with
them (600). All the men boast in the tavern, all my friends and age
mates. I shall not make complaint against my elders. Yet I am angered
at my father and at that hypocrite[18] Uncle Hasan. They have not instructed me in anything, Peter, neither in raiding nor in fighting in the
regular army. They have taught me nothing of raiding, let alone waging
war, Peter. I have not known where duels are fought, nor in which
direction the imperial cities are located, nor where the landing places
are by the imperial sea, nor the green plains beside the sea. I have remained like a woman. That is what I told my father, and I have left him.
I have sworn an oath, Peter. God's faith will not fail; the sky will come
together with the earth before I will fail you. If you take me into your
courts—but to be by your side, Peter, to drink with you as two dear
brothers—not to be a servant to anyone, but to be your right hand, I
shall guide your army, I at the head, and you behind me. By my hope
in God, I shall lead your army to march across Bosnia and to plunder its
towns—a thing which my faith cannot tolerate—to take captives, and to
cut off heads. You will marry off the men of Bogdan to Bosnian maidens, and adorn your ramparts with heads. God will see, and the Border
will see, what sort of comrade you have gained, such a one as no other
has found.'

"All this will Peter do for me. He will put me at his left hand.

When I am his guide and he my firm support—not like my father and uncle, but like a gray falcon—I shall lead the army of Karavlah[19] and Kara Bogdan from Bogdan in an attack on your Bosnia, and I shall give you much black woe. Peter will receive me well. He will stable my horse beside his own wondrous star-hoofed steed, which has wings beneath its girths (650). Then you will see what fierce troubles are!"

When Hasan Pasha Tiro heard that, tears flew down his cheeks. They rolled down his cheeks like pearls over white cloth. And he thought: "Woe to Almighty God! What have father and uncle done? Were they to let their one and only son go from them, they would remain wretched old men without anyone in the world. Yet with sorrow we might forgive them this. But it is worse that Smail's son should break the wings of all Bosnia, that his black deed should fall upon Bosnia. It would be sorrowful news indeed for all men that the house of the alaybey has fallen in ruin, that father and uncle have betrayed their son. We shall see their woes now, and after them the Border will fall, and after it will come the destruction of the empire. Mehmed the hadji's son is no laughing matter, such a son of such a sire, as no mother will again bear, nor has ever before borne."

When Hasanaga heard what that falcon, his brother's son, said among the agas, tears raced from his eyes and rolled down his white beard, just like pearls over white silk. The old man leaped to his feet, stretched forth his arms and embraced his dragon son, kissing him between the black eyes, where the gray falcons kiss. "My Mehmed, honor of our house, would you really do that, son? Would you really pluck out the eyes of your old father and uncle, and your dear and aged mother? Your father married three times and your uncle four. God gave issue to neither of us, not even to your father, Hadji Smail—God preserve him!—except you alone. I, my son, have none. We both have wound our four arms about you, my son. Day and night we thank God that the decree of the sultan, his mandate with the command, will pass from us two old men to you in your youth (700), that our candle be not snuffed out. We can scarcely wait, my son, to see that fulfillment of our desires, that we give the command over to you, that you take your place at the head of the thirty captains. We have been waiting to find a wife for you. We pray God that we both may see this, dear son, with our own eyes. Were we to see the command pass to you and a wife at your side worthy of you to serve me and your father, were we to die, we would have no regrets. You are our one and only desire; were anything to happen to you, how could we endure the loss of you? You are our pride and mainstay. The command means bitter warring. You have grown up, son, accustomed to all good things. You are still young in years, a child, and the Border is a rough cloak. The thirty captains are no laughing matter, each with a thousand chosen blood-stained heroes. The warriors of Unđurovina[20] are tough men. It is not easy to please them. They are men of many humors. When you were born, son, your head rested upon a pillow, your brow touched on gold, your locks were strung with pearls from your mother's pearly lap. When you were born, son, cannon boomed in every city in all the Border, in Bosnia and Hercegovina, and in Unđurovina. The agas and beys came to celebrate with me and Smail. The agas here know all that, son. They informed the sultan of the news.

"The sultan sent a firman to your father and to me, your uncle: 'I congratulate you both on the birth of your son. May long years and good fortune be his, may the title of alaybey fall to his lot, as it did to his father and to his uncle Hasan.' And for a name for you, my son, we gave to you none other than that of Mehdija,[21] the imperial pontiff of Islam. That your life should be the surer and longer, my son, (750) we brought in three other women to nurse you besides your mother so that you might feed in greater abundance and grow better in time and get greater strength. We could scarcely wait for you to grow up and so four nurses gave you suck, first your mother, then the other three. Day followed day, and when four years had passed, you had grown so that you were like any other child of eight years. Then we sent you to school and brought you to the feet of the imam.[22] Yet we could not bear to send you from our home to the school, but the imam taught you at our own house; you studied until you were eight years old, my son, and if you had studied yet another year, you would have known the whole Koran by heart. Then we took you from school.

"When you were twelve, another firman came from Stambol asking me and your father: 'Smailaga, how is the boy? Will he be like his father and his uncle Hasan?' And we praised you to the sultan: 'O Sovereign, most humble greetings. The auspices are favorable and it appears that he will turn out well. He will not bring disgrace upon us.'

"When your thirteenth year came, my son, the imperial chamberlain arrived from the halls of Sultan Sulejman, bringing an Egyptian chestnut horse for you, one which had been bought from the Shah of Egypt. Golden-winged, its mane reached to its hoofs. Then a two-year-old, it was like a horse of seven. The trappings were fashioned in Afghanistan especially for the brown horse when it grew up. The saddle was all of coral; the upper part woven of pure 'fined gold. Beneath the saddle an Osmanli cloth, not like any other, my son, but of Syrian damask silk, that it should not chafe the horse's back. The saddle of gold, (800) the trappings of gold. On the Egyptian chestnut horse next to his skin are silken girths, soft silk that they may not chafe his flesh. The upper part of them is ornamented with pearl. If God grants, my son, you shall see them when you become the alaybey of the Border. It is now nineteen years, my dear son, since that day when you were born, and today is the ninth year since the brown horse with its trappings came to you as a gift. Whatever the sultan could think of by way of trappings for the steed was prepared for him. We hid the horse from you and made a separate stable for him. There is no other horse with him. Two servants are in the stable and four torches burn the whole night long beside your horse. They exercise him within the stable. Every twenty-four hours they rub him down four times, not like any other horse, but with a scarf of silk. The horse has been so well cared for that he has seen neither sun nor moon, my dear son, for nine years. Were one to lift the blankets from the horse, one would note that the hair had been shortened and a black fly on the horse would be brushed from him by his wing.[23] The horse is waiting for you, Mehmed, when you become alaybey and lead the emperor's armies and captains.

"And clothes came for you, my son, from the sultan as a gift because of your father's prestige, out of affection for your famous father and my dear brother, Hadji Smail. Among the clothes which have come for you is a pearl breastplate of silk of Damascus the noble.[24] There is more gold than silk on the coat and fine spun trousers. On all sides spread branches.

"A Persian sword came especially made for you, my son, (850) of fiery Persian steel tempered in fierce poison, which cuts angry armor. Its scabbard is adorned with pearl, the whole hilt of diamonds. When it was finished, they sent the sword to Mecca, and gave it to the guide, who took it to the Elder of the Kaaba, who put a passage from the Holy Book on it and blessed it. No ill can befall him who bears it. Before him shall the ranks take fright. In Mecca with the blessing of the sultan they gave the sword its name, 'Hadji Persian Sword,' because it was made for you in Persia and taken on a pilgrimage to Mecca. Hence it is called the 'Hadji Persian Sword.' Woe to him who stands in its way. On the hilt are three imperial seals, and two, my son, of the Elder of the Kaaba. Upon the fur cap which was given you are two plumes such as neither I nor your father have—how then would any other?—but only you to whom the sultan presented it! These clothes, yours and your horse's, these arms the sultan gave you and your horse, together with the plumes, and your wondrous sword; if you were to gather all these treasures in one heap they would be worth a good Bosnian city.

"Why, my son, should the sultan do this, if not because you have a father and uncle who have pleased his magnificence? You know your father was alaybey for full twenty-seven years and was at the head of thirty captains. He fought all up and down the border, and gave aid to every Moslem—but first of all to his magnificence, the sultan. Everywhere he proclaimed the honor of the sultan, and brought glory to his own name. On all sides, my son, was the name of your father known and respected. When your father's limbs grew old and he could no longer hold himself on his white horse, nor keep the stirrups on his feet, nor give the horse full rein, nor cut with the sword as he had learned, (900) so many battles had he won, so many wounds had he received, my son, that when he advanced in years, his old legs would not ride horses nor his aged body fight duels, nor his old hands cut off heads. Especially had his body grown old and weak. An aged frame cannot endure the poisoned swords of the enemy, my son. He grew old, and I had reached your years, and somewhat more. Then your father, my brother, Smailaga, set out for Mecca and Medina, to make the pilgrimage. He let his beard grow and departed for the Kaaba. In Stambol he stopped to visit his sovereign. He was announced at the palace. The glorious sultan issued an order that he be admitted, and he flew to his majesty's hand. The sultan embraced him with both arms and congratulated him on his pilgrimage. 'My lord, may your journey be blest!' 'O glorious sun! May your empire be likewise!'

"The sultan kept him there a whole month. And your father made petition before him: 'O sultan, the waging of war is no longer possible for me. My hands are incapable of dueling. Nor can my body endure biting wounds. Dead hands do not sever heads, nor dead limbs fight duels, nor ride horses. I have made a pilgrimage to Mecca and there sworn many vows. I shall drink neither wine nor brandy. I shall not lie, nor swear falsely. I can still sit and rule, with almighty God's help, and your gracious leave. But, O golden sun! take the command from me, and, as it is within your power, give it to whomever you wish.' But the sultan would not let him think of its leaving our family: 'Since there are no sons to rise to your place, then let the command go from brother to brother!'

"When the hadji returned from Mecca, and with him a messenger from Ali Otman[25] and an imperial representative, then was the command transferred from the hadji to me. (950) The imperial decree was read—here it is in my bosom even to this day. For twenty years have I been alaybey under charter of Sulejman the Magnificent. Now begins the first and twentieth year. It is full four years now that I have been imploring the hadji, your father: 'O my brother, Hadji Smail! Prepare a petition for the sultan. Let him take the command from me, for my limbs have grown old. I can no longer keep myself on my horse, nor go with the army against the enemy—how then could I engage in duels? I could not withstand sharp saber wounds. An aged frame cannot endure swords. My brain is clouded[26] and my mind has begun to fail me. No longer am I capable of speaking wisely.' In this way did Smailaga beg me: "A little patience, brother Hasan! If God grants—and all good things are from him—our son will come of age and then will the command fall to him and not leave our house, the command and imperial decree, and the charter of Sulejman the Magnificent. Wherever the charter is, there is God's help also. And the imperial charters belong to our house.' Thanks to God and to this day when we two old men have found our son ready, that the command might pass from us two to you, our only one. Now are we greatly comforted, my son. Now shall the command not pass to other hands. It is not necessary now to send you to Stambol, for a decree has come from the sultan to the vizier with three horsetail plumes[27] in Buda. Whenever we desire to transfer the command, you must go to Buda, to our good friend, the imperial vizier. He will take the command from me, and bestow the charter upon you. He is our good friend. (1000) Thanks be to God, the time has come. My son, now shall I leave my place. Here with us is Hasan Pasha, our golden wing, the sultan's representative. He has four scribes who render his answers to the glorious sultan in Stambol. Hasan Pasha will fashion a decree for us, and the fifty heroes and agas together will ratify it. Great good fortune is it for us, my son, for it is not necessary to call them into council, to put their seals upon the decree. They are now all gathered here. Under the imperial sign and mandate all the agas will set their seals. And Hasan Pasha will ratify it, and give it into your bosom.

"At evening, when the assembly adjourns, we shall go to your father's house to tell him how things are. Then fly to do your elder homage. Let your father send you to Buda to receive the command unto yourself."

Thus spoke Cifrić Hasanaga, and all the Turks in the council answered: "Thanks be to God in the highest! For at last we shall see the father's son in command over us." Cifrić Hasan jumped to his feet. Hasan Pasha issued the order and the four scribes hastened to fashion a decree for the hadji's son, stating that the command should pass from father and uncle to young Mehmed. Straightway they fashioned the petition and the fifty heroes signed it, they and the sixty agas of Kanidža, and the four elders of the city, the two fortress commanders, twelve captains, and the twenty Turkish standard-bearers. They all set their seals upon the petition. The scribes wrote it, the heroes signed it, and all put their imperial seals upon it—then did Hasan Pasha ratify it and give it to Cifrić Hasan, who delivered it to his brother's son, (1050) to Mehmed, the son of the hadji.

Then the imperial Turk Hasan Pasha Tiro offered up a prayer, and all the Turks responded 'amin," a prayer for the success of Mehmed's journey. They wished him then a happy journey: "Blessed be your paths, my son, and wide to Buda, free of any sort of care. Receive then the command, and may it be blessed to you, even as it was to your father and your uncle. If God grants, my son, may you accomplish such heroic deeds as did your father, and leave behind a good memory. May your wings extend more broadly throughout the Border, and may they bear you up as did your father's! May your enemies be beneath your feet, like the shoes and nails beneath your chestnut horse. May you accomplish all you undertake."

Then the gray falcon leaped to his feet and flew to Hasan Pasha's hand. He kissed his heroic hand and that of his uncle Cifrić Hasan—then in turn he embraced the two fortress commanders and four elders, each aged bey, chieftain, leader of a thousand,[28] and captain. The standard-bearers stretched forth their arms: falcon embraced falcon. In those days prosperity and contentment reigned among the Turks, and they loved one another. From love for that golden dragon, from love and great joy, tears fell from their eyes and raced down their heroic faces, like pearls over white silk. The time of breaking up the assembly was at hand, when each aga sought his own abode.

Cifrić Hasan took his brother's dear son, the son of Hadji Smail. He walked first and Mehmed followed, as they went to the lordly house.

That house was like the sultan's palace. The roof was of yellow copper. The house was four stories high; each story was painted, and the balconies were hung with fine draperies. In the courtyard were four guard-houses, each with twenty guards,[29] (1100) whom Hadji Smail and his brother Cifrić Hasan kept, paying for all they wished.

They entered the hallway where the staircase was carpeted with fine cloth. The palace was just like a vizier's. When they came to the uppermost story, to the chamber where the hadji sat, they opened the door. Hadji Smail was sitting on the cushions between the windows. He wore a blue fur-lined mantle and held a long silver pipe. The tobacco was burning, and he was drinking unsweetened coffee.

Hasan greeted his brother, and the hadji bade him take his seat in his accustomed placed at his side. Young Mehmed crossed his arms in front of him on his belt of weapons and waited upon his father and uncle, even as a new bride serves her husband or her husband's brother, or his father or mother. The aged Smailaga observed the lordly countenance of his dear son from the corner of his eyes, over his pipe. The rose did not bloom upon the boy's cheek. One would say that he was ill, or had quarreled with someone, so changed was he. In all their lives his father and his uncle had had neither son nor daughter save him alone—may God protect him! Thus did he speak to Mehmed: "My Mehmed, shining light of our house! Why do you look so sad, my son? Are you ill, or have your quarreled with someone? Has the drinking in the tavern with your fellows made you ill? Why is your face darkened, why are your cheeks thus?" Young Mehmed shrugged his shoulders and kept his peace. But now his uncle spoke for him. "No, my brother, Mehmed has not fallen ill, nor has he quarreled with anyone. Drink of no kind has he taken, (1150) how then overmuch? But Mehmed is angry with us, and rightly so, for he has great reason. Today the council gathered, the first meeting for a long time. Hasan Pasha was there with his fifty warriors, the two fortress commanders, four elders, forty agas, and twenty beys, and with them the twelve imperial captains and the three and twenty standard-bearers. In their conversation over the unsweetened drinks, the men of the Border began their boasting of what one had better than another: who was a better hero than another, who had killed more enemies or won more duels, who had carried away a Hungarian captive, an old man or a maiden; who had married off a comrade, or kept a better steed. One boasted of the weapons in his belt, one of his arms, another of his battlespear. They talked of who had a better rifle of Dubrovnik or who the better sword at his side; who had got him the better wife or begotten the better son or reared the better daughter. One boasted of his daughter, or of his sister or of his brother's daughter; one of his son or of his brother's son. Each in the tavern boasted of something, but our Mehmed was sore distressed. He neither boasted nor lit his pipe, nor did he drink of wine or brandy, nor join in heroic banter. The younger man's head hung low, God forgive us, as though it had been severed. His fair countenance was darkened. I could not question him because of my affection for him, nor could I bring myself to speak to him.

But Hasan Pasha Tiro, from his seat at the head of the assembly between the windows, saw how our son was downcast. His falcon eyes did not move, nor did his cheeks bloom as we are wont to know them, but his fair mien was darkened. Hasan Pasha's heart was touched, and he summoned me to his side and secretly whispered to me: (1200) 'O Hasan, do you know what is wrong with your brother's son, Meho, son of Smail?' 'No, my lord, on my very faith, my heart is breaking for him, but I have not asked what troubles him, nor can I.' Then the wise imperial Hasan Pasha Tiro spoke a word of wisdom: 'Hasanaga, go and sit beside your brother's son. When half an hour has passed, ask Mehmed what is wrong, that we may see whether he will tell us, God be with him!' I obeyed the pasha and took my place beside our Mehmed, dear brother. When half an hour had passed, according to the command of Hasan Pasha, I said: 'Mehmed, shining light of our house, why do you hang your head thus, my son? Have you fallen ill? You are breaking your elder's heart. Has some thought come to your mind of which your uncle knows not? Or is it because we two have grown old, that we have lived long?' Then Mehmed answered me: 'Uncle Hasan, how foolishly you speak! If your old age weighed upon me, I would not serve you as I do, my uncle, three or four times a day: first, uncle, when you make your devotions at dawn and recite your prayers; then do I serve you, uncle, as a newlywed waits upon her husband or her husband's brother, or his father or his mother; the second time, when you have your midday meal; then do I serve you, even as at dawn; the third time, when the night falls. God has seen all this, so has the Border. But, my uncle Cifrić Hasanaga, let the lords of the Border boast, let them boast, for they have something to boast of. Some have led bands of warriors and raided with them. Some, my uncle, have marched with the army, and some have looked upon the borders of our empire and know where they are, and they have learned where raiding is best and where to lead the army in war. One boasts about battles or a captive, another of a horse or arms. These men have whereof to boast; but I, uncle, have nothing. By the health of my father and uncle, I am ignorant of raiding, to say nothing of armies and war. I know not where lie the imperial marches nor the boundaries between the two empires, nor where the sea beats upon the shore nor where the coastland is, to say nothing of fighting a duel, either to lose the head from off my shoulders, or to win, and at least to leave some memory of a name behind me as have done all these dear lords of ours. It would be better, Uncle Hasan, if I were a woman rather than a man; then would I embroider, spin thread, sit among the maidens, and wait for a suitor.'

"Smailaga, my beloved brother, thus did your son, Mehmed, speak to me, nor shall I tell you all he said. And I replied to him: 'My Mehmed, shining light of our house, other than God we have no one, my dear son, but you alone. We married several times, I, four, Smailaga, three, but I had no issue, neither son nor daughter; Hadji Smail had but you alone. May God preserve you! If good fortune is ours, you will live and be happy and suffice for both of us. But, my son, we cannot bring ourselves to send you with bands of warriors or with the great army, as you are too young. But we expect and pray God, our son, that the imperial command will pass from us both unto you; that, my dear son, we will marry you off and see a daughter-in-law within our halls, my golden star, at your side. Then, were we to die, we would not be sorrowful, for we have had all good things: we have ridden good horses and enjoyed all happiness and every gift, (1300) even that of ready money in our coffers. Your father has been alaybey with imperial pay by firman and order[30] of Sulejman the Magnificent, the greatest ruler in this world, for seven and twenty years. Smailaga has commanded[31] all Bosnia and the Border; he has led his thirty captains, each with a thousand men.[32] Everywhere, my son, he has warred and broadened the imperial border. Well has he found favor in our sight and in the eyes of the Border and the empire. Your father's name is famous. The seven kingdoms know of him. When your father's limbs grew old and the muscles of his arms grew weak, his legs could no longer hold the stirrups, nor could he wield the sword and fight duels. No longer could his flanks bear the wounds of swords when they grated upon his bones, for he had received many wounds from rifles and from sabers, from swords and battlespears.

"When your father saw that he could not longer hold the com-

mand, he let grow the beard upon his face, took the necessary
gold and set out for Mecca. In our holy city he walked around the
Kaaba and became a hadji. On the way back he went to visit the sultan
in the palace of Ali Otman,[33] even our Sulejman the Magnificent, to the
illustrious hands of Sulejman; he wished to kiss him, but the sultan
would not have it so. But he himself embraced him and bade him sit by
the throne. The sultan showed him great favor—he favored him always—
and kept him for eleven whole days within his palace. Then the hadji
made petition of the sultan: 'Have mercy, O Emperor, our shining sun,
take the command from me, for my bones have aged and dead limbs do
not ride horses nor dead arms fight battles. My old body cannot (1350)
endure the saber cuts of enemies. Grant the charter to whomever you
please. I have made all sorts of vows; I shall not drink wine or brandy,
nor speak falsely nor forswear myself. For I have arrived at the edge of
the grave, and when one's time to die has come, there is no avoiding it!'
Then the sultan said to him: 'Lord Smail, why do you speak of my giving the command to anyone else? As long as I and my house live, as long
as Bosnia remains in my hands, the command in Kanidža, my son, will
fall to no other house but yours. You have no son to whom we may
give it, but let it go from brother unto brother.' Then the sultan issued
the order and he gave the command over to me. He delivered to Smailaga the firman with his seal, and the imperial envoy, departing from
Stambol, in due time arrived in Kanidža. There he read aloud the sultan's firman, ordering that the command pass from your father over to
me, Hasan. And now, my son, twenty, nay, even one and twenty years
have I held it. Now I am old and I find the command difficult to main-
tain. I cannot ride my horses any longer nor keep myself in the face of
the enemy nor yet endure the saber wounds upon my body, whoever
my enemy may be. For four years, my son, I have begged Smailaga to
prepare a petition to send to Stambol to Sulejman the Magnificent. But
the hadji will not let me think of this. 'Have patience, my brother,
Hasanaga, until our little son has come of age.' I have waited for you,
my son, and for this moment, for which God be thanked!

    The time has come for us to give the command over to you. Now it
is easier, my dear son, to bestow the charge upon you than it was before,
for now the authority in such matters has been given by the sultan to the
vizier in Buda, who is our good friend. This is a happy chance for you and
me. We would have to summon the council, (1400) all the beys and imperial agas, the captains and the standard-bearers, Hasan Pasha and his war-

riors, that we might draw up the request for transfer of the command. It is our good fortune that the council is assembled. Here is the council; here is the pasha; and here are the fifty warriors.' I rose to my swift feet and approached Hasan Pasha Tiro. The pasha summoned his four scribes, and we fashioned a request for Mehmed. The fifty warriors countersigned it and the agas in turn set their seals upon it, the forty agas and the twenty beys, the twelve Turkish captains and the three and twenty standard-bearers. When we had fashioned the request for your son, the pasha ratified it and gave it into my hands, and I bestowed it upon your beloved son, Smailaga. Then the Turks gave thanks, and said: 'Blessed are we all that we have seen the fledgling of our alaybey and that his house shall not fail, for the gray falcon will now assume the command. We are all content and happy that you should be our leader in battle. May you hold the power even as your father did under the decree of the sultan and with imperial pay and golden marten.[34] May it be happy for you as it was for your father and for your uncle, Cifrić Hasanaga, and may all of us share your happiness.' Then Hasan Pasha rose and offered up a prayer over your son; we all followed and responded 'Amin'; 'May good fortune attend him and may he accomplish what he purposes. May his enemies be beneath his feet, even as the shoes and nails beneath his horses' hoofs.'

"That is why Mehmed is sad. He is embarrassed before his father and uncle. Yes, brother, the young man is proud and jealous of his honor. Thanks be to God that we have seen this with our own eyes. Now let us but ask one more favor from God, my dear brother, that we may marry him off, that God give us a mighty friend through marriage, whose house would be of equal fame with ours (1450) and whose daughter would suit our son."

Now when Cifrić Hasan had finished his discourse, telling all to Smailaga, and the hadji understood his brother, then he addressed his son: "O Mehmed, shining light of our house, you have made too great haste, my son, and I am afraid we shall not carry on with honor. You are young in years and you have been brought up surrounded by good things. You have experienced no difficulties, neither yourself nor have you seen them in those about you. You have not known poverty or scarcity of any sort. Whatever your heart desired you had enough of, and may you have it thus in the future also. The Turks in Hungary are hard to deal with, and the Border is a bloodstained garment. The Borderers are good people, but their temperament is volatile and you, my son, are not skilled enough to judge them as would please the Turks. Hence you might overestimate yourself. Among men of nobility one must not be conceited; you must be humble before them all. Take the advice of your elders, and embrace those of equal age, and kiss the younger between the eyes, so that they will not hesitate, my son, to die or to be killed for your sake, nor to fill dungeons with their bodies. You have as yet neither beard nor moustache. Listen, therefore, Mehmed; this is my last advice to you: if today you take the command upon yourself and during my lifetime any evil rumor should come to my ears concerning you from the Border, from any youth younger than yourself—we should not even speak of your elders—that you have been unjust with any man, then as long as my right arm can strike and as long as I have my sword hanging from its peg—your father has but you alone —by my faith in God, which never fails, I shall have no son, even if you are my only one.

"Go now from my room. For seven years now, my son, I have kept it secret that the sultan sent you rich garments. Ever since the time when Bosnia was established (1500) no one has seen such raiment, certainly never worn such. There it is, my son, in the hamper by your dear mother's pillow—your dear mother, who, for my sake, in my old age, lost her youth in caring for you. She keeps it there beneath her pillow. Those garments were made for you against this very time and season when you should come to take the command. Tell your mother to change your clothes. I shall call the steward Husein and his brother, Ibrahim, who, for seven years, have cared for your horse. Then you shall see a chestnut horse, my son! I shall not say whether I shall send you to Buda or not until you return from the women's chambers and I see you in your dress array, that I may judge whether you are worthy to be alaybey, whether your fur cap suits you, the golden cap with its twelve plumes, and the feather of the alaybey at your brow, and the Persian sword blessed at Mecca at your side. That sword is no trifle and I desire to see it by your flank to judge whether you are a hero worthy of that Persian saber. Only then shall we see, my son, whether I shall send you or not."

Smailaga's son Mehmed listened to all this. He was a gray falcon bred of a falcon; a good father has a good son. Mehmed was not at all abashed at his father's and uncle's chafing with words which were now sweet and now harsh. He ran to his father's right hand and kissed it, both his father's and that of his uncle Hasan. Then Mehmed went to the

door of the room and strode through his father's courts until he came
to his mother's harem. There he raised the curtain at the doorway and
the son went to meet his mother in the room. He greeted her and ran to
kiss her hand. She kissed her son between the eyes and gazed into her
Mehmed's face, her dragon son's. She was surprised to see that his face
was somewhat drawn, not at all as it used to be. (1550) One might say
that he were ill. His mother had given up her whole lifetime and cast
her youth at the feet of an old man in order to bring up such a son.
When she saw Mehmed's face, she rose and embraced her son, crying:
"My beloved son, what ails you? God be with you! Do not tell me you
are ill, my son, for that would wring my heart and make me mourn.
May God preserve us from that; may God's help be ours!" Then Mehmed said to his mother: "O my mother, be not so foolish. If God grant,
and we have hope in almighty God, you shall not mourn for me. But
now I bring greetings from my father. You have here a hamper inlaid
with mother-of-pearl in which is the raiment which the sultan sent for
me. You must change my garments that I may go in full dress array
before my father and my uncle, Cifrić Hasanaga. Smailaga has a great
longing, mother, to see me thus arrayed; I know not what he will do
with me. If God grants, all will go well."

The lady rose and offered up thanks. In her heart she was thinking
of something else; that, perhaps, Smailaga wished to marry off her son
and was preparing him to go courting. His mother could scarcely wait
for that day to come when she would see a daughter-in-law at her son's
side. Then she took her son's clothes, which were like a pasha's, and
opened the gold-adorned hamper.[35] From it she took a bundle[36] of silk
embroidered with gold. It was not tied with knots but had been pierced
by golden pins. She untied the golden bundle, and garments of gold
poured forth—may God be praised—it was as if the sun shone. First of
all his mother put upon him linen of finest silk cloth. Every third thread
in it was of gold. Then she gave to him a silken vest, (1600) all embroidered with pure gold. Down the front of the vest were buttons fashioned of gold pieces which reached to his silk belt. There were twelve
of them, and each contained half a liter of gold. The button at his
throat shone even as the moon and in it was a full liter of gold. The vest
had a gold-embroidered collar whose two wings were fastened by the
button. At the right side of the collar above the button was the likeness
of Sulejman the Magnificent and on the other that of the imperial pontiff of Islam.[37] Then she gave him his breastplate. It was not of silver

but of pure gold and weighed full four oke. On his back she fastened it
with a buckle. She put on him his silken breeches, which had been made
in Damascus, all embroidered in gold, with serpents pictured upon his
thighs, their golden heads meeting beneath his belt and beneath the
thong by which his sword was hung. Then she girded on him two Tripolitan sashes and his braided belt of arms, which was not like other belts of
arms, but braided of golden threads and embroidered with white pearls.
Therein were his two small Venetian pistols forged of pure gold; the
sights were diamonds and pure pearls. They shone even as the moon.
Both pistols fire without flint and take a full liter of powder, breaking
fierce armor and burning the hearts of heroes. Between them was a two-
edged sword which severs heroes' hearts. Its whole scabbard was decorated with pearls, and its hilt was forged in gold. Upon his shoulders was
a silken cloak, its two corners heavy with gold. Gilded branches were
embroidered round about and upon his shoulders were snakes whose
heads met beneath his throat. Down the front hung four cords, (1650)
braided of 'fined gold, all four reaching to his belt of arms and mingling
with his sword-thong which held his fierce Persian blade.

Then with an ivory comb his mother combed out the sheaf-life
queue and bound it with pearl. She put on him his cap of fur with its
twelve plumes, which no one could wear, neither vizier nor imperial
field marshal nor minister nor any other pasha save only the alaybey
under the sultan's firman.[38] Upon his head waved the plumes, and the
golden feathers fell over his forehead. The imperial plumes were made
after two fashions, half of them were stationary and half mobile. Whenever he rode or marched, the stationary plumes hissed like angry serpents, and the moving plumes revolved. The hero needed no watch, for
the plumes revolved three or four times an hour.

Then his mother put on him his boots and leggings and sent him
in before his sire. When Mehmed came before his father with his Persian
blade beneath his left arm, like a light gray falcon, he approached his
father's right hand and kissed it, he kissed the hem of his garment and
his hand. Then he did the same to his uncle. And, retreating three or
four paces, he stood at attention before his father, in his glorious array,
in boots and leggings, with his fur cap and plumes; then he let his Persian
blade drop at his left side, his left hand on its hilt, and his right resting
on his belt of arms. He waited upon his father and uncle even as the
nobles upon the sultan in Stambol.

From his cushion-seat his father watched him full quarter of an hour without a word, (1700) and Mehmed did not move; so proud and jealous of his honor was he that he would have toppled over rather than budge from that spot without permission from his dear father. He is a blessing to the father who begat him, as well as to the Border and, indeed, to the whole empire. His father opened the casement window and called Osman, the standard-bearer, from his guardhouse and coffee hearth.[39] The younger man answered his elder; Osman ran from the coffee hearth to the top of the staircase opposite Smailaga. He folded his arms over his belt and waited to hear what his elder would say. Then Smail, the hadji and former alaybey, addressed him: "Osman, my golden wing, with you, my son, not only the whole Border flies but also Hasan and the hadji. My son, you are like a dragon's brood. For twenty-seven years you have carried our green[40] standard before your alaybey. Seven years did you serve me and twenty my brother. Such was the great service which you performed for us. There is none other like you, nor shall there ever be, nor shall a mother ever again bear such a one. You have never, my son, bowed your face before the rifles of the enemies of our faith. My dear son, your manly chest has always been unbuttoned. You have ridden hard and cut down the enemy, you have scattered whole companies of Germans. Now, Osman, the day of destiny has come. Well have you served me and my brother Hasan; you have pursued the foe well and well have you withstood his onslaught; may good fortune follow and overtake you!

"The time has come that the command pass from us two old men to a younger. Now, Osman, by the bread you ate in our house, shall you serve Mehmed even better than you did either of us. The boy is still young and foolish. But you, my son, are more than wise. (1750) May you guard him from all evil and in every difficult pass may you protect him from all enemies; for Mehmed is still young and foolish. I shall lay this command upon him, that he take advice from you, Osman, that he not depart from it, and that he obey you even as his own father."

Then Osman addressed the hadji thus: "Had I not sworn to serve your house, to be to it like a sword in the right hand and the wings upon the shoulders of a falcon, I would not have left my own house in Orlovac[41] and my seven brothers, the seven Hamzagići. I came to you in Kanidža and saw that your house was the first, that you were mother of all Bosnians, and of all champions of the sultan. I came to serve you, to share with you both good and evil. With you I prefer to live and die, rather than to stay with my seven brothers, long life to them. My youn-

Market day at Bijelo Polje in 1935. The two-story building in the upper foreground is the *kafana* where Parry first met Avdo.

ger brothers have married, but I remain still without a wife. They all invited me to their weddings that I might give gifts to my sisters-in-law. You know well I did not go, either to celebrate their weddings or to bestow gifts upon my sisters-in-law. They met to divide my father's substance and they summoned me. I did not go nor did I take my share, but I fashioned and sent them a well-writ letter: 'I shall not come for the dividing. Divide among yourselves my portion: if anyone of you is alive when I die, let him grant a little something for my soul. My share of life's goods is here with the hadji and his brother. I live well by the health of the bey. Of all have I enough and more, noble is my treatment. I have sworn that, even as I have lived with them, so shall I die in their service.'[42]

"O hadji, my great benefactor, my first and last master, well shall I guard your son. In the hope of almighty God (1800) and with his help, as long as my head remains upon my shoulders nothing shall befall your son. I shall be to him as his right hand and as a sharp sword at his side."

Then Smailaga thus addressed him: "I kiss your eyes, O standard-bearer, even as my son's. You are indeed as my own son. This is your commission with Mehmed. Prepare yourself, Osman, my son, yourself and your dapple-gray steed. Array yourself in those garments which you wear only twice in the year, on both Bajrams,[43] even on the Day of Pilgrims and the Bajram of Ramazan, and which you wore when we went before the sultan. And upon your horse, my son, put the trappings and saddle of gold. Thus shall you escort my son to Buda, to our friend the imperial vizier with three horsetail plumes; he is our good friend. But there are all sorts of dangers in Buda, and you must care well for Mehmed. I fear more for him there than if he were in a great war. Now call Husein the groom and let him prepare that Egyptian steed which was reared for this very day. This will be his first journey. Let his master assume the command and all else will fare well."

Then the hadji stretched forth his hand and opened a hamper behind him. He took out a thousand Venetian ducats with not a single lesser coin among them. He wrapped them in a kerchief embroidered with gold and threw them from the window to his standard-bearer: "Here, Osman, my son, are ducats for a safe journey to Buda. The responsibility is yours, my dear standard-bearer: take care that no harm befall you and that you bring no shame upon yourselves or upon us two old men. Let no one reproach you or me, in my old age. Should disgrace come upon my last years, (1850) then would I never forgive you."

Osman listened and obeyed, and took the golden kerchief. Then he called the two standard-bearers: "My brothers, go down to the stable and prepare my dapple-gray horse in those trappings and armor which Smailaga commanded." While the standard-bearers were carrying out his orders, Osman prepared himself within his chamber.

Osman called Husein the squire:[44] "Husein, steward[45] of the bey, Smailaga has ordered you to prepare that chestnut horse which came from our sultan, and which our master reared for his son. Now has God granted that we have seen this day; Mehmed, the hadji's son, is leaving for Buda. Prepare the horse in those trappings which came from Stambol."

And when the steward heard, he went down to the manger where the chestnut horse was. He unfastened the twelve buckles forged of silver and took from the horse his twelve blankets. Then he called for the groom Ibrahim, and they brought a caldron of warm water and a piece of perfumed soap.[46] They washed the horse's coat as they had trained him to expect. With a sponge they dried him and they smoothed his coat with a towel. Then with a key they opened a hamper ornamented with gold and brought forth the horse's trappings. First they took a Hungarian saddlecloth and placed it on the chestnut steed. On this they set the coral saddle which was adorned round about with gold. The coral was decorated with Egyptian agates of various colors, one of which was worth a golden florin. The gold was yellow, white was the pearl. Among the pearls were agates, some blue, some green, some yellow, and some red. On the background of gold and pearl the colors of the agates were enhanced. On the front of the saddle instead of a pommel there was a sphere of gold worth a chest of ducats. The holsters for his pistols (1900) were of Syrian silk, embroidered with white pearl. In them they put his two Venetian guns, covered all with gold. Their cover[47] was adorned with so many golden sequins that you could scarcely see the Venetian cloth; around them was a border of Venetian ducats. Over the saddle were four girths and a fifth beneath to protect the horse's flesh, whenever the steed jumped or galloped. All four were woven of silk and the one next to the horse's body was of black marten fur, while the outer ones were adorned with pearl. The stewards tightened and buckled the girths and adjusted the crupper on his back; the crupper of silk was ornamented with ducats and a moon-plate made of gold glittered on it. The two shabracques were of gold and down the horse's breast hung shining bosses. On them diamonds flashed. He fas-

tened the martingale from the girth to the double-ring snaffles; all the
fastenings were of gold. Next came the golden breast-strap. Over his
mane from ears to shoulder they cast a piece of embroidered mesh from
Egypt, fastening it under the pommel of the saddle. The embroidery
was of gold. Through it the dark mane hung, shining through the gold
like the moon through the branches of a pine tree. They brought then a
golden bridle and attached the Egyptian reins to the four chains on the
bits that fitted over the horse's teeth and were fastened under its neck.
All four were ornamented with pearl and the bridle beside them was of
gold. Down each cheek flashed a band of pure gold, the two fastened by
a clasp between the ears. Atop the clasp shone the morning star and in
its center a diamond. (1950) There is no darkness before the horse, but
midnight is as bright as midday.

My God, thanks be to thee for all things. When they had harnessed
his mighty steed with golden saddle and golden shabracques, with girths
and martingales and shining bosses on its chest, a golden mesh over its
mane and the golden breast-straps, the bridle, and bands covering him
from the tips of his ears to the bottom of his cheeks, no hair was visible
except a bit of tail, no mane at all. The yellow gold confined and covered it. The horse was like a mountain vila, and people say that it had
wings. It knew not how to speak and yet it knew the way to go. When
he bared his two nostrils and snorted, he was so strong and fiery that
from them burst forth smoke and blue flame. The two stewards led the
steed into the courtyard.

When Smailaga the hadji and his brother Cifrić Hasanaga saw him,
they opened the window and leaned forth their foreheads against the
jamb, their beards out the window, and all four hands upon the sill.
Then Smail called his one and only son: "Ah, Mehmed, here is your
horse all caparisoned and ready. Care well for the horse as though it
were your own head, for he has been long idle in the stable. Seven years
is not a short while to lie and do nothing. All the first day, even unto
noon tomorrow, calm him, do not drive him overmuch, until the stiff-
ness leaves him, and the numbness departs from his jaws. But then, after
noon tomorrow, my son, I do not think you will even see where the
horse is flying, to say nothing of stopping him. Mehmed, my dear son,
if fate is with us, you must not long delay, (2000) for I can hardly await
your return. Proceed wisely; do not perish foolishly, for Buda is like a
whole province, my son, or like a small kingdom. Buda, you know, has
just been taken from the Magyars into the hands of the sultan,[48] and

they gave us much trouble. The city is not yet peaceful and well ordered. They are still shooting in some parts. Yet I think the vizier will
not keep you long in Buda, my son. Farewell and God be with you."

He accompanied Mehmed down the stairs. What a sight that falcon
was to look upon as he descended the stairs in his golden raiment, his
sword at his side, and the quivering plumes upon his head. He resembled
nothing more than a flash of lightning from the clouds or a shower of
lightning bolts. When the gray falcon came to his horse's side it was a
glorious thing to look upon, glorious for the whole kingdom to have together in one state two such creatures, and glorious, too, for his elder
to have begotten such a son, so noble and wise, with strong heroic heart
and manly form and countenance, and strong right arm to bring harsh
woe upon his enemy.

When Mehmed came into the courtyard the stable opened and the
gray stallion all adorned came forth. You should have seen it! It was
but a little inferior to Mehmed's own horse. Indeed, had it been as long
in the stable as the chestnut horse it would have surpassed him! Its trappings, however, were different, for they were those of a standard-
bearer, but not much inferior. The two standard-bearers led him in,
holding him by two ropes to the bridle and bits. When the gray stallion
saw the hadji's horse it suddenly reared and lifted the standard-bearers
a whole meter from the ground; I wouldn't say it wasn't a whole spear's
length! (2050)

Then they quieted the horse, and from the guardhouse, from the
coffee hearth, the gate opened and forth came Osman the standard-
bearer, dressed in silk and gold. On his head was a golden cap with seven
plumes, three stationary and four mobile. The stationary plumes hissed
like angry snakes, while the moving ones turned on their pivot four
times an hour. When the hero was journeying afar or fighting in the wars,
he needed no timepiece for the plumes turned and told him what hour
it was of day or night. The golden feathers fell over his forehead and
some backwards over his neck. They struck against the young man's
shoulders like lightning bolts. Osman's cloak was woven and had upon
it braid of gold. Golden branches were embroidered on all sides, and
serpents were woven on his shoulders, their heads meeting beneath his
throat. Had you not seen them before, you would have sworn the snakes
were living. The breastplate upon the young man's chest was of gold.
His breeches, which suited him well, were of scarlet Venetian stuff,
with golden stripes upon his thighs and branches embroidered between

the stripes. The embroidery was of gold and the fabric of scarlet; the two colors contrasted well with one another. Around the young man's waist were two silken sashes and a woven belt of arms with golden weapons. At his left side was his sharp sword[49] with which he had won many duels. In his hand was a Dubrovnik rifle, which held a full liter of powder. With this he brings down eagles from beneath the clouds, holds up ships upon the sea, and intercepts the imperial post. No mother ever bore a hero like that mighty falcon, Osman the imperial standard-bearer of the alaybey. His eyes were dark, his forehead broad. Osman's moustaches were of such length that they fell over his breastplate (2100) and covered it and his weapons. Were you to see him from afar you would say that in his teeth he carried an unskinned black lamb. As the young man strode to his horse the two old heroes watched and gave them their blessing. Smailaga addressed his standard-bearer: "O standard-bearer, my golden wing, take care not to delay, for I give my son into your keeping."

Then the stewards led forth their horses to the hadji's mounting stone and with a cry of "Allah be with us!" the two youths leaped to their steeds. In their right hands were their shining rifles, which they hung over their saddlehorns. Their two-edged swords shone as they hung down the steeds' sides. How tall their Arabian steeds were! They were long as a bolt of cloth and as high as a mountain fir tree! But tall as they were, the youths' swords were even longer. Ever did the swords strike against the nails in the horses' shoes and play about the steeds, even as a serpent about a dry thistle. First rode Osman, and behind him Mehmed. They left the courtyard and entered the heathrows,[50] making their way to the plain of Kanidža. Dear God, thanks to thee for all things! By the way the horses moved you would say they were flying. They raised their hoofs into the air and spewed foam over their flanks and over their riders. The foam fell on their rounded rumps and from the rumps it fell to the plain; one would say that lambs were being born. From their nostrils flames emerged and set fire to the mesh on their forelocks. Clouds of smoke billowed before them as if Venetian rifles were being fired whose smoke was poisoned. Like hares they crossed the level plain; like wolves they took to the mountains. All day long until nightfall, like two fiery dragons on phantom steeds, they crossed the ranges. In one day they covered as much ground (2150) as any other men in two.

At nightfall they found themselves in the village of Vukašiće[51] before the dwelling of Vukašin, the village elder[52] and their family's best householder. Vukašin and his spouse were both at home; when they saw the hadji's son on his winged chestnut horse all submerged as he was in pure gold, he shone like the moon. His forged saber glided over his horse's side like a serpent around a dry thistle. The steed spread his two jaws. Were you to cast into it a Bulgarian cloak[53] you would not fill his gaping jaws. One would say and swear that it was an imperial field marshal upon the horse; his trappings were better than a field marshal's. Behind him rode Osman on his gray horse as though on a slender mountain spirit. He, too, was one of the mightiest heroes in this fair world. His raiment was a bit different from that of Mehmed, but his horse was mighty beyond reckoning; the horse was mighty and mighty was Osman.

Vukašin recognized them and spoke thus to his beloved spouse: "Do you see those two noble lords in golden garments, with gilt imperial caps upon their heads, gilt caps and gilt plumes, astride their richly caparisoned horses?" When his love heard Vukašin she said to her husband: "Vukašin, my dear master, what is this rare wonder? Never before have I seen such dragons on such richly caparisoned steeds. Glorious is that youth. Blessed is the mother who bore him, and the sister who swears by him, but most blest is his true love because she knows his caress upon the couch. And that mighty one upon the gray steed! Mighty is he and more than awesome. O my husband, I pray you, as my own spouse, what is that he carries in his teeth? (2200) It looks like an unskinned black lamb with legs hanging over his chest." Then spoke Vukašin to his love: "My dear one, it is not a lamb in his teeth, but those are the moustaches of that hero, the standard-bearer of Hadji Smail, Alaybey of Kanidža. There is no fiercer dragon among the Turks nor mightier nor more worthy than Osman, the alaybey's standard-bearer." Then she spoke to Vukašin: "I see that he is mightier than the mighty. But, Vuk, who is it on the chestnut horse, who is that gray falcon?" "That, my love, is the son of Smailaga. No other issue has he or his brother than this one alone." When his love understood his words she offered up a prayer of gratitude: "May God and all his saints preserve the son of his father from all evils! In all the years, Vuk, that I have been your love, and dwelt in your abode, many Turks have come to us, all the elders, captains, beys, and imperial agas, leaders under the imperial decree. But such heroes have never come and never will come again." And Vuk sustained her words: "Truly, my love, never." Then she spoke to Vukašin: "Vukašin, my dear master, it seems as I look

upon these dragons, that they are coming straight to our dwelling."
"My love, what thought is in your young mind? They are my prime
friends. Know, my love, that from the time when Hadji Smail, the dear
mother of the Bosnian people, began to rule and judge in Bosnia and
became alaybey in Kanidža, and about Kanidža, no one would say that
we were subordinates, but that we were like their other heroes. All value
us as they value their own eyes, and we, my love, revere them as our
agas. Now I shall go to the courtyard and open the gate (2250) that I
may call the servants in the courtyard to take their noble steeds. I shall
take the Turks by the white hand and do you run to receive their long
rifles." Thus he spoke and rose. He flew quickly down the steps and ran
to the courtyard and opened the courtyard gate. The two winged steeds
entered with their imperial heroes. Vuk placed his cap beneath his arm.
They greeted him: "Good evening, Vuk!" And he to them: "Welcome,
my lords! our golden plumes and feathers!" They dismounted. Vuk
spread his arms and embraced Mehmed, son of Smail, and kissed him.
"Blessed am I, O falcon's seed, that I may receive the dear son of Hadji
Smail, the foremost alaybey of Kanidža." "Be thanked for thy hospitality, Vuk. May God preserve your line from great distress and from
enemies' hands." Then Vuk embraced the standard-bearer, Osman:
"Welcome, wing of the alaybey!" "Blessings upon your house, Vukašin." Then his love came in like a white mountain vila and bowed and
kissed their hands, and took their long rifles. Servants took their stallions and loosed their girths, and drove them a little around the courtyard that the horses might not feel fatigue.

Then Vuk took the two gray falcons by their lordly hands and led
them to the painted dwelling. He made them sit upon purple cushions
and he took off their boots and leggings. He put costly mantles about
them and lighted their silver pipes while his love hung their rifles and
their golden swords upon shining pegs. Then Vuk started the fire under
a kettle on the hearth to prepare fresh coffee for them. While the coffee
was brewing, he gave them some sweet sherbet with water, and his wife
brought from another room (2300) a table inlaid with mother-of-pearl
and covered with Venetian stuff. She brought also two casks, both
weighing four oke, one of red wine of seven years, the other of brandy
which Vuk had put aside, as it were, for them. And those casks were as
noble as the lords themselves. They each held half a liter. Then Vuk
answered: "Which will you first, strong coffee, wine, or brandy; which
would you like? Choose, my lords and heroes. Happier am I that you

came to my dwelling to rest, that you have visited your faithful subject than I would be at a great gift from someone, uncounted coin, or good unridden horses." "Thanks, my friend, many thanks to you. May all good things fall to your lot." "To your lot, my lords, and mine." Then he poured out coffee for them, two cups before the youths had turned away fatigue, two for them and the third for Vuk. Then cup followed cup. Vuk took off his cap and spoke: "May God in his great wisdom grant happiness to Hadji Smail, happiness to him and protection to his son, this golden star of the heavens, from the sharp swords of the enemy, and from sore distress and evil." Then Mehmed said to Vuk: "May the same fall to you, Vukašin, and to your noble issue."

When they had both exchanged greetings, then the true love of Vukašin once again kissed Mehmed's hand and that of Osman, the standard-bearer, and that of Vuk, her lord and master. The Turks made Vuk sit beside them on cushions. "If you wish us to stay the night, Vuk, and enjoy the hospitality of you and your wife, may God grant that you receive us in your dwelling as it seems best to you. (2350) Let us, then, drink." Then Vuk beseeched them as they drank: "I pray of you as though you were my elders. I could scarcely wait to hear those words. You cannot refuse my hospitality. It is indeed dear to me to have guests within my house." "Thanks to you, Vuk, for this kindness."

He sat between them on the cushions. His wife did not remain long. Soon the fried chicken came to make their drinks the sweeter. Then the mistress of Vukašin's house pushed back her sleeves and made pies and prepared wheat cakes. Young servants slaughtered barren sheep, some drove bees from the hive. From the way Vuk ran about you would think a son was being born to him, an only son in a family of girls. His wife was even busier. Vuk prepared for these dragon heroes so much lamb and fried chicken and so many wheat cakes and sweet honeycombs that one would think that ten people had come to his home, instead of the two youths from Kanidža. Were they to sit for a whole week, they could not have eaten all of it.

Then stewards walked their horses, and as they led them, the horses regained their spirits. They stripped them of their saddles, their trappings, and armor. They flung blankets over the horses that the tired steeds should not become chilled, measured out barley for them, and tied them in their stalls beside Vukašin's stallion. When the horses had eaten their barley, the youths groomed them and rubbed the sweat from them, drying their manes with cloth. Finally they replaced the blankets on the horses. Meanwhile in the upper chamber the young men were taking their fill in the white dwelling of Vukašin, that good master of the house. Many and fine were the ornaments and furnishings of his home. There was Venetian stuff and dark-hued velvet, such as are to be found in the houses of rich agas or beys, (2400) for Vuk had been born among Turks, and he believed and lived in their fashion.

Then a lively conversation arose, and Vuk said to Mehmed, Smail's son: "Mehmed, my golden shining star! How is Hadji Smailaga, and your uncle Cifrić Hasanaga? Does your father still go to the assemblies? And how are things along the Austrian border? Does your house still have the command, or has another succeeded your father while you were growing up? Your house must keep the command." And Mehmed answered Vukašin: "Vukašin, my father is well, praise be to God, and my uncle Hasan also, and all the Turks around us, like the dusky wolves on the mountains. Each who wishes spends his life raiding, and the army still follows its alaybey. But father does not go to the assemblies. The Turks gather at our dwelling, and converse in our white halls. Long since my father gave over the command to his brother Hasan, my uncle, while father himself went on the pilgraimage to Mecca, and there, like other pilgrims, made vows of abstinence from wine and brandy. And he who does not drink is not fitted to be a bey and lead armies and raiding parties. For twenty years now, Vukašin, my uncle has been alaybey under the decree of our sultan. But both uncle and father are now very old, and find their happiness in me. Yesterday with our agas and beys they drew up a decree for me, our Turks put their seals upon it, the fifty warriors signed it, and Hasan Pasha confirmed it. So today, Vuk, they have sent me to the vizier in Buda, who, my father says, is a good friend of himself and of my uncle. The imperial mandate and the command are to pass from my elders unto me, young as I am."

Vuk rose and crossed himself and did obeisance before God, (2450) offering up a prayer of thanksgiving. "Praise be to God, and to this day, when our ears have heard such glad tidings, and our eyes see their desire. And yet, my son, I wonder somewhat at what your father said about the vizier, that he is a good friend to you. I do not trust the viziers, not only on my own account, but even more for that of a bey such as your father and uncle, who are the keys of all Bosnia, keepers of the sultan's storehouse. And so, my son, Mehmed, take great care, and tell Osman to watch over you well in Buda. The viziers are traitors to the sultan."[54] Mehmed and Osman thanked him.

Then came the lordly feast, and what a feast it was! For Vukašin's house was bounteous. They supped and the crumbs were cleared away, and after supper they drank red wine. When the time for sleep came, twin girls beautiful as mountain vilas came into the room. They wore many-colored skirts decorated with pearl, and two belts with buckles of pure gold about their waists. Their hair was carefully combed, and in it shimmered strands of ducats. On their arms were crimson sleeves. Many-hued flowers trailed along their breasts and among them necklaces of ducats and gold pieces. The yellow necklaces fell over their white breasts, the colors contrasting with one another so that one would say they were lovely oranges from the sea coast. The two girls drew up their sleeves and skirts and taking the youths' hands and hems would have kissed them, but the young lords did not allow themselves to be kissed.

The maidens waited upon the young men. They brought in a silk mattress in which there was no wool, neither from lamb nor from full-grown sheep, but only the feathers of birds from the sea coast; (2500) on it they spread a silken sheet on which was more gold than silk and two pillows of Venetian velvet. On the pillows were covers embroidered with gold. They spread also a silk coverlet. Then the maids returned to their own quarters, and the two youths took off their belts of arms, their fur caps, and golden garments. They lay down beside each other and slept.

They slept, but Vuk did not fall asleep, nor his wife either. They watched all night in that room, not sleeping, nor did they blow out the candles. Thus all night they waited upon the sleeping youths, lest they wake from their dreams and seek water or wine. When half the night had passed, when two hours after midnight came, when small birds begin to sing and cocks to flap their wings and crow, Osman rose from the couch and kissed Meho's fair cheek. "Rise, my golden star! Dawn is near, and we must prepare to depart. While the young men are harnessing our stallions, we must make ready. Far have we to journey today, even to the village of the Vujadinovići.[55] The days are short, and the distances between overnight rests long. You know your father's orders."[56]

When Vukašin heard that, he said to Osman: "Are you jesting or do you speak in earnest? You two heroes cannot leave here so quickly, after but one night in my dwelling, except over my dead body, or by cutting off my hands. You must not leave my home for at least three or four days." Then Meho and Osman turned to him and said courteously:

"Vukašin, honored host! We embrace you as our own brother. God be praised that we have seen you, Vuk. Your bearing has been most honorable. We have had more than enough of everything, praise be to God. But if you were to give us all your possessions we could not stay another night, because at home we swore (2550) that unless we were killed or captured we would spend no more than one night anywhere. Therefore, you who are our glorious golden fortune, if you wish us to think well of you as long as we live, do not hinder us, for you have no good reason. There must be no further talk of this. We beg you as our own brother, for we must obey the commands of our elder, that you may not suffer our displeasure." Vuk and his wife were so sad at this that they burst into tears, and Vukašin said: "I am boundlessly sorry, but I would not displease you. Rather I praise you as I would a kinsman for your obedience to your elder, that imperial hero, Hadji Smailaga. But give me your promise, if you wish not to displease me either. When you have finished your task in Buda, you must spend the first night of your return journey with Vujadin in the village of the Vujadinovići, but the second night, my lords, if God wills, you must come to my house. Were you to pass me by and turn away, you would displease me and I should never forgive you." The two dragons cried out to Vuk: "Vukašin, dear host! If it is God's will, when we return we shall visit you."

Then Vuk rose and called the young men: "Take the shining coverings from the steeds and put on the golden saddles and trappings. Quickly prepare the horses." Three of Vuk's servants arose and prepared the two winged stallions. In the time it would take a mother to suckle her son the two dragons were ready. Then came Vuk's wife. She took the saddle bags from the horses, wrapped fried wheat cakes and other food, lamb and chicken in a silk kerchief, (2600) and put it in the violet-hued[57] bags, which she then placed on the steeds, and the servants drew tight the straps that held the saddle roll.[58] The youths put on their long socks and boots, and girded on their sharp swords. Down the stairs of Vuk's dwelling they went, preceded by Vukašin himself, who accompanied these two dragons of the sultan. His wife carried their long rifles in her own hands. When they came to the courtyard, the young men brought the horses to the mounting stone, and the heroes mounted. They shook hands with Vuk, and Vukašin's wife gave them their shining rifles and they fixed them on the saddle horn.

Then you should see Smail's son! Mehmed the hadji's son put his hand into his pocket and gave the lady twenty ducats. "Here, Lady Vukašin,[59] give these twenty ducats to your two daughters. Let them prepare the better for their weddings! May peace and good fortune attend them!" But Lady Vukašin was wise, and she swore by both her eyes: "O golden dragon, Mehmed, son of Hadji Smail, by my life and my eyes I do not desire your shining gold pieces. O Mehmed, do you wish to pay for lodgings in my dwelling as if you had been in a tavern or inn? Do you really want to pay for lodging and service? I would rather that my eyes be gouged out, mine or those of some one dear to me. I cannot accept this." Then Mehmed said to Lady Vukašin: "O Lady Vukašin! Be not foolish! I am not paying for lodging or service. Last night's hospitality was not for gold, but for love and kinship, that remembrance may last forever and never be lost or forgotten. It is for that I bestow this gift upon your daughters. (2650) They are as dear to me as my own sisters." With tears the lady received the ducats, and kissed the horse's eyes. "O chestnut steed, golden are thy wings! And the master you carry is pure gold. May he live many years! May all the good things which his mother and father have planned for him come true, and when he marries may you be the maiden's horse!" "Many thanks, Lady Vukašin. Many thanks as to an elder sister. May you also receive your heart's desire and marry off your sons and daughters, later finding pleasure in the knowledge of their peace and happiness!"

Then he applied the spurs and slackened the reins. The chestnut understood, took to his hoofs, and tossed the bit. He would not go through the iron gateway, but cleared the wall and was off over the heath. He cantered playfully across the green plain, behind him Osman on his spotted gray. He flew over the plain even as a star across the sky. They passed through villages and crossed mountains. A whole day they rode until dark night came, and they had covered as much of Bosnia as they said they would before nightfall, for they had come to the house of Vujadin.

Vujadin happened to be at home, and with him his wife and their two sons. They were looking from the window when the two imperial dragons came in sight, all in gold and plumes and with full-panoplied stallions. They were like imperial pashas, but much finer riders, and their array was much better than that of a pasha or vizier or even the great field marshals of the sultan. Vujadin's two sons[60] flew to the window and pressed their foreheads against the glass. When they saw, they marveled, and called out to their father. "O father, come and see a great wonder we have never seen before! Here are two heroes on golden steeds. They must be either pashas or viziers!" (2700)

When Vujadin spied the son of Hadji Smail in his plumed cap on which was the feather of an alaybey, and beneath him his winged horse, and when he saw the standard-bearer behind Meho, that mighty hero and his fine gray horse, Vujadin was distressed, for that was Hadji Smail's son in person with Osman on the white steed. All the border knows Osman, and all the kingdoms know him. Then Vujadin said to his sons: "Rise quickly and run to the courtyard gate. Draw the four bolts, two of wood and two of steel, and open the courtyard gate, both portals for these two imperial dragons. Greet them and stand at attention as if they were pashas or viziers. For you these men are indeed pashas and viziers. Thus shall you do all night, neither sleep nor sit, but cross your arms on your breasts. You shall not speak, but wait upon the heroes, to honor them as best you know how, that you may bring good repute in after years to me and to your house." Vujadin's sons looked, and then ran like wolves of the mountains. They opened the courtyard gate, and the two heroes drove in their horses. "Good evening" cried the heroes. "Good evening" replied the youths in the courtyard. The young men bowed before them, and the heroes took them in their arms.

Then came Vujadin from the castle to the bottom of the steps, and called a welcome to the heroes, taking them by their lordly hands. His two sons took the horses by the bridle and led them up and down. Then Vujadin's wife took the two long rifles from the saddle horn and carried them to the upper chamber of the house to the masters' room, where but few guests are admitted. That room was kept for such heroes as these. It was strewn with Venetian cloth. Round about were silk couches with pillows covered with white silk embroidered in the center in gold. They parted the curtained doorway of the room and entered. Then came Vujadin's two dear daughters-in-law, like two white mountain spirits. They took off the men's boots and socks and the swords from around their waists. When the two youths sat down they gazed at the ornaments of the room, at the cushions on the couch, all silk embroidered with gold. In the middle of the room a table was spread, covered with Venetian cloth, and on it a metal platter, on which was a service for various drinks. There were coffee urns with golden trays, and cups of crystal. Next to this service was a table of mother-of-pearl pitchers and four three-liter glasses covered with a silken napkin. Around the table were four chairs, studded with metal discs from the coastland. When the two imperial dragons entered, Vujadin bade them be seated, filled their glasses, and did honor to his guests. "I am indeed pleased, imperial lords, that you have come to my dwelling." "Thank you, Vujadin, we have found you and rejoice that we had a friend to visit." "Thank you. You are welcome, Turks. I greeted you below in the courtyard, and now again in this chamber. How are you, Meho, son of the hadji, noble offspring of an illustrious father? It seems to me as I look upon you in my old age that you will not be much different from your father. No, you will not be any less noble than he. God bless you, my dear son! Do not disappoint your father!" Then he greeted Osman. "Welcome, lordly plume! Pride of the Border." (2800) "May all good things be yours, o Vujadin!" "Now Mehmed, how is your father and your uncle Cifrić Hasanaga?" "They are both well, thank you." "How are things on the Austrian border and how are the lords of the Border? Do you still lead your raiding bands over the mountains, your raiding bands and your large armies? Do you march as far as the Austrian empire, broadening the borders of Sulejman's kingdom? Have the young men become better than the old? How does it seem to you, Mehmed? Are the old men better than the young?" And Mehmed answered Vujadin: "Opinions are divided, but mine shall ever be that the old men are better than the young." "Bravo! my dear son. If God grants you will be an honor to us." Then he sat beside them on a chair and filled a three-liter glass. Aged Vujadin filled all three glasses and glowed with satisfaction.

In the meantime the young men were walking the heroes' steeds, driving fatigue from them. They took off the golden saddles and trappings and all the girths. Then they sponged the horses and dried their manes with a towel. They covered them with blankets, gave them barley, and waited for the beasts to eat it. Then they put hay into the mangers, closed the door of the stable, and went upstairs in their father's house and renewed their serving. They put their caps on the pegs and stood bareheaded before Mehmed and Osman the standard-bearer. Shaking hands with them once again, they asked their guests if they were well and happy, asked after their homeland and all the lords of Kanidža. Then Vujadin's two sons stood at attention like two dusky wolves from the mountains. Vujadin's two daughters-in-law brought in all sorts of food. The cup went round, (2850) and the ruddy drink flowed. Then talk arose among them. Brandy is ever a talker. Evening came and they supped, and when they had supped and cleared away the crumbs, then came more wine and brandy.

Finally the couches were spread for sleep and the youths settled comfortably. All night the young men watched over the lords, lest these heroes, tired from drink, should be disturbed and seek either water or wine.

When dawn broke Osman called Mehmed: "Ah, Mehmed, we have overslept." Vujadin and his two sons tried as best they could to make their guests stay, but it was of no avail. Then Vujadin's sons prepared the two falcons' horses. Meantime the youths were ready and descended to the courtyard. The daughters-in-law brought their long rifles. The sons led out their horses, and the youths mounted. They had passed a comfortable night. Now the day star shone and dawn unfolded its wings.

Mehmed put his hand into his pocket and gave each of Vujadin's daughters-in-law five gold pieces. They swore they would not accept them: "No, Mehmed, you shall not pay for your lodgings. These are not inns or taverns, but a house for good men." But Mehmed would not listen. "That is not pay, my children, but gifts of love. Let the girls buy combs and powder."

Then he rode his chestnut steed to the courtyard gate, Osman behind him on his gray stallion, like a star across a clear sky. Just as dawn spread its wings, the two youths were riding by the cool Klima[61] near Buda, four hours away. The Klima is very muddy (2900) and great beyond telling. Silently the quicksand works. There is no horse who could cross it without being sucked down by the quicksand. There is only one bridge over the Klima and this is called Čekmedže bridge.[62] It has twelve arches, for the Klima is long and wide. The riders crossed the bridge and set out over the plain of Muhač.[63] The sun's rays began to light up the very tips of the peaks.

Mehmed the hadji's son looked forth over the green plain of Buda, when suddenly a wondrous coach came forth from the city. It was covered with fine cloth and drawn by twelve Bedouin mares covered with fine stuff from the top of their heads to the green grass below. Two were white as swans, two black as ravens, two gray as doves. Two had white spots on their hoofs, two had spots on their noses, and two were pied black. The last two were bays.[64] These were the reserve horses. Beside the coach rode fifty warriors on fifty Syrian Bedouin mares in full war panoply. Their saddles were of moroccan leather with Janissary girths. In their teeth were bits of steel. The heroes on them wore crimson trousers and short cloaks and caps like the Janissaries, with the sign of the Janissaries on their caps.[65] This was the army of Sultan Sulejman.

They carried war spears at their shoulders and sharp swords at their left sides. The Syrian steeds were as graceful as a mountain vila, as long as a strip of homemade cloth, and as high as a mountain pine. They flew like swallows. In the heroes' hands were quirts with which they spurred on the Bedouin mares beneath them. (2950)

In the lead was a captain,[66] strong and mighty beyond telling. On his head was the imperial studded cap, with a single plume over his forehead. On it was written the captain's name. He was leader of a hundred men and rode a chestnut bay stallion, with imperial Osmanli saddle, studded shabracques on either side, shining bosses down his chest, and martingales from the snaffle beneath his neck. His reins were decorated with wild animals, especially a wolf and a fox. What a cloud of smoke surrounded the steed! From his nostrils spouted smoke and blue flame, as though fires were burning within him. They lighted up the coats of the fox and the gray[67] wolf. Great was the noise of the horses' hoofs, still greater the rumbling of the wondrous coach, and greatest of all was that of the imperial captain. Strong he was, and fine and mighty! His moustaches were dark and his brow broad. His arms were thick at the wrist and the sword at his left thigh was sharp. As high as the stallion stood above the ground, the sword was still longer. It was longer than two arm-spreads. As the horse galloped, the sword resounded and struck the rocks, making as great a noise as would a whole band of men. At his shoulder was a bone-breaking spear three arm-spreads in length, weighing twenty-four oke. On one side of the lofty steed's saddle horn was a brass mace, and on the other a two-barreled gun, two-barreled, taking four bullets.

When Mehmed saw him: "O Osman, my dear brother! How dashing these imperial heroes are! How mighty are their Bedouin mares! And what a mighty man their leader is, he who rides the chestnut steed! What a wondrous golden coach, with its Bedouin mares! See, Osman, how it is hung with fine cloth. (3000) What can this wonder with the warriors be? Who can it be who rides in this coach? They must be pashas or viziers, or some pasha's harem." "I know not, Mehmed."

They rode forward a little. Then they heard—dear God, thanks be to thee for all things—a mighty weeping within the coach, so great that the sound reached the heavens. Mehmed asked Osman the standard-bearer: "Osman, my very dear brother! Can it be true, or have I heard amiss? Listen, Osman, to the weeping in the coach." "I hear, Meho, by my faith. I have never before heard such wailing." Then the son of the hadji said to Osman the standard-bearer: "I cannot resist asking the captain of that band what creature it may be that wails in the coach. Osman, my golden wing, I shall quickly ride and ask the imperial captain whence the sad weeping in the coach comes." "Go, Mehmed, I shall not hinder you."

Meho, urging on his horse, applied the spurs lightly. When the steed spread its wings one would say that a vila[68] was flying through the air. Straightway the son of the hadji came among them, saluted and reined in his horse. The warriors received his salute, but the captain did not turn his head. Mehmed reined in his horse before him. "Wait a bit, imperial captain. I am a stranger from afar. I just happened to see these imperial soldiers on their Arabian mares with Janissary saddles, these warriors in red breeches and Janissary cloaks, caps and imperial marten insignia. Fine are the youths and fine their clothes, and passing fair are the imperial sabers at their sides, and the war spears at your shoulders. All the young men are like wolves of the mountains. And their leader is the handsomest and best equipped of all. We saw also the coach with you, (3050) and the various Bedouin mares which draw it. When my companion and I saw this, I was so pleased at the sight of you that I could have taken wing. And thus I urged on my horse to come nearer to you. Then something struck my ears. When I heard the great wailing in the coach my joy was turned to heavy grief, and I have ridden here to ask you truly, brother, what is wailing in the coach. Is it a vila or a fierce serpent? or is it some supernatural thing? Were it a vila, it would be on the mountain tops, were it a serpent, it would be beneath some stone, and divine creatures fly in the air. Tell me truly, is it a maiden in distress thus wailing?" Then the imperial captain spoke: "Away from here, drunken stranger! you must either be drunk or mad. I see that you are a very brazen fellow. Get your horse out of the way and drag your great cape out of here! Talk no longer of what concerns you not, or you will straightway lose your head. I perceive that you are of noble lineage, from some mighty family. Beware or I shall bring sorrow to your mother, who will wail forever because of me. I am in the employ of the imperial Porte. When my superior gives me an order, and says 'Do this, or that!' I must obey his command, lest I lose my head or my reward. Therefore he who hinders or opposes me will lose his head!"

At that moment Osman rode up on his dapple gray and demanded of the two warriors: "What is wrong between you? May God be with you both!" And the imperial captain spoke: "Away, you two troublemakers.[69] You must be some kind of imperial bandits. Do not anger me and my warriors, lest we cut off your heads, or take you alive." When Osman looked from the corner of his eye and saw that gray falcon, Mehmed, the son of Hadji Smail, (3100) he noticed that Mehmed's eyes were filled with blood, and that his eagle hair bristled beneath his plumes like a wolf's in the month of December. His heroic heart was quivering, and his breastplate began to shake. His right hand went to his belt and he took his sword. But he was a little wary of Osman, and feared that the standard-bearer might not do as Mehmed wished. He knew not what his intentions might be. But Osman was a falcon, without peer. There was no treachery in him, but thus he addressed Mehmed: "Lord Mehmed, you are so foolish! Why do you turn and look at Osman? Have you not the daring, or do you not trust me, if you attack your enemy? Did not your father, the elder hadji and alaybey, send me to be of help when you were in a tight place? On, my courageous one, Mehmed, make your choice! Do you wish to fight with the fifty warriors or with the imperial captain himself?" When the falcon understood these words, like thunder and lightning from the clouds his arm bent, his saber flew and the captain's head was off. He fell dead, and his horse remained standing there.

Then Mehmed turned to see what was happening with Osman. Fifty flintlocks fired a volley at Osman the standard-bearer, but of what avail was it to fire on him? The rifles harmed him not. The cloud of smoke settled and Osman disappeared. They attacked like lightning in the heavens with the sharp edge of the sword. And then the imperial traitors saw that firearms harmed him not, nor the sharp swords at their sides. But Mehmed was in a dilemma; for he dared not leave the coach, lest the swift horses run away and carry the maiden with them, for the mighty steeds were startled by the battle, (3150) and one would say that they were possessed, and that they were pawing the clouds with their hoofs. But the warriors turned their backs, and in the time it would take a mother to suckle her infant son, twenty-five had lost their heads, and twenty-five had fled in all directions like white sheep before wolves. When the cloud of mist rose, Mehmed saw what Osman had done to the warriors and realized there was no need to help that fiery dragon.

Then the youth ran to the coach to hear what was being said amid the wailing. The voice was a shrill girl's voice. The first words she said were: "Beauteous faith, my great wound! O holy word, my heart is torn! Creed of the Turks, sorrow thou forever! May Buda be destroyed by fire, and may a gypsy executioner kill its vizier! May the waters of the Danube roll over all the vizier's chieftains! For thus did the vizier treat my father, Zajim Alibeg,[70] and a hundred of the chief men of Buda." When the hadji's son understood what the maiden was saying in her weeping, his hero heart ached. He took the tempered spear from his horse, cut away the hangings of the coach, and saw a white vila of the mountains sitting therein, a maiden in great sorrow. Her hair was so long that she had twined it about her waist, but she had torn it on the right side because of her great sadness. The maid's face was as white as a ball of snow, yet from sorrow she had bruised her skin so that her dark eyes were closed.

When Mehmed saw the girl's white face and flowing hair, his senses reeled, and he thought in his heart: "Praise be to God! Can this be true? (3200) Could any mother have borne such a daughter? I wonder from what line and family she is?" Then Mehmed spoke: "O maiden, my dear eyes! my golden one! be not troubled! You must not weep, for it is a sin against your faith. Tears will make your head ache. God will bring relief from this distress. Tell me—may you live and bring happiness to your mother!—who has done you this wrong, who has captured you, sweet soul, and to whom were you being sent? Tell me as you would tell your own heart!" But because of her great grief the maiden thought that one of the warriors or the captain was questioning her, and the young girl said: "Go away, traitors to the sultan! God grant you lose your heads even as you have lost your firm Turkish faith. You have taken pains to suppress it. God grant, that He may overcome you!"[71]

And Mehmed said to the beautiful girl: "Swear not, beautiful maid! This is not a warrior from Buda, dear heart, but I am a stranger. With God's help, with Osman's golden arm, I have met and defended you. You will not be enslaved today, and as for the future, it will be as almighty God wills. I see that you are of noble lineage, and by your bearing that you are of lordly station. From your white face shines great loving kindness. I desire nothing in this world but to see your two eyes, whether they be gray or blue. Then were I to die, I would not mourn."

When the maiden understood what he said, she opened her eyes. Something cleaved Mehmed's heart like a highly tempered sword. So greatly did the girl please him, so great was his happiness. Then he said to the maiden: "Dear heart, who is your father? Look well at me on my horse. Maiden, what is your name?" When the beautiful girl heard, she gazed up at him, (3250) she gazed and was glad, for straightway she loved him in her heart, and cast away all her troubles. She began to talk freely with him. "Dear heart, dragon on horseback, dear heart, even though it be shameful to talk thus openly with you, I cannot help myself. I am Fatima, daughter of Zajim Alibeg, scion of one of the best and oldest families in Buda. We were among the founders of the city. Life in Buda had not its equal anywhere else in the world. Nowhere were there such riches and nobility, such agas and beys, such stallions as theirs, such lofty dwellings, so much silk, such lavishness of decoration. But where there is good fortune there is also bad. It is now fifteen years,[72] dear heart, since a decree came from the sultan to my father Zajim Alibeg. I was only a year old. 'Zajimbey, imperial plume! You have preserved Buda well for me, defending it from the enemy without my help. Now my hopes run high. I am sending you a vizier with three horsetail plumes,[73] the best in my inner council chamber, and with him a pasha of the Janissaries with fifty thousand troops and fifty imperial cannon, so that my vizier may be at your disposal and give satisfaction to you. For the beys there will be plumes, for the agas imperial marten insignia, and for all others medals on their breasts. The pasha will join you with his army in defending Buda and the Border from enemies of the faith, under the leadership of my vizier.' "[74]

Speaking thus, she said to Mehmed: "Dear heart, I shall say no more, but do you tell me who you are, whose son you are and what your name is, what your house and lineage are. Are you married, or are you now on the way to seek some maiden for yourself?" Mehmed spoke thus to Fata:[75] (3300) "Dear heart, Fatima, daughter of Zajim! I know well your house and your father, for my father told me all that you have told me just now. But, I know not, whether, because of your youth, you would know of my house and lineage. For you grew up a maiden in the women's quarters, and could not ask your father Alibeg whose were the best houses, and who had sons, and of what sort, which was better than the other. There was no way for you to know this, Fatima. Now I shall tell you truly. Perhaps, Fata, you have heard from someone or other of broad and noble Bosnia. Bosnia is the golden wing of the empire, and the Border is its lock and key, and a firm defense. My heart, I am from the imperial Border, from the city of Kanidža. Perhaps you have heard, beautiful Fatima, of Smailaga of Kanidža. I am Mehmed the hadji's son, dear son of Smailaga and brother's son to Cifrić

Hasan. Fata, dear heart, we have been alaybeys for many years past, forty-seven indeed, under the decree and mandate of the sultan. The sultan himself knows of my father. And, Fatima, though I should not boast thus, the Austrian emperor and several of the kings know of him also. My father married three times and my uncle four. Uncle had no children, and only with his last wife did my father beget me. No other sons or daughters has he. I am the only hope of both old men. Now they have grown old and left the life of battle. With trust in God they have awaited my growing up, and now they have sent me to Buda that my father's command and that of my uncle Cifra Hasanaga should pass to me, under the command of Sulejman the Magnificent, and the seal of our friend, (3350) the vizier with three horsetail plumes in Buda."

When Fatima heard this she cried aloud and her anguished cry reached the heavens. "Golden star, Mehmed the hadji's son, how can you speak of him as your friend! You ask me if I know anything about you, dear heart, and your father. When I was eight years old and had finished school,[76] my father placed me in the women's quarters. Those quarters are furnished in mother-of-pearl. Fate will have it, perhaps, that you will see for yourself, so I shall not describe it to you. Yet, wherever you may go, you cannot see its equal. Now you are to destroy the vizier. Dear heart, let Fata tell you about this friend of yours. He is ready to ruin Buda and give it over into the hands of the Magyars. At that time when the decree came of which I told you before, telling how the sultan was sending the vizier from Stambol to defend us from all evils, and with him a pasha of the Janissaries and an imperial army with cannon to protect Buda and the Border from the enemies of the faith, my father read the decree and gathered together the lords of Buda, all the agas under the sultan's charters, just a hundred heroes, my heart, beys and agas. These are they who wear plumed caps and ride gold-caparisoned steeds. They prepared their mighty horses and led forth four teachers and four hundred pupils from the seminary,[77] each with the Koran under his arm. They went ahead two days' journey from Buda and there they met the vizier and welcomed him. The teachers read the prayers and the pupils said amen, and all the imperial beys and agas, and whoever else happened to be with them. Then they brought the vizier and the pasha of the Janissaries to Buda. For two days with prayer they called upon God on behalf of the vizier, that with the help of almighty God (3400) and the favor of our illustrious sultan he might arrive at Buda under good auspices and with all the good fortune the

Turks might desire for him. They brought the vizier to his palace, to the halls where he was to rule. They decorated the whole palace with silk and curtained the bay where the vizier sat with soft broadcloth. Beneath him they placed a silken rug embroidered with gold, and on his shoulders a golden mantle. He rested for a whole month, and every morning four prayers from the Koran were offered up before the vizier that he might judge well in Buda. Then the council began to gather. For a year and a month the chief men of Buda came in audience before the pasha. They all made speeches of welcome to him and came better to know him. The vizier asked them all for their names and their families, to what house each belonged and of what sort it was, what manner of hero each was, until he had seen through the heart of all and knew who were the true defenders of the Turkish faith and who were less loyal to Islam and who would be willing to rule as he did in Buda; such men he put into the council.

"The pasha of the Janissaries had an order from the sultan that he should do nothing with the army without the command of the vizier of Buda. Now when he had made the fortress so strong that he could do whatever he wished—all Buda is in one citadel, and the stronghold within its walls is the surest in the world—he built guard-towers at every exit and entrance gate of the city, and placed a detachment of Janissaries under an army commander in each. His orders were as follows: 'Neither at night nor in the light of day shall anyone come into or leave Buda on any side (3450) without the guard having first searched him well, lest he be carrying some letter or some sealed and stamped petition!'[78] And when he had thus isolated the city, he had another guardhouse built before the gate of the castle, a guardhouse of executioners with their black leader. They had sharp swords in their hands. Their heads were black as coal. Their heads were black but their teeth were so white one could see them even at midday. Their clothes were of leather. One would fall into a fever at the sight of them, and God knows whether one would ever get well again. Then the vizier ordered the captain of the executioners: 'If anyone wishes to come to see me in the palace, take his name and surname, and ask him what he wants of the vizier. If he has some complaint, if he wants to complain that he is hard oppressed, cut off his head. Don't bring such men to me. Then when dusky nightfall comes, make arrangement with the fifty guards, and under the cover of night throw them into the Danube. Let the fish of the Danube devour them. If any other wishes to come to see me, ask him who he is and what he wants. If he says: "I wish to have a friendly conversation with the vizier," bind him and cast him into prison. And as for the third group that stays at home and will not venture forth . . ."[79]

"O lord Mehmed, my life, we had received him so gladly, and brought him with prayer and rejoicing to Buda! But our prayers were of no avail. He came to Buda not for our good, but under evil auspices.

"In the third year, dear Meho, a hundred and fifty imperial heroes who defended the empire from the foe had given their lives and not deserted their country. Fifty he had given to the executioners and no one knows where their bodies are. Fifty he bound, hung a stone about their throat, and threw into the Danube, and in torment life left them. Fifty he herded together (3500) at night from their couches and sent them by night into exile to Bagdad, never to see their homes again.

"At that time, I, unhappy one, was but four years old, Meho, my heart, when all those misfortunes struck us. Then my father's turn came, my father, Zajim Alibeg, and the vizier sent him to Bagdad. O Mehmed, when my mother saw what was happening in Buda, that the masters of the greatest houses in Buda, they who defended the fatherland, were all gone, when all Buda indeed saw this, there was immeasurable sorrowing. All were silent us though they had neither mouth, nor mind, nor tongue. Our matrons laid aside their fine silks and took the wondrous kerchiefs from their heads and the pearls and coral from their throats. And they arrayed themselves in black cloth from their heads to the green grass. My mother was left in our house (O, I cannot tell you all!), young and childless except for me alone. She hid me behind nine doors, and in hiding she taught me, and in hiding, dear heart, sorrowing, light of my eyes, I grew up.[80] My mother and I thought that the traitor would know nothing about me. Would that God had granted that I be blind and ugly rather than too beautiful! I know not, but people say that it is true; for my praise arose in Buda. 'Fata of Zajim Alibeg is more beautiful than anyone even in the sultan's palace. There is no sultana like her.' And that praise reached the vizier. The traitor was seized with great desire, and he sent the people of Buda who approved his rule to me, to ask my mother for my love, dear heart. When mother and I heard of this, (3550) I scorned the suitors, my mother even more than I, shamed by the thought of giving my fair face to our enemy to kiss. He had closed our house and exiled my father. He had taken all our property, our inns and stores. You will never see such possessions, nor can I describe them all to you. There is a square in

Buda with fine houses and dwellings on both sides, with stores and gaily decorated inns, a whole quarter of an hour long. Meho, my heart, they were all ours. The vizier took them for himself, and their revenues[81] were given over to him. Then, there is a village on the plain of Buda, dear heart, beside the Danube, a village with hundreds of serfs, even three hundred. That is a great possession, a fief worth any other four. And this chief of traitors took that from us too, and now they call it Vizier's Plain.[82] When the vizier's suitors returned to him without the kerchief of betrothal, and when he saw that I had not accepted my enemy's ring, even yesterday he took me by force, and this morning he is sending me off to Bogdan, to exchange the true faith for a false one, to blacken my youth in Kara Bogdan. And you, Mehmed, dear heart, say that the vizier is your friend! O my heart, my life, for the sake of God, if you acknowledge Him and believe that He is one and all-powerful, flee back to where you came from. For now you will lose your life here in your youth. Forget about your decree!"

But Mehmed, the falcon's son, spoke thus to Fata: "Fata of Zajim, pure golden one! You are good and beautiful. But as I look upon you, it seems that your words are somewhat foolish. Would you really send me away, Fata? All Bosnia and the Border and all Hungary have heard and are rejoicing (3600) that I have gone to Buda to assume the command. My aged father, Hadji Smail, has scarce been able to await this day, and feels now that he has begotten a son worthy of him. But, Fatima of Zajim Alibeg, why do we spend the time in talk? Why dally thus? You have seen me. Do you like me? Would you take me and be my love? I love you and take you, Fata. But, Fatima, you must not take me because all this has happened. You must give yourself to me as if it had never been, as if your father were still in his home and your possessions were still yours."

And Fatima said to Lord Mehmed: "Mehmed, precious jewel! When I was with my mother in our home at the time of our great sorrow, she often said to me: 'Fatima, I bore a beautiful daughter, and I have brought you up to dark days. I thought I should bring you up at your father's side, the imperial alaybey,[83] in his happy and prosperous home, until you were of age that I might give you to Mehmed, that worthy son of Smailaga. That would be the marriage of mountain spirit and falcon! And the two houses would be especially well matched. Mehmed, my heart's keeper, you ask whether I know about you, who you are, my heart, and what sort you are. I have seen your heroism and your heroic heart. I see your falcon eyes and the beloved cheeks beneath them. I swear to you, nor would I lie, that were I to die seven times—and it is hard to die even once—were I able to die and then come to life again, I would die and live again an eighth time to be your love. But there is no happiness for us this way. When I heard your rash words just now, that you will not return but go to the vizier, I knew that I would never be yours, that I must not even think about you.[84] (3650) I now see where my lot lies. But I beg of you, and humbly kiss your boots, beseeching you in the name of your faith in God which is firmer than stone, either kill me or give me the knife, that I may cut short my dark youth, not because of my being taken away into captivity, but because of your death, Meho. May I never hear nor see with my own eyes such youth destroyed. I could never endure your loss." Then many tears fell from her eyes across her white cheek, like pearls across white linen.

Then Mehmed said to Fata: "O Fatima, what a foolish maid you are! The vizier has frightened you terribly. May a gypsy's sword strike him down! If God grants, Fata, it will not be long before the vizier comes to judgment before Tale of Orašac.[85] And Tale will find an executioner who will cut off his head, that he cause no more dark sorrow. But, Fatima, we have delayed long. Osman will be angry at us. He has overcome the imperial heroes and seized their Arabian steeds. He has tied them behind your coach and now waits the command of his elder. Whatever I say, he will accomplish. Fata, give me your right hand that I may put you on my horse, seat you on the soft saddle-roll behind me, and place your white feet in the stirrups. Put your arms about my waist, Fata, over my belt and over my heart. I shall cover you with my woolly cloak, whose top is all of gold, which shields me from the sun and rain. Let me take you to your dear mother and ask her again whether she will agree to give you to me and call me her son-in-law. I shall give the orders to Osman."

Now Fata said to Meho: "O Mehmed, heart in my breast! I shall not give you just one hand. Take both, my love. But no hand will be of any use to you, (3700) neither mine nor yours, my dear." "No, Fatima, do not be foolish! Things do not happen according to the words of men, but according to the judgment of God." Then he lifted Fatima onto the horse and she grasped him about the waist. Mehmed covered her with his cape, seated her on the saddle-roll, and put her white feet in the stirrups. Then he called out from his horse: "Standard-bearer, our gold-

en wings! I have become betrothed to this maiden, if such is God's will
and if her mother will agree. I am taking her on my horse now that I
may more quickly carry Fatima to Buda. But, Osman, you turn the
coach about and tie behind it the slender Arabian mares you have taken
from the warriors. Then mount your dapple gray and drive the coach.
Come as quickly as you can, and don't delay, my right wing!''

Then he turned the chestnut horse by the bridle and went off
across the plain towards the city of Buda, like a star across the clear
sky. The brown steed flew over the plain. He had acquired such great
strength that he scarcely knew he was carrying two instead of one.
Straightway they came to the city gate and entered the square that
crossed Buda. Buda is a vast city and has no equal. Mehmed had never
been there before and knew not where to turn. So in a whisper he asked
Fatima over his shoulder. She was hidden by the cape. ''My Fata, heart
and soul! I have never been in Buda before, and I know not where to
turn the chestnut horse to find your house.'' ''Mehmed, my dear eyes!
Turn left from the square, and you cannot err. The square is half an
hour long. No one can cross it in less, but with your winged horse it
will not take more than a quarter of an hour. Yet I beg you, as my
master, (3750) do not keep your eyes fixed on your horse's mane, but
turn your gaze on all sides. All the buildings you see on both sides of
the street used to be my father's, as I was telling you beside the coach,
all those inns and shops, but now the treacherous vizier holds them.''
Then Meho raised the horse's rein. Glory be to God for all his gifts! The
steed's hoofs smote the marble pavement and struck living fire. The
bystanders in Buda, looking at Meho, said one to another: ''From the
time of the founding of Buda such a mighty one has never been here,
such a winged chestnut stallion, nor such a golden champion! Blest be
the mother that bore him, and the sister who swears by him! Blest also
be his love who shall embrace him, either now or in the time to come!''
And the old men called out to one another: ''I am a hundred years old,
and I have seen the imperial armies and their commanders, I have seen
pashas and viziers, but not even in my dreams, to say nothing of waking,
have I seen such a one as this!''

The young man drove on his horse and gazed at all that Fata
pointed out, and he thought in his heart: ''What Fata said cannot be
true. Why, that would be half of Buda!'' Just then he arrived at the end
of the street, and Fata said to Mehmedaga: ''My heart, Mehmed the
hadji's son, go forward a little further and then turn to the left. You

will pass three or four houses and their gateways. When you come before the fifth courtyard you will know that it is ours. It is easy to recognize. It is a good two stories high[86] and of blocks of hewn marble. Father had each stone colored white or red or blue or yellow.[87] Some of them even have three colors on them. (3800) There is nothing like it in all Buda. It is roofed by yellow copper. Giving onto the courtyard is the entrance gate with its knockers. The inner door is of steel; the outer one on the street is of mother-of-pearl and rounded like a hero's rib case.[88] Both knockers on the outer gate are of silver, and the discs in which they are set are also of silver. In form they are like a maiden's breasts. Above the door sleeps a gray falcon. Beneath him shines a golden cord and on it a little bronze bell. Whenever anyone wishes to enter or leave, the falcon cries out and the bell rings, and the sound is heard in my father's house."

Lord Mehmed, the hadji's son, listened, but he thought Fata was mistaken. Not even the sultan has such riches. But at that moment he came before the gate, and he was struck with amazement. From the saddle of his horse he raised the knocker, and one side of the door flew open; then the little bell struck, and the falcon above the door crowed.[89] When he opened the other side, he discovered that the wall of the courtyard was two arm-spreads thick. Then another gate confronted Meho, a door all of steel. And he thought in his heart: "What Fata said was indeed true." When the steel door opened, he rode his horse into the courtyard. It was long and wide and paved with marble slabs, large as copper trays. Each slab was fastened with a tie-bar. The courtyard shone like the ice along the streams in winter. When he looked about he saw a fountain with twelve running spouts, every pipe of pure gold. Nearby, beneath an almond tree, a pleasant summerhouse had been built, strewn with Persian rugs woven with gold. (3850) In the summerhouse by the lordly fountain coolness reigned, and it was refreshing, even as though one was sitting on a mountain plateau. When the hadji's son saw the fountain with its golden spouts and the summerhouse with its ornamentation and Persian rugs, he thought in his heart: "Ah, my father, Hadji Smail, we say, and rightly, that in Kanidža and around Kanidža, in all our thirty districts there is no more pleasant place than ours. But, father, your riches are nothing. Were you to sell all your possessions you would not be able to build a courtyard like this and embellish it thus. Indeed, if you were to spend all the treasures in your coffers, you could not make such a fountain as this nor such a lordly and beautifully decorated summerhouse." But how his head whirled when he saw Alibeg's house! It had four stories and was a great edifice. It had sixty rooms, each decorated in its own color and spread with silk. The balconies around the house were covered with bright latticework and studded with metal ornaments from the coastland, and behind the lattice hung fine cloth draperies. All the staircases of the house were covered with soft carpeting and draped with broadcloth and velvet. When Mehmed saw it his head reeled. He stared in amazement at this dwelling and its brilliant doors like a young calf, nor could he even dismount. The house had a roof of burnished copper. Instead of a peak there was a minaret rod with star and crescent[90] topped by a golden orb worth a thousand ducats. In the night this shines over the house and the courtyard and by its light one can see as well as at midday.

Then Fata said to Mehmed the hadji's son: "Why, my heart, do you not dismount, (3900) and take the maiden from the horse's back?" Just then Mehmed heard the wailing of Alibeg's wife from the highest room of the house. She had besought each room, seeking solace in her house, and for two nights and two white days in every room of the dwelling she had wailed and had mourned for her husband and for her precious gem, the maiden Fatima. Now she had come to the end as she arrived at the highest room of all and was wailing over her house: "Woe to the house of my lord Zajim! When I was betrothed to an imperial noble personage, and when I had been wed to Zajim, the sultan's champion, I thought that I should never mourn in my youth over this house, but sing gaily day and night, and carry one little child in my arms, while the bey would send a second one to school, and a third would reach the age of carrying arms. But it happened not as I had thought. A woeful fate came upon us and now the house is deserted. I would not mourn if this had come from God's judgment, but it is the workings of that mighty traitor to the sultan, that traitor, the Vizier of Buda. The cowardly wretch despoiled me of my faith, for I have been left alone on this earth, and a villainous rascal has consumed my bey's possessions. Did my heroic lord deserve that this be done to him? O black misfortune, no son remains, no heir for this lord. Nor did they allow Fatima to rest in peace, my Fatima, my dearest happiness. With her I concealed my grief for my unhappy lord. I shall die and never hear of such a man again. Fata reopened and renewed those sore wounds and dark evils. I bore her into a world of gold, wrapped her in golden swaddling clothes, nursed her on a golden couch, soared with her and viewed the world.

But today the Vlahs[91] have captured her. May misfortune fall on the sultan's traitor! May the crops fail him, (3950) and a gypsy's sword[92] destroy him! My treasure has been lost; those evil men will bring great sorrow to my Fata. Why should I, a wretched and mourning mother, wander alone about the house? By my faith I shall not!" She struck the glass of the window with her hands, her eyes began to roll, and she was about to jump from the lofty house.

Mehmed the hadji's son did not dismount. He heard and understood what the lady was saying, and the falcon cried out even as a stag roars. And the courts and balconies reechoed. "O my lady, wife of Alibeg! What is wrong with you? Why do you not place your hope in God but instead roll your eyes and throw away your faith by jumping from the window? Tear the veil from your eyes, come quickly down and take back your Fata!" When the wife of Zajimbeg heard that, she thought that she had gone mad. She had long since given up all hope of Fata. She thought her daughter had already reached Bogdan. Then the lady looked into the courtyard and saw the gray falcon on his tall black-maned steed; tall and slender was the chestnut horse, like a mountain vila, and the youth on him was mighty as a dragon. The young man raised his cloak and showed Fatima's face, that the mother might more quickly comprehend that in very truth it was Fatima. Meho untied the belt and strap and with his arm he took the maiden from the horse and set her down in the courtyard in the same way he had taken her from the coach. When the lady saw the dragon take the girl in both his arms, she rubbed her eyes to see if it were really true. While her mother was rubbing her eyes Fata called up from below beside the horse: "What are you doing, wife of Alibeg? Have you lost your mind? Hasten to come down and take the horse, and receive the imperial lord! Do what you will in welcoming Fatima back. Fata will welcome herself, until what time the evil judgment (4000) of our traitor should again fall upon her."

When the wife of Alibeg came downstairs in her haste she lost her veil and her golden coif. Bare-headed she ran, even as a fair mountain vila from the top of a fir tree. She seemed only a bit older than Fatima, for her youth had not disappeared. Three years after her marriage with the bey she had borne Fatima. Now she was left a window in her youth. She cried her blessings and her thanks to God. But she paid no attention to Fatima, nor indeed to that hero Mehmed the hadji's son, but she embraced the chestnut horse. She raised each of his hoofs and kissed them, and thus she spoke: "Golden steed, with golden wings! You carry a good master! I know not who or what he is, but may almighty God and all his saints preserve him from all evil! God reward him with a long life and sweet reputation, even such as has Hadji Smailaga the alaybey of Kanidža on the Border. They say that he has begotten a son who is much better than himself, and all we Turks pray that he may live in happiness many years, this gray falcon of lord Smail the alaybey. And even such a prayer for happiness, heroic steed, do I, unfortunate and mourning one, offer up for your master, for he has brought me Fatima, and defended her from the might of the enemy at least from now until sundown, even though it may not be longer." "May your prayers for his eternal happiness be accomplished before God! Proper indeed are the prayers you utter for this dragon in the courtyard, that he may live out his life like Mehmed the hadji's son, the proud offspring of the alaybey. May both our prayers be fulfilled for this warrior of the chestnut steed! Receive your daughter and your son-in-law, mother! (4050) Look upon this golden one. People say that no mother ever bore a hero such as Mehmed, the hadji's son, whom the wife of the alaybey bore. O mother, many times have you said to me: 'When you are grown-up, my gem, Fatima, I shall marry you to that good son, Mehmed, son of the alaybey.' Now is your prayer fulfilled and God's gift of happiness has been granted. Here is Mehmed! And here am I! He met me on the plain of Muhač, traveling on his own affairs to Buda. A mighty hero who was with him and will soon arrive here scattered the imperial warriors. In the time it takes a mother to suckle her son, he had beheaded twenty-five warriors, and Mehmed the hadji's son had killed their imperial leader. Soon Osman will arrive with the wondrous coach, which the Syrian mares draw, and with the other horses, captured from the warriors which have been hitched to the coach."

The mother took her daughter and Mehmed the hadji's son in her arms. She made him sit on the bench in the lordly summerhouse, and putting her arms about his neck kissed him between his black eyes. From her eyes tears of joy and happiness fell on him, and also tears of sorrow that he had come there; for surely he would lose his life in Buda because of what he had done. "Why did you not flee back to Kanidža? You could then have married Fatima and known whom you were loving and with what house you were allying yourself. But as it is now, my dear son, alas and alack, you will not marry Fatima or any other, but the sword of the dusky executioner at the command of the treacherous vizier." Thus she spoke and fainted, falling into the young man's lap, as though her life had fled. But God granted that the fountain of water was close by, and Fatima bathed and washed her mother's face until she opened her eyes. (4100) Again she complained to the youth. "O you who are the happiness of both me and your father, why did you come with Fata to Buda? Why did you not flee with her to Kanidža? In but a short time now you will lose your life."

Mehmed the hadji's son said to her: "Why, Lady Ismihan,[93] are you so frightened of this traitor, the vizier of Buda? My father sent me here to assume the command from his shoulders and from my uncle Hasan's. For they have both grown old, mother. My father cannot wait any longer for the command to pass to me, if it is to come in his lifetime. Would you really send me back, my lady, to my father without the imperial decree, to bring shame on the honor of the alaybey? The maidens would sing as they danced: 'Shame on Mehmed, son of Hadji Smail! He dared not go to Buda to receive the imperial mandate. He picks up women from the streets and does not know who or whose they are. Nor does he wait for his father to marry him off as he should, with wedding guests and musicians, with violins and palanquins,[94] with agas and beys and the ceremonial standards of the sultan.' You know well, lady wife of Alibeg, what the Turks of Kanidža would say of my father and uncle. They would say that our house's nobility was dying out, and that it had no even half-decent son. Indeed, would it not be better for me to perish than to return in shame to Kanidža? Heroism cannot be bought for gold, but is given freely for bright honor. And so I say to you, my lady, that my father sent me here and told me not to delay but to return quickly. But fate had it and God decreed that I should defend this maiden and love her in my heart. I told your daughter Fata whose son I am and from what house, and asked her if she would take me and be my wife, not because things had happened as they did, but just as if she were free (4150) and prosperous, as when her father was here.[95] And Fata gave me her word that were it possible to die seven times and then live again she would go through all those deaths to be my betrothed. I am just as devoted to Fatima as she to me—no, even more. And so I said that I would take her to her mother and ask for her consent.[96] But, wife of Alibeg, I do not ask you to give me Fata because of the vizier. I swear and give you my solemn word. In the name of God and his mercy, and on the life of my old father, who has many friends, for all Bosnia and the Border and beyond love him, I swear and pledge my word that if you will not give me Fatima, I will not be angry with

you. Marry her then to whomever you desire, and hide her no longer
from anyone. The vizier will trouble her no more."

When Zajim's lady heard that, she said to Mehmed: "Mehmed, you
are even as my own son. Know you not that all that Fata said to you
beside the coach was true? I tell you on my steadfast Turkish faith, I
would rather see Fata married to you than to the sultan himself or to
one of his sons, to be sultana in Stambol. There she is, Mehmed, and
may she bring you happiness! But I fear—may almighty God protect
us!—that I shall see great sorrow come upon you, my son. It would be
more than I could bear, far more, to see your flourishing youth destroyed by the vizier."

"My lady, do not be foolish!"

Just then a great fanfare was heard in the streets, and the lady
cried out that the vizier's men were coming from the traitor's palace to
take Mehmed. Yet not a single one of them appeared, but rather a coach
drawn by Bedouin mares, with others tied behind it, including even the
chestnut stallion of the imperial captain. The gate of the courtyard was
open, and Osman drove in the silver coach (4200) and all the horses. In
the courtyard of Zajim Alibeg there was a marble stable, and at the
mangers were the fifty mighty steeds of his elite guard whom he had
always kept in service. Such was the might of Zajim Alibeg. Mehmed
leapt from the lordly summer house and embraced his standard-bearer,
while Fatima took the chestnut horse and the dapple gray, and led them
about the courtyard. Mehmed seized Osman by the hand and seated him
in his own place. Then he opened the door of the stable and led in the
stallion and mares, and drew the coach into the stable too. He tied the
horses at the marble mangers. When Osman had rested a bit, Mehmed
returned to him, and they sat beside one another.

The lady wife of Alibeg flew about like a fair mountain vila for her
son-in-law (if so it fell out) and for the mighty standard-bearer Osman.
She brought them a sweet sugared drink, and then she said to Mehmed
the hadji's son: "My Mehmed, fair light, it is not right to sit here in the
courtyard. Let us go into Alibeg's house that you may sit and rest yourselves. God has given us of all his bounties. There is every kind of food
and drink, and we must partake in honor of Zajim Alibeg and to the
health of you and Fatima." And lord Mehmed answered: "Thank you,
my lady, wife of Alibeg"—it was not yet midday—"if God grants, there
is time for me to do all I have to do. Now I am going with Osman before
the vizier, for him to affirm my command. When I return, I must seek

out the courthouse and the judge, that I may be betrothed to Fatima
and bring the writ of betrothal to my father."

When the wife of Alibeg heard that, she sighed deeply (4250), her
eyes filled with tears. "Mehmed, my son, my joy! I know what your
writ of betrothal will be. It will be the executioner's sword. How will I
ever get over your loss!" And again she fainted. When they had revived
her, Mehmed said: "Listen, my lady, wife of Alibeg! Now indeed I see
that you are mad. By God's faith, just one word more! If, when I return,
I find your face wet with weeping, I shall not even spend the night here
in your house, nor shall I take your Fata. Know you not that you are
beside yourself? I have told you about the alaybeg my father and how
proud the Border is of him. I swear by the merciful God, believe me, in
a short time I shall go to the vizier, and he will receive me well, embrace
me, and place me at his right hand. He will keep me there as a guest,
and he will without delay affirm my mandate. He will say nothing of
that highway encounter. He will ask me nothing, for he does not dare. I
swear to you as to my own mother, if anyone tries to spy upon me, or
to whisper secretly with someone else, or if I see any executioner, or if
anyone questions me at the gate, either me or Osman, God will see and
the Border will hear what Mehmed will do to the vizier and the people
of Buda and all their sentinels. With God's help I will kill the vizier and
all of them. I will dye their palace in blood. And whoever attempts to
flee from me will never succeed, for Osman will be in the courtyard
holding our horses and waiting for me. When Osman hears what I am
doing in the palace, even if his own dear father were with the vizier and
all the others, he would kill him for my sake."

Then the gray falcons rose, (4300) and they mounted their spirited
steeds. Along the streets they went like two golden dragons on wondrous winged stallions. And what havoc the horses raised in Buda!
Wherever their hoofs struck they kicked up the marble paving stones,
which flew from the streets into the shops. They did great damage to
the merchants and shopkeepers. All Buda ran to watch them, to see
those dragon youths on their winged steeds. The two men of the Border
passed through the center of Buda. It was on the edge of the city that
the palace of the vizier was who ruled over Buda.

The vizier had understood what force it was that had attacked his
coach and the imperial warriors and scattered and killed many of them.
He had heard how they had taken the Arabian mares and returned Fata
with the coach and the horses to Buda. The vizier asked his sentinels:
"Would you be able to know who they were who attacked and trod my

command under their feet?" And they said to him: "Your excellency, we did not know them. We did not recognize them as being anyone from Buda or from round about. We can report, O vizier, that there was one mighty hero on a chestnut horse, who had neither beard nor moustache. No one could describe to you his beauty and the nobility of his countenance. We cannot say, nor believe that any human mother bore him. It must have been some woman sent from God. The other hero rode a dapple gray. We shall tell you something of him, his might and his glory. He was terrible to look upon, but even more so to fight with." Then the vizier remembered, and he said: "I know who they are! They are mighty youths from Unđurovina. That young man on the chestnut horse, that fair vila, is Mehmed the hadji's son, (4350) the dear offspring of Smailaga a fierce serpent, and my elder, one nobler than I. As long as Hadji Smail and his brother Cifrić Hasanaga and especially Mehmed, the hadji's son, dwell in the Border, Bosnia will never be subjugated. The sultan favors them above all us other pashas and viziers. Mehmed son of Smailaga has come to Buda. His father has sent him to me to assume the command, for me to affirm his mandate. Be very careful what you say, either to him or to one another in his presence, for you will regret it. He will deprive us all of our heads. There must be no warring with that house. When Mehmed the hadji's son comes, I shall treat him with honor. He will fly to kiss my hand because of the honor of my rank and my imperial charter; but I shall not allow him to kiss my hand. I shall embrace him with both of my arms and kiss him between the black falcon eyes. Leave everything you are doing and prepare a mandate for Mehmed, and I shall put my seal and covenant upon it, in accordance with the command of Sulejman the Magnificent. I shall pray him to spend the night here, but he will not. Now call the guards at the gate. Let the executioners go to their quarters. Not a single one of them must be at the gate when Mehmed comes before the vizier and when he leaves. He would cut off their ruddy heads. Let not one of you be at the gate, or you will lose your heads. Nor would it be pleasant for me. Let the devil alone, for he would bring greater evils upon us."

The younger men ran immediately to the gate and removed the executioners. Before the mighty heroes arrived the vizier's courtiers had taken away all his guards from before the gate of the vizier's palace. (4400) The vizier sat on the balcony of the palace, which was lofty and near the plain that surrounds Buda. On that plain gardens had been planted, and in the gardens maidens were dancing a kolo. The imperial traitor watched them from the palace where the vizier ruled.

At that moment the two Border warriors arrived and rode their horses from the street into the courtyard of the vizier's palace, where no one usually can enter, not even on foot, without the permission of the vizier. But these youths waited not for leave. They rode their horses right up to the palace. As one they dismounted and rested the reins on the saddle horn. Mehmed put his hand on his sword and gave his horse over to Osman the standard-bearer. "You take my horse, my golden wing. Walk the animals up and down and be on the watch for trouble, so that you may come to my aid, Osman. Watch carefully, golden wing. You must not betray me now we are at the vizier's, for you know what we have done. See that no attack is made on me!" And Osman said to Meho: "O my Meho, how foolish you are! If I were a traitor, I would not have been with your father and uncle, Cifrić Hasanaga, for twenty-seven years."

Meho went straight up the stairs until he came to the floor where the vizier was. He looked at the council chambers. One door followed another, some draped with woolen cloth, others with velvet, some studded with mother-of-pearl, others with silver, and still others painted with different colors. Mehmed went through each of the chambers, and he counted twenty-six of them. Finally he came to the balcony where the vizier was sitting near the latticework. Seven men of Buda waited upon him. His clothes were embroidered with gold. Over his shoulders was a blue woven mantle, (4450) and around his head was wound a turban of green silk. In it were seven imperial plumes, and on one was written 'Three horsetail vizier.' He was the highest officer in Buda, governing both the civilian and the military. On his breast were imperial medals, some of gold, some of pearl. Meho the hadji's son recognized him by the plume on his forehead on which was written 'Three horsetail vizier.' The youth placed his hand on his sword, gathered the skirts of his tunic about him, rolled back his sleeves, and flew to the hem of the vizier's cloak. The vizier stretched forth his arms and addressed him as his own son. "Golden youth, whence come you, from what city? Come you from Bosnia, or the Border, or from Unđurovina, my son? From the look in your eye and from your noble countenance I should say you are of some very splendid house, and of good lineage." "Thank you, your excellency, imperial vizier. May God exalt you for your praise!" Then, once again he flew to his hand, but the vizier would not allow him to kiss it. Mehmed said to the vizier: "O imperial vizier, I am from the Border, from the aged city of Kanidža. I am the son of Smailaga. Perhaps, pasha, you have heard of him. I am his only son, none other has he." But the traitor had the manners of a true Osmanli. How sweetly he embraced the youth and kissed his black eyes! He pressed him to his left side and put his left arm about him.

Then the traitor cried out to Mehmed: "Is it true, indeed, my son, as you say, that the dragon's nest has hatched, and a young dragon has come forth and flown to my palace? My dear son, my two eyes, how is your father Smailaga? Has he grown very old, my son? Does he still assemble the gathering of nobles, does he still go to the tavern?" (4500) "O pasha, our golden plume! Yes, my father has grown very old, and he has made the pilgrimage to Mecca. But you must know about all that, O vizier. Whoever wishes his pilgrimage to be acceptable in the sight of God must refrain from frequenting the tavern. And so the chieftains come to my father's dwelling, and there consult him." "And how is your uncle, Hasanaga? Does he still hold the command?" "He, too, O pasha, has grown old. Both my uncle and my father sent me to you with special salutations, and orders to kiss your hand on their behalf." Again he attempted to kiss the vizier, but the latter would not think of it; instead, he made the youth sit beside him on the cushions, clad as he was in full array, and with his boots and socks. The vizier signaled to the servants, and they lighted a water pipe for Mehmed, brought him coffee on a tray, and did everything to make him comfortable. The vizier entertained him not as a young man, but as though he were his elder both in years and rank.

Then the vizier said: "Mehmed, my black eye! Why did your father send you to me? Was it as a guest, or have you business in Buda?" And Meho answered him: "Your imperial excellency! My father sent me that the imperial command should pass from my father and uncle to me, that your authority should affirm this, under the decree of Sulejman the Magnificent." Then Mehmed took the mandate from his bosom and gave it to the vizier, even the mandate which had been drawn up in Kanidža, which the fifty heroes had signed, and upon which all the agas and imperial beys in turn had put their seal. And Hasan Pasha Tiro had confirmed it and referred it from Kanidža to Buda. When the vizier had read the mandate, he offered up thanksgiving to God. "Praise be to God, my son, for I have seen with my own eyes the renewing and perpetuating of your line, my dear son, for another generation." (4550) Then he laid a strict command on his scribes: "Leave all your other work and serve this mandate! Take it that we may confirm it and put our golden seal upon it." And the vizier's scribes arose. Some of them wrote and gave their papers to others, and these witnessed the signature. In each of the rooms in turn, they served the mandate. In not more than half an hour it came before the vizier, and the vizier confirmed it immediately and sealed it with the imperial seal. Then he took it in his right hand and gave it into Mehmed's right hand: "Here, Mehmed, our right hand! May it bring you good fortune and joy for many years! May your father, dear son, live to see you wed! Then invite me to be your wedding elder. Put the mandate in your bosom, my son, and make merry here with the vizier, from the palace watching the maidens dancing and singing in the garden."

But Mehmed rose to kiss the vizier's hand. "Thank you, O pasha, you whom we emulate![97] But you must not detain me. I cannot keep my father waiting." The traitor was a true Osmanli,[98] and he straightway rose. "Nor, my son, would I think of so doing, and destroy your father's good opinion. Go, my son, and may your journey be happy. Give special salutations to your father and uncle from me. Tell your father, Smailaga, that he must come and be my guest here for at least a month." "Thank you, O pasha, I will tell him. May your meeting be auspicious!"

Mehmed went to the door and found Osman his standard-bearer. Osman was walking both the horses, leading them with his left hand, while his right was free (4600) to grasp his sword quickly, should the occasion arise. Mehmed came down the stairs to him and gave him greeting. Straightway they mounted and entered the streets. Then Osman turned to Mehmed: "How did things go with the vizier, Meho?" "Well, Osman, it is hard to say. I wonder at the complaints of the Turks here. If we hadn't had that experience this morning on the green plain, my brother, I would not have believed all that has been said against the vizier, were it my own father who told me." Then Osman laughed. "O, Mehmed, how foolish you are! That's just what these traitors are like. They always make favorable impressions. But if anything should go wrong, you would see what sort of friend this vizier is!" And he took a letter from his bosom, and said to Mehmed: "Look, my young and foolish boy! This morning when you had taken away Fatima, and I had tied our Bedouin steeds to the wheels of the silver coach, I found this letter beside it. It was by the body of that captain whom you slew. When his head rolled away, his cap fell off, and by the cap was this paper. See what it says!" Mehmed took the letter from Osman and

read what it said. It was signed by the three horsetails vizier. He sent
greetings to his blood-brother in Bogdan, General Peter. "General Peter,
light of my eyes! Since the day we became blood-brothers I have not
sent you any gift. Now I am sending you a maiden as a present, Fata,
daughter of Zajim Alibeg, who has no equal in the empire. Marry her,
and beget falcon-children.[99] And, General Peter, light of my eyes, that
is not all. I shall send you a better gift, the heads of the two alaybeys
and of their only son. When God grants that that time come, (4650) it
will not be long before Bosnia falls into your hands, and as for Buda, I
have hopes that we will rule Buda even before I send those heads to
you." Mehmed read the letter three times and could not believe his eyes.
Then he struck his thigh so violently that his trousers were almost rent.
He put the letter in his bosom next to the mandate which the vizier had
given him.

Soon they came before the house of justice and rode into the
courtyard. When Mehmed saw the palace of justice, where judges gave
judgment, and compared it in his mind with the vizier's palace he was
taken aback. "Brother and standard-bearer, how can it be that this is
the palace of justice? This palace is even finer than that in which the
vizier rules." "O Mehmed, how foolish you are! The vizier built them
for his chief conspirators. All the planning of woes and destruction is
done here. From here come the judgments and the ready executioners.
All the witnessing for the vizier is taken care of in the hall of justice by
the twelve judges. If any trouble comes for the vizier, from the sultan or
from an imperial firman, it is they who justify his side, for they admin-
ister the law, and hold in their hands the religious statutes[100] in which
the sultan's faith is absolute." Then Mehmed was amazed and grew
somewhat wroth at these judges, these imperial traitors. He gave his
horse into Osman's hands and proceeded up the stairs. Angry, the youth
entered the building and sought the entrance to the high judges' chamber. Before it he found two guards, who announce anyone to the judge.
Mehmed approached and gave them greeting, and they perforce answered it. The young man's face flamed even more, (4700) and he
spoke: "Guards, is the judge here? I have business with him. I am a
stranger and must complete my business as quickly as possible." The
two guards looked at the young man and saw that he was almost un-
controllably angry, that his eyes were clouded and shot with blood. The
guards moved slightly from his path; and it was lucky for them that
they did not try to hinder him. Mehmed raised the curtain in the door-

A typical house in the town of Bijelo Polje in 1935.

way and went in among the scribes. He gazed about the judges' chamber. It was long and wide. Around it were seated the twelve judges, with the supreme judge of Buda at their head, that guardian of the law[101] and arch traitor even more dangerous than the vizier. On the lower side of the same room, reaching from one end to another, was a table with twenty-two scribes behind it! Each one had a pen in his hand. The chief justice gave orders, and the scribes wrote them out. The chief justice was a great scoundrel. He was leaning against the window and had laid his turban on the table. Mehmed came into the room angry, in anger he stopped, and in anger he gave greeting. The judge was the worst of all infidels; he did not wish to gather his legs under him, nor was he willing to answer his greeting. He was furious because Mehmed had come in without asking permission, without waiting until the judge had given him leave to enter. But that is the way things were in Buda, such were its sorrows, and such were the murders of the heroes of Buda. The falcon's lips trembled. The judge was so angry that he had turned his face to the window and refused to look at the hadji's son, but was looking anywhere else. When Mehmed saw what the traitor in the hall of justice was doing, he grasped the hilt of his sword and struck it on the floor. Because of Mehmed's great strength behind the blow one would say and swear (4750) that the hall of justice was about to fall and the floor collapse on the ones below. Then he drew his sword and swung it naked in his hands. The poisoned weapon gleamed like a flash of lightning from a dark cloud. When the traitor heard the quaking and saw Meho the hadji's son with the naked sword in his hands,—the hero's hair, bristling like a wolf's fur in December, had raised his plumed cap, and he gnashed his teeth in his jaws, even as a saw when men cut wood, and from his teeth living fire darted—when the traitor saw Mehmed, all the judges leapt to their feet and put their hands behind their sashes and fell at Mehmed's feet. The pens of the scribes were turned to stone, and the blood left their fingers, which stiffened even as if they were dead. And the traitor, the chief of the judges, nearly lost his mind from fear of the might of that falcon's son. The scoundrel's lips became stone, as though his head had been severed. He tried to say something, but could not. His tongue stuck in his mouth. He tried to say 'aman,'[102] but his jaws were paralyzed. His head and beard began to tremble. Then he jumped to his feet and cried out: "Aman, aman, my son, aman, aman, and have mercy, my son! Do not kill an old man. I have a wife and young children. You are young, my son, and you will marry. Do not destroy your

youth. My son, I am under the command of the vizier, and have important affairs on my hands which must be completed by midday. If I and
my people in this room do not finish this task we shall lose our heads.
I did not know you were a stranger, but I thought you were from Buda
and could wait a little while." Then said Mehmed: "Do not lie, imperial
traitor! (4800) Even if you have much work to do, it was not at all difficult to answer my greeting, nor to turn your head, you pig!"

No one else spoke, for they could not. Then again the traitor
begged for mercy: "Aman, my son, there is your sword, and here my
head. I have sinned. Do as you wish, my son! I realize that you can do
whatever you desire in the name of the merciful God." "O traitor, pray
to your God whom you rejected so long ago! Yet for my father's sake I
dare not kill you, for he laid this command upon me: 'Go, my son, and
may success and happiness attend you! May you make the journey to
Buda without misfortune!' O chief of scoundrels, I warn you, although
I shall not disobey my father now, if God grants, when I return to Buda
with the wedding guests to take my bride, it will go hard for many a
one here." The dog said nothing to the young man, but he let his beard
sink upon his chest and hung his dog's head as though it had been
severed. Then Mehmed said to the traitor: "Traitor, order your servants
to make out a license for me right away that I may carry it to my father,
Smailaga, for I have been betrothed to a maid of Buda." When the traitor heard these words: "Praise be to Allah! Mehmed the hadji's son!
Alas, what a mistake I have made, my son! Why did you not say whose
child you were? To think that I have been keeping him in my own
palace! Sit down, sit down, sit down, my dear son!" Then the judge
took him and seated him on the cushions beside himself. He threw a
blue fur cape[103] over him, and servants lighted his pipe and brought him
unsweetened coffee. Ah, if you could have seen that whoreson! By
Allah, he sat on his haunches before the young man, the way children
sit before their master in school. But Mehmed said to the judge: "Sit
here beside me. I cannot allow you (4850) to sit thus before me, for
your beard is streaked with white, and you are the keeper of the Koran
and dispense its wisdom to all; albeit you have renounced it long ago,
someone will teach it to you!"

The judge had scarcely recovered his breath, but he came and sat
beside the young man. The judge had scarcely revived when he said to
Mehmed: "May great good fortune be yours, my son, and very long
life! To what maid have you been betrothed? Whose is she, who is her

father? We shall have the servants prepare the papers. Forgive me for
having been so slow." "Her name is Fatima, daughter of Alibeg, one of
the noblest lords of Buda." The judge sank his head between his shoulders and lowered his head and beard. "Forgive me, Mehmed the hadji's
son! Someone must have deceived you. They are probably giving you
another maiden under her name, in order to praise her the better to
you. This Fatima, of whom you speak, my son, was at home until
yesterday. But yesterday a command was issued and the imperial warriors went and took her by force from her mother. They gave her over
to people in the vizier's palace. And I cannot tell you further what he
did with her last night." Then Mehmed said to the judge: "I know everything that happened to her. But you do exactly what I told you. Do not
dare to deceive me." And the judge said quickly: "Put everything aside
and write out the license papers." They all jumped at the command, fulfilled it, and gave the document into Mehmed's hands, saying: "May she
bring you good fortune, and may she bear you falcon-children, a daughter first and then sons, that the daughters-in-law may not overtake the
daughters in the house.[104] And in due time, may you marry off your
sons to a worthy house. May you give your daughters in marriage to the
house of Zajim, even as you took your wife from the Zajimovi." Mehmed would not say "Amin!,"[105] nor even "Thank you," (4900) for
their good wishes were perverse and meant quite the opposite. The
young man saw that they were traitors and would have nothing of their
congratulations and well-wishing.

    The young man rose like a gray falcon, and, thrusting his hands
into his pocket to pay the judge for the document, Mehmed asked him:
"How much is your fee?" The judge rose and said to Mehmed: "Even
if there were several such documents, there would be no charge for
them; I do not want a penny from you." Mehmed threw down two
gold pieces and left the room. When he came to Osman his countenance
was changed, and Osman asked Mehmed the hadji's son: "God preserve
you! What is wrong? Why this change in your face? You are not ill?"
Then said Mehmed to Osman the standard-bearer: "No, my brother, I
am not ill, but that unbeliever of a judge has angered me." Then they
both mounted their noble steeds and entered the streets to return to
the house of the wife of Zajimbeg.

    And now let me tell you about Lady Zajim. While she was waiting
for her son-in-law, ever worrying lest he lose his head, lest the treacherous vizier murder him, thrice she fainted in the palace. When the sound

of hoofs was heard in the street, and the heroes rode into the courtyard, those two dragons from Kanidža, both the lady and her daughter ran to meet the young man and his standard-bearer. Lady Zajim greeted Osman, the standard-bearer, while Fatima welcomed her lord. The lady had found servants to care for their caparisoned steeds when the heroes would return. Lady Zajim was well able to entertain her son-in-law and Osman in the palace. She led Osman the standard-bearer into the house, and the servants pulled off his boots. Meanwhile Fata led Mehmed by the hand, and her mother and the standard-bearer followed. She led them to the room at the top of the house. When the youths entered they looked about them in amazement. Were I to try to tell the brilliance of the room, I could neither describe nor even recount it. The young men's heads swirled at the beauty and richness of the room. But they both acted wisely. They simply looked at one another. One could not measure the honor which was done them, nor could one say whether the mother or the daughter was the better, nor which of them wore more jewelry, or had the more ducats on her headdress, or the more necklaces at her throat. They did honor to their guests and crossed their arms. Both the young men were dazzled at the honor done them, and at the richness of their hosts, and at the great abundance of everything in their dwelling. They brought forth all kinds of drinks, and the young men drank, while the ladies waited upon them. No one has ever seen, nor even dreamed of, such possessions. Neither pashas nor viziers had ever heard of or seen such things.

Then dark nightfall came, and the silver candlesticks were lighted, twelve on each side of the room, and others scattered about. They lighted also the golden candelabra, that there might be more light in the room. But indeed there was no need of light from candles or candelabra, because of the gleam of ducats from the women's throats, Fatima's lovely face, and all the jeweled ornaments of the room. Then came time for the lordly meal. They brought in a cloth of silk and spread it in the brilliantly adorned room. They set up a table of mother-of-pearl and on it placed a metal charger, all of silver and engraved in gold. There was food of all sorts, and they ate a lordly supper. When the meal was over, the table was removed and the crumbs brushed together and folded in a fine napkin. Afterwards they sat and talked, and the two ladies waited upon them, that mountain spirit, the daughter of Zajim Alibeg, and Lady Zajim, his wife.

When the time for sleep came, Fata put down two white mat-

tresses, one beside the other. (5000) She spread them in the room, and
the youths gazed at them. They could not say or tell of what sort they
were, nor of what they were made. Then the women laid cloth of finest
silk on the beds and placed pillows on them, pillows of broadcloth or
velvet; they were all stuffed with muskrat fur so that whoever should
lie on them should not find them heavy. Then the youths lay themselves down on the beds. There was no need of quilts, for the mattresses
flowed over and covered them like the foam of the sea. Straightway
they both fell asleep amid all this luxury, even as though they were
dead. But the ladies did not go to sleep, nor put out the candles in the
room. Thus they did honor to their sleeping guests.[106]

When the cocks crew, sleep left Osman, and he awakened his
brother Mehmed. "Arise, Mehmed, shining light of our house!"[107] Both
falcons rose, and when they had washed and rested, coffee and all sorts
of drinks were brought. Before the dawn had come they had satisfied
their hunger and thirst. Then said Mehmed, the hadji's son, to the mistress of the house: "Dear lady, dear to me as my own mother, Destiny
has been fulfilled, and Fatima is to be mine. May she bring me good
fortune!" "Yes, so be it, my son! I have given her to you." "And now,
my lady, I have something to ask you. If God grants, I shall go to Kanidža, and I shall tell my father, the alaybey, all that I have done here. Now
tell me, my lady, in how many days or weeks, whether fifteen days or
not, from the time I leave here should I bring the wedding guests? And
how many shall I bring? And tell me, my lady, shall I have a coach or a
spare mount prepared for the maiden?"

Lady Zajim smiled and said: "My Mehmed, dear to me as my own
sight, why do you not take Fata with you now? Do you really dare to
leave her, my son, and go away, lest the treacherous vizier seek to drown
her somewhere? Then would great shame be added to grief." Then said
Mehmed to her: "My lady, dear to me as my own mother, we must not
think of taking her now. Praise be to God, I see clearly that you are rich
in all worldly things. Even if all Buda were Fatima's, and you were to
give and deed all your possessions to me, you know that, though I might
wish it, I would not dare take away your Fata without wedding guests,
for fear of my father, Smailaga. Were the emperor to give me the whole
empire, what good would it be to me, if my head were not on my shoulders? For my father, Hadji Smail, would surely kill me. But, my lady,
even if my father were to say to me: 'My son, marry Fatima without
wedding guests!' I would sooner lose my head than destroy our honor

and good name. You know my lady, what has happened, where Fata was being sent, and who it was brought her back, and what befell after that. Were I to take her with me to Kanidža, not only all the folk but even our young maidens would immediately sing of me, for rumor is a traveler: 'What a fine lad is Mehmed, the hadji's son! The world says that there never has been, and never will be, such a falcon as he is. Devil of a falcon he is! He does not dare gather wedding guests because of the imperial three horsetails vizier!' What could I answer?" Then the lady said to him: "My son, do as you wish. Now, as for the maiden's trousseau, why should you waste your gold, my falcon, for my Fatima, since Fata has enough clothes to last her whole life long, without renewing a single silk thread, to say nothing of silk cloth from Stambol! My son, her wedding dowry is forty horses, with burdens bound in velvet and covered with Venetian satin. As long as you have your health, there will be no lack of gifts. Mehmed, you are as my own son! Do not ask me about the wedding guests. (5100) When you tell your dear father what happened here with Fatima, he will know how many wedding guests are necessary. As far as I am concerned, my dear son, if you are able to gather wedding guests, we, in the absence of my husband, Zajim, would be able to care for them without asking anyone to give up his house, even were you to bring a hundred thousand. Nor would it be crowded for them; there would not be nine in one house, but only three or possibly four. The groom's attendants[108] will stay at our house, and, if you want to bring them, the bride's maids also and the leader of the wedding guests, and with him whomever he may desire, from one to a hundred. Gather more wedding guests than is necessary. I do not think it possible to avoid a war, either with our vizier, or with Peter of Kara Bogdan. Thank you, my dear son! By the soul of my departed husband I have money and possessions enough. Whatever you spend in gathering and leading the wedding guests here, I will make up to you every penny and ducat, when I come, if God grants, to visit my one and only daughter. As for the time when you will come for her, my son; come in fifteen days, if you wish, or in a month, whenever you may wish. I am ready to entertain the guests at any time from this very day up until a year."

Thus she spoke, and then ran and kissed her son-in-law between the eyes, kissed that golden dragon on both cheeks, and he kissed the lady's hand. Then her ladyship bowed over Osman's hand. But Osman would not allow her to kiss his hand: "O, my lady, it would be a sin to do that! I could not bear to have such fine ladies kiss my hand."

The door of the room opened and four maidens came in. (5150) In their hands were four trays[109] holding forty gifts.[110] Fatima was carrying five gifts separately, which she put down at her mother's side. They put the gifts and the forty golden bundles before Mehmed. What wonderful golden gifts they were! Each was fastened together with a feather, and on each was a golden apple. On the apples was written that those gifts were for the chiefs of the wedding guests. Mehmed called Osman the standard-bearer: "Osman, bring in the saddlebags of blue silk.[111] Bring yours from your white horse and mine from my chestnut stallion." The younger[112] immediately obeyed his elder. He flew to bring the saddlebags, his own and Mehmed's. Mehmed took the golden bundles and gave the forty to the standard-bearer, that Osman might put them into the saddlebags and give them to Mehmed's old father, that his father might present them to whomever he wished.

The tray which had five bundles on it was especially for Mehmed. One of them was for Hadji Smailaga, another for his lady wife, one was for Cifrić Hasanaga, and another for Mehmed's aunt, Hasan's lady. One was for the dear bridegroom himself. Let us now tell you about the gifts. Those five were worth all together five hundred ducats, but Mehmed's was finer than any other. As you looked at his bundle you saw that it was all woven of gold, and on it were two clasps of 'fined gold. On one was a picture of Fatima, and on another that of the hadji's son. These had long ago been fashioned for him. Mehmed took the bundles and put them in his saddlebag.

Then the youth's face became clouded, for he had no money with which to reciprocate in gifts. Osman had a hundred ducats, but that was nothing compared with the gifts they had just received. But Lady Zajim was wise. (5200) "Mehmed, my golden treasure, why do you change your countenance? You did not journey here to woo Fatima, my dear son, it was fate that brought that about. I give you my word before God, that even had you come expressly for Fatima and brought whole sacks of gold, I would not have let you spend a penny of it. What would I do with your gold, since mine will become yours and enter your house the moment Fata is married to you?" "Speak not thus, lady! If there be any salvation from the appointed death, if your husband Zajim Alibeg is still alive, and if I escape with my life from the vizier, my father will seek out your husband, across the kingdoms, wherever he may be. You are young, and your heroic husband is young also. If God wills, and he may, it might yet be that you will bear more children, and then I shall

fly with my brothers-in-law as a grey falcon with wings." The lady said:
"It's possible, if God grants. If the time comes of which you speak, even
if but half of the wealth which the vizier took from my husband were
redeemed, it would still be plenty for my lord. All this which is given
to Fata, all I have told you of, that is all her own, for I inherited it from
my mother. None of the bey's possessions are mingled with it."

Mehmed was dazzled at such immense riches. The lady took
Meho's saddlebags. In one she put the wedding gifts, and in the other
light cakes.[113] She did not mix pies and pastry but sweet cakes made of
pure honey and butter. Then luncheon was brought, and Lady Zajim
asked him: "Now, indeed, my Mehmed, there is no shame in this.
Fatima is promised to you. We shall bring the imam[114] of Buda, and he
will marry you two. Stay with her a month, and nothing will be said
against it. (5250) Then were your judgment day to come, my eyes, in
the war at Buda, you would not be sorry to die, for you would have
kissed Fata's fair cheeks." Fatima fled to the door, and Mehmed addressed his mother-in-law: "Thank you, my lady, for thus fulfilling my
wish. But why do you not think of your daughter? Were I to be with
her a month, and then my day of judgment come, Fata would be a
widow, and her maiden virtue would be lost. No, I cannot agree to that.
I do not intend to kiss Fata here. But I do intend, by my hope in almighty God, when I have won the battle with the general, and we have
seized the vizier in his palace, and given him to Tale for judgment, when,
my lady, we have stained the great plain of Buda with blood of horses
and of heroes, when we have stirred the waters of the Klim so that it
flows, half water, half black blood, past the city of Buda, and carries
caps and fur hats, and the tricorns of Peter's heroes, then, my lady,
whoever has conquered may take Fata to himself, to love her whenever
he awakens."

The lady's tears fell. Mehmed raised the shutter on the window
and discharged his two pistols, like two thunderbolts from a black
cloud. And Osman shot off his two coral-handled pistols also. When the
shots rang out from the palace of Zajim Alibeg, the treacherous vizier
heard them and knew what had happened. His heart trembled in his
breast, the wretched[115] medals on his chest shook, and the Otman
plumes upon his head quivered. Then he called out to his courtiers:
"Let Meho proceed! I swear by God's faith, which cannot lie, that Meho
will not take her away without bloodshed, without dead and wounded."
The word went throughout all Buda, men and women ran out and said

to one another in the streets: "Fata, Zajimbeg's daughter, is betrothed to Mehmed son of the alaybey." (5300)

Then Mehmed cried out to Lady Zajim: "Call the youths to ready the horses!" The servants prepared the horses, while the young heroes made themselves ready. Then the door of the room opened, and Zajimova Fata entered. She gathered her skirt about her, rolled back her sleeves, and flew to her lord. She kissed the edge of his tunic and she kissed his hand, his heroic boots, and the prayer carpet before her husband. He kissed Fatima on both cheeks. Then the two lords turned away. Two serving maidens carried their rifles. The two ladies went before them to the courtyard. When they came to the head of the stairway, a young girl was standing there. She was a bit less beautiful than Fatima. She stood before Mehmed and spoke: "Mehmed, our new alaybey, may Zajimova Fata bring you happiness! and may your new command be blest! It is the custom in Buda, that when such a one as Fata falls—of course not many such do—that we tell off, O alaybey, what Fatima owns, when the fated day comes. You see that plain in front of us, with two large villages on it, many towers that are like palaces? Each village has a hundred houses. That the girl has inherited from her mother. Do you see this square in Buda? That is not, as Fata told you, Zajim Alibeg's property. It comes to her from her mother. The whole block of houses on the right hand side of the street, from this palace that we see to that one yonder that is opposite us with yellow tiles shining like the moon is hers. The caretaker of her estates, he who manages her possessions, dwells there. The room which is opposite us has nothing in it but waxened cloth and pure gold." Then Mehmed said to the girl: "Long life to you, and good fortune! (5350) For you speak well in accordance with custom. Neither pennies nor ducats are treasure, but one's treasure is what is dearest to one's heart. I am the son of that hero who would give his head for the sultan and for his country, and for another hero, and for people like this who are oppressed. Long life to us and to our sultan!"

Then the young men went downstairs and mounted their ready horses. They flew like two gray falcons, or like the day star, across the heavens. Day followed day and night's lodging followed night's lodging until the time came when they arrived in Kanidža. News reached imperial Kanidža and came to Mehmed's uncle and father. He who brought the first news was given countless treasure. The second to arrive was rewarded with unridden horses, and the third with uncut cloth. Then they brought the news of the hadji's son to imperial Hasan Pasha Tiro. Hasan Pasha issued an order to fire the cannon from the battlements, to celebrate the arrival of the new alaybey. When Mehmed and Osman the slender standard-bearer flew up, they dismounted from their glorious steeds. Servants took their horses. Both young men went with haste to where Hadji Smailaga was sitting, Osman first, and after him Mehmed. Osman gave Turkish greeting, and the two agas received his greeting. Then Osman rolled back his sleeves on his arms and kissed the hands of both his elders. They gave him welcome and made room next to them for him.

"Be seated, Osman, our golden wings!" Osman took his place and then Mehmed flew up. He kissed the hem of his father's robe and his hand, and that also of Cifrić Hasanaga. Then he stood aside to wait upon them. The gray falcon folded his arms before his father and uncle. Now his father gave him welcome and asked how he was. "My son, how was your journey to Buda? (5400) Did you have any difficulties with our good friend, the three horsetail vizier in Buda?" "No, father. I have never been received better nor more honored than at the hands of that imperial vizier. He issued the mandate without delay and asked after you and Uncle Hasan, sending you especial greetings. He invites you to come to Buda as his guest for a whole month whenever you may be able." "Thanks to the pasha for his gracious greetings! My Mehmed, shining light of our house! How did you like Buda? You have not been there before. Did anything strike you with amazement?" "My father, Hadji Smailaga, it is a goodly city without an equal. I saw nothing to wonder at. But why did you say to me: 'Go to Buda to our good friend, for there is friendship to be found.' My father, Hadji Smailaga, when I came to the broad Klima by Buda, we crossed the drawbridge. The sun was high over the peaks and mountains. We set out over the level plain, and there we saw a wondrous sight. A silver coach appeared, drawn by twelve Bedouin mares, bedecked with fine cloth from the crown of their heads to the green grass. Before the coach, on a splendid stallion, rode an imperial captain, a mighty man without an equal. He was only a little less than the sirdar,[116] but alike in moustache and in eye, fearsome of aspect and broad of brow. Both he and his horse were attired as Janissaries. A cap, however, was perched on his head and on the cap a golden feather, which read 'leader of a hundred men.' (5450) With him were fifty warriors on fifty Syrian Bedouin mares. They were mighty and spirited, and their trappings, father, were wondrous. Their saddles were of Moroccan leather like those of the Janissaries. Spears rested on their shoulders. On their thighs were crimson breeches and on their backs Janissary cloaks. The sabers at their sides were all alike. I cried out to my standard-bearer: "Standard-bearer, brother dear, that is a finely decorated coach which those splendid Bedouin mares are drawing. Fine also are the imperial warriors who ride beside the coach. But finest of all is their leader.' (O, my father, he was a mighty one among the mighty.) 'O Osman, would you perchance know who is in their coach? Are they pashas or viziers or the harems of pashas or viziers?' 'No, Meho, by my faith, I do not know!' And we urged our horses forward. Then the sound of screaming from the coach met our ears, an outcry, my father, like that of a snake beneath a stone, and the sound of it reached the heavens. Amidst the screaming these words were heard: 'May Buda be destroyed by fire, and may a gypsy slay the vizier! For he has clad Buda in black, separated the dear one and his beloved, and slain the heroes. Some he has thrown alive into the Danube, some he has given over to his executioners, and some he has exiled to Bagdad, to the third empire.[117] No house in Buda has been spared from slavery at his hand. The vizier has enslaved the heroes' daughters. He seizes slaves and sends them off to the enemy. He betrays Turkish faith for unbelief. He has worked evil for so many years that there is nowhere any brave man to carry a petition to the sultan, to stop the oppression of the enemy. My fine faith is now an open wound! My belief is a heart torn asunder! O Turkish faith, O sorrows eternal! My mother has become a black mourner,[118] for she remains without anyone (5500) among all her riches. Not even I remain to her any longer. And her husband was driven into exile long ago.'

"O my father, when I understood these words, my heart danced, my breastplate clattered, and many thoughts pressed upon me. 'Is it true that the vizier has been doing that?' And, my father, I could not believe that it was so, for you had told me that he was a friend unlike any other you had ever had. I rode forward and gave the Turkish greeting. He was not willing to receive my greeting. The captain did not turn his head, neither to me nor to Osman. Then I asked their leader: 'O wretched one, young aga of the Janissaries, what is the crying in the coach? Is it a vila or a fierce serpent, or some supernatural apparition? What is the terrible thing in the coach which the warriors are taking away by force?' Then, father, you should have seen the captain. He immediately rushed at me, began to put his hand on the hilt of his sword, saying: 'Away, drunken warrior! Are you mad or drunk, or did your father bring you up a fool? Urge your horse from the road, draw up your cloak. Don't talk a lot of nonsense, or your ruddy head will fly from your shoulders.' If Osman the standard-bearer had not been there, I would have fought with the man. I would not have left that captive to go into the enemy's hands, though I were to lose my head."

When the alaybey heard Mehmed tell of the oppression of the people, the south wind blew from his nose, and rain fell from his forehead. His jaws rocked back and forth like boats on the sea, and he parted his beard in four strands. He began to look at the sword hanging above his head, and thus he spoke: "You whoreson, a whore bore you! Here you are boasting in the tavern that you know nothing of fighting? Did we not teach you anything (5550) about fighting for a woman? Shame upon you in God's assembly even as there is shame upon you today in battle. Did you fear those fifty warriors and their leader? What will you do tomorrow in the face of the enemy in the camps? To leave a captive maiden! The imperial warriors were carrying her off, and you did not dare defend the girl!" "It was because of you, father, that I did not dare, for when I left, you said to me: 'Go, my son, and good fortune attend you! See to it that your journey is without mishap. Do not delay, but return here quickly!' " "Mehmed, whoreson! A mishap is one thing, but honor is still another. Then as soon as you arrived at Buda, you dog, you bowed before the vizier! Shame upon your mandate! Disgrace to the command! But by Allah you will not hold it long!" Then like a living flame the hadji acted. One would say and swear that he was no older than thirty years. The gleaming saber flashed from the peg. Good God! He was about to kill the boy and send the flower of his youth to the grave! But Osman jumped up and put his arms around the alaybey.

"What are you doing? Have you gone made? It is not as Meho was telling. Your son was only making trial of you. If he had done such things do you think that I would not have rebuked him for them? The facts were as Meho said, but Mehmed is his father's child. He attacked the warriors and killed their leader. I helped him a little. We attacked the warriors, killed half of them, and frightened the rest out of their wits. Then your Mehmed took out his battle-axe and cut the curtain cord of the coach. When the curtain fell we both saw a maiden sitting in the coach. She was like a white mountain vila. (5600) But she had torn out her hair on the right side from great grief and had lacerated her cheeks. She had closed her black eyes. We could see that she was of good family, even though her clothes were dyed black. Then your son Mehmed asked her: 'Young maiden in the height of your grief! Whose daughter are you? What is your name? Of what family and house are you? Who was the mother who brought you up?' O hadji, the girl thought that the warriors were speaking to her. She did not open her black eyes, but she held her head with both hands, weeping and wailing. And thus she spoke to Mehmed: 'Go away, traitor to the sultan! You are all traitors to the sultan, since you serve a traitor, destroy the honor and faith of the sultan, and lead the faithful into the hands of the infidel. Our faith cannot forgive that.' And your Mehmed said to her: 'Golden one, dear to me from the bottom of my heart! I am not an imperial warrior, but a stranger from afar.' When the girl understood his words, she opened her eyes. If it is useless for me to tell you of her, how much more so is it for your Meho! She cut us both in twain with her eyes as with a poisoned sword, so noble was her bearing. O commander, if fate wills it so, and you see her with your Mehmed, then will you realize that what we say is true.

"Then she recognized us as strangers and saw what we had done, how we had put an end to her captivity and saved her from the warriors. Then the young girl cried out and said to your son: 'My heart, my eyes, O youth on the chestnut stallion! I am daughter of the best of houses. I am Fatima, daughter of Zajim Alibeg. That is the foremost house in Buda. It was we who founded Buda.' Then she began to tell of her woes. When she was only two years old (5650) a firman came from the Osmanli, and in it was an imperial blessing. 'You have preserved my honor well and Buda has but recently been taken from the enemy. Now, my lords, I have arranged to send a vizier to Buda and with him a military commander, a Janissary pasha, with an army of fifty thousand men and fifty battle cannon, to fortify Buda against the enemy. The vizier will govern you and my lands. The military pasha with his army under command from my vizier will protect you and the Border and take from you the burden of the enemy.' Then, O hadji, the girl continued: 'When they heard this announcement, my father Zajim read it aloud, he gathered together the agas and beys and read the imperial firman to them and they rejoiced at it. Dear heart, the most select agas and beys went to meet him, even those who wear the imperial plumes and ride steeds with golden trappings. They took four teachers and four hundred students from the seminary. Each one had a leather bag over his shoulder, and in it was a Koran, God's book. Two days' journey from Buda they met the imperial vizier, and the agas did homage before him; for the sake of the firman they approached the hem of his cloak. The teachers intoned the prayers, and all the Turks said amen, and all the children too, that the prayers might be accepted, that the vizier should come to us under good auspices. For two days they read the Koran. Then we set him up in his palace, which was all decorated with beautiful cloth and pure gold. For a year the people came to do him homage, stranger, as they should before a vizier, and that they might look upon the justice and fairness of the sultan.

" 'But Buda is all within one walled city. The whole army was under the vizier's command. He took the full name of every imperial aga and bey, the name of his house and tribe. (5700) Thus he found out who it was who was defending the country, the imperial fatherland, and the sultan's honor. They would give their lives, but they would never abandon their country. At each of the four gates of Buda he set up guard houses and sentries. These were Janissaries with their own captain. The vizier ordered the captains to have the guards stop and search anyone, either day or night, who wished to enter or leave the city, to see whether he carried some letter or petition. When he had imposed these restrictions, he took all the others who approved the vizier's order and agreed that he could do what he wished, and put them in a chamber in his own palace. There he had a strong guardhouse built, and there he stationed twenty executioners, with black heads and shining white teeth. In command of them was a dusky captain of executioners. And this is the command he gave them: "Inquire of anyone who wishes to come to see the vizier who he is and what is is he wants. If he says that he has come to complain about something, cut off his head and cast his body into the cold Danube. As for any others who come to me, ask them what they want of the vizier. If they reply 'we want to sit with him and talk,' bind them and throw them into prison. I'll decide what to do with them later." When he had thus established a reign of terror, he executed fifty and bound fifty alive. He hung a stone about their necks and threw them alive into the Danube, that their souls might leave them in torment. Those that remained in the palace didn't dare to move anywhere. He took them from the palace at night and sent them all into exile to Bagdad in the third kingdom, that they might never see their home again. Thus he exiled my father, and I was left alone young and innocent. In secret my mother brought me up. (5750) She thought that nobody knew of me.

" 'When my father was exiled I was four years old. That traitor has now ruled there a full fifteen years, and I, alas, am just nineteen. The maidens and widows of Buda, whose homes the vizier had clad in mourning even as that of my father Zajim Alibeg, saw me. All unknowing of what would happen, they praised me. "Fata, the daughter of Zajim Alibeg, has no equal, even among the vilas on the mountains, certainly not among mortal women." Thus the treacherous vizier heard of me, and sent suitors to woo me, imperial traitors of Buda, asking me to marry my enemy. But I drove the suitors away: "Go away, imperial traitors! I shall not take my enemy in marriage, even were the sky to fall upon the earth!" The vizier became angered at me. Yesterday he took me prisoner, and this morning he is sending me with these warriors to Kara Bogdan, to a certain General Peter.' When Mehmed understood her words, Zajimova Fata said to him: 'Golden dragon, whose child are you? From what place and house are you? Who is your father, and what is your golden name?' He said: 'Mehmed the hadji's son, the dear son of Smailaga. Perhaps you have heard of him.' 'Yes, I know well, for my mother told me: "The house of Smailaga is foremost. That hero is the key of Bosnia. When you are grown up, my precious Fatima, I shall give you to the hadji's son. Let a vila mate with a falcon. Let a family find another suitable to it, and thus be renewed and continued!" ' Then, my hadji, Mehmed asked Fatima: 'Would you take me for your love? You see me; do you like me? But do not take me because of this incident, because the vizier has captured you and sent you away. (5800) But just as if your father were still in Buda, to be seen and talked of by people.' And Fatima said to your Mehmed: 'I would take you, Mehmedaga, even if I were to die seven times and, were it possible, come to life again; I would be your love even the eighth time. But, my heart, I shall not have you, for now you will lose your life. It is fated for me to witness that sorrow on top of all the others, to see your flourishing flower of youth destroyed. But if you wish me to be your love, take me on your horse and flee with me to Kanidža. If God grants that we arrive at your father's and that your father saves us from the vizier, all will be well. Otherwise we shall never be safe.' She begged him to do this and cried out to him, but that did not influence your son. 'There will be no talk of that, Fata. I am the only son of my father and of my uncle, Cifrić Hasan. I shall not marry without my father knowing it, without returning you to your mother and asking her to give you to me.' "

Even then it was with difficulty that Osman the standard-bearer

appeased the old alaybey. He listened to it all, but he held onto his
sword. Finally Osman said to the alaybey: "My elder, it is a long story,
but let me tell it to you briefly. The boy took Fata onto his horse and
then said: 'Osman, golden wing, turn the gilded coach around and tie
the captured horses together. Then follow in my path to Buda. I have
taken away Zajimova Fata!' I obeyed your one and only son. I bound
the horses, both stallions and Bedouin mares, and Mehmed carried
Fatima away. Her lady mother me them there. Had he not come upon
her at that very moment, she would have hurled herself from the palace,
but he succeeded in dissuading her. There the lady entertained him, and
Meho told her what he had done. She implored him in the name of
God: 'But why did you not take Fata to Kanidža, rather than bring her
here and lose your head?' (5850) He told her just what he had told
Fata. 'With hope in God and in my father's health, nothing will happen
to your Fata. She has given herself to me, and I have taken her to be my
love. If you agree with Fata, do not say that she is already promised to
another. Marry her off to whomever you wish. Keep your doors open
and free. The vizier will not trouble your Fata.' Then the mother gave
the girl to him and blessed her. At that moment I drove up the gilded
coach. We drove it into the bey's stable, and then we both rested a
while. Afterwards we mounted our noble steeds and went to the vizier's
palace. There there were neither hindrances nor executioners, nor was
your son stopped at the gate. I remained outside to walk the horses,
and listened to what was going on upstairs, that I might be of help to
your son. The vizier received him well. He has already told you that the
vizier approved the decree and blessed your son. Mehmed came down,
and we mounted again. Then we went through the square of Buda and
found the palace of the chief justice. Let me tell you what happened up
there. If God grants, there will be time. Upstairs Mehmed received his
marriage license and came down with it in his bosom. Then we returned
to Lady Zajim. We spent the night in her house. Let me tell you what
there was in that house and describe the elegance of the courtyard and
of the staircase. Let me tell of the balconies and their splendor, of the
stairs and how they were made, of the wall of the courtyard, and of the
doors of the gateway. I would tell also of the pearls and precious stones
on Fatima and the wife of Alibeg, her mother, when we saw them, of
the golden diadems on their heads and the golden necklaces on their
breasts, of the jewels and pearl in the room. Then I would describe what
we had to eat and drink, what we slept on, and how we slept and rose

early. They honored us in every way, with food and drink they overwhelmed us. They brought forth a rich engagement gift for Fatima.
Then Mehmed asked the wife of Alibeg: 'I am returning home, now,
how long shall we wait before we come for the girl? A week or a fortnight? or a month or two? And what sort of clothes shall I cut out for
your daughter, an only son for an only daughter? Shall I bring a coach
for her with young bridesmaids in it? Or shall I bring a finely caparisoned horse for her?' And she replied: 'Do everything according to your
own desires.' In regard to the wedding guests, she said to ask you. 'When
you tell him what happened here he will know how many to gather. For
my sake and in honor of Zajimbeg my husband, you might bring a hundred thousand. In Buda there are a thousand houses of Zajimovi, all of
the same family. There are beys and widows, and innocent mothers with
little children. The vizier did the same to them that he did to me, my
dear son. Nor will I make it hard for the wedding guests, but give them
comfortable quarters. There will nowhere be as many as nine quartered
together, but they will be in groups of three and possibly four. And I
will keep them here an entire week. Then you can take my precious
Fata and load her forty packs of clothes, wrapped in cloth of Venice
and covered with Venetian satin.' Lady Zajim did not allow him to say a
word about Fatima's trousseau: 'My dear son, Fatima has enough
changes of clothes for her to wear one after the other from today to the
end of her life, and she can wear gold besides. But health and long life
to you, my Meho, to you, my son, and to my Fata, and to me, my son,
and to your mother, and to your father and your uncle Hasan. May the
honor of your house remain forever bright! May you accomplish what
you plan! May your enemies be beneath your feet! And do not fear, my
son, for what you will have to spend for the wedding guests! Spend the
money, make an account, and when, if God grants and fate allows,
(5950) I come to visit my daughter, I will recompense you for all you
have spent. Fata has a large inheritance from her mother beside all her
father's possessions.'

"O, my alaybey, were Osman to tell you of that family and of its
nobles, of the wife of Alibeg and all her wealth in Buda, over and above
what Alibeg had and what the vizier has robbed them of today, and
were you to bring in four scribes I could not finish describing it to you
in fifteen days, nor could the scribes write it down. But peace and good
fortune to us all!

"When the dowry had been settled with Alibeg's wife, she gave us forty gifts for the forty chief wedding guests. And then special ones for you and your Mehmed, one for you and for your beloved wife, one for your brother Hasanaga, and one for Hasanaga's wife. You will see them when they are brought in. Grandfather, you are a hundred years old, and you have seen all sorts of things, but I wager you have never even heard of such as these. Besides the forty other gifts those five alone are worth five hundred ducats.

"But when we had put the gifts into our saddlebags, our expressions changed, for we had no money for gifts in recompense. We had not set out with intent to woo a maiden, and thus had only enough for the expenses of traveling. But the lady was wise and saw our distress. And as soon as she saw it she realized why it was. Then she said to your Mehmed: 'My son-in-law, do not be distressed. You did not come with intent to woo a maiden, nor did your father send you here for Fata or for any other, but you took with you only what you needed for the trip to Buda and back. That is my first word. And even if you had come to Buda especially to woo Zajimova Fata, you would not have had to spend a penny here. My son, what do I want of guineas or of yellow ducats, since it will all go to your house!' (6000)

"And your son said to Alibeg's wife: 'You must not speak thus, my lady! It will not be as you think, but as almighty God grants. God shall grant and fortune will bring it about that there will be some betterment of destiny. With hope in God, and the health of my father, if Zajim Alibeg is alive, Smailaga will find him with the help of the sultan. When we have given our aid and overcome the treacherous vizier, he will bring back your bey to Buda. You are a young and good woman, and with you he will beget children, and then shall I have new brothers-in-law, and with them I will fly like a gray falcon with his wings.'

" 'My dear son, may it be so, if God grants! May it be so! We shall look forward to it. Now I give you my inheritance from my mother, but the possessions of Zajimbeg remain untouched. If he had but half of what the vizier has stolen he would have enough and to spare of all kinds of things.' But to tell the rest in brief, O hadji, here are the gifts, here the decree and the command, and here is a wife for your son. Only your daughter-in-law is not to be won without cost. I tell you, Smail alaybey, your strain has not degenerated, but you have begotten a good dragon. You will never be ashamed of him, neither before God in fair combat nor before the sultan in any council."

Then Hadji Smailaga rose and stretching out both arms embraced his one and only son. He kissed him between the black eyes where the gray falcons kiss. Then he cried out: "Bravo, my son! For you have preserved our honor unsullied. Now, my son, do not worry. Take with you Osman the standard-bearer and stroll wherever you wish. Treat your comrades and gather your friends in the cafés and taverns. Do not worry about us here. (6050)[119] Now I see that I have a worthy son, and my heart is full. Long life to you and your father and to your uncle Cifrić Hasanaga, and to level Bosnia and Unđurovina, that golden wing, and to our Border. I know what I shall do now, what letters I shall send and how I shall raise the Border, for the sake of the shining honor of my son. I shall not spare money nor would I fail to sacrifice my own head, nor that of my brother, if we can but have, with hope in God, the fulfillment of our desire, to see that vila married to our falcon, and do what he will to the vizier, his enemy."

Then Mehmed unclasped his breastplate and put the mandate down before his father, the well-writ letter of the vizier of Buda, his father's first friend. Mehmed, said to his father: "See, father, what sort of friend you have! This letter about you was sent by the vizier to Kara Bogdan. He was giving Fata to General Peter in exchange for a brotherly alliance,[120] that he might kiss her whenever he awoke. That was not all. He was about to present his brother with the heads of the two alaybeys, yours, my father, and Uncle Hasan's, and along with them a third, your son's. This is what the vizier said in his letter: 'If God grants, my dear brother, when the time comes that I send you these heads as gifts, Bosnia will straightway follow, and you may have dominion over it. I shall give Buda into your hands, even before I send you the heads.' There you are; see what a friend you have!" And Smail the alaybey said to his son: "Now, my son, I have seen and understood. He has raised his hand against our faith and destroyed so many families! Now I see what would have happened to me. But God will grant us to see even more."

Now he embraced Osman. "Osman, shining light of our house, (6100) I have often asked you: 'My son, do you wish us to find you a wife?,' but you would not even let me speak of it. Now, my son, the time has really come when with these wedding guests we marry off our son. I will seek a maiden for you in Buda; someone whom the wife of Alibeg will tell us of, someone like Fatima whom she gave my son. I shall marry you off to that maid, as I wish during my lifetime, if God but grants. Seven or eight times I have offered to marry you off and give you half my possessions, but you did not wish to have my property.

You desired to preserve it for my son. Now, in our hope in almighty God, there will be plenty for both of you. You shall have my heritage and he shall have Fatima's, and Hasan has his own. If Hasan dies some day, then his property will also be ours. But, my son, this is scarcely a sufficient reward for what you have done for me. I shall never be able to repay you."

Osman kissed the old man's hand, then both young men went to the door of the room. The old man took the gifts before him and began to divide them. Of the forty bundles he gave thirty to his thirty captains. Then there was one for Sirdar Mujo Hrnjica, who was commander-in-chief of the whole army, and there was a good one put aside for Halil, who was to be the girl's protector.[121] Another good one was put aside for Tale, because Tale wouldn't move without it. Then there was one for Mustajbeg of the Lika. Six others were for his six standard-bearers, the wings of the whole Border.

Then dusky nightfall came, and Hasan and the hadji said their evening prayers, they and both their wives, who bear heroes. The mother of young Mehmed the hadji's son had devoted all her life to him. She was as young as a mountain vila. She rejoiced and wept not for her son, as she prepared him for the wedding guests, for bloody deeds and battle. (6150) She flew about and sang a song, and in this song these are the words she said: "Praise be to God, for he has given me a son, who will enlarge the empire of the Ottomans, and be of assistance to all its heroes, and who will take captives from among the enemy! May his honor be bright and his right arm strong and his blade keen! May he accomplish whatever he undertakes! I do not weep at the loss of my son, if only he overwhelms the traitor to the sultan and does not yield the land to his enemies." And Smail encouraged her: "Bravo, Lady Ismihan. I have seen your nobility and your youth compared to my age. You have served me well. God was good and you bore a son. Such are the women who bear heroes."[122] Then the lordly supper came. They supped and cleaned away the crumbs. Then they slept and passed the night.

When the time of dawn was near, the hero Hadji Smailaga summoned Omer the standard-bearer from the guard post of his house. And when the young man had come to his elder, he approached and stood ready to serve. "My dear son, standard-bearer Omer, I am celebrating two joyous events. The new command has fallen upon my son (may it be blessed to him, for he is worthy of it), and he is marrying a maiden who must be won in battle, because she has two challengers, Peter of Bogdan and the Vizier of Buda. The sun will soon rise and shed its warmth, and the congratulating will begin. Take care that you do not blacken our honor! Call out forty of the honor guard; for you, my son, are their leader. Bring forth the keys of my wine cellar where the wine is in casks, and strong rakija beside it. Divide your honor guard into groups to meet and welcome our guests, to honor them when they are in our house, and to escort them at their departure. For at least a month or more, (6200) the agas will come to visit me, to congratulate my son on his appointment as alaybey, and to hear me tell of the marriage. Serve us well, and do not worry! Draw and distribute drinks of all sorts. Do not concern yourself about how much will be left. If Smailaga lives, he will obtain more for the wedding itself."

He sent Omer back to his post and called his steward,[123] he who governs the ramparts and cannon. And he said to Husein: "Go now to the fortress gate[124] and fire the two great cannon, which announce a festival of joy. The Border knows which are for war and which for feasting. Let all know that I am marrying off my son. Let the agas come to pay their respects. May we give them good entertainment!"

When Smailaga had given this command, Omer went to the honor guard and told them what his elder had said, and they scattered in all directions. They opened the gate of the courtyard and brought beverages from the cellar. They put them in every room in the house, set out glasses and tumblers, and beakers of 'fined silver. All the tables in each room were alike, and the glasses and tumblers also. There were all kinds of different drinks for everyone alike and tables for the imperial agas. While the house was being readied, the cannon were fired from the battlements. They spread the news to all corners; the sound went out over the black earth. The captains and commanders of a thousand[125] heard in Kanidža and nearby, and they rejoiced: "Praise be to God! Mehmed has returned from Buda and has received the command. He has brought joy to his father and to the whole Border."

The happy news went from town to town, to every town and province. In some places cannon boomed, in others guns[126] were fired, and thus the news passed from one to the other. There was rejoicing in every part of the Border, as if each man were marrying off his own son, (6250) or daughter, or celebrating the circumcision of his child. Then was there real happiness among the Turks; for they were thoughtful of one another. Mutual respect is good warring and penetration on every side.[127] The agas began to set out to congratulate Hadji Smailaga. He who was near went on foot, and he who was from afar on his horse. Who was the first to arrive? The first was Hasan Pasha Tiro with his fifty warriors. They alighted at the bey's house, and the pasha gave greeting to Smailaga and to the hero Cifrić Hasanaga. He congratulated them on the arrival of their son, on his safe journey from Buda, and on his appointment to the command. And the joy continued. Wine and thrice-distilled rakija were drunk. Then Smailaga said to the pasha: "Golden pasha, imperial right hand! My son has been betrothed." And he told him to whom and of what sort she was. "O pasha, you are our lock and key. Will you come to our help?" And the pasha said to Smailaga: "What is this you are saying, O hadji? Praise be to God that you begot such a son and that he has had such success! I would not feel sorry to die for him, with twelve thousand soldiers at my back, the imperial army and Janissaries. I will be the first to join the wedding guests, if God grants, whenever you wish." Then he embraced him, and Smailaga said to the pasha: "Thank you, imperial hero!"

Then Hasan accompanied the pasha to the door, and the other leaders of Kanidža, that white city, came pressing forward. First were the two imperial fortress commanders, and then the four elders, each with his own standard-bearer. They thronged to Smailaga's dwelling, gave greeting, and embraced. Then they took seats one by the other and congratulated Smailaga. And he said to them: "Many thanks, agas! I am celebrating two happy events. (6300) My son has been made alaybey and has become betrothed to a maiden, Fatima, daughter of Zajim of Buda. But, my brothers, Fatima will not be won without a fight. She has two challengers, Peter of Kara Bogdan and the imperial vizier in Buda, who has ruined imperial Buda." Then he told them the whole story, all that had happened to Fata and what Mehmed had done with her. "And now, my brothers, you our four elders, and you our two imperial fortress commanders, help me in this! When I gather the wedding guests, will you feel sad to give up your life for me in my old age, in the service of every Moslem, for the sake of the honor of Sulejman the Magnificent, as we see whether we can find some way to help and to outwit the vizier? Just see how the traitor works! He offers the emperor's lands to the enemy. He is ready to hand over Buda to him, and Bosnia would not stay free long once Buda was gone. And you know that if that should happen, the whole empire would fall!" Then the imperial elders said: "O alaybey, imperial reflection! You know you need not have put the question, for have we not sworn as long as any one of us lives to serve our sultan and emperor and be true to our whole fatherland, and to sacrifice ourselves for the sultan? Then why not, O imperial reflection, for you, also? But look you to the rest of the Border, to the parts around Kanidža and the more distant regions. Write letters and summon your captains. Tell your heralds the appointed time and place. As for level Kanidža and its surroundings, it is not necessary to send letters. Merely fire the two great cannon, and all thirty of your captains will be ready before your gates with all that is necessary for the wedding, both for the wedding journey itself and for the fierce battle." Smail thanked them well: "Blessed are you, golden wings of the empire! (6350) As long as there are such as you Bosnia will not be lost."

And so they drank and made merry, and one after another they thronged there for a whole month of days and a week more; day and night the men of the Border came to the white courts of Smailaga. Hadji Smail, his house, his riches, and his great nobility were worthy of respect. No one here was angry with him, but all did him every honor. And when the month and week had been fulfilled, the aged Smail prepared himself. He threw his cape over his shoulders and took his silver pipe. Then the servants prepared his stallion, even as the courtiers serve the sultan in council. Two young honor guardsmen went before him through the streets of Kanidža to greet Hasan Pasha Tiro.

For two full days before this, Hasan Pasha had risen early and had spread the word that the assembly of chief men should be called together in the pasha's courts in Kanidža, that they might come to agreement with one another how the men of the Border should be summoned, how letters should be sent throughout all of muddy Bosnia, lest no one be forgotten in letter or in summoning; not to be sure, for fear that there would be fewer men, but that someone might feel hurt and say: "Look at Smailaga! Why is he disdainful of me on account of his one and only son and the golden wings of all of us? He is marrying off his son and does not invite us!"

And so the chief men were assembled in the white courts of Hasan Pasha, but there was no word from Hadji Smail. Then they saw Hadji Smailaga come into the courtyard and dismount from his white steed. The pasha cried out to his twenty warriors: "Go immediately down to the outer courtyard to meet our hero! Let ten honor guardsmen escort him and another ten care for his horse. Put it in the stable next to my spotted charger." (6400) Then straightway the servants obeyed the pasha and received the elder hadji. They took his pipe from his hands and from his shoulders his cape of blue and gold. Others led his white steed into the dark stable.

When the hadji came into the house, the chief men of Kanidža were all assembled, even the two fortress commanders and four elders and Kanidža's thirty captains. They were sitting one beside the other. Each one was served by a standard-bearer, leaning on a supple saber. When the hadji came among them he gave them greeting. In answer to this greeting from such an imperial hero all rose to their feet and made room for him next to the pasha, and all embraced him. Then they asked the aged hadji: "Are you tired, elder, from looking at your son's celebration and from entertaining in your court?" And Hadji Smailaga answered them: "Can one become tired when there is so much rejoicing; when the chief men gather at my court and do not turn away their head? Ah, my brothers, one is never tired of such honor."

They they began to talk of many things. The pasha said to the aged alaybey: "I have gathered the chief men to see if we cannot help you in some way, to come to agreement with one another about the sending of letters and the summoning of broad Bosnia, lest anyone be left out. Not because there would be fewer men (if we are fortunate there will not be), but because someone might feel hurt and say: 'Look at the aged hadji! He is marrying off his one and only son amongst us all, but he has not invited me!' " Then Smailaga stretched out his arms and embraced the imperial hero. "Golden wings of the city of Kanidža! Great good fortune is it for us that you are amongst us. But you know now what to do. You are wise and yours it is to command. I have grown very old, and my brain has lost its vigor.[128] (6450) I might make some mistake and hurt some one. All my life I have never failed anyone in love, neither I nor my brother. And I have great hope in almighty God that Mehmed will rule well." Then the pasha said: "Now the time has come to send the letters, for Bosnia is long and broad. It will be a whole month before the letters are written and distributed, and another fifteen days before the wedding guests are assembled. Already a month has passed since Fatima was betrothed to our son. It will be full three months before the wedding guests are gathered and leave, before the army arrives at Buda."

Thus spoke the pasha and thus he made his reckoning. Then the twelve imperial scribes knelt at the tables among the beys. And the pasha ordered his fifty warriors to prepare their fifty Bedouin mares, and the imperial captains also to ready themselves, that the warriors might distribute the letters. The honor guard in the hadji's court also had work to do in Kanidža, to obey the hadji's commands, to be ready to do whatever he ordered. Now the scribes took their quills and white paper free of writing.

To whom will they write the first letter? To Pašić Ibrahim in Travnik.[129] And this is what the pasha said to him: "My friend, Pašić Ibrahim, the command of all the armies and the imperial territories has been left in your hands in Travnik. My dear comrade, have you heard what has happened in Kanidža? how the hadji, the aged alaybey, has given over the command into his son's hands, and also betrothed his son to the well-born Fatima far away in crooked[130] Buda? Therefore, my friend,[131] we are gathering the wedding guests. These are not guests for an ordinary wedding, because we expect a great battle. Fata, O pasha, was betrothed against the will of two other suitors, (6500) a general of Kara Bogdan and the imperial vizier in Buda. My friend, you have twenty thousand Janissaries with you in Travnik, and we all know you to be a hero, we know the nobility of your house. Come, my friend, and join the wedding guests with twelve thousand followers and twelve great cannon, that we may discover what is happening in Buda!" This he sent to the city of Travnik, and gave this command: "O captain, give Ibrahim my special greetings, and tell him not to delay coming with his army. We must meet in fifteen days."

Then he wrote a second. To whom did he send it? To the bey of the broad Lika, because he was a Turkish bey with firman from the sultan, ranking above any vizier. "Bey of the Lika, reflection of the sultan! Receive greetings from Hasan Pasha. There is rejoicing in Kanidža. Hadji Smailaga is marrying off his son, our new alaybey. But he has chosen a maiden to be won by battle, Fata Zajimova of Buda, whose happiness has been taken away by the Vizier of Buda and by Peter of Kara Bogdan. Come, O bey of beys, and prepare your dove-colored horse and your seven standard-bearers and twelve thousand men of the Lika and twelve imperial cannon! Do not delay long, O bey of beys! We depart in full fifteen days. We shall proceed as if to a wedding, but we expect also that there will be a battle." Then he called his imperial captain: "Carry this letter to the broad Lika!"

This he sent, and then wrote a third, and directed it to Upper Vrljika, to the aged elder of Vrljika: "O elder of level Vrljika, imperial hero! Have you heard how the aged alaybey Smail has found a maiden for his son, our new commander, even Fatima of Buda, who must be won in battle and whose happiness has been taken away by two challengers, (6550) even Peter of Kara Bogdan and the treacherous vizier in Buda. I pray you, as my own brother, to gird on your belt of arms, to gather the men of Vrljika, and to bring with you your standard-bearer Velagić on his chestnut steed. Without Velagić Selim we cannot march. We are preparing as if for a wedding, but we shall also march as if to war. Hence, my lord, do not tarry; the latest time is fifteen days. Let us see what is happening in Buda!"

This he sent, and then wrote a fourth to go to Banja Luka, to the hero Fetibegović. Thus did Hasan Pasha write to this bey: "Fetibeg, our reflection, have you heard of our rejoicing? Hadji Smail of level Kanidža has betrothed Mehmed our new alaybey to Fata Zajimova of Buda, who must be won in battle. Prepare your Bedouin mare, O Fetibeg, and gather the men of Banja Luka, an army of seven thousand, all mounted, none on foot! For the journey to Buda is long. This is to be not only a wedding, but also a great battle. Fatima's happiness has been taken away, as The Vizier of Buda is planning to give her over, my dear brother, to our enemy. General Peter of Kara Bogdan. Prepare for a wedding, but expect a battle!"

This he sent, and then he wrote another, to Fatić Omeraga of white Jajce, the stony: "Golden aga, Fatić Omer![132] You are the head of all Jajce. Prepare you sorrel and gather all the fiery heroes of Jajce, as many as you can! We have found a maiden who must be won in battle for our new alaybey Mehmed, son of Hadji Smail, even Fatima of Buda. She has two challengers, Peter of Kara Bogdan and the three horsetail vizier (6600) who is doing his utmost to betray the Border and destroy the whole empire. So I pray you, as if you were my own brother, to gather as many wedding guests as you can! We depart in fifteen days."

This he sent, and then he wrote another and directed it to Upper Lijevno to the Turk Ljevak Omeraga: "O Omeraga, wing of Lijevno, of Lijevno and Lower Duvno, have you heard of the city of Kanidža and of Hadji Smail? He has betrothed his son to Fata Zajimova of Buda, a maid of the best family. But Fata's happiness has been taken away by our enemy General Peter and the treacherous Vizier of Buda, who has draped the city in black. So I pray you, Omeraga, my brother, to gather as many wedding guests as you can. There will be a battle at Buda, a battle to be celebrated in song and story. I pray you, as if you were my own brother, not to delay. We depart in fifteen days, Omeraga, at the latest."

This he sent, and then he wrote others. Now he prepared twelve letters and sent them across the Una to Unđurovina,[133] to the twelve imperial captains who lead armies without firman from Sultan Sulejman and without written orders from the vizier. Thus the pasha wrote: "My brothers, Beys of Una, have you heard, imperial lords, of our Hadji Smail in Kanidža, that imperial city, the most blood-soaked spot in all Bosnia? He has found a maiden for his son Mehmed, the new alaybey, a maiden who must be won in battle, the famed Fatima, daughter of Zajim Alibeg. There has never been anyone like her until now, and never will be hereafter. But she must be fought for. The imperial traitor, the Vizier of Buda, is betraying her into the hands of General Peter of Kara Bogdan, who is attempting to destroy the empire. (6650) So I pray you as my own brothers—for the sultan's army is in your

hands, and you have been given authority by the sultan: you are the golden plumes
in our midst—to gather a mighty army and come to our aid! Let us march to Buda,
my brothers, to see what the imperial traitor is doing to our fatherland, which we
have dyed with our blood. He who has annihilated Buda, who has wrapped it in a
black shroud, will soon encompass us also. Arise, heroes of the sultan, to protect
our homeland! In fifteen days the wedding guests will gather in Kanidža." Then he
summoned twelve warriors. They mounted twelve Bedouin mares and bore the
twelve letters abroad to the twelve captains of Una.

    Then he wrote two messages to the two beys of the two imperial Janjas, the
two Janjas and the two Bijeljinas, even to Filduš and Fildiš,[134] and thus Hasan Pasha
entreated them: "I pray you, imperial lords! Have you heard of our Kanidža? Hadji
Smail has found a bride for his son the alaybey, Fatima, daughter of Zajimbeg of
Buda. But Fatima cannot be won without a struggle. The Vizier of Buda is betraying her into the hands of General Peter of Bogdan, who is endeavoring to destroy
the empire and our Bosnia, which is its lock and key. So I pray you, imperial beys,
to raise the two imperial Janjas and come with as many wedding guests as you can,
my brothers. Prepare as for a wedding, but we expect there will also be a battle."

    These he sent, and straightway he wrote others. One he sent to bloody Tuzla,
to Mehmed the imperial captain. Another he sent of Gradašac, to the Turk Brkić
Ibrahim. Hasan Pasha thus entreated both beys: "Raise as large an army as you can!
The alaybey of Kanidža is to be married to Fatima of Buda, who must be won by
battle, (6700) because this maiden's happiness has been taken away by the pasha
of Buda."

    These he sent, and wrote still others. One he sent to the bey of Brčkovo, to
that Turk, Šahić Alibeg:[135] "My hero, bey of Brčkovo, read well what the letter
from your friend Hasan Pasha Tiro says of our Hadji Smail! He has found a bride
for his son, the daughter of Zajimbeg of Buda, Fatima, who must be won by battle.
This maiden's happiness, however, has been taken away by our enemy Peter of
Bogdan, aided by the Vizier of Buda. So I pray you, as if you were my own brother,
to gather as large an army as you can from the Sava region. Then come at its head
on your black-maned courser, that we may defend our homeland, which the vizier
is betraying to our enemy. We depart in fifteen days."

    This he sent, and then he wrote another, even to Delibegović in Osik: "Osman-
beg, peer of an imperial pasha! Read well what this letter from your friend Hasan
Pasha Tiro says! Have you heard of our Kanidža and of our Hadji Smailaga? He has
found a bride in Buda for Mehmed, the new alaybey, the good Fatima, daughter of
Zajim Alibeg. But Fata has two challengers, General Peter of Bogdan, aided by the
treacherous vizier, a traitor to the sultan, my dear bey, for he is doing his utmost to
betray the empire, to fix our heads upon stakes to decorate the enemy's cities,

even as he has already done until now in Buda. So I pray you as my elder. Gather Osek and the men of the Border, and come at their head on your own mouse-colored steed to join our wedding guests. We cannot march without you!"

This he finished and then he wrote twelve messages to be sent to the twelve imperial captains in the city of Cazin, each of whom commands a thousand men. And thus Hasan Pasha implored them (6750): "I pray you, leaders of Cazin! Have you heard of Kanidža, that bloody place, and of our Hadji Smailaga? He has found a bride, Fatima of Buda, who must be won by battle, for his son the alaybey, who has but recently assumed the command, and who with his sword will receive his baptism of blood in our imperial Buda. I pray you, insofar as you are able, mount your steeds and prepare your standard-bearers! Gather the adventurous men of Cazin, who defend their homeland from the enemy, who sacrifice their heads, but do not surrender their land. We depart in fifteen days. Come as quickly as you can!"

These he sent, and then he wrote seven messages to be sent to bloody Bihać, to the seven imperial captains, even the two Kozlići, the three Huremagići, and the two Poprženovići from the depths of Bihać. Thus Hasan Pasha wrote them: "Captains, heroes of the sultan, blood-stained warriors from Bihać, you are ever heroes of the sultan! Have you heard of our Kanidža, where old Smail the alaybey lives? He has found a bride for his son the new commander, the beautiful Fata Zajimova in Buda. But she must be won by fighting. The vizier has taken away her happiness in order to give her to General Peter of Bogdan, an enemy of our faith. If we do not put a stop to this, he will soon betray the empire, and the Magyars will overrun Bosnia, the Germans and the Magyars together. Our faith will be subject to the infidel. So I pray you in the name of merciful God, gather as large an army as you can. The men of Bihać are blood-stained heroes. We cannot go without you. And I pray you not to delay, not longer than fifteen days, if possible. Be in Kanidža on the twentieth."

These he sent, and then he wrote a letter and directed it to the commander of Klis. "Commander, head of all Klis, (6800) read well what the letter from our Hasan Pasha Tiro says. Have you heard of our Kanidža, of our hero Smailaga? He has found a bride for his son Mehmed the new alaybey, Fatima of Buda, the dear daughter of Zajim Alibeg, who must be won in battle. Her happiness has been taken away by the imperial vizier in Buda. He is giving her to our enemy General Peter of Bogdan. And so I pray you as mine own bey, gather as great an army as you can in Klis and near Klis. Do not delay, but hasten to Kanidža. We depart in fifteen days. Come and help us, O bey, not only for the sake of Hadji Smailaga and his son Mehmed, but for the sake of God and our empire, for the faith of every Turk, that we may wipe out our enemy. O bey, you must not delay the army. Come at its head on your piebald steed."

This he sent and wrote another letter, and addressed it to the city of Sarajevo, to the Turk Sehidić Pasha. "My dear brother, Sehidić Pasha. Read well this letter from your friend Hasan Pasha of Kanidža, that blood-stained place. Mount your Syrian mare and gather together the young men of Sarajevo. Pasha, I need twelve thousand young men, handsome as maidens. I do not wish any without breastplates, none that have not imperial plumes on their heads. Nor do I wish horses without full panoply. For, O pasha, the army of Sarajevo is the flower and ornament of all Bosnia. You shall go before us even as the sultan before his courtiers. We cannot go without you. We must fight a battle near Buda, that, if almighty God grants, we may put an end to the vizier and bring complaint against him before the sultan. Let the sultan see whom he has sent, how he has betrayed the imperial cities, taken captives and slaves, and executed many heroes. Let us ask the sultan (6850) if he is in agreement with what the vizier is doing."

This he sent and then wrote another letter, and he directed it to Tarić Omer the captain in level Visoko.[136] "O Tarić, young lord, see, my son, what this letter from your friend Hasan Pasha Tiro says. Have you heard of our Kanidža, of our alaybey Smailaga, whose name is mighty, and whom the sultan and the Christian kings both know? Whenever anyone was in need he has gone to their aid and has warded off evil from all, keeping steadfast the foundations of all Bosnia for forty-seven years, for he has held the imperial command. Now, my son, captain Tara, he has found a bride for his son Mehmed the new alaybey, Fata Zajimova in Buda. But Fatima cannot be won without a struggle, for she has two challengers, one, my, son, General Peter of Bogdan, the enemy of our faith, and the other, still worse, the Vizier of Buda, who is working day and night to betray Bosnia and the Border, and to mutilate the empire of the sultan. So I pray you as my own son to gather all of Visoko and level Zenica, and to summon also Šahić, the standard-bearer of Maglaj. Let the standard-bearer gather the men of Maglaj and come on his piebald horse to Kanidža, he on his piebald and you with him on your jet-black steed. We cannot go without the two of you."

This letter he sent, and then he wrote another and addressed it to the city of Mostar, to Mostar the noble market-town, to the Turk Ćemalović Bey.[137] "Ćemalbey of Hercegovina, wings of all Bosnia, see, my brother, what the pasha writes, even Hasan Pasha Tiro of Kanidža. Have you heard what has happened here to our former alaybey, to Smailaga the imperial hero? He has found a bride for his son Mehmed, the new alaybey, Fata Zajimova of Buda. (6900) But Fatima is not to be won without a struggle. Her lot has been made hard by the treacherous vizier, the betrayer of our whole country. He has enslaved Fata and is sending her to Bogdan, to give her to General Peter, to honor thus with a gift the enemy of our faith. He is giving up our faith for unbelief. Bey of Mostar, our pride, I pray you as my own brother to raise all Hercegovina. Tell the hero Ahmet Ljubović[138] to mount his white horse, and let him bring Dževetić Bey from Trebinje on the borders of Hercegovina. And come yourself at their head, to be of help to us in the name of God and with his aid. Let us see what the vizier is doing."

These he sent, and then he wrote other letters, even two to the sources of the Cetina,[139] to the two imperial beys of Cetina, the hero Babahmetović and the Turk Zenković Bey. And thus he implored them: "My lords, even as my own two brothers, see what the pasha writes, even Hasan Tiro of Kanidža. Let me tell you what has happened here to Hadji Smailaga, our foremost protector of the faith. He has found a bride for his son Mehmed, our new alaybey, Fatima of Buda, who must be won in battle. Fatima's happiness has been taken away by the treacherous Vizier of Buda, and by our enemy General Peter of Kara Bogdan. The vizier and the general intend to drape Bosnia and the Border in black as they have already done to Buda. So I pray you, as my own two brothers, to gather as large an army from Cetina as you can, my dear brothers, so that you may help us."

These letters he sent and wrote two more. One he addressed to Sirdar Hrnjica, commander of the entire army of Bosnia. And thus Hasan Pasha wrote: "O thou our golden plume, (6950) honored one, Sirdar Hrnjica, commander of all the armies of Bosnia, have you heard what has happened in Kanidža that imperial city? We have a new alaybey, the dear son of Hadji Smail. We have given him the command and have found a bride for him, that with God's help and with yours we may marry him off. Prepare your spotted horse, your white one with ears hanging. As long as you are with us good fortune is ours. Your white horse is a fortunate one for a Turk, and your brother Halil is the protective wings of the whole Border. You know, Mujo, what your place is. You are the commander of the whole army. Smailaga desires your Halil to be the groom's representative with the girl. This honor is given to your house, that you are the leader of every army, and Halil, Mujo, is groom's representative for every young man's bride among us. There is no summer without St. George's Day, there is no brother until a mother bears him, there are no burning coals without an oaken stump, nor battles without your family. And so I pray of you, as leader of the army, mount your white horse, and bring Halil. Bedeck yourself like an imperial vizier, and Halil like a pasha's courtier. And, Mujo, gather three hundred of your men of Kladuša, men of evil father and of worse mother, who cut off the heads of heroes, who sever heads and bind men alive. It is your army of Kladuša that tears the souls from the living. O Mujo, when your swords whistle through the air, all the enemy groans before them. Then, our golden wings, come with your heroes to help us. We send special greetings to you Hrnjičići. Without you we cannot go."

This he sent and then wrote another, and addressed it to Oruljce, that

broad village between the Lika and Vrljika, to the hands of the hero Grdan
Osmanaga, and his son Grdić Husein.[140] "O hero Grda Osmanaga, see what
the pasha writes you, (7000) even Hasan Pasha, your right wing. Have you heard
what has happened here to our former alaybey, Hadji Smail of Kanidža? He has
found a bride for his son Mehmed, the new alaybey, Fatima the daughter of Alibeg
in Buda, one of the best families. But Fata cannot be wôn without a fight. The vizier
together with our enemy General Peter has taken away her happiness. And so, Grda
Osmanaga, mount your white-hoofed mare, bring your standard-bearer, Grdić Husein, on his dapple-gray steed, and bring with you also a thousand heroes. Do you
know, Osman, where your position will be? Your company has always taken up its
position at the standards where there are fortifications and barricades. This time
take your place at the drawbridge over the Klima, on this side of the plain of Muhač, on Mount Šemeško. There we shall dig a ditch and construct barricades, twelve
barricades along the ditch, and behind them the twelve cannon of Mustajbeg; these
shall be the forts and trenches for your army. While the wedding guests go to Buda,
however many there may be, and return, at the Mount Šemeško you must hold off
the mighty army of Kara Bogdan, so that they may not capture Mount Šemeško
and bring the beginning of disaster upon us. We shall add to your army either that
from Udbina or Donji Otok, from Vrljika, or from Cetina. It was long ago discovered that wherever you took your position at the standards you always brightened
our honor and brought confusion to the armies of the enemy. That is why they call
you 'Grda Osman.' "

He sent this letter off straightway, and then the pasha wrote another
and sent it to level Udbina, to the aged Ćejvan in Udbina and to his son Mehmed. He told him the whole situation. "Gather the army of Udbina. The men of
Udbina are blood-stained heroes, (7050) young men like wolves of the mountain.
Each one of them is a match for seven of the enemy. Mount your swan-white horse,
my lord,[141] and bring your son on his chestnut steed. Come to our aid, Ćejvanaga. Bring
as large an army as you can."

This he sent and wrote another, and addressed it to Captain Hadži of
Meki Do on the plain of Udbina. "Captain from the plain of Udbina, heed
well what this letter from our Hasan Pasha Tiro says. We have found a bride
for our new alaybey, Mehmed, the son of Smail, but she must be fought for,
the jewel Fatima of Buda, the dear daughter of Zajim Alibeg. But Fata cannot be
won without a fight. The vizier has taken away her happiness, the vizier and the
general of Bogdan, our great enemy, with him. And so, hadji, prepare your Bedouin
mare and gather the men of Donja Udbina, of Udbina and Meki Do, and come to
our aid. We depart in only fifteen days."

He sent the letter off and wrote still another, even to Otoka and to Ribnik, to

the Turk Alagić Alija. He told him the whole situation. After sending this, he
straightway wrote another and addressed it to the village of Orahovo, to the Turk
Begzadić Rizvan. When he had dispatched this, again he wrote a letter, and sent it
to Stijena Žuta, to Zukanaga, the imperial captain. This he sent and wrote another,
and sent it to Orlić Mustafaga,[142] telling him all that had happened. After he had
dispatched this note, he wrote another, and sent it to Alem Kadunić.[143] Then he
wrote again and addressed the letter to Vlahinjić Alija.[144] (7100) This he sent off
and wrote a new one, this time to Šarac Mahmutaga.[145] This he dispatched and
wrote another, directing it to Kunić Hasanaga.[146] This he sent off, and a final letter
he wrote and sent to Ramo of Glamoč, telling him the whole situation.

Then he began to ponder. There were no more letters to be sent.
The pasha had told every man who had carried a well-writ letter to fire
off his pistols from horseback and to cry out, like an imperial crier:
"Whoever intends with God's help this day to defend his fatherland, let
him join the wedding guests of the hadji. Today it shall be known in
Buda, when we go to accompany Fata Zajimova, whether Bosnia will be
lost forever, or whether it will flourish for many years to come." Then
Hasan Pasha Tiro said: "Now, O hadji, I have not disturbed you. I have
written letters and dispatched my warriors, but I have not called into
service your own honor guardsmen. Now send your men out wherever
you wish, old sir, and give them whatever orders you desire. You have
five hundred serfs. You have pasture lands on the mountains; your serfs
will do your bidding and dig a ditch in the plain of Kanidža. Drive in
your cows and oxen, slaughter your sheep and fattened rams. Gather
the wedding guests and accompany them hence. Give them food and
give them drink. Even then you will not spend very much, if fate and
almighty God are kind. All the leaders of the wedding guests who come
to the wedding will bring you some contribution. One will bring cows,
another oxen, one sheep, another rams, someone will give you horses
covered with blankets, and some will bring ready money, and later, if
fortune smiles on you and Fata marries your son, there will be enough
left so that you will then be able to buy Kanidža and all the villages
around Kanidža.

"I have invited all I knew, (7150) but I have not invited him who is
the best of all, Lički Tale of Orašac. If I write that kind of letter to Tale,
since Tale will not pay any heed to the warriors anyway, he will not
leave his house or even listen to you. You know how Tale is accustomed
to act. Without money he won't stir his limbs. Send him some ducats
by your guardsman Husein. Let him prepare his sorrel and take some

ducats in a gold-embroidered kerchief, and let him go to Tale in Orašac. And tell your guardsman Husein to be careful and not lose his head foolishly. Let him approach Talaga wisely, and not waste foolish words. When Husein comes to Tale's house, he will find that it is of three stories. On three sides it is propped up by forked sticks, and it is not covered by a roof on three sides. On the fourth side it is patched together with boards. There is a courtyard of birchwood around the house and in the courtyard a gate of alder wood, which has neither bolt nor bar. O Husein, my dear one, dismount from your horse right before the courtyard, then listen, my son, before the gateway, to see whether you can perhaps hear Tale within the house. Listen to what Tale is saying, whether he is talking with his mother, with his mother or with his true love, or with his sister the mad Aziza, or whether Tale is, my son, in the courtyard sharpening his sword on the whetstone, or in the stable shoeing his mouse-gray steed. If God and mighty good fortune grant, you will get along easily with him in the courtyard. But, as long as Tale is not in the house with his mother, he will not be in an angry furor and you may call Tale to the gate. But don't be bewitched by the devils and attempt to open the door to the courtyard, Husein. It has no fastenings or hinges, but is propped up by a forked stick of boxwood. It might fall and crush you, and you would lose your head without having drawn your sword." And Husein said to the bey: "My dear pasha, and you Smailaga, (7200) where it was easy to deliver letters, you gave them to the warriors, to distribute to the Turkish heroes. But you send me to mad Tale to lose my wretched head. I would rather deliver all your other letters in all four directions, than that single one to the fool Tale." Then Smailaga said to him: "Here, my son, are fifty ducats. Give them to Tale of Orašac, approach his right hand, my son, and give Tale greetings from the hadji. Tell him I have found a bride for my son. Tell him where Fatima is from, of what house she is, whose daughter she is, and who her challengers are. Let him prepare himself and his mouse-gray steed, and the Turk Hodža Šuvajlija, and his standard-bearer Belaj."[147] Husein was not pleased at this, but he had no other choice. "And, my son, give him these fifty ducats, and say: 'This is for you, Tale. Hadji Smailaga has sent it to you, that you may leave it at home for your wife, your old mother, and your little children. When you arrive in Kanidža, Tale, more ducats will be waiting for you. You will not lack for expenses. If Allah is kind and we complete a battle with the general and with the vizier, that imperial traitor, and overcome both those forces, then

Tale, if we have our old good fortune, your mouse-gray horse will not be able to carry your treasures.' Say this to him and then return, and you will see what Tale says as to whether he will come or not."

Then the guardsman prepared his black horse and mounted and led it to the gate of the town. He crossed the plain and entered the mountains; he passed through villages and traversed the ranges. Finally he arrived in Orašac at the house of Tale of Orašac. When he came up to Talaga's house, he found everything just as the pasha had described it to him, and the guardsman Husein was struck with amazement; he wondered how Tale's children could survive in this great squalor. (7250) The guardsman went quietly alongside the courtyard until he arrived with his horse before the gateway. There he dismounted from his black steed and went to listen and find out where Tale was, with whom he was talking and at whom he was swearing. Troublous doubts seized on Husein, but fortune was good to him. Tale was not in the house, but he was sharpening his sword in the courtyard. Tale was making so much noise with his sword that one would say a whole band of men had started a great quarrel.

Thus Tale was speaking to his sword: "My sword, do you wish to be deserted! I have sharpened you every day in the week, for full three months. I lie here hungry and thirsty in my house, and my miserable children are dying. I don't put in an appearance before my wife; I don't dare come into her sight, for she curses me and is quite wretched; 'Away from here, you ugly Turkish clown! What are a wife and little children to you, since you're not able to provide for them at least a crust of dry bread? They have never become used to eating butter and eggs and vegetables!' A curse on Bosnia and the Border, for the agas of old times are gone, those who used to raise bands for raids and whole armies to attack infidels. They used all to receive me well and keep me well. I always had ducats in my pocket. I was able to buy drink for myself and give something to my wife. And the young people used to get married more often and to invite me sometimes to their weddings. Of course, no one used to invite me to be the elder wedding guest, but only to be their chief herald.[148] But those times were more profitable than these. I would take my drum and go from wedding guest to wedding guest. One would give me a penny, and another perhaps four. Of course there weren't any ducats, but I realized a guinea or two from the young men, and from the girls a silk bundle with trousers and a shirt in it, and a golden pillow cover and kerchief. I put the trousers on my own legs right away (7300) and gave the shirt to my wife. She would make three shirts out of the one, and give one to my old mother, put one on her own back, and give the third to my mad sister Aziza,[149] so that she wouldn't run naked around the streets. I would twist the kerchief around my head in place of a turban, and weave in my plumes, and the children would make fun of me. I would hide the pillow cover from my true love and give it to my crazy sister and say to her: 'Crazy Aziza, gather a trousseau, in case some one will marry you.' Damn her![150] No one wants her. Crazy girls don't get married. She is worse than all my other sorrows."

The guardsman Husein heard all this that Tale was saying to his sword. "It's wretched for Tale![151] The old people have died. No longer do raiding bands gather, nor armies. Young men have become wiser and marry their wives secretly without gathering wedding guests or anything else. I have fallen upon great sorrows! Now, my sword, I shall sharpen you just this once more, and wait a week. Then I will take you to the blacksmith and have him make two swords out of you. I shall sell one of them to feed my children, to feed them and defend them from evil. Hell, no,[152] I can't even do that! I haven't a penny, how then a ducat, to pay the smith his fee. And there is no way out of that either. If I were to sell my spirited mouse-gray horse, I have neither barley nor hay to stuff him and make him fat. If he were fat—may the wolves eat him! —I might exchange him and take an even worse horse. I wouldn't ride him uphill, just a little on the level plain, but not a bit uphill, but he might carry my long rifle.[153] No one would want him as he is now, not for a single wretched dinar!" And now the guardsman Husein thought: "It seems to me, looking at Tale, that he has fallen on great misery. He is in need of a shiny penny and of yellow ducats. (7350) If I give him fifty ducats and tell him there are more in Kanidža, he will not kill me."

Then the guardsman Husein called out from the street in front of Tale's gate: "Hadji Tale, may God give you health! Come out here and open the gate. I am one who was sent to you. People have sent me to you." Then Tale spoke to him thus: "Who is calling me from the street? I am not a shepherd with his flock, but the hero Tahiraga.[154] I am sharpening my sword and preparing for war." And the guardsman Husein said to him: "Tahiraga, by my faith! Your gate is not like any in our Border. It hasn't either a knocker or a bell. But I have heard people say, and now I see with my own eyes, I have heard people say that I should be very careful, that the gates are not fastened to anything, neither by rings nor by hinges, but they are propped up by forked sticks of box-wood. If I were to kick them they would fall, and the boxwood branches would crush me. Thus I would die without having drawn a sword." Then Tale spoke as follows: "Who told you about that? A curse upon[155] his father and mother!" He left the sword on the whetstone and took away the supports from the alder gates and opened both sides. Tale rubbed his hands. His palms were as dirty from the whetstone and the sharp sword as if he had been mixing charcoal. Husein was in a quandary, be-cause the pasha had ordered him to kiss Tale's right hand. "How shall I kiss his hand?" he thought, but there was no help for it, so he flew to his hand. Huso was lucky, however. Tale wouldn't let him! Huso put his hand in his pockets to give him the kerchief with the ducats.

Then Tale spoke as follows: "Where are you from, stranger from afar? What have you in that kerchief, my son, dinars or small change?"[156] (7400) "Hadji Tale, may God give you health! They are neither dinars nor small change, but yellow imperial ducats.[157] I am from level Kanid-ža, friend of Hadji Smailaga. The alaybey has sent me to you, the alay-bey and the Turk Hasan Pasha Tiro. They send you special greetings. The hadji has found a bride for Mehmed the new alaybey, Fata Zaji-mova of Buda. But Fatima cannot be won without a fight. The vizier has taken away her happiness and given her to General Peter. He sent her off with fifty warriors. Mehmed had gone with Osman the standard-bearer to the Vizier of Buda and had met the fifty warriors, Tale, with their imperial captain. They engaged in combat with them and killed the imperial captain and twenty five of the warriors. The rest fled to Buda. He took Fatima back to Buda, became betrothed to the jewel, Fata, and assumed the command from his two elders. Now old Hadji Smailaga is preparing a wedding and gathering wedding guests. He sends you special greetings, and asks you to prepare yourself and your mouse-gray horse, to bring Hodža Šuvajlija, and Belaj the standard-bearer, and three hundred men of Orašac. There are fifty ducats here to give to your true love. Don't leave a single one for yourself, for there are others waiting for you, Talaga, for the expenses of your trip to Buda. If God's help be with us, and we overcome their two forces, if, Tale, our old luck holds, your mouse-gray horse will not be able to carry the money you will earn." But Tale flared up and began to curse. "Why that Meh-med! the bastard![158] So he went down to Buda and stole my bride-to-be! Didn't Mehmed know, the whoreson, that Fata was my betrothed, and has been for a whole year? (7450) I have sent her seven letters, asking her if she will have me. I don't know what the bitch is doing. She hasn't given me any answer. Three times I have been to Buda and walked around the city, but I haven't seen her. Tell Mehmed, the son of Hadji Smail, that if it were not for my friend the hadji, I would challenge him to a duel, that we might decide with the sword who would take Fata. Alas and alack, I had thought to take her to be my wife, that I might live on her property. But the young bitch deceived me! So give my greetings to Hadji Smail. I cannot offend him, I shall come with my comrades to join the wedding guests, but I won't even exchange a greeting with Mehmed,[159] because he has stolen my betrothed." The guardsman heard him at the gate, and had he dared, he would have burst from laughing at Tale.

Then the hadji's friend mounted his black horse and returned to Kanidža. He told the whole story to the assembly at his aga's house. For a whole hour he told of his conversation with Tale. All listened to the guardsman Husein. No one drank wine or brandy, but all laughed at Tale of Orašac. Then they began to drink anew.

Smail called both his village elders,[160] Marijan and Mališa, to come to his house with the men of the Border. When his two village elders came, they entered and gave him good day, put their hands over their hearts, and flew to the hem of the pasha's robe. They embraced the pasha and the hadji, the Turk Cifrić Hasanaga, the two fortress commanders and the four elders, and then moved aside to wait upon them. The hadji made room for both his village elders on chairs near him. He gave them red wine to drink and served them, drinking a toast with them, he with his coffee cup and they with their glasses. (7500) "Your healths, my friends! I had hoped to see you before. Now I am celebrating two events. The command has passed to my son, and at the same time he has become betrothed to a maid of noble house and lineage. People say she is a perfect match for my son. But her happiness has been taken away by the vizier, our traitor. My children, the vizier wanted to send her to Bogdan as a gift to our enemy, the General of Kara Bogdan. But my son Mehmed happened along, with Osman, my golden wings, my standard-bearer. God granted that they destroy the warriors and take away the wondrous coach. He has wooed her against the will of the vizier, and he has taken the command upon himself. Now I am gathering Bosnia for my son, as though the men of Bosnia were going to a wedding, but in reality they are setting out for a mighty war, one to be remembered forever. Even now, my children, I have sent the letters of invitation and set the date for the assembling. O my village elders, will you be of help to me? You are the elders of my serfs. Take serfs and tenants and dig narrow trenches to build fires in. I shall give over to you the mountain pastures and corrals, cows, and oxen in droves, sheep and lambs in herds, to deal with as you see fit. But by no means must you use your own sheep. God be praised, I have enough of everything myself; I can take care of this wedding! If fate is kind to me, and Fatima comes to Kanidža with my son Mehmed, the wedding will easily[161] be worth the pains. Be of help to me, entertain the army before it leaves, and meet it when it returns. But, village elders, I do not wish to force you in any way, unless you really desire to help (7550) in whatever way you and my serfs wish."

Then both elders arose: "Our hadji, our reflection! What are you saying? Your grandfather and your father were judges among us, O hadji, your grandfather among our grandfathers, your father among our fathers, and you these many years among us. You are our very wings. You never use force against us, but always protect us from others' violence. May God preserve your only son! May his joy be complete! May he live and lead the army even as his father and uncle have done! May all go honorably and well with them at Buda; may they destroy the traitor's power and look their fill on his discomfort! May they kill the general, and may the wedding guests bring Fatima back with them! May she be blessed to your son for many, many years! May you live to see her serve in your home and bear sons!" "Thank you, thank you, my village elders! May you too obtain what you desire!" But the elders said: "O hadji, we are yet somewhat angry with you. Why have you left us only to act as servants? Among your five hundred serfs, each house has at least two men, and many of them four. All of them are happily married, and their houses are full of children and sons. Why do you not take one of the two village elders and make him a company commander, to lead five hundred serfs, that we may join the wedding guests. In the name of God and your own health! We have horses and saddles, and you could arm us quickly. Then would God and the Border see how your serfs would help you. Even if they should all lose their lives there, one or two would be left in each house. We have a ready abundance of children.[162] We would not notice the difference at home, and they would be of help to you. Let the rest of us wait upon you!" "Thank you, my elders. (7600) The time of need has not yet come. I am keeping you like golden wings for that time in the future when Mehmed must help the sultan against some mighty king. Then you will do deeds to be remembered. You have always been incomparably loyal to us."

Then the two young village elders left; Smail called his forty guardsmen and spoke to them as follows: "Guardsmen and retainers,[163] you know where the storage chamber of Sulejman is, over which Hasan Pasha has charge, not the storage for weapons, but for tents. It was prepared for us for an emergency, when we might wage war with someone, so that we could have tents for battle, to use wherever we needed them. Hasan Pasha stored them away. There are a thousand Janissaries there, without weapons, without steeds, and without their sharp swords at their sides. They will help you pitch the tents on the plain. Put them up in sections according to their colors, first the white, then the red, thirdly the blue, fourthly the green, and fifthly those colored yellow. The imperial army will lodge in some, the Janissaries from the two Borders, those from our Border, and those from Travnik. Let the Janissaries take the white tents, and all the armies of the beys, the red and blue ones. Let the armies of the agas take the green tents, and then those of the sirdars and company commanders, the elders and the captains, and the rank and file of the Border can use the yellow tents. Thus the commanders will know where their armies and their standards are, and in which tents they belong." The young men ran across the plain. The Janissaries opened the storage chamber. From the bottom of the level plain of Kanidža to the foothills of the mountains is a space of exactly six hours' journey. In this place they pitched the tents by kinds, (7650) even as the old man had ordered. It was all done in two days and two nights. They had scarcely finished, when the serfs drove in the steers and herds of Smail the alaybey. They dug ditches in the plain and lit fires in them. Then they put the meat of oxen and sterile cows, of sheep and wethers on the fire. The smoke from the huge fires under the caldrons wove its way to the heavens. One would say that the mountains were burning.

And when the time and the season came, Hasan Pasha called his Janissaries. They prepared the horses of Kanidža, and then he gave them the following orders: "My four thousand Janissaries! Take your places in order upon the plain! Whenever any Bosnian hero arrives, be he pasha or commander of a thousand, elder or imperial captain, aga or imperial beylerbey, or the chief imperial company commanders, who command five hundred men, give greeting to him. This do every day while the army is assembling. It is fitting for a hero to do honor to heroes in his own household and leave remembrance of himself, that they may praise us as long as the world lasts." So the army of Janissaries scattered. The four thousand Janissaries sat themselves down to await the Turks. They stuck their spears in the ground before their tents and tied their horses to them. Then the divisional standards were unfurled. Fifes squealed and drums beat, and from the ramparts cannon roared before dawn in the city of Kanidža.

Now Mount Kozara rumbled, and the pasha and the hadji turned their gaze in that direction. A standard shone, plumes glistened, and the imperial pasha from Travnik came out upon the plain on his mighty swan-white steed. He had an imperial cap of gold with Janissary's plumes in it. Before the pasha were twelve mercenaries, leading twelve reserve mounts, (7700) entirely blanketed in fine cloth from the top of their heads to the green grass. These were gifts to Hadji Smailaga. Behind the Turk Pašić Ibrahim rode twelve divisional standards and twelve thousand Janissaries, on mighty stallions and Bedouin mares. The equipment on all the horses was alike, their saddles and their trappings. The weapons on the horses were all the same, and their bits and reins, and the rifles across their saddle horns. The heroes too all wore the same uniforms; red breeches on their thighs, and the coats of Janissaries on their backs. Their caps and plumes were all alike, and the spears across their shoulders. The army filled[164] Kozara. The standards waved, and the sharp swords hung by the horses' sides; one would say they were dusky snakes. Pašić himself was dressed in pure gold, and his swan-white horse in golden trappings. Behind him were twelve cannon, and the supply and ammunition train. The pasha carried a sack of gold coins to spend on the trip to Buda, from the time he left until he returned. Hasan Pasha Tiro saw the pasha across the plain, and his trumpet blew on the ramparts. The well-trained Janissaries arose and stood at attention before the tents, they and the guardsmen of Hadji Smail. When Pašić Ibrahim arrived he salaamed in response. Then pasha sat beside pasha, and the hadji together with them. The two pashas shook hands and inquired after one another's peace and health. The pasha congratulated the bey. "Congratulations on the passing of the command to your son, and on Fatima who has been betrothed to your son!" Servants placed a cloak about the pasha's shoulders and lighted his water pipe. At the tents the Janissaries of the pasha (7750) unfurled their standards and stacked their war spears around the tents. To the spears they tied their mares, all Bedouin mares from Syria. The cannon were placed at the edge of the plain beneath Karashko Mountain, by the passes through which they will go to Buda. There they stayed and rested.

There was no wind, but Mount Kozara rumbled; the clover grass cried out, and divisional standards came into view. Hungarian heroes struck up a song, and the beylerbey from the broad Lika emerged onto the plain riding a tall dove-colored horse. He wore a golden helmet with twelve imperial plumes. It is impossible to describe that mighty hero, to tell how powerful and noble he was. He was dressed in clothes of gold, and his dove-colored horse was tall in its trappings. Sorry would be the pasha or vizier who might be compared with the mighty bey of the Lika. His harness was better than a vizier's. Before the beylerbey were twelve mercenaries, behind him seven standard-bearers. And what standard-bearers! And what horses! They were winged, and the youths on them were like dragons. Their breastplates were of gold, and they had imperial plumes. By their thighs hung their swords and over their shoulders their bone-breaking spears. The staffs of the standards were encased in metal and tipped with golden apples. The banners waved over the young men, and the ornaments of gold touched even to the third reserve bearer. All seven standard-bearers were gathered around Mustajbeg, even as seven nobles around the sultan. Behind them was an army of twelve thousand men, all men of the Lika, all imperial cavalry, Hungarians like living fire. After the mighty Mustajbeg had appeared and behind him his twelve cannon and the supply and ammunition train, the beylerbey advanced across the plain, and the trumpet of Hasan Pasha blew. The Janissaries stood at attention, and the guardsmen received the bey. (7800) The army of the Lika went to the tents, but they led the beylerbey to the hadji. When the bey arrived in the house, he salaamed, and the pashas arose. They took one another's white hands and gave greeting to the Bey of the Lika. Then they made room for him by the pasha, and they shook hands. They inquired for one another's peace and health, and the bey congratulated the hadji: "I congratulate you on the passing of the command to your son, and on your son's wedding!" "So be it, O bey, and may your desires also be fulfilled! May you marry off your daughters and sons!" Servants brought drinks and served them; they lighted his water pipe and threw a purple cloak about his shoulders. His army joined the others at the tents, and his cannon were placed near the others.

It was not long before Mount Kozara rumbled, although there was no wind; divisional standards came in view, and pistols were shot off in pairs. An imperial beylerbey appeared on a tall black horse. He was entirely submerged in yellow gold, and his black horse had trappings of gold. He wore an imperial cap with twelve plumes. Both the horse and the warrior shone as the moon. Before him rode twelve mercenaries, and behind him twelve standard-bearers. Merciful heavens, who was this beylerbey? It was Fetibegović from Banja Luka, with twelve thousand Turks, all horsemen, not a single man on foot. The riders wore breastplates on their chests and on their heads imperial plumes. The horses had trappings and saddles, and on their breasts were gleaming ornaments. When the pashas saw the bey, they all jumped up in their excitement and pleasure, leaned their foreheads against the win-

dow, and thanked God for such a bey. From Mount Kozara the bey came to Kanidža. When he emerged upon the plain of Kanidža, the trumpet of Hasan Pasha blew,
the Janissaries stood at attention, and then the guardsmen welcomed Fetibeg. Some
of them led him into the house to the hadji, (7850) and others took his horse to the
stables. When Fetibeg came to the pasha, he salaamed and stood among them. They
all arose and welcomed him, then they sat down and gave him greeting. They inquired
for one another's peace and health. When they had said that they were well, servants
lighted his pipe and offered them all various kinds of drinks. Each took whatever he
desired. And now Fetibeg congratulated Hadji Smailaga: "I congratulate you on
your new alaybey, and on Zajim's daughter as his wife. May she be blessed and
fortunate!" "So be it, O bey! May you enjoy good health!" And so they sat and
rested themselves.

There was no wind, but Mount Kozara rumbled, and there appeared an imperial commander, Omeraga of Jajce, on a tall gray horse. What a hero Omeraga
was! He was a mighty youth in rich clothes, and his steed was mighty, as though it
had wings. Behind him came a green divisional standard and a thousand heroes of
Jajce, all horsemen, not a single one on foot. They rode stallions and mares, Bed-
ouins from Syria. Their commander was fine and mighty; behind him was a mighty
standard-bearer, and behind the standard was a mighty army. The beyler bey descended Mount Kozara, and the men rejoiced at the sight of that aga, his horse, and
his mighty standard-bearer. He came down from the heights of Kozara onto the
green plain of Kanidža. The trumpet of Hasan Pasha sounded, and the Janissaries
leaped to attention before him and saluted. Some guardsmen took his horse, and
others the hero himself; him they led to the hadji's house and the horse to the warm
stable. The imperial hero salaamed, and they all greeted him and gave him a place of
honor. All sat in order, one beside the other. (7900) Then he congratulated Smailaga
on the new command for his son, and for his son's happy marriage to Fatima of
Buda. Smailaga replied: "Thank you, my friend!" Once again the glasses of wine flew
around, that the one might drink to the other's health and honor and to a successful journey for the wedding-guests of the new alaybey. Thus they sat and took their
satisfaction.

There was no wind, but Mount Kozara rumbled, and the pashas and beys
gazed towards it. An imperial hero came into view on a tall stallion. He was entirely
submerged in pure gold, wore an imperial helmet and imperial plumes, a steel
corselet on his breast, and a bone-breaking spear on his shoulders. One would say he
was an imperial vizier. His decorations were exactly like a vizier's. Behind him were
four standard-bearers and an army of four thousand men. All the pashas and beys
arose to gaze at this mighty hero. He was mighty and noble, without a single peer.
But they were all amazed at one thing. Every aga and every imperial bey and all the

other imperial elders, imperial captains, and company commanders wore his sword on the left side, but this warrior was wearing it on his right thigh. Who is this? What can this strange thing be? Why is he wearing his saber on the wrong side? Then Mustajbeg of the Lika spoke: "Pashas, our golden wings! Do you not really remember him? That is Ljevak[165] Omeraga. He cuts off heads with his left hand, and that is why he carries his sword on the right side. Do you not see, imperial pashas, that is Ljevak Omeraga! With his left arm he has cut his way from Lenger to Silitor.[166] The kingdoms fear him. He is a fierce serpent without peer." Then the pashas thanked God for him and for his horse, his mighty standard-bearers, and his strong army. The young Omeraga came down (7950) from Mount Kozara to the green plain, and the trumpet of Hasan Pasha sounded. The Janissaries stood at attention. Gazi Omer salaamed in Turkish fashion. Some guardsmen took the aga, and some his horse. They led the horse to the stable, but the imperial aga went to the hadji's dwelling. All in order received his salaam and greeted him. They made a place for him among them. Drink stood ready for him, and he congratulated the hadji on the command and on the wedding. He replied: "Thank you, Omeraga!" And so the conversation and the entertainment continued.

There was no wind, but Mount Kozara rumbled. The lords of Kanidža looked and saw how Mount Kozara was enveloped as in a net. Praise be to God for his help! One would say that the army of the sultan was coming under the command of imperial generals. The two pashas were amazed, and asked Mustajbeg of the Lika what mighty force this could be coming from Kozara. "Imperial pashas, our hope! Those are the twelve imperial captains from beyond the Una, from Unđurovina, who raise an army without a firman and without a decree from the vizier. Each one has a standard-bearer and a thousand heroes. Each one is an equal of seven men. Those youths are like wolves from the mountains, and they are as handsome as mountain spirits." Then the pashas thanked God for this. "Thanks be to God and to this house, since we have such champions as these. We can still rule with ease, rule and reign." The captains came out upon the plain, and the trumpet of Hasan Pasha blew. The imperial Janissaries hastened to come to a salute before each of them, and they each returned the salute with a Turkish salaam. Then the guardsmen received the horses and the heroes. They led the horses into the dark stable, and the captains to the white dwelling. The imperial champions salaamed. All those in the hadji's dwelling (8000) greeted the beys on their feet and took them by their white hands. They made room for each of them and greeted them. They inquired for one another's peace and health. The eyes of all flew to gaze at this mighty force and these heroes. Now golden cups were brought, and pleasant conversation passed amongst them. The armies mingled with one another, and men began to dance heroic kolos.[167] The divisional standards waved in the wind, the Bosnians sang as they danced, the drums of the pasha beat, and the fifes and trumpets sounded. The stallions neighed and the mares whinnied. The tents were like cities, and the standards like clouds in the sky. The battle spears were like a thick forest.[168] O dear God! Those were mighty armies on the broad plain of Kanidža. One would say that a firman had come from the sultan and the imperial commanders, that they had gathered the whole army for a war, that the sultan was fighting with the emperor. The ranks of the army rejoiced, and so also the bey in the white halls.

There was no wind, but Mount Kozara rumbled; the lords looked out from the halls, and two imperial beys appeared, two heroes from the two imperial Janjas, from the two Janjas, the two Bijeljinas, even Fildus̆ and Fildis̆. Both beys had their own horses, both of them gray. The beys wore golden helmets, and on their backs crimson capes, woven with golden branches, with snakes meeting on the shoulders. They wore corselets of steel and carried mighty battle spears on their shoulders. Along their thighs hung their sabers, which glistened as the lights in the heavens. Behind them were two standard-bearers, and behind them two thousand men, all horsemen and splendid fighters.[169] O dear God! What an army that was! And what commanders it had! The commanders were like imperial nobles, and the army was inspired,[170] (8050) with spirited horses beneath it. The black earth trembled beneath them. In the hall all rose to gaze upon the two captains, Fildus̆ and Fildis̆. They thanked God for them. The captains arrived upon the plain, and the trumpet of Hasan Pasha blew. The Janissaries stood at attention before them, and the two beys salaamed. The guardsmen received them both. Their horses were taken to the dark stable, and the captains to the hall of the bey. The two heroes entered and salaamed to the assembly. Then all the lords arose before the beys in return to the salaam, because of the salaam and the honor of the guests. They made room for them next to the pashas. Cups were ready for them. They drank and gave greeting. They inquired for one another's health, and congratulated Smailaga on his son, the new alaybey, and on his happy marriage. He thanked the beys. Thus they sat and rested themselves.

There was no wind, but Mount Kozara rumbled. Before their eyes Kozara was enveloped as in a net. A mighty army overran it. When the lords looked from the halls there appeared from the heights the captain of Tuzla on his tall horse, all dressed in silver and in pure gold, his horse in fine trappings. With him were lower and upper Tuzla, two standards, and two thousand men, all young men as handsome as maidens, and as strong as mountain wolves. They were all alike, all arrayed alike. Their breastplates and tunics, the helmets on their heads, and the spears on their shoulders were all alike. The horses beneath them, the trappings on their horses, and the agas' swords at their thighs were the same. The men looked at them and thanked God for Tuzlić. A short time after that Brče Ibrahim came (8100) on his swan-white horse, which was like a spirit of the mountains. Behind him were a hundred horsemen, all young men like wolves from the mountains, who know how to move in close and how to withdraw quickly, and how to carry away a wounded comrade. All the men gazed and thanked God that Bosnia was still so proud that it could bring forth such heroes. As long as it could do that, it would be easy to govern, to govern and to rule. Both the beys came out upon the plain, and the trumpet of Hasan Pasha sounded. The Janissaries stood at attention, and the two falcons salaamed and dismounted. Guardsmen took their horses and went with them to the stable, but they led the beys to the others. When lord met lord they salaamed and took their places in the middle of the circle. The imperial lords received them and found a good place for them. They each gave greeting in turn, and saluted them with ready glasses. They inquired for one another's peace and health, and they said that they were well. They congratulated the hadji on the passing of the command to his son, and on his happy marriage. And he gladly replied: "Thank you, agas, all has been done with the help of God and to the health of yourselves and the sultan." The army mingled with the rest of the army, the beys with the beys, the imperial agas with the elders. Thus they spoke, and then rested themselves.

There was no wind, but Mount Kozara rumbled, and an army came out across Kozara. The clover cried out, and the needles fell from the pine trees. All the men looked, and saw the bey of Brčkovo, an alaybey who looked like an imperial vizier, on his tall black horse. He was dressed all in gold, and, by God and the Rosary, the harness of his black horse shone like the sun. With him was a young man on a chestnut horse. He carried a divisional standard in his hands. The standard enveloped him, and the tassels of the standard enveloped the reserve bearer. Behind him rode a thousand horsemen, (8150) agas and freebooters from beyond the Sava. When the beys saw this bey[171] coming from Kozara onto the very broad plain of Kanidža, the trumpet of Hasan Pasha blew, and the Janissaries came to attention. The bey gave them the Turkish salaam and dismounted. They put his black horse in the stable. His army joined the other armies, and the bey joined the beys. He salaamed and stood in the middle of the gathering. All the beys extended their arms and embraced the bey from Brčkovo. As they embraced him they greeted him and made room for him, and then they drank his health. When they had said that they were well, the bey congratulated the hadji: "Congratulations on the passing of the command to your son, and on your son's bride!" "My friend, may God give you all you wish![172] May the things of your desire fall to your lot! May you ever be a hero, my friend!" Thus they sat and took their satisfaction.

Mount Kozara groaned aloud, and all the lords gazed from the halls. Twelve company commanders came in sight on twelve winged stallions, even as twelve imperial pashas. The commanders had plumes, and on their breasts breastplates of chain mail. On their shoulders were bone-breaking spears, and at their thighs hung sabers. The harnesses and trappings of their steeds shone like the moon. Behind them were twelve standard-bearers, like twelve fair spirits of the mountain. The horses beneath them were spirited and the men on them were like fierce serpents. The golden standard covered the imperial standard-bearers, and the tassels covered their reserve bearer. The lords thanked God for such men and for the army of twelve thousand, all horsemen, not a single one on foot. All the lords saw the commanders and praised God for the imperial commanders of Cazin, their golden standard-bearers and their mighty army. (8200) The two pashas gave praise to God: "Thanks be to God and to this hour, for we have seen the good fortune of the Moslems, and their blessedness!" Then the commanders came out upon the plain, and the trumpet of Hasan Pasha sounded. The Janissaries stood at attention, and the company commanders dismounted. The guardsmen took their horses, their blanketed steeds, into the warm stable, and they led the imperial agas to the white halls. They mingled with one another and extended their white hands in welcome. They sat down one beside another and gave one another greetings. They asked after one another's peace and health. Dear God, thanks to Thee for all things! If one were to see these heroes with the hadji, the elder alaybey, one would say and swear that they were imperial courtiers in council. So large was the army which had gathered, that the steam from men and horses rose to the clouds. Were an apple to fall from the sky, it would not fall upon the ground, but on a man or horse. The lords took their satisfaction. They drank wine, and the smoke from their pipes arose. So they sat and were satisfied.

Mount Kozara quaked, and the lords gazed from the halls. Seven company commanders appeared from rich Bihać and the Border. Behind them were seven standard-bearers. In their hands were divisional standards. The staffs were gleaming and the spheres on them were of gold. The banners themselves were embroidered with gold. Across Kozara, among the evergreens, there was so brilliant a reflection from breastplates and plumes and sharp sabers at the thighs of the heroes, so brilliant a reflection arose that it was like the sun shining through the branches of a pine tree. Both the pashas saw the chieftains, and they both rose to their feet, and they asked the bey of the Lika: "Bey of the Lika, who are those men? From what imperial Border do they come? They are mightier than any of us, (8250) and their chivalric stallions are better. They are more richly arrayed than all the rest of us." "My two pashas, they are from Bihać and the Border. Bihać is the most distant of the Borders, and the shining wing for all of us. The sultan has turned his attention to them, more, my pasha, than to all of us. Well, let him! I do not mind. For they are our best heroes. On every side they have preserved the honor of the Turks and maintained the boundaries of the sultan's empire. My pasha, whenever anyone is challenged to a duel from the land of the emperor or from Hungary, from whatever land it may be, then the beys come forward for him, and fight bloody duels for him.

All of those seven company commanders have won seven duels each. Their seven standard-bearers have won at least as many, if not more. Theirs is the whole army. O pashas, they are blood-stained heroes, who never turn their backs in combat, nor do they leave behind their comrades. They carry away all dead and wounded. There is no mingling with them. Both the sultan and the Border know of them." The pashas thanked God. The company commanders came out upon the plain, and the trumpet of Hasan Pasha sounded. The Janissaries came to attention before them. The seven commanders salaamed and dismounted from their seven horses. Young men took their horses. The army mingled with the army, and the lords with the lords. They all rose to their feet before them, and cleared the best place for them. And again they passed around the glasses. To each a glass of wine came, and with it a greeting. They inquired for one another's peace and health. They all said that they were well. They all congratulated the hadji: "Congratulations on the passing of the command to your son!" And the hadji thanked them all.

They had not yet completed this exchange of greetings when Mount Kozara opened, (8300) and Pašić Sehidija from white Sarajevo came forth on his tall swan-white horse. The lords gazed at him from the halls. Dear God, thanks to Thee for all things! From the rich panoply of that imperial pasha, one could not tell which was better to look upon, which was mightier of limb, or which the more worthy, or which had more gold upon him, man or horse. Before him were twelve mercenaries and a servant with a sack of gold coins, for the pasha carried ducats with him, so that he and his army should not suffer want anywhere on the journey. Behind him were twelve standard-bearers, and behind them an army of twelve thousand men, a splendid army from Sarajevo. There was not a young warrior who had not a breastplate, and imperial plumes upon his head, and a horse with gilded harness. When the Turks saw them from the halls, this golden army and Pasha Sehidija, out of admiration they all rose and thanked God for them. Then when the pasha and his mercenaries and his army came before Kanidža, the trumpet of Hasan Pasha sounded, and the Janissaries stood at attention. The imperial pasha dismounted from his black horse. The guardsmen took him by the arm and brought him up the stairs to the hall. When that falcon came amongst them they had all risen to receive him. They salaamed and extended their arms, and kissed one another's white faces. They made room for him among the pashas, placed a purple cape over his shoulders, and lighted his water pipe. Straightway two youths came before him to wait upon him as long as he remained there. Such was this mighty warrior, and such were his chief nobles. He congratulated the alaybey. "O elder alaybey of Kanidža! Golden wings of our empire! I congratulate you on your son, the alaybey, and the bride he has chosen. May she be fortunate, for our sakes, and for yours!" "So be it, pasha, and may your honor shine as brightly as the day star!" Such was the talk among them. (8350)

Mount Kozara opened again; they gazed from the white halls, and now Captain Tara appeared on his tall chestnut horse. Behind him were two standard-bearers; one was from level Zenica, and the other from the city of Maglaj, from Doboj to lower Derventa. With these men were armies of fifteen hundred, and with Tara an even fourteen hundred, all young men from proud Bosnia. They were arrayed differently from the men of the Border. On their breasts the breastplates were beneath their cloaks, and on their heads the plumes were on the side. Their stallions too were differently arrayed. They had no ornamental finery, nor golden saddles, only harnesses for battle. Every youth had a rifle on his saddle horn and a bone-breaking spear in his hand. When the pashas saw Tara, they looked and liked him well as he was, without ostentation, without great display. Thus were both the captain and his army. The youths were as pretty as maidens, and one could see that they were of good stock, of fine family, and of Turkish faith. The pashas could not take their eyes from them, but one praised the captain to the other. When the captain arrived at Kanidža, the trumpet of Hasan Pasha sounded, and the Janissaries stood at attention. Captain Tara salaamed and dismounted. The guardsmen took his horse and led it to the dark stable. They led the captain to the other heroes. He salaamed, and the Turks received his salaam and gave him great honor. They gave him greetings, and after each of these a full glass of wine. Thus another glass was always ready for him when that was drunk. They inquired for one another's peace and health. They gave thanks, and replied that they were well.

They had just taken their satisfaction when Mount Kozara rumbled, and the lords gazed from the halls. Who was the first to appear on Kozara? Mehmedaga of the city of Konjic[173] on his dapple-gray horse. (8400) The aga was as finely arrayed as an imperial pasha. His dapple-gray was as slender as a spirit of the mountains. Behind this hero was a company of five hundred, all youths as handsome as young girls, though each was like living fire. They gave praise to God for him.

Who emerged after him on Kozara? Ćemalbey from the city of Mostar on his tall sorrel steed. The young man was not yet twenty, but he had twelve plumes above his forehead, to show that the sultan himself knew of him, that he was a valiant knight and right hand[174] of the sultan. His panoply was like that of a vizier, and his bearing was better than a vizier's. Behind him were a thousand heroes, men of Hercegovina, like living fire. Who came first after the bey? Bey Ljubović from level Nevesinje, even Ahmetbeg, on his shaggy chestnut horse. Let me tell you of the hero Ahmetbeg Ljubović. In the room of Hadji Smail there were gathered an even seventy heroes, thirty agas and forty beys. When they saw Bey Ljubović, his panoply and richness, there was not one of those beys who could compare with the person of the glorious Ljubović.[175] No mother has ever borne anyone like him, nor has any mare ever borne a steed like his. He was distinguished and noble, ready and proud, and strong of arm. His adornment suited him perfectly, as did the golden saber at his thigh, and the golden trappings on his chestnut horse. I cannot begin to describe any of this for you. May God protect him from all evil for the sake of his father and his aged mother and all Bosnia! The bey was scarce twenty years of age, and had already won twelve combats and four for the sultan. When the pashas saw the bey, they rose before him, that they might see him better.

Who emerged after him on a mouse-gray stallion? Bey Dževetić from the city of Trebinje. (8450) That bey, too, was like a spirit of the mountains. With Dževetić and with Ljubović were five hundred heroes; but one of them was better than any six others. Such were the forces which gathered at Kanidža. The Janissaries stood at attention, army joined army, beys joined beys. The horses were led into the dark stables. Bey Ljubović and Bey Ćemalović with Bey Dževetić of Trebinje, all three, one after the other, joined the chieftains with the hadji. All three stood in the midst of the circle. All present rose before them. Then all three sat down one beside the other. They made a wide place for them, gave special welcome to each one, together with the giving of a glass, to some wine and to others brandy. This lordly gathering was proud! The Turkish army filled the plains. They congratulated Smail-aga, and he returned their congratulations with thanks. They were all very satisfied.

Then Mount Kozara opened, and when the lords looked from the halls they saw the two beys from Cetina, Zenković and Babahmetović. Babahmetović was riding a chestnut horse, and Zenković a tall white one. Both were encircled by their beards. On their backs were green cloaks, and about their heads were green turbans, in which plumes were fixed. On their foreheads were imperial caps of fur. One could see that they held firman from the sultan, that their beyship was granted by his decree. Anyone who saw these two imperial beys and the fitting apparel on the beys and on their horses could not escape saying that they were two imperial viziers. With them was an army of five hundred heroes, men of Cetina, like living fire. On the two beys their sabers shone, the hadji swords at their thighs shone, as though the men themselves were only youths of twenty years. The pashas' eyes were filled with tears. They could not take their gaze from the two beys and their antique trappings, (8500) their pride and their perfection. You can never gaze your fill at such beauty. Then the two pashas asked the bey: "Bey Mustajbeg, model for us all! Who are those two imperial beys?" and the Bey of the Lika said: "Those, O pashas, are the two beys of Cetinje, who hold permanent imperial firman. The sultan knows of both of them." The pashas thanked God at that. "Yes, he should know! There is reason!" The beys descended with the army, and the trumpet of Hasan Pasha sounded. The Janissaries stood at attention. They took the beys from their horses and led them into the white halls. All that were in the hadji's house rose before the two beys. They made room for them between the pashas. The younger ran to kiss their hands in honor of the sultan and his firman and because of their lordly age. They brought coffee for the beys, for the two beys did not drink wine. They had not drunk when they were young; why should they now in their old age! The two beys shook hands with the aged Hadji Smailaga. "Hadji Smailaga, a blessing on your son's new command! May it bring him good fortune and happiness! May his honor and yours be bright!" "So be it! So be it! imperial heroes!" Then they seated themselves and rested.

Then Mount Kozara opened, and when the lords looked from the halls, they saw Sirdar Hrnjica, commander of the whole army,[176] on his spotted-white horse. Behind him was the stalwart Halil, riding his Malin as on a demonic spirit.[177] If you could only see the sirdar! He was mighty in his array! The sirdar's forehead was as broad as two spans, and between his brows was the space of a man's hand. His eyebrows fell down over his moustaches; through his eyebrows he made a peephole and through it his murderous eyes pierced. He was terrifying beyond compare! (8550) His moustaches stretched from shoulder to shoulder and covered his breastplate and arms. Through his moustaches the breastplate shone as the sun through the branches of a pine tree.[178] The muscles on his arms were as large as a hero's trunk. A sirdar's cap was on his head; he was twofold an imperial sirdar. On his shoulders was a tunic woven of threads of Venetian gold. On his thighs were crimson breeches, decorated with branches woven of gold. All the seams were covered with gold braid. Along his thigh serpents were woven, their heads upon his hip. At his hip hung a sharp two-bladed sword, two arms-breadths long. It waved about his white steed as a serpent around a dry thorn tree. On the horse were trappings of gold. Over his chest were plates of gold, covered with shining bosses ornamented with gold and pearl. The martingales were hung with medallions and fastened beneath his jaw to the bit with clasps of pure silver. There was a net woven of 'fined gold about the white horse's neck from the tip of his ears to the pommel of the saddle. There were two plates of pure gold reaching from his ears down both cheeks, meeting and fastened at the ears. Between them shone a morning star, and on his croup shone the moon.

When the pashas saw the commander-in-chief, all three looked at one another. "Who is this mighty one? Do you know him? Can it be true that a human mother bore him, or was it one of God's creatures who descended from the sky?" The hairs on the pashas' heads bristled as they looked upon the mighty Mujo of Kladuša, and they asked the Bey of the Lika: "Bey of the Lika, we pray you in God's name, who is that awesome one on the white horse? How mighty and powerful he is! We have never even heard of anything like him! What a sheep he carries in his teeth, black and dead, but unflayed!" And the bey spoke these words to the pashas: "Imperial pashas, do you not recognize him in truth? Do you see his imperial cap of fur (8600) and the two plumes above his forehead? On one is engraved the sign of the commander-in-chief; he is the commander of the entire army. On the other is the

mark of a sirdar, for he has two imperial commissions as sirdar. That is Sirdar Hrnjica. Throughout all the lands of the emperor, in every great city, on every great
rampart, far and wide, carved in marble are to be found likenesses of the sirdar and
his horse. Whenever women quiet their children, either in the cradle or in their white
arms, they frighten them with Sirdar Hrnjica: 'Hush, my children, or Mujo will
come!'[179] And you ask the bey who the mighty one is on the white horse!" At that
the pashas gave thanks: "Blessed is our sultan Al Otman for such sirdars in Bosnia,
for such commanders for the army!"

Then behind him appeared the stalwart Halil Hrnjičić on his black horse, on
his Malin, as on a demonic spirit. Halil was to be Fatima's protector.[180] Dear God,
praise to Thee for all things! How handsome and noble he was! He was finer than
any maiden. The youth had neither beard nor moustache. His black queue[181] covered his white neck, as if a black raven were perched there. He had divided it into
two strands; one stretched down his back, the other held tight the plumes on his
forehead and on his fur cap. His hair was black and his cap was of gold. One would
say that a serpent was entwined there, a black serpent across the hero's forehead.
From the plumes feathers waved across his neck and his dark queue. His hair was
mingled with the gold, which glinted even as the sheen shed from a dragon in the
clouds. His forehead was like a magic charm, and his brows like sea-leeches. His
cheeks were like white parchment,[182] and their cheekbones were red as two roses.
His eyes were like a falcon's, and his teeth were small as a demon's.[183] (8650) Like
the broad wings of a swallow, his lashes flickered over his eyes. About his neck was
a collar of gold, one plate on each side of his neck. Beneath his throat was a clasp
of ducats which weighed a liter of gold. His golden breastplate fastened on his
breast, the buckles joined on his shoulders. Girding the boy were two sashes of
many colors and a belt of arms woven all of pearl. In the belt were two small golden
pistols which fire without flint. Their sights were precious stones, and the rings on
the barrels were of yellow gold. Between them was a venomous handjar[184] which
cleaves the hearts of heroes. The entire hilt was of 'fined gold. The three straps
across the youth's chest were of woven gold. They met at the thong on his thigh, at
the thong which held the bright sword of Hrnjica's son, which could cut both flax
and coats of mail. On his thighs were white trousers of white Venetian velvet.
There was more gold than cloth. A bone-breaking lance rested on his shoulder. To
its midpoint it was encased in fine cloth, and from its midpoint the lance was
stained with blood. At the tip of the lance was a dragon's head and in the head two
elephant's tusks which crush the bones of heroes. On the black horse were two harnesses of gold fastened to the coral-decorated saddle. The saddle was studded with
gold and strings of pearl and various kinds of coral, some blue, some green, some
yellow, and some red. It glistened as when the moon shines. Above the golden sad-

dle on Malin were placed equestrian weapons, and over the weapons a protective covering from Dubrovnik. It was neither forged nor hammered, but of pure woven gold. Around it was a border of three-ply braid decorated with gold coins. The blanket was worth a thousand ducats. What a man was the stalwart Halil! What a pleasing face he had (8700) and what kind eyes! When he looked at one, it was like a caress, and when he smiled, it was as if pearls were gleaming!

The three pashas leaped to their feet at the sight of the stalwart Halil Hrnjica, his features and his glance, and they asked the Bey of the Lika: "Bey of the Lika, model for all of us! Whose face and form is that? What spirit bore him? What sister swears by him? What mother gives him her blessing? Blessed be the mother who has nothing more than such a golden dragon! There is nothing like him in all the army, neither in the army nor among us." In those days there was great good fortune among the Turks! They loyally supported one another. When the pashas asked the bey these questions, the bey praised him still more highly:

"Do you three pashas in truth not recognize him? The two kingdoms know him. In Hungary and in the land of the emperor, wherever there is a maid ready for marriage who is embroidering cloth on a frame, the branches form for her the image of Halil, the background is the face of Hrnjičić, as her fingers and little hands ply the needles. And the maidens throughout all the empire sip him at table even as shepherds sip warm milk. My pashas, when the maidens in the empire begin to dance, they all weave Halil into their song." Then all three pashas swore an oath: "Let them sing! They have reason to be troubled!"

With the Hrnjičići were three hundred men of Kladuša, offspring of evil fathers and of worse mothers. They carried steel hooks, and when the armies mingled in battle, dark indeed were the toils of any who withstood them. At their thighs were sharp sabers[185] which tear out the life of heroes. They carried poisoned lances at their shoulders and caps of mail upon their heads. Beneath them their horses were spirited. Over the horses was only a blanket covered with leather to which were fastened plates of steel. In their hands were sharply pointed pikes[186] (8750) which cut through opposing armies.

When the pashas saw Mujo and Mujo's army, their flesh crept, but they softened a little with Halil. When the commander-in-chief came out upon the plain, the trumpet of Hasan Pasha sounded, and the two cannon on the ramparts boomed in salute to the sirdar, commander of the army. The Janissaries stood at attention. The mighty Hrnjica dismounted from his white horse, and behind him Halil dismounted from Malin. The men of Kladuša went to the edge of the green plain, nor did they mingle with any of the army. The two Hrnjičići went to the hadji's house, and their horses in full panoply were sent to the stable. All received the sirdar standing. He salaamed, and the agas received his greeting. All three pashas stretched forth their hands and made room for him near themselves, Mujo next to them and Halil opposite. The might of the one surpassed all the heroes, and Halil nobly graced their circle. Now they set a glass before Mujo, no, not a glass, but a gleaming tankard, a tankard of two liters of wine. Then the two Hrnjičići congratulated Smail on his son Mehmed and on his new command, and on Fatima, daughter of Zajim, for the son. And the hadji said: "Thanks to you, Hrnjičići!"

On Kozara there appeared a border warrior on a tall sorrel mount. His clothes were neither of gold nor embroidered, but were all of leather, and over them he wore a belt of arms and his weapons. On the youth and on his horse, on the standard-bearer behind him, and on his thousand heroes the clothes were all alike, all of dark moroccan leather. And their caps were all alike. About their caps were wound turbans, and in the turbans were imperial plumes. The weapons of horses and heroes were all the same and all of one color. The sabers at their thighs were alike; (8800) and the lances at their shoulders were all alike. The face of each in turn was darkened as if fire had scorched it. One could see that this was a select army, with a good leader at its head, and a mighty and strong standard-bearer.

The three imperial pashas saw him and they asked the Bey of the Lika: "Mustajbeg, whence comes this army, and whence the army's leader?" "O pashas, our golden wings! That is Grdan Osmanaga, and the standard-bearer behind him is Nagrd Husein. Those clothes were made especially for his army. When the rear guard is in danger of being hard beset and an army must be left before the cannon, before the cannon and the attacks of the enemy in the course of wars and marches through other states, there Grdan and Nagrdan take their stand, no matter who comes to attack them. If God grant, when we come to Buda at the point opposite the city where the Klima flows, there is a drawbridge, and on this side of the drawbridge there is a height, a high mountain. There we must leave Osman to dig a trench in front of the cannon, to make platforms in the trench on which to rest the cannon, so that their muzzles may be turned in three directions, eight cannon facing in each of three directions. When the wedding guests leave for Buda, this will prevent Peter from surrounding us and from setting an ambush at the bridge. The river Klima is very treacherous, and all horses cannot cross it without great struggle and misfortune. We must excavate a chain of seven bastions and leave seven thousand men; we must station an army in the entrenchments to wait with cannon for the general, and we must make Osman its commander." All three pashas marveled at the way in which the men of the Hungarian border knew how to direct the campaign, what was wisest and most necessary to be done; it was as if they were accustomed to directing armies. Grdan Osman arrived at Kanidža, and the trumpets of Hasan Pasha sounded. (8850) The Janissaries stood at attention. Grdan Osman and his standard-bearer arrived, salaamed, and dismounted from their horses. The guardsmen took their horses; they led Osmanaga to the hadji's house and their fine Arabian steeds to the warm stables. Osman salaamed to the nobles and they received his greeting well. They made room for him near Mujo, that one awesome hero might be seated by another. They placed the standard-bearer Nagrd Husein next to Halil Hrnjica, that one handsome hero might be seated by another. Greetings and compliments were exchanged. They quaffed ruddy wine in abundance. Osman shook hands with the hadji and congratulated him on Mehmed and the noble Fata. And the hadji said to him: "May Allah reward you!"[187] Thus they spoke and took their ease.

Mount Kozara quaked, and the pashas and beys looked in that direction. An imperial company commander appeared on a tall silver-footed horse; behind him was an imperial standard-bearer, and behind the standard-bearer were three hundred horsemen. Who was the imperial commander? It was the hero Ramo of Glamoč, and with him three hundred men of Glamoč. Ramo arrived with his army before Kanid-ža and the trumpets of Hasan Pasha sounded. The Janissaries stood at attention and saluted Ramo. He salaamed and dismounted from his silver-footed horse. Some guardsmen took his horse, and others took Ramadan and led him to the hadji's house, while his horse was taken to the warm stables. Ramo salaamed in their midst, and they gave Ramo greeting and welcoming. They cleared a broad place for him, and the ready servants brought him a tankard. He congratulated the hadji on the new command for his son and on the marriage with Fata. The hadji thanked him well.

Now the pashas' eyes flew from one standard to another and chieftain after chieftain appeared. An aged warrior appeared (8900) on a tall dark horse, a leading aga in fine array, with good dress and fur cap. Behind him he led a standard-bearer on a long-maned chestnut horse. Of all the standard-bearers who had arrived thus far there was not such a one. All three pashas asked the bey: "Who is that, O bey, on the dark horse?" "That, O pashas, is the Elder of Vrljika; behind him is Selim the standard-bearer, and behind the elder is the army of Vrljika, an army of five hundred men."

Now Mount Kozara quaked again, and the agas of Udbina emerged. With them appeared Kahriman Ćehaja who brought Mehmed. Ćejvan the Elder rode his cropped mare, and Mehmed was riding a dapple-gray. Behind Ćehaja were three hundred men of Udbina. These passed, and another emerged, even Hadji Kapetan on his white horse from Meki Dol on the plain of Udbina on his tall stallion. Behind him were three hundred men. Hadji was like an imperial pasha. When he had passed, another elder approached. Dear God, who was this hero on a silver-footed dapple-gray horse? It was Zukanaga from Žuta Stijena, and with Zukan were a hundred horsemen. Zukan was better than forty men, and the dapple-gray was better than forty horses. Zukanaga came down across Kozara; Zukan passed and another hero arrived. Beneath him was a slender Bedouin mare, a Bedouin mare like a slender mountain spirit. Dear God, who was the hero? It was Alemkadunić of Čekrk. He passed, and another lord arrived on a tall fox-red horse. Behind him were a hundred horsemen. Dear God, who was the hero? It was Šarac Mahmutaga from Otoka, that imperial city. Mahmut passed and another emerged on a tall swan-white horse, and behind him were a hundred horsemen. Dear God, who was the hero? It was Šabanaga Zović. (8950) Šaban passed, and another aga arrived on a tall spotted-gray horse; he wore breastplate and plumes, and behind him were a hundred horsemen. Dear God, who was the hero? That was the hero Kunić Hasanaga. Behind him was another on a chestnut horse; that was the hero Kurtagić Nušin, and with him were a hundred horsemen. Behind Nušin another appeared on a long-necked chestnut horse. Dear God, who was the hero? It was Bojičić Alija. In a short time—it was not long—another appeared on Kozara on his tall piebald horse, and behind him a hundred horsemen. Dear God, who was the hero? It was Gavrić Alibeg of Pripor, that tiny province. He passed, and another aga arrived. Dear God, who was the hero? It was the warrior Vlahinjić Alija, and with him a hundred horsemen. These were all imperial standard-bearers, all the standards, one after the other. Last of all came the four standard-bearers Huso Vilić, Alija Ibričić, Tanković, and Arnautović.

When this force had gathered beneath Kanidža, they thought that there was no one else. For six days and seven nights, all day and all night, the army had been gathering. Now the three imperial pashas said: "O hadji, our protecting wing! We have all been pashas in your lands; one for three years, one for more than four, and one his father begat here. Had a firman come from the sultan and told us that Bosnia was like this, that it had so many heroes, that it had so many champions, and agas and beys, so many imperial company commanders and imperial captains with commissions, and alaybeys who are such falcons, we should all have hanged ourselves in turn. We did not know that Bosnia was like this, nor that it nourished such champions, (9000) nor how pleasant and rich it was. Praise be to God and to God's gifts! Blessed is the sultan in the city of Stambol, who will hold empire as long as Bosnia is his. Now beylerbey[188] and Sirdar Hrnjica, the army has gathered in its tents. At noon this will be the second day that the army has filled the mountain valleys; we have filled the tents with soldiers. Isn't it time to recite the prayers for the favorable journeying to Buda; to send heralds into the army ordering the warriors to tighten their girths, inspect their belts of arms and their weapons, the long rifles at their saddle horns, and the sabers on their straps. Let the cannoneers make the rounds of their cannon; let the men look to the armor on the horses who draw the ring-fitted cannon! Let the provisions and munitions be prepared; let the hadji's son prepare for combat!" Thus spoke all three pashas, and Mustajbeg said to them: "A little patience, imperial nobles! There is a fairly great army beneath Kanidža, a fairly great army, even as the leaves on the mountain, and many good battle commanders, praise be to God, pashas and commanders of a thousand and sirdars and imperial elders; and we have good captains, and plenty of chieftains and company commanders, and standard-bearers like mountain wolves. But the best of our comrades is not yet here, even Tale Ličanin from Orašac." When the pashas heard the beylerbey they all three marveled. One said to the other in secret: "Brother, did you hear Mustajbeg? Of all of us here he says that there is still some better. Sejdić Pasha, our brother, do you know of this Tale, whether he is so mighty? You were born in noble Bosnia, in the white city of Sarajevo. Do you know whether Tale is such a one?" Sejdić Pasha of Travnik cried out: "I have never seen him, but I have heard of him. I have heard that many saints are with Tale, and there are mighty powers on the side of his army."[189]

In a short time—it was not long—(9050) although there was no wind, Kozara rumbled. The pashas and commanders of a thousand and all the nobles looked from the halls. An imperial standard-bearer appeared. He was bareheaded and his mare was unshod. He had turned the standard upside down; the staff was on high and the flag was down below. He was sitting backwards on the mare; his head was turned towards the tail, and his back to the pommel of his saddle. All three pashas leaped to their feet and began to nudge one another with their elbows and to marvel at a strange sight they had never seen before. Then it was not a long time before someone in a derviš elder's turban appeared behind the man on the mare; the beard on his cheeks was tangled, and he was riding a tall dark horse. He had tied the horse's bridle to the pommel of the saddle, and in his two hands he held two things; an ivory comb and a blue flask in which were four liters of wine, and in the other he held the imperial[190] Koran. At this man, too, the pashas marveled. His beard was fine and his turban was green, and he wore the clothes of a priest, but the flask was very extraordinary. The book has no comradeship with the flask. The priest had seized the ivory comb and was combing his beard in an attempt to smooth it out. But his beard was very tangled and from it fell clots of dust. He was smoothing his beard and covering everything around himself with dust. He was reading the prayers and tippling from the flask. The pashas clapped their hands together and leaped to their feet in consternation, but the beylerbey looked at them from beneath his eyes, from beneath his eyes and over his dark moustaches.

In a short time—it was not long—Tale appeared on his mouse-gray horse. Put the priest to one side and forget the standard-bearer at the sight of Tale on his mouse-gray horse. How had Tale bedecked himself? Talaga's breeches were of goat's leather, and on his back was a jacket[191] of donkey's skin. On his head was a fine white skullcap, and he wore boots and long socks. The pashas did not take their eyes from Tale, nor from his standard-bearer, nor from their priest on the dark horse. What were the boots like on Tale's feet? (9100) His toes protruded from the boots, both knees from the breeches, and his elbows from the cursed jacket. Through the tears in his cap passed his queue. About Tale in place of a belt of arms was tied a belt of reeds. On his chest was no shirt of any kind, how then any breast-plate or armor! In the belt of reeds were two small pistols. The flints fouled his belly. The pistols had neither butts nor locks except the two which held the flint. And this is how he had decked his mouse-gray horse. The reins were reeds from the river bank. There was neither proper saddle nor pack-carrier on the mouse-gray horse, but only a blanket from a smelly goat. Over the blanket hung a broken-down saddle of sorts. The boards that were next to the pommel were so cursed old that they were broken and patched with a metal plate. He had saddle pistols in the saddle holsters. The saddle holsters were so good that they had been patched in three places with burlap, and not a half hour passed but that the pistols fell from the holsters. From one side of the pommel on the mouse-gray horse hung a nail-studded club and from the other hung a huge rifle. Its rings were of pure copper, but old and covered with verdigris, and in two or three places they were tied together. There were no stirrups on the saddle but only two slings of reeds, and they were both broken away from the saddle frame and hung loosely down the mouse-gray horse's flank. The reins of reed had broken against the mouse-gray horse's teeth. Tale's legs hung free, and the cursed mouse-gray horse frequently trotted a bit and often grazed on the grass at the side of the road. Tale tried to kick the horse with his feet, but there were no stirrup slings, and his two legs dangled free and his boots struck against the stones, which nicked his boots. Tale's toes had broken through them.

Behind him came three hundred men of Orašac. On their heads were caps from Eždeg's hand,[192] all red in color. On their thighs were red breeches, (9150) and the warriors wore dark jackets.[193] From beneath them their long knives pro-truded; not one of them had any other sword. But at their shoulders were bone-breaking lances.

When the pashas saw this marvel, they could not restrain themselves, but they asked Mustajbeg of the Lika: "Bey of the Lika, model for us all! Is that the famed Tale? You spoke well, Bey of the Lika, when you said that there was no better man among us all than Tale! In the name of God, what is that creature? What has that shameful creature to do with us? You will only disgrace all our elders. Whoever sees him will only mock him, and great difficulties will come upon us." The bey rose upon his right knee, and thus he spoke to the pashas: "I pray you, as person-ages of great power amongst us, not to deceive yourselves, and not to mock or laugh at him. Such is Tale's nature. He does not bedeck himself especially either for war or weddings. Were an imperial firman to come now and summon him to appear in council before the sultan, he would approach the sultan even as he is now." The pashas marveled at this, and then again the bey spoke; "O pashas, do you see Tale? In battle up and down the empire, along the imperial border and in Hungary, where there are most strongholds, where platforms have been excavated in the trenches and great cannon placed upon the platforms, there it falls to the lot of none to attack the cannon and the breastworks but to Tale alone and his three hundred men of Orašac. He cuts off heads and reads the prayers over them, and he seizes strongholds from the Germans. If today, as seems likely, the vizier attacks us and there is a battle beneath Buda, you will see what Tale is like." "In the name of God, O Bey of the Lika! Then is Tale as you say he is. But what is the name of that priest who disgraces himself even in the sight of God? He combs his beard and covers himself with dust; (9200) he reads the liturgy and tipples from the flask. The book has no comradeship with the flask." "Do not be troubled, my three imperial pashas! He is like unto Tale of the Lika. Both of them are accompanied by saints."[194] Again the pashas implored the bey: "By God, what say you about the bare-headed one with the blinded eye, Bey of the Lika, the one on the unshod mare who carries the standard upside down and rides his mare backwards? What is he, and who is he, my bey?" "He, imperial heroes, is a great woe-bringer beyond measure, and a mighty youth without an equal. His mother was left a widow, and she had him after a year's time. She married seven times, and he cut down his seven stepfathers. Finally, O pashas, he was wroth and cast down his own mother into the fire. Woe, woe, and the Woe-Bringer[195] he remained. People gave him that name, for wherever he is, there is nothing but woe. Up to now God has been our help always, and he has brought woe only to our enemies." Then had the pashas exhausted their words.

Tale descended to the plain with the army, in the midst of all the imperial host, and then Tale cried out loudly from his mouse-gray horse: "Hadji Smailaga, it is easy for you to raise the men of the Border and to gather the men of the marches in order to take Zajim's daughter Fata, who has riches in loads and will make you rich and pay for the wedding three times over, but, O hadji, by my faith, it is not easy to obtain Fata. Many a mother will mourn, many a dear sister will be left without a brother, many a young love without her husband. O hadji, hearken to the witless Tale! Fata would not be cheaply won even by me, Tale of Orašac; for Fata is my betrothed." The agas smiled at this, and the three pashas more than all the rest. Hadji Smail summoned his steward:[196] "Bring Tale a hundred ducats, and give him coin on the level plain. (9250) Let him be quieted and let him cease from shouting! Lead him to the wife of Smailaga, and let him take his rest in her dwelling!" At that the steward Husein ran and met Tale with a bag of gold crowns. He placed the coins in his belt of arms and flew to his right hand: "Here, this is for you, Tahiraga! It is for you to spend until we come to Buda; for all three imperial pashas are up there,[197] Sejdić Pasha from the city of Sarajevo, and Pašić Ibrahim from Travnik, and Hasan Tiro from level Kanidža." Then Tale spoke thus to the steward:

"What care I for pashas? They are imperial robbers! Who pays any heed to pashas and viziers? You know, chamberlain—may the dogs attack you, wretch—how we are always waging war? We wage all the wars, and the pashas live as masters! See, chamberlain, what our pashas do! They take captives, they give them to the enemy! They consume money, they sell cities!" At that Tale crossed the streets to the dwelling of the wife of Smailaga.

When the wife of Smailaga saw him, the lady ran to the courtyard to Tale. She met him at the courtyard gate, and Tale dismounted from his mouse-gray horse. The lady flew to Tale's hand and wanted to take him into her house, to her brilliantly adorned room, but Tale spoke thus to the wife of the hadji: "Our lady, wife of Smailaga! I shall not go upstairs to the room, but I shall stay here in the hearthroom and sit a while and take my rest. A plague upon you, wife of Smailaga! Why do you let your mad husband do these things? He has gathered the men of the Border and of the marches. He is devouring your son's inheritance. If it were Fatima's destiny that she come into your house, were she to find you penniless and without possessions, then Fatima would continually find fault with you. What say you, O my poverty-stricken[198] lady! You see, my lady—or perhaps you do not see, because you are young—that you will have to sell the cloak from your back. You must not send the wedding guests to Buda." The lady flew to Tale's hand, she flew to him, and then she smiled. (9300) "Tahiraga, our golden wings! I do not regret what I shall spend for the glorious honor of the Moslem faith and for the honor of our Al Otman, if God but grant that all may turn out well and fortunate, that victory in the battle may be in your hands, and that you may bring an end to the traitor." The lady seated Tale and rested him with drink of all kinds, with bitter coffee and with strong brandy. When Tale had rested well, darkness fell upon the earth. Then the Turks took their sup, and they began to dance on the plain. Dear God, the Bosnians sang and all night long their rifles cracked.[199]

On the morrow when dawn had appeared, Tale of Orašac arose early and began to shout in the streets. Tale was seeking heralds and criers, while upstairs the nobles were beginning to mingle together. The sirdar cried out to the Bey of the Lika: "O Bey, summon the three imperial pashas. Let the pashas summon their servants to prepare their horses. Tale is seeking criers down along the plain. Even now will he give the command for the armies to move." The bey declared this to the imperial pashas, and the pashas dispatched their servants to the stable. They watered their stallions and placed fine barley before them. Thus they made their horses ready, while all the nobles were making their preparations.

The two imperial pashas made themselves ready, and the hadji and his son made preparation. The stewards readied the mare, the Bedouin mare of Cifrić Hasanaga. Others readied the chestnut steed of Mehmed the alaybey. Mehmedbeg prepared himself in the very same golden array in which he had assumed the commission of alaybey and in which he had wooed Fatima. Osman prepared his own dapple-gray horse, and the hadji summoned the standard-bearer; "Omer, my very dear son! Tell my brother Hasanaga to take with him a goodly supply of gold crowns; tell him, my son, and tell Mehmed also. Let us be disgraced at no point in our journey, my son, either on the way to Buda or in Buda. (9350) Let them take money with them in their saddlebags! We have labored for so many years that there is sufficient for this day, and afterwards, too, if almighty God grants." The younger man straightway obeyed his elder. Osman delivered the commands of the hadji.

They struck their tents, and they made ready the reserve horses for Fatima and her escort, if fate granted. The herald of Tale of Orašac cried out, Sirdar Hrnjica's white horse neighed, and the flagstaff of Husein the standard-bearer rang. The leaders mounted their horses, each in his turn, and all the battalions of Bosnians wheeled in order. Each knew its own leader. First came the three imperial pashas, then twelve thousand Janissaries, then the Bey of the Lika on his dove-colored horse, then the twelve thousand men of the Lika, then the army of Pašić of Sarajevo, and behind it that of Fetibegović, with Fetibegović at its head, then after him came Ljevak Omeraga and his army from Lijevno, then the twelve captains from the Una and behind them twelve thousand men; then after them the chieftains of Cazin, and the agas and beys of Bosnia, and the three great beys of Hercegovina; then came the two beys from the sources of the Cetina. And that was almost half of the army.

Now came the turn of Sirdar Mujo. The sirdar always marched in the middle of the army, and behind Mujo the thirty company commanders, those of Otoka and Udbina, those of Bihać and of the Upper Lika, and then those of Kladuša. Then came the great army of Vrljika with the three imperial elders at its head, the two from Kanidža and one from Vrljika. After them marched the other imperial commanders, each as his order and turn came.

There arose the clang of lances on shoulders, the thud of sabers on men's flanks, the clatter of the nails in the horses' hoofs, the lowing of the cattle from Srijem, and the creaking of the wheels beneath the cannon. The division banners waved, the imperial drums rolled, (9400) the fifes sounded shrill, the trumpets blared, and the small band struck up a tune. The Bosnians began to sing in pairs, and their Venetian rifles cracked in pairs. Dear God, praise be to thee for all things! How great were the Border and the marches! One would say that it was an imperial army, with four imperial marshals, which the sultan was sending against the emperor.

Now see Tale of Orašac! He summoned the priest Šuvalija: "Wretched priest, may your mother lose you! Summon thence our standard-bearer. Let him lead forth our three hundred men from Orašac and hasten after us to Kozara,[200] that we may seize the pass at Kozara through which the army will march, that we may see, priest Šuvalija, how great an imperial army has marched forth, how many will return from Buda, and whose bones will remain there." The priest and Tale hastened to Kozara, and behind them their three hundred men of Orašac. From Kanidža to the summit of Kozara is an even four hours. Tale and his horse occupied Kozara, and there he erected a gate. On one side he placed Šuvalija, and on the other side Tale stretched himself. Then he shouted thus at the top of his voice: "Commanders and imperial pashas! Each one of you draw up your army. None must march anywhere except through this gate of Tale's, past me and my priest, so that I may make a count of the Border and the marches, that I may see what armies will depart for Buda, how many will depart and how many return." Each commander in his turn hearkened to Tale. First the pashas appeared at Kozara, and last of all the battle cannon, the pack-horses, the provisions and munitions departed from Kanidža. Tale began to count. The army passed by all day until sunset, and then he made an end to the reckoning. Except for the pashas and the commanders and the cannoneers, and except for those who drove the munitions and the provisions, (9450) and except for Fatima's forty pack-horses, Tale reckoned an army of just one hundred thousand men, and thirty and two more. Then Tale shouted at the side of his mouse-gray horse; Tale shouted and Kozara echoed: "Dear priest, this is a day fraught with ill omens! Something gnaws at me; the signs[201] are unpropitious. I fear that half of this army will not arrive. Yet one should not believe a dream. See what the book says, O priest!" The priest scanned the holy book,[202] and then he said to Tale: "Tale, the book says nothing about how many of the army will perish. It says only that there will be a battle." Then said Tale to the priest Šuvalija; "Tell me no more!" But the priest said to Tale of Orašac: "Let none who will perish in this battle have any regrets, Tale;

for in a brief time the traitor would have betrayed our empire. It is honorable, Tale, to defend oneself and to perish for the faith and for the fatherland. My book says, Tale, that the gates of all our eight paradises are open for us, and that the houris of paradise will emerge and receive the souls of the blessed." Then Tale said to the priest Šuvalija: "O priest, forget about the houris of paradise and your encouraging speeches! What good will your houris of paradise be for me, when my children begin to die from hunger?"

At that moment twilight fell upon the earth. The army passed the night at Brešljen. The troops camped among the evergreen trees, and the chieftains pitched their tents. The next morning each arose early. They marched at an easy pace all the second day until dark. Where did they camp the second night? Above the village of the Vukašinovići. All night the wedding guests sported and danced the kolo on the plain, and the chieftains pitched their tents. On the following day they arose early. Where did they camp the third night? In the midst of the plain of Bey Šemešić. (9500) Then in the morning they arose early, and they marched the whole day through until twilight came. Where did they camp the fourth night? Beside the Klima, where stands the drawbridge.

There they passed the night, and before early dawn they chose four thousand men, all youths as handsome as maidens, and they took up the artillery tools which broaden the roads for the cannon, and on the high level ground opposite the Klima, above the drawbridge over the Klima, they dug a trench for the cannon and wove green cradles. They rested the cannon on the cradles. They divided the cannon into three groups, eight cannon on each of three sides. They constructed earthworks for the cannon and for the ammunition for the cannon. Beside that, on several sides, they dug trenches and connecting ditches as dugouts in which the army could take shelter. There they left the seven company commanders from broad Bihać the bloody, the worthy Grdan Osmanaga, with his standard-bearer, Nagrd Husein, and with them they left an abundance of provisions and ammunition. And Tale of Orašac told them how they might protect themselves on each side as long as their heads remained upon their shoulders, so that they would not surrender the high ground by the bridge; for if the forces of Bogdan occupied it together with Peter's great cannon, of all those who had gone to Buda not a single soul would escape, and Bosnia would be left without a man. The vizier would seize it easily and destroy our empire.

Then the wedding guests set out onto the bridge. The news came to the city of Buda that the wedding guests from the Border were departing from the bridge over the cold Klima. But for a full month before that the lady had sent the news to all the kin of Zajim Alibeg and to the other heroes of Buda. "Will you prepare your homes for the wedding guests all at my expense?" All had leaped up and said to the lady: "Our homes are always in readiness for you, and as for the expense, my lady, do not be embarrassed, (9550) if some one of us receives ten of your guests. Our houses have not been burned. We can receive and entertain the guests for a week or for ten days." Then when the news arrived that the wedding guests were departing from the Klima, the lady straightway spread the news throughout Buda to the young men and to their mothers. The houses had all been prepared, and so the youths readied only their horses; the number of hosts who went forth to receive them was in accordance with the number of Bosnian wedding guests.

It was two hours before sunset when the wedding guests arrived before Buda. Their hosts stood at attention before them on both sides, as if they were Janissaries, and they took away with them in different directions the wedding guests who were before Buda. When not a single guest remained, it was just one hour before sunset. Neither Buda nor the Border was any trifling matter in the days when the city was still strongly built and before the traitor had destroyed it. The guests did not divide into groups of nine for their lodging, but in threes and fours and fives; nowhere in nines. The hosts received their guests well, both the wedding guests and their horses. They provided rest for the horses and they furnished an abundance of drink for the wedding guests. All three pashas, together with the mighty Mustajbeg of the Lika, and the Sirdar, the commander-in-chief of the army, the three elders, the twelve captains, and the twenty and four powerful beys, found their lodgings in the dwellings of Alibeg's wife; whereas Halil and the thirty protectors of the maiden, and Mehmed the new alaybey, lodged near Fatima's harem, awaiting the time when Fata would depart from the harem. A lordly supper was brought forth for each man, and to each man in his lodgings it was announced that it was a custom of old in Buda that whenever wedding guests came from any place to Buda, guests from nearby might remain for two or three days, and those from father away for a full week; none there would speak of departing before a week had passed.

There the wedding guests rested well. Throughout the night rifles cracked, (9600) and the guests began to vie with one another from the houses where they were lodged. They reveled, and then they took their sleep. Early in the morning the wedding guests arose and drank their fill of many kinds of drink; they partook of food, and then they gathered in the marketplaces and throughout the streets. Cymbals clashed and trumpets blared, and the Bosnians danced in the gardens; in the gardens with the maidens each flirted with whom he wished.

There they passed the first day, and then they spent the second night, and again they passed the third day; then day after day and night after night for six days and seven nights. The next day was the time for their departure. Then came an order from the Vizier of Buda to the three pashas and the Bey of the Lika, and to Mujo, the commander-in-chief of the army: "Men of the Border, imperial golden wings! My heart is filled to overflowing that this imperial golden flower has come and adorned all crooked[203] Buda. I have not slept for a full week now because of my great love for you and my yearning to see you. I am sending other ready hosts for you. Now can I know whether you are my wings. If you wish and desire it, since you have been six days with the lady, pass yet another three days with me, the vizier, and may a fourth be to your good fortune. If you do not wish and desire it thus, at least I shall know that you do not love me." Such words were powerful. The pashas were satisfied with them. Neither the Bey of the Lika nor any of the other chieftains would have been content to remain, but all three imperial pashas were afraid that the vizier might bring complaint against them before the sultan, and that he would either do them injury or cause them to lose their heads! They implored the Bey of the Lika: "Bey Mustajbeg, we implore you earnestly. If you ask each of us three in turn, leave it thus as the vizier requests!" The bey cried out: "Ask Mujo, for in his hands is the command of the army." The pashas made their plea to Mujo: "Heroic aga, if you ask us, (9650) keep the army here these three days more, that the imperial traitor may not bring complaint against us, that we may not all three lose our heads." Mujo said: "Let me ask Tale."

Mujo leaped up; it was not far to the house of Fata's uncle; only a hard-packed street separated them. Mujo came to Tale for a talk and told him of the request from the vizier. "All three imperial pashas implored the Bey, and Mustajbeg asked me, and I said that I would ask you. Today, Tale, it is all in your hands. Whatever you say, I shall not countermand it. But the traitor has gone to expense; he has done us honor and requests us graciously: 'If you wish and desire; yet

A typical scene on a side street in Bijelo Polje in 1935.

if you do not desire this, at least I shall know that you do not love me.' As for us, Tale, we care neither more nor less; for the three pashas it is distressing and more." Tale spoke softly thus: "May God destroy Hadji Smailaga for wishing the pashas to join the wedding guests, as if the men of the Border and the marches were not enough! Traveling with pashas is hard. It is indeed hateful to me to associate myself with them, but such was our destiny, Hrnjičić! Listen, Mujo, to what Tale says. The vizier is not ordering our wedding guests to stay here. His heart will survive the anguish, if he can deprive us all of our heads! But news has come to him from Bogdan, from his brother the general, that all the general's army has not yet assembled against the wedding guests; and so the vizier wishes to delay us here until Peter arrives at the Klima and digs trenches and fortifications, and until he can destroy Grdan Osman and our seven company commanders and occupy the Klima and the bridge. Then you will have lost your head. The vizier will attack you from the rear, and Peter will attack you from the front. No more than two full hours would pass before not one of us would remain. Then what would our orphans do? What would become of the empire of Sulejman? When Bosnia and the Border pass from his hands, (9700) let him depart whenever he wishes from Stambol; let him flee to Mecca and Medina where the sultans of old held empire." Mujo did not think that that would be, but he was inclined to sit a little and to drink wine in beakers-full. So Mujo began to take exception to Tale: "Come, Tale, don't be foolish! Things will not actually come to such a pass!" "All right, Mujo, but hearken well to Tale! This is what I see, you old deceiver! Wherever you find an opportunity to sit and enjoy yourself, as at this reception in Buda, to drink the ruddy wine and all kinds of beverages, and to lay your hands upon the choicest meats, there you find it pleasant to linger. But see this, Hrnjičić! From now on whatever you drink will mean wounds for many a man! So, Mujo, whenever you wish, tell the pashas and the Bey of the Lika that we shall not depart for three days."

Mujo told them what Tale had counseled, and they sent an answer to the vizier: "Many thanks, star in our heavens! At your request, we have stayed." When the vizier received the answer, he prepared a message for the general and dispatched it by an imperial hero. This is what he said to him in the well-writ letter: "Brother, as quickly as you can, gather an army, the largest and most evil you can muster, and in great haste a large number of cannon! Assemble your army beside the cold

Klima. Do not do this tonight, but tomorrow evening and day after tomorrow; it is not far. Prepare the greatest force you know how! Then, my brother, General Peter, tomorrow evening, when midnight has passed, I shall fire the cannon from the battlements, as if in rejoicing in honor of the wedding guests. Let the booming of the cannon be heard throughout Buda, so that the Turks will not hear your cannon when you are about to do battle with the rear guard, with the detachments that the wedding guests left behind them on the great mountain." When the traitor had dispatched the letter, he sent another letter to Mustajbeg and to Hrnjica, the Turkish Sirdar: "Thank you, Turkish leaders of the armies, (9750) for having hearkened to my request. If God grant, in the name of the sultan, I shall strive to return your kindness. Hearken to me, Bosnian chieftains! I shall declare a festival during all those days and during the nights, until the wedding guests depart."

The Janissary hosts appeared and led the guests from their lodgings to the ones which the vizier had arranged. Then the cannon boomed in Buda, two together, and twelve at one time, and forty on one fuse. The roar reached beneath the clouds and the black earth trembled. The vizier took the pashas and the chieftains and all those who were leaders. He had prepared dwellings especially for them. They passed the night, and it was well with them. The traitor himself received them standing, and many a time did he do them honor. But whatever moves forward always arrives swiftly, and that woeful request was soon fulfilled. On the third day the chief men leaped up. The pashas shook hands with the traitor, and then Mustajbeg from the broad Lika did likewise, and Sirdar Hrnja from ancient Kladuša, and the elders and imperial beys also. The vizier said farewell to them with a prayer of thanksgiving that such honor had come to his courts.

The herald of Tale of Orašac cried out: "In the name of Allah, the well-adorned wedding guests are ready! In the name of Allah, the well-adorned maiden is ready!" There arose the clatter of the nails in the horses' shoes upon the street; there arose the clang of battle lances, the clash of sharp swords, and the neighing of stallions and mares. The maiden's protectors prepared their horses. Halil went to the harem for Fatima. The bridal veil was put upon the maiden. In accordance with custom he put the ring on Fatima's finger and led her forth by the right hand. Her pack-horses were loaded, their burdens wrapped in fine cloth and covered with Venetian velvet. A golden horse awaited the maiden, and Fatima mounted. The wedding guests gathered in the streets, bey behind bey, and aga behind aga; the alaybeys passed one after the other, and the company commanders one after the other. (9800) Buda could scarcely contain both the great number of Bosnian wedding guests and the friends who were to accompany them. By the time the guests had prepared themselves and had brought themselves and the maiden out of Buda to the middle of the level plain, black night had fallen upon the earth. In the middle of the plain the wedding guests halted, and their friends returned to Buda.

Now let me tell you about the vizier. He saw that the wedding guests were about to spend the night, and he saw their companions turn back to Buda. Then the vizier summoned the commander of his army. "Shut the gates at all four entrances to the city! On the battlements and in the imperial blockhouses turn the muzzles of the cannon on the roads which lead to Buda, in the direction in which the wedding guests carried Fatima away! When the wedding guests meet the general, and shots are exchanged between the two armies, and fierce battle begins, order your army of imperial Janissaries to take their places kneeling on the battlements. If the wedding guests wish to wheel and to flee hither to Buda, if you let any of them reach the ramparts alive in disobedience to my order, your life will be forfeited. The sultan will deliver you to the executioner. Keep close watch on the wedding guests with your spyglasses, and fire upon them on the plain with the cannon, so that none may reach us here. No matter how long the battle lasts, whether it be a day or two days, no matter if it continue a week, the army dare not leave the strong ramparts around Buda, nor must it allow anyone to come hither, by imperial order and decree." The military knows no other way; the younger man hearkened to his elder. The vizier sent forth heralds throughout Buda: "From the morning of this very day, let none dare to leave his house or to open the courtyard gate of his house, nor to call to one another to ask where the battle is taking place. Whoever opens his door, I will hang alive, and whoever asks questions, I will throw into the Danube." (9850)

The next day, when dawn broke, the wedding guests began to stir, to prepare to depart and to carry away the maiden. When the guests had tightened their saddle girths and belted on their shining weapons, when Halil had prepared Fatima and her forty pack-horses and the three hundred protectors beside Halil, dawn had come and the sun had risen on the heights, though not yet upon the plains. The sky was clear without any clouds. The three imperial pashas gazed from their tall imperial

horses; as far as their eyes could see, from where the Klima meets the
Danube, and all along the bank of the Klima on both sides, a cloud of
heavy smoke had settled. The three imperial pashas pondered on what
the cloud meant which had descended upon the Klima. Wherever their
eyes could reach, there was no sign of the Klima or of the bridge. They
looked up into the heavens, but there was no cloud in the sky. Was it
possible that a mist had risen from the water, that the Danube had begun to be misted over and had sent forth a mist before the rain along
the cold water of the Klima? This was a great marvel to them, and they
asked the Bey of the Lika: "Bey Mustajbeg, imperial reflection! We are
pashas, strangers from afar. We have never come to Buda before, nor do
we know the character of the Danube. The sky is clear and there is no
cloud, nor is there any rain from clouds to make the mist rise from the
Danube and settle on the plain beside the Klima. There is no wind that
the wave might dash the Danube against its banks. Do you know what
this means? You have come here many times before." The bey looked,
and then he marveled, and he said these words to the pashas: "I have
come here many times before and stayed for a full week, sometimes in
the summer and sometimes in the winter, but I have never before seen
this marvel." Then he hastened to Hrnjica Mujo and asked Mujo if he
knew anything of it. (9900) But Mujo marveled even more: "This is the
first time my eyes have seen this." The commanders began to gather,
and the imperial elders with them. The younger men kept asking their
elders, and they all said: "This is the first time we have seen it; we have
never even heard of it before." Then Mujo looked around, but Tale was
not nearby. When the sirdar from his white horse caught sight of him,
Tale was terribly angry. Together with his priest and his company and
with his standard-bearer Belaj he had ridden his mouse-gray horse apart.
He was not mingling with the wedding guests. Sirdar Hrnjica realized
that Tale was terribly angry. Mujo folded his arms on his chest and then
cried out: "Woe is me, mother, would that I had not asked Tale a short
time back, but today our mothers will mourn, and from today until the
end of time!" Then he hastened to Cifrić Hasanaga: "Hasanaga, by your
faith! You are the closest friend to Talaga; there is love between your
houses. You have not angered him in anything. Let him tell you— implore him courteously—what that cloud means from the Danube."

Hasan hastened and mounted his Bedouin mare and flew to the
side of Tale of Orašac. The old man dismounted from his Bedouin mare
and threw his arms around Tale's neck. Tale returned his greeting even

more warmly and more handsomely. Then he said to Cifrić Hasanaga:
"What is the matter with you, Cifrić Hasanaga? What is the matter with
you—may God be with you!" Cifrić Hasan said to him: "So be it, Tale,
you are as a brother to me from the same mother! So be it, Tale, and
do not be angered at me." "Why should I, O hero, Cifrić Hasanaga?
What is the matter with you? What misfortune is yours?" "Tell us what
those clouds are; are they from the sky or from the Danube, or is the
Klima filled with silt and has it from its clay sent forth the mist?" Tale
said to Cifrić Hasan: "Hasanaga, that is not a mist, O sorrowful one, nor
does it come from the clouds, nor is it a mist, brother, from the Danube,
(9950) nor has the Klima, nor its clay, sent forth a mist before the
dawn. Tell Mujo and the Bey of the Lika that the wine which we drank
with the vizier has become hot and has now sent forth steam from the
Danube and along the entire length of the Klima. This is a toast from
the vizier, Hasanaga, your recompense for having taken Fatima away
from him and for having cut down his imperial champions. Now look,
Cifrić Hasanaga! All four gates of Buda have been shut. On the walls
stand the Janissaries. They have leveled their rifles at us, and the muzzles
of the cannon are turned towards us, so that we cannot go back. Neither
can we move forward. That mist before us is not from steam but from
animals; it comes from the nostrils of Peter's stallions. Last night, and
from the very first night, there was a battle against the unfortunate
Osman and the seven company commanders of Bihać. What was our
good fortune, brother, has departed from us. Now the heights before us
are occupied. The rear guard which was ours has disappeared—woe to
their mothers! There are their earthworks. We had twenty cannon,
Hasanaga, and four more, and they have fifty. We had seven company
commanders there with seven thousand men and the eighth was with
Osman. I swear to you, Cifrić Hasanaga, that they have twenty more.
Now go and tell Mujo this from me, and let Mujo do as he knows best!"

Tears fell from Hasanaga's eyes and ran down his white beard, like
pearls over white silk. In tears he returned to the sirdar. Then Tale summoned Hrnjičić Halil: "Make Fatima dismount from her golden horse,
and unload Fata's pack-horses. (10000) Freely pitch her tents and do
not send away her protectors." Straightway Halil obeyed Tale. He
pitched a tent and led Fata into it—it was the tent of the three imperial
pashas—and he carried into it Fata's gifts. The drivers released the pack-
horses and let them crop the clover on the plain.

When Hasan returned to where the sirdar was, he told Mujo what

Tale had said. From Mujo's nostrils the south wind blew, from his forehead rain fell, and from his eyes tears streamed down the dark-brown moustaches of the sirdar. Bey Mustajbeg's face lost its color.[204] He hung his head upon his chest as if it had been cut off long ago. Mujo lamented loudly and drew up his white horse. When the wedding guests saw that their chieftains were troubled and had hung their heads, they began to stir about. Mujo implored Cifrić Hasanaga: "I dare not go to Talaga. I have done wrong to all, but Tale in particular have I not obeyed. Tell Tale that I kiss his hand, and on your own part kiss him between the black eyes. Kiss Tale and implore him in the name of God that he come to our aid with the great help of God. There is no help which I can give today but to hearken to what Tale may say. Tell Tale that he has my firm promise that whithersoever he sends me, whether with the army or alone, with trust in God and with God's help, I shall not return until I have carried out his orders or until my severed head yawns." Then Hasan went off weeping. He approached Tale and embraced him; he kissed his raven-dark eyes. "This greeting is from me, O our golden pride, that I kiss you between the raven-dark eyes; as for Mujo, give me your right hand! Mujo salutes you. He realizes what he has done, and today he mourns that he did not hearken to you. In the name of God, Tale, give us aid! Mujo can do nothing, (10050) but thus he gives you his word. Whithersoever you send him at your command, whether with the army or alone, he will not return without having carried out your order or until his severed head yawns." When Tale heard Hasanaga, he shook his head and said to him: "I should like to place Mujo alone by himself in the front ranks, that he might see how wine is drunk, how ruddy wine is drunk in Buda, while we lose our heads here. Yet, were I to see him perish, that would not be pleasing to me, though I would not regret his wounds. Let us do thus, Cifrić Hasanaga. Take a standard from one of the standard-bearers, a standard, whatever it may be, and carry it to one side apart from the wedding guests, half an hour away either to the left or to the right. When you have stuck the standard into the hard ground, return to the wedding guests. Then tell Mustajbeg of the Lika to dispatch heralds among the wedding guests and let the heralds cry out thus: 'By your faith, O Turks, do you see that two states are pursuing us? The traitor pursues us in the rear, and the enemy awaits us ahead. We must move forward; it is worse to go back! The garrison which we left has now been scattered. The army of General Peter is there, and he has more cannon than we have. Their muzzles are pointed toward the bridge. There is no possibility of passing through without loss of life, and not a little loss but much. In spite of that, and in the name of God, for the sake of the faith of all Moslems, for the sake of the homeland of innocent orphans, for the sake of the honor of our sultan, is there any who[205] would not regret perishing today, who would not think of his innocent children who have been left alone in the house, who would voluntarily sacrifice his life, put aside his armor and expose his blood to sword thrusts, strip himself of his outer clothing and stand only in his linen breeches; who would take his sharp sword in his teeth, (10100) having naught else to which to return it, and his shining rifle in his right hand, who would cling to his horse with his stirrups and shout as loudly as his throat could endure: 'Allah! Allah![206] Help me in your strength!'; who would fall upon the enemy? If his judgment day should come, it would be better for him to perish here than to become an imperial vizier, or even to be the sultan in Stambol. When he perishes, his shroud is already with him.[207] The enemy will not maltreat him, in order to strip him of his clothing and his armor, and to foul his body destined for paradise.' This is the only way, Cifrić Hasanaga. We need not one, nor ten, but a hundred and more; the more we have, the better it will be. Then, my brother, Cifrić Hasanaga, when we see how many are our volunteers, then with God's help I shall accomplish what we must do."

Now Cifrić Hasanaga returned weeping to Sirdar Mujo's side. When he arrived beside the sirdar, Mujo was lamenting loudly and tugging at his white horse. Then he implored Cifrić Hasanaga: "Hasanaga, in the name of God, what did Tale say to you, brother?" Hasan told him truly all that Tale had commanded. Bey Mustajbeg agreed with him, and straightway he sent forth four heralds, and the four heralds cried: "Turks, our brothers, in the name of almighty God! Do you see where we find ourselves? There is no possibility of advancing forward, nor can we turn back. When the time comes that we must die, there is no escape; here it is our turn to die. If we stay here for two or three days, the enemy will attack us. Since the evil day has come upon us and great suffering from the enemy, are there any true Moslems among us? Let several volunteer; for we need not ten nor fifteen, but more than a hundred. Whatever there are more than a hundred, (10150) so much the better will it be for us. There is the standard over there apart from the wedding guests. Now if there is among you any who will give up his life and will now sacrifice himself, let him strip off his clothing, his silk and his armor, and let him break the scabbard of his sword and put the blade

between his teeth and take his proud rifle in his hand; dressed only in
his linen breeches, and trusting in God and his right hand, let him
straightway emerge from the wedding guests and fly to the division
standard which has been placed to one side. Let them emerge one after
the other, that we may see among our wedding guests how many volunteers there will be ready to lose their lives in the name of God and
for the sake of the Turkish faith, for the honor of our sultan, for the
sake of our innocent orphans, and for our country and our fatherland!"
For a full hour the heralds cried out among the wedding guests on the
green plain. But no mother had borne a son who would lay down his life
in the name of God nor rally with his horse to the standard. Each held
it bitter to die. The herald shouted for two full hours. Again there was
none at the standard. The herald shouted for three full hours, and yet
there was none at the standard. All three pashas let tears fall; the leaders
wept, and so did the commanders of a thousand. The army sat disgraced and unhappy until midday came. The herald cried out nor did he
desist until one hero flew forth; he stripped himself of his clothes and
his shining arms, broke the scabbard of his sword, took his rifle in his
right hand, and, dressed only in his linen breeches, flew with his horse
to the standard. Dear God, who was that hero? It was the Turk Cifrić
Hasanaga. There is no summer without St. George's day, nor brother,
until a mother bears him, nor will any stranger's heart ache![208]
    Each of the chieftains saw this, that of all the young men there,
(10200) and of all the men of middle age who had left kin[209] in the
house, one a brother, one a brother's child, one a son, and one a brother's son, none would come forth except the aged Cifrić Hasanaga. In a
short time—it was not long—three imperial champions also came forward
on their three horses and in their white linen, which would be suitable
for their shrouds. Dear God, who were those agas who joined Cifrić
beneath the standard? They were the three imperial elders, two from
Kanidža and one from Vrljika. All four, Cifrić Hasan and all three elders,
had white beards. Then the pashas began to weep, and they said one to
another: "Up until now there are only old men and no youths!" In a
short time—it was not long—two champions rode forth on their horses
and joined Hasan beneath the standard; they too wore only white
breeches, and the scabbards of their Persian sabers had been broken.
They both joined Hasan. Dear God, who were those agas? They were
the two aged beys from Cetina, and they both had white beards. In a
short time—it was not long—twelve champions came forward; they too

wore only white breeches and the scabbards of their sabers had been broken. They joined Hasan beneath the standard. Dear God, who were those agas? Those were the twelve Turkish captains from beyond the Una, from Undurovina. Then, when there were eighteen, the wedding guests began to stir; the young men began to whisper and to speak. One began to scold the other: "What are we doing? This is a disgrace and a great sin in the sight of God! Did we not come hither to wage war at Buda? Is it not for that that we prepared ourselves! We are looking at what is before us, and we can see what will come upon us. It is better to die like men than to live like women, bereft of honor." They began to strip off their caps, their golden breastplates, and their arms. (10250) The Turks began to scold one another. In less than a minute or two, in groups of ten, they flew forth from the wedding guests and approached the divisional standard. When two hours had passed, two hours beyond the middle of the day, Tale reckoned to himself how many imperial volunteers there were who were ready to sacrifice their lives in the name of God. There was an even thousand riders! Tale raised his two hands to God: "So be it, O God! Be Thou our help, since yours is the power, against the enemy!"

Then Tale mounted his mouse-gray horse and came among the pashas and the wedding guests to the side of the bey and Sirdar Mujo. Then he spoke to them thus from his mouse-gray horse: "Would it not have been better, imperial pashas, if we had not stayed with the vizier? Even if the battle were still before us, the Klima would not have been taken, nor the drawbridge over the Klima, nor would our garrison have fallen, that army and those champions who were the mightiest among us. But we shall march forward to our destiny. Now, since it has been done, now stretch forth your white arms, embrace one another and kiss one another. If anyone has done anything blameful in his life to anyone else, forgive one another this day. He who dies here today will not regret having perished. The doors of paradise are open, and he will reap the reward for his life. Blessed is he who will perish, but more blessed he who survives. He shall receive the name of hero." Tale spoke, and the army said, "Amen," and none stayed away from the battle! "Now, brothers, I go to join Hasan. When half an hour has passed and darkness falls upon the earth, I shall prepare myself and my mouse-gray horse and I shall take with me the priest and my company and my standard-bearer Šaćir, as I have always done, and I shall send forth our volunteers. Let them attack the drawbridge. (10300) The cannon will fire upon them, forty cannon from the high cliff. The smoke will fall from heaven to the earth. Who dies will be blessed of Allah;[210] who survives will have a weighty trust. Let him not turn his horse back to the wedding guests, but let him ride forward to the camp. Let him cut down the enemy as long as his fate allows. When the smoke from the cannon falls, I shall ride forward on my mouse-gray horse. If God grant—and our hope is in God—as I have always done, I shall ride with my company straight at the cannon, at the cannon and the earthworks. Then, agas, in the name of God, do not hesitate or watch me to see what is happening to me and Hasan! But tighten the saddles on your horses—all you chieftains know your armies—and attack the bridge in the name of God with your armies, one after the other. Leap over one another. Let not the living mourn for the dead, but let each man consider with himself what he does in the name of God. When your rifles are loaded, fire them only once, both your long rifles and the pistols on your horses. As soon as you have fired the long rifles, hang them from the saddle, but do not reach out your hands for your small pistols, the small ones in your belts; for afterwards you may have need of them to save your life, if God grant—and good fortune is from God. If anyone fills his rifle a second time, it will remain as a remembrance of him for his wife, that she may look upon it in place of her husband. Then seize your sharp swords, my brothers, and call upon God! Fall upon the enemy, and then—whatever God grants to us and to them!" Tale of Orašac was not one to be trifled with, for God's powerful aid is on his side, and the help extends to every hero. All the agas rejoiced as if they had already finished the battle and the victory lay in their hands.

Tale joined Cifrić Hasanaga and the thousand Turkish volunteers. (10350) Tale saluted them, and all the Turks returned his salute. On this side the army assembled. Each man sought out his leader, and they waited for the time to come when their leader would give them the order whither to advance with him. They tightened the straps on their breastplates and stretched forth their white arms. All the Turks kissed one another, and each one forgave the other for whatever he had done which was blameful. When Tale had saluted and opened conversation with the agas, he spoke thus: "Volunteers, you are the elect of God, because you are willing to sacrifice yourself for the sake of God and the fatherland! Nightfall has almost arrived. We have not a full hour to delay. You also tighten the straps of your breastplates and stretch forth your white arms and kiss and forgive one another. God's help will go first; follow it, and Tale will follow you, and the whole Border will follow us. My brothers, the auspices are favorable. In the name of God, there will be blood shed. Shining honor and combat are before us. For whoever perishes it shall go well, and whoever survives will live well; even he who perishes will leave his children blessed, for they will not suffer sorrow at the hands of the traitor."

Straightway the Turks tightened their horses' girths. They stretched forth their white arms, kissed one another, and forgave one another. When dark nightfall came, Tale cried out all was ready. Cifrić Hasan mounted his Bedouin mare, and behind him the three imperial elders, and then the two beys from the sources of the Cetina, and then the twelve captains from beyond the Una, and behind them all the volunteers. Shouting the name of Allah, they flew across the plain until they came to the drawbridge. Just four hours passed as they flew over the broad plain. Dear God, thanks be to thee for all things! When the volunteers attacked, they and their cursed[211] stallions and horses (10400) and Bedouin mares from Syria, when they galloped onto the marble of the bridge, such a clatter arose from the horses that one would swear that they were destroying the bridge. When they came to the middle of the drawbridge, their thousand ring-decked rifles cracked, some straight ahead, some to the left, some to the right, and some wherever seemed best.[212] When their fire had subsided, the general's garrison was prepared and met it; they had been expecting it. Forty cannon boomed in one volley. One would say and one would swear that the mountains were descending to the level plain. The roar reached the heavens; great thundering passed over the earth, and the dwellings in Buda were shaken; the Turkish folk cried out. The Janissaries who were serving there wept; they were not weeping because of the enemy, but they were weeping because of the treacherous vizier, and for what he was doing to so many heroes, to so many imperial champions.

Now let me tell you of Hasan, of the hero Cifrić Hasanaga and his thousand heroes.[213] The first volley overwhelmed half of them. They died blessed and fell into the Klima, and their horses were left alone. The five hundred who remained did not turn their heads to look at the dead, but they moved forward to the attack. They hung their shining rifles immediately on their saddles and seized sharp steel. Then they attacked the trenches. A second volley was fired by the general's army, and this one too was from forty cannon. Behind Hasan Tale did not hesitate. With a cry to Allah he attacked with his thirty men of Orašac.

From below the Klima for four hours cannon boomed on all sides. The Turkish wedding guests did not retreat but rushed upon the encampment in one attack after another. Smoke fell from the heavens to the earth. The sound of groans arose around the river Klima. Rifles were fired on all sides, and cannon from every cliff. So great was the roar of the cannon that the rifle fire could not be heard. (10450)

When bright dawn appeared, there was no dawn which anyone could see because of the great smoke from the cannon, from the cannon and the slender rifles, and from the steaming of horses and heroes. Were anyone to stand and look—were he able to see for the smoke—along both banks of the cold river Klima, he would see that the corpses had clogged the bridge, the sad corpses of sad Turks. The river Klima was running with blood; it was half water and half pure blood. It was flowing slowly and carrying away caps and plumes of the Turkish wedding guests. The corpses had fallen about the Klima. The quiet-flowing Klima was not carrying them away, but the corpses had clogged the Klima. From dawn until white noon there was a great roar and a dread battle. Dear God how frightful was that battle! A mist fell from the heavens to the earth, and comrade could not recognize comrade, to say nothing of Turk recognizing infidel! Only their words divided them. The Turks shouted: "Allah and Alija!," and the infidels called upon their Mary. At an hour past midday, the rifle fire became a little less frequent, but the cannons boomed on without ceasing, even the general's great cannon, lodged about the cold Klima, one hundred and twenty and four in all, two in some places, four in others, and in others ten or twenty, but forty and four at the drawbridge. The cannon boomed and the earth trembled for an entire day until black nightfall. One knew not which side was losing more men, which side was losing and which winning; nor could anyone see anyone else, neither who was crying out in anguish nor who was singing. Only the din of battle arose in the camps. Knives flashed and blood flowed; sabers whistled, and the wounded groaned for an entire night right until dawn. When dawn had broken and half an hour had passed, Tale seized Peter's earthworks and Peter's forty cannon; from them he offered the call to prayer, (10500) and he cut off the heads of the cannoneers.

Then Tale looked around him. What had once been Turkish cannon were all overturned and covered by the black earth. About the cannon and about the cannoneers on every side corpses had fallen. From the ravages of powder and lead the heroes' turbans had been burned off, and their breastplates and coats as well. All the heights were adorned with corpses, and the valleys were flowing with blood. There were not only Moslems there, but they were mixed with Peter's army. One could not say which there were more of, when the armies mingled. It could not be said truly that Turks had not fought there without great woe and without great bloodshed. Hot tears fell from Tale's eyes. He was not weeping because of the battle, but he was weeping because he could see nothing of what was happening on the plain and on the banks of the river; he could not see who was losing and who winning. With him were three hundred men of Orašac. All the sashes about their heads and the plumes on their heads had been torn off by rifle bullets and by shot from the great cannon. On the heroes were neither breastplates nor clothing, and on their horses neither manes nor tails, but hot bullets had carried them all away. All their swords to the very hilt, their right arms to the shoulder, and their fine steeds to their knees, were dripping with black blood. Tale listened from the high level ground. It was more than halfway through the second day. One could hear neither cannon nor gun, to say nothing of slender rifles! Only the groaning of heroes from the sore wounds about their bodies could be heard. One cried out: "Woe is me, mother!," and another: "My father and my mother!," and a third: "Take me up, comrade! My sore wounds have overcome me. Were someone to lift me up and give me some water to drink, I think I would be easier." Another shouted: "Tread me down, comrade! My spirit is in my throat, (10550) and I would part from it!" Another shouted: "Take me up, brother!" But in war there are no brothers. Horses flew by without their heroes, and heroes without their good horses. Stallions neighed and Bedouin mares whinnied. All that Tale heard, but could not see.

Then Tale said to the priest Šuvalija: "O priest, take the holy Koran, and find a prayer in the Koran which will be accepted. Do you read the prayer and we shall say amen, that God may send us a wind from the Danube to drive away the mist beside the Klima, that we may see what has been done, that we may see how the Klima flows, whether it is carrying shakos or fur caps, whether there are more shakos or more fur caps. Last night, O priest, when the night began, the Klima was flowing half-filled with blood, and it was carrying away only our corpses." The priest opened the Koran and read a prayer to almighty God; the priest read the prayer, and all the Turks said amen. Their prayer was accepted by God, and he ordained as he had the power. A strong wind blew from the Danube about the Klima and all the plain, and it lifted the mist to the airs of the heavens. When Tale of Orašac looked, he said: "Dear God, thanks be to Thee for all things!" Along both sides of the cold river Klima, for a whole hour and more of the field of combat, lay corpse upon corpse, hero upon hero. In three places the Klima was dried up; it was filled with corpses. "One can easily cross over the Klima on the corpses, wherever one wishes. When the troops pushed forward through the heavy darkness of night and the great smoke from the cannon, when the two forces were carried forward, they did not look to see where the bridge was, but the armies exchanged blows on the river Klima; they trampled the living and cut off heads. The quiet-flowing Klima did not carry corpses, but the whole river became clogged with them. Last night it was flowing half-filled with black blood, but this morning it is flowing with blood alone. Yesterday at midday (10600) it was carrying only fur caps; an hour before nightfall it was carrying both shakos and fur caps, but now it carries only shakos. Dear priest, our woes are great; dear brother, of all those wedding guests, one hundred and thirty and two thousand, there is none now at our side except our poor orphans. One hears neither cannon nor guns, nor does one see anyone pursuing another, nor can one hear rifles on the distant borders. Have the armies been driven off to some place farther along the Danube?" Tale sat himself down upon a cold stone; he took his head in his two hands and pondered what he would do for the life of him.

Then Tale's eyes caught sight of something below the drawbridge where there were twelve hollows and twelve towers by the arches. From one of the hollows there emerged a youth bereft of clothes. He was leaning upon two staffs beneath his two heroic arms. One would say on looking at the youth that his legs had been broken. He raised his legs and walked upon the staffs. With difficulty he walked up from the bank of the Klima. When he had moved nearer, Tale asked the priest and his company: "O priest, see that border warrior carrying the two hazelwood staffs. He is coming straight towards us, O priest. Would you be able to know or to recognize who the youth is, from whose army he comes?" "I know not, Tale, by my faith! How could I recognize him or know him, since the bullets have torn away his clothes, and his countenance is blackened with powder, even as a black coal upon the hearth!" When the hero came up to Tahir, he stretched forth his arms and put down the two staffs. He embraced Tale with both arms. "Tale, is that you, my comrade and my brother?" When Tale heard the words, he recognized the hero from his speech. Dear God, who was this hero? It was the hero Grdan Osmanaga! Hot tears came to Tale's eyes, and he kissed Osmanaga about the throat. (10650) "Osman, my dearest brother! Are you really alive, imperial hero? What happened with your company?" Then Osman said these words to Tale: "Why, O Tale, do you ask about the company, when you see, Tale, that we have all perished; all have perished and none remains." "Osman, my dearest brother! Where are your fierce wounds? Have your legs been broken?" "Brother Tale, ask not about my wounds, but see my darkened countenance. My legs have not been broken, but the nerves in my legs have collapsed. It is today ten days since the garrison was taken from me. I fled beneath the bridge to save my life, beneath the bridge into a hollow. Not even a fox would be able to curl up in there, but I was there and I gathered my legs under me. I have eaten nothing, nor have I had water to drink."

Tale shed tears from his eyes, and then he asked Grdan Osmanaga: "Osman, my dearest brother! Would you be able to tell me something about the seven company commanders from Bihać and their seven standard-bearers? Tell me how it was; tell me what happened." "I know nothing, Tale of Orašac, because a mighty army was upon us, and our army was buried, Tale. When they attacked us, Tale, it was dark, no moon was shining, and a fine rain was falling, so that comrade could not see comrade. Out of the darkness the armies fell upon us; Tale, I swear to you, there were thirty thousand men. They did not give us time to drag out our cannon, nor did we know in which direction to fire. They leaped upon us in the trenches; they buried their fingers in our pigtails and offered us and our heads their sharp swords. We stood there as if we had lost our minds. We did not draw our sharp swords; we could not, they did not give us time. We could draw only the sharp long knives from our belts, and we did what we could with the long knives. There was a great battle in the trenches. (10700) The infidel fell upon us and we upon the infidel, and the great mountains echoed. We caused much woe, they to us, but we more to them. Since the greater force was against us, we accomplished heroic deeds for two reasons; one because of fear, and the other for the sake of our honor. A sword struck me across the strap which protects my belt; the strap was severed and both my many-colored sashes, and the silken jerkin beneath them. It reached the flesh beneath my shirt. There is a hole where there is no flesh on the right side beneath my shoulders. A hero's hand would fit into it."

"Well, brother, Grdan Osmanaga! Can your sore wound be healed? Are you easier? Can you be healed? Or are you in pain so that you may die?" "Tale, my fine brother! That wound will easily be healed; it is beside my heart, but the other wound within my heart I cannot heal. It is a sore wound; the Border lost the battle! What will Bosnia do with me, dear brother, and with you, Tale?" Then they sat down one beside the other.

Both agas were listening when a rumbling sound was heard from the Danube. The sound was wrapped in mist, but the mist was not alone; for from it emerged a border warrior on a spirited horse. He was wearing only white linen breeches and he was riding his horse as if it had wings. At his side were twenty or thirty men, each riding a spirited horse, each wearing only white linen breeches, and each carrying on his shoulder a pike with a head fixed upon it. The man who was at their head was also driving a captain before him, whose hands were tied behind his back. Tale said to Grdić Osmanaga: "Have courage, Grdić Osmanaga! The Turks have begun to gather together. Now do I know that we have won the day, in spite of the fact that many have perished, brother. (10750) There coming from below are twenty or thirty men clad only in white linen breeches. One can see that they are volunteers. Each is carrying a head upon a pike, and one is driving a captain whom he has captured alive." Then Tale rejoiced at this. As they came nearer and nearer Tale tried to recognize the man. Dear God, who was this hero? It was the champion Cifrić Hasanaga on his cropped-tailed Bedouin mare. He saluted and dismounted from the mare, and with him also the thirty horsemen. They stretched forth their white arms, embraced and kissed one another. Tale complimented each man upon his battle prize and Hasanaga upon the captain whom he had captured alive. Such was the custom among the Turks, that if anyone captured an enemy alive in battle, he gave him to Tale for judgment. Thus he gave the captain to Tale, and then they sat down one beside the other.

They began to ask questions of one another. Hasan asked Tale what had happened. "What happened here, Tale?" And Tale asked him: "What happened there?" Tale said to Cifrić Hasanaga: "Hasanaga, imperial hero! You see what has happened here. Yet must we be thankful that our honor is still intact. Neither cannon nor gun roars any longer; perhaps one of ours, but not a single one of theirs. God granted to me —and good fortune comes from God—that I put to flight their strongest garrison and took from them forty cannon, and there are all kinds of good things left. But you, my brother, Cifrić Hasanaga, how far did you pursue the battle? Was the greater part of the fighting cut off? Do you know, have you heard, whether any of the Turks has survived except for yourself and your thirty comrades? I do not ask you, Hasanaga, my brother, about all the Bosnians from Bosnia. You could not know them or know what happened to them. I ask you only about the leaders. Do you know anything about the three imperial pashas? The pashas worry me more than any others, (10800) because they are high officials of the empire and of the faith and they are strangers from afar among us. But I know not what happened to them." "I shall tell you about them, Tale. All three remained on the riverbank, all three pashas, one beside the other, with six thousand Janissaries at their side, and six thousand perished for the faith." Tale gave thanks to God and kissed Hasan.

"I have someone else to ask you about. Did you see Mustajbeg of the Lika anywhere?" "I saw the Bey of the Lika at the point where the Klima and the Danube meet, and with the bey were his seven standard-bearers. There were no clothes on a single one of them; the shot of battle had torn them off as well as the manes and forelocks of their horses. Their swords were bloody to the hilt and their right arms to the shoulder. Their horses were bloody to the knees. Each standard-bearer, Tale, each one had a single bound captive. Their shakos were no longer on their heads so that I might see the insignia on their caps; hence I do not know, Tale, whether they were captains or Bogdan's standard-bearers. With the bey were six thousand men of the army of the Lika, and each had a head on a pike. Six thousand were no longer with the bey." "Yes, my brother, Cifrić Hasanaga. What you tell me is very good news. I would give an eye were I to hear for certain that half of the wedding guests had escaped. And from what you say, Hasanaga, from what you tell me of the pashas and of the bey, half of the army has escaped. Now Cifrić, my dearest brother, do you know anything about the greater bey,[214] even Fetibegović of Banja Luka?" "He is down there at the end of the plain, Tale, He is waiting for his standard-bearers. More than half of the army is with him."

At that news Tale gave great thanks. "Yes, my brother, Cifrić Hasanaga, do you have anything to tell me of the commander-in-chief of the whole army, of Sirdar Hrnjica of Kladuša?" "He is there by the River Danube, and with him are two hundred men of Kladuša (10850) and his brother Halil. They have heads in heaps, Tale!" Tale roared, and the plain echoed. "That is like Halil—may the dogs attack his mother! Did the whoreson abandon Fata for the traitor of Buda to capture?"

"Quiet, Tale! Do not speak foolishness! Halil is such that he would protect Fata! But you know that house of falcons. He would sacrifice all for the faith. There is no summer without St. George's day, no hero until his mother bears him, no flame without an oak log, and no battle without their house.[215] Let me tell you, Tale, We know well what the wedding guests did. Of all that the guests accomplished against the leaders and the men of Bogdan, half was done by the Hrnjičići and half by the other guests. You should have seen the inspired sirdar; how he rode his horse down through the ranks of the enemy and made a path through their ranks with his right arm and with his sword! Before him, Tale, heads yawned! He made a broad path before his white horse. Two wagons could have passed along it, nor would a third have been crowded! I saw that, Tale, with my own eyes. He cut down the enemy in droves. Slender rifles fired upon him, and bullets fell as hail from the heavens. Their might did not hinder him, and God's help was with Hrnjica. No bullet struck him, nor was Mujo afraid of them. In the midst of the fiercest of the battle he cried out to his brother, the stalwart Halil: 'Have courage, my shining honor! Let us see if we can scatter the enemy and cool Tale's anger!' " At that tears fell from Tale's eyes.

"But what more shall I tell you, Tale? There are many agas left alive and many leaders of the army. Of those who survived this battle, Tale, of both Hrnjičići, there is much to tell, but one is to be praised above all. Let me tell you truly who it is. It is Bey Ljubović of Hercegovina and his five hundred comrades. (10900) He captured one of their army generals alive, Tale, and in full battle array. He will bring him to you for judgment, and you will see what a mighty man he is. It is frightening to look upon him from afar, to say nothing of fighting with him! And the troops that were with him—I know not, Tale, how many they were—fell to none other than to God and to Ahmetbeg and his fierce Hercegovinian youths! As many troops as there were, Ahmetbeg annihilated them, even Bey Ljubović and his army. I shall tell you truly, Tale, of all which I heard and saw and of all which I could know, Tahiraga. No tower in our Border will be extinguished. But, Tale, I must tell you that our house has been extinguished."

Tale raised his hands above his head and brought them down hard upon his knees. "What is that, O hadji, my brother, Hasanaga? Surely Mehmed has not perished?" Then said Hasanaga to Tale: "Tale, my brother, as if we had the same mother! I have not seen him with my eyes. Yet I have seen with my eyes that the whole Border has assembled, that is, all that remained alive. I have seen all the chieftains. Each man on the plain is asking his comrade: 'Do you have any news to tell of Mehmed, the new alaybey?' And each answers the other, Tale, that he knows nothing of him either dead or alive. And at that, brother, my heart grows cold; from one end to the other it is cut into small pieces! Each of us is a hundred years old, and between us we have no child, either girl or boy, but God and him alone. And I ponder and think on this, that our hands be not bound as long as we live and our hearts beat beneath our belts. But, whatever almighty God grants! Praise be to God for this day, when we have overcome the might of our enemy and have lost so many brothers, even if our Mehmed is among them!" (10950) Tale's heart was broken at the words of the aged warrior, but he dared not show it for fear that Cifrić Hasan's mind might snap.

As they were talking, the Moslem army appeared, those who had returned from the battle and had conquered the enemy of the faith. They had scattered the enemy army, and it would not be raised again for a long time. Bey followed bey and aga followed aga as they assembled. They had fashioned great stretchers and were carrying the wounded from the Danube; the dead they would care for when the army had reassembled. As each aga who had a living captive arrived, he gave him to Tale for judgment. Each man placed his heads on the heaps that we might know our debt and tell of it. For two days the army gathered. Then they said that there was none else who would arrive, either alive or wounded. They went to seek the scribes. They congratulated one another on the heads they had won and exchanged hearty compliments on having brought to nothing the great force of the enemy. When they had drawn up the reckoning of dead and wounded, it came to exactly sixty and seven thousand. Then they furled their standards. and the drums and imperial trumpets ceased to roll and blare. Then a herald shouted in the ranks: "Let the fleeter and the younger of the youths bring our dead from the Danube to the junction with the Klima, here to where the living stand. Let those who are skilled in swimming bring as many as they can of the dead from the water to the dry land!" The army of the Border and the Marches was no trifling matter. The army leaped up in droves by the bridge and the broad Klima, and they fashioned graves for the dead. They did not fashion them one for each man, but one grave for forty men. It was a whole day before they had gathered them, and they passed the night guarding them. (11000) During the second day they scarce had time to bury them, and again they spent the second night there.

Then in the morning they arose early. Each man pondered, each bethought himself; each man knew who of his comrades was wounded and who had perished. Then each gave thanks to God and took his comrade's bones into his arms and placed them in the ground as was the custom. Hasanaga wept and wailed, and the Turks gave him courage. "Be comforted, our brother, Cifrić Hasanaga! Our children too have perished; to some of us a son, to some a brother's son, to some, O aga, both brother and brother's son. Yet do we not shed tears for them, and there is no brimming of tears to our eyes." Then said Cifrić Hasanaga: "My brothers, by my faith! I weep not for our son, for the fact that the youth has perished gloriously; but I weep that I know nothing of Mehmed, my brothers, either dead or alive. I know not whether he has been left in the Danube or in the Klima. When I return safely to Kanidža, what shall I tell Mehmed's father and his unhappy mother? His father and his mother will ask me: 'Did you lower him into the earth, so that the ravens would not pick out his eyes and the eagles mutilate his face?' I shall not tell them what I do not know. He lived like a man, and he perished as a man. Now in truth among all the Turks, the agas would have forgiven all else, but Mehmed never to the end of time. For he was a dragon above dragons, and his maiden had been wooed, and betrothed, and carried off. Now we cannot abandon Fata, nor give her to another man of the Border. That sorrow will overwhelm Mehmed's father and mother with grief even more than the loss of their only son."

As they were speaking a black cloud appeared from the Danube, and from the cloud billows arose, and from the billows emerged a border warrior on a winged chestnut horse. (11050) But it was not easy to recognize him. He had neither plumes nor fur cap. He was wearing a breastplate, but it had been blackened. His coat was all torn and it hung from him like a wolf's skin. Before him walked a Bedouin mare, and on the mare was a rogue in bonds. He came nearer and the heroes arose. When he was near the army, the young men gazed at him with their raven-black eyes and the older men with spyglasses. Then all said: "Blessed are we to the end of time! That is our new alaybey, and he is driving before him a general in bonds, even Peter, the leader of the armies of Bogdan!" When the Turks had come to this decision, Cifra Hasan said: "Is it true?" and the spirit within him wavered. They persisted until they had restored him. Then Mehmed arrived with General Peter. Tale shouted to his cannoneers and they fired four cannon in salute. Mehmed drove up General Peter and presented him to Tale of Orašac. The whole Border congratulated him. "Blessed are we in this gray falcon! We do not regret having perished as long as the hearth of the alaybey has survived!''

Then Tale shouted to the youths. Those who were bound they impaled on stakes of oak that they might guard the drawbridge, that the living might fear the dead! The rest they put to the sword. They left General Peter untouched. Then all the men of the Border asked Tale: "Tale, what will you do with General Peter?" "Leave Peter alone! I need Peter; I shall need Peter when I come to the vizier. If God grants and fortune ordains, and I lay hands upon the vizier, I shall judge them both before me, as to which of them is the more guilty." All the men of the Border looked at one another, and the Turks began to murmur: "See how Tale is against us! He wants to close all our towers and leave the Border deserted so that the foxes may bark in it." Then the soldiers shouted to their commanders: (11100) "O chieftains, implore Tale not to attack Buda! The heart of each one of us has been consumed by fire: one because of the loss of a brother, another for the loss of a son, one for the loss of his brother's first child, another for his own brother's son. And Fatima has stayed there on the edge of Buda for so many days. It is better for us to unfurl our standards and with our shining glory before us take Fatima home for Mehmed, hold the wedding festival, scatter the wedding guests, and rest for a full month. Then after that we could raise Bosnia, even those of us who are here and some others besides, and go to Buda." And thus the commanders said to Tale: "Tale, the army is no longer able to attack Buda and the vizier. Their hearts are sick and their limbs are exhausted."

Then Tale said these words: "O chieftains and scoundrels! Are you frightened, my beys, after five days of this battle? Of what use is it that we have struggled and that we have lost so many lives? As far as this Peter and his army are concerned, if the vizier had not incited him, Peter would not have gathered the army, nor would he have attacked our wedding guests. As it is we have ground Peter to dust, and extinguished all our army, but we have gained no plunder, not a penny or a ducat! By my glorious faith, I want neither rifles nor heads! There they are; you take them to your loves! Let the wife take the place of the husband who dared not go to Buda to seek out our enemy. No, thank you, timid agas! Whoever dares not, let him say so here and now! But I dare in the name of almighty God with my three hundred men of Orašac and with Mujo Hrnja and his army. Mujo swore to me in your presence that he would not betray anything which I said. We shall return the army to where Fatima is. Halil is there with the maiden's protectors. We shall leave the wounded aside. (11150) I shall go first on my mouse-gray horse, if God grant, with the priest on his dark horse, and Šaćir Belaj on his mare.

"When I approach near to Buda, I shall cry out to the pasha of the Janissaries: 'Imperial pasha, model for all Turks! The entire military command is in your hands. In the name of God and the Turkish faith, turn your guns away from the Turk. You see, pasha, what the vizier has done to us, how he has returned treachery for good faith, and has ruined lives for so many years. You have looked on at that and have done nothing! You see how he was beginning to take captives and to marry Turkish women to the enemy. We have prepared a petition against the vizier, the imperial traitor, accusing him of murder and seeking his life. You govern the army of Al Otman. You look upon him, yet you do not help us. If you are a Turk and swear by the faith, if you believe in God the merciful, and if you love our glorious sultan, you must not turn your guns against us. I give you God's word, imperial pasha: I have sixty and five thousand men with me, and until I have destroyed every youth among them I shall not let the vizier escape. Nor will it be comfortable for you either!' It may be that God grants—and good fortune is from God—that the pasha is a true defender of the faith and will come to our aid. If God grant and fortune ordain, and I get the vizier in my hands and bind him with General Peter, he shall declare to me each of the traitors in Buda one after another. If God grant, when I have struck them down, blessed will be he who comes into Buda. You know—may sorrow find you out—that not even fifteen days is a trifling matter when a brutal bandit falls upon a city among the unfortunate beys and rich property-owners who have ready money in pack-loads, to say nothing of what it would be like for fifteen years! Were the vizier to unlock the treasury, one would dare to vow and swear that the treacherous vizier in Buda and the cadi, the judge,[216] who is a worse traitor than the vizier, have at least half as much ready money (11200) in the treasury as our sultan. If God grant and we accomplish this, if God grant—and good fortune is from God—and the Border attains this, each of you will become rich. If God grant—and my hope is in God—I shall divide it fairly with each of you, with the best as with the worst, and with the worst as with the best. Do you know, unhappy ones—may you remain without eyes—if you accomplished this, what gifts there would be from the sultan? For all those who died in battle, the sultan

would bestow upon their houses, upon their houses he would bestow
the rights and title of a spahi;[217] for the infant children and the widows,
a decree of privilege for the children and money for their mothers.

"If God grant, my dear brothers, that I enter Buda with the army, I
shall return Zajimbeg's Fata to her mother, Alibeg's wife. Let her rest, her
and her pack-animals, until we have come to a little understanding with
the pasha, until we come to an understanding and are freed. When Buda
is in our hands, and, if God grant, we have rested well, I shall make
ready Mehmed the hadji's son and bring him to Alibeg's wife and say to
her: 'With my blessing!' The priest[218] will read prayers and the lady
will proclaim anew a wedding festival. Our new wedding will be a splendid one. When we accomplish that, in the name of God, I shall send all
three imperial pashas, the Bey of the Lika, the sirdar, the twelve captains from beyond the Una, the two beys from the source of the Cetina,
and the twelve company commanders of Cazin, and I shall prepare a
well-writ bloody petition and tell the sultan the whole truth; and I shall
send the vizier and the general and the judge of Buda[219] and with them
all the others to Stambol. Let the sultan try their case. Let the Vizier of
Buda tell our sultan whom of the men of Buda he has delivered to the
executioner, whom he has cast into the Danube, whom he has sent to
Bagdad. Then the rest is between the sultan and the vizier.(11250) My
hope is in God the merciful, that the favor of the sultan will be towards
us, with the help of almighty God, that no other pasha will come to
either Bosnia or imperial Buda except one of us or one whom Bosnia
approves. We shall live even as God wishes. We shall await the firman in
Buda and send the news to Kanidža. My hope is in God the merciful,
that beside Mehmed the son of Smail the alaybey many youths will be
married. Is it not better, brothers, if God grant, to remove such an
enemy, to do what we desire, to marry the young men and give the
maidens in marriage, and until such time as the imperial firman arrives,
to dispense the treasure and divide it fairly; to let the youths flirt with
the maidens, to let these old men who are married ride their horses and
walk throughout Buda?"

Tale spoke and the Border hearkened. They all were in agreement
with this. "Just so, Tale, and may it be well! May almighty God be our
help!" "So be it, brothers! It shall be, if God wills!" Tale spoke, and
none said him nay. They mounted their noble steeds. The divisional
standards were unfurled. The small military band began to play. They
carried their wounded before them. Near to where Fata was they low-

ered the wounded onto the plain. When the army had come up, they found Halil Hrnjica; the youth had performed deeds of heroism and returned to protect young Fata.

There they passed the entire night, and in the morning before dawn,—let me tell you the good news—an imperial warrior came from Buda before dawn. He sought the tent of the commander-in-chief of the army, Mujo's tent, where were also three imperial pashas and all the beys and chieftains. They were sitting one beside another, and as they sat they were talking of what would be done in Buda that day, how they would fight with the Turks, thus making the heart of the enemy rejoice. (11300) Now the imperial warrior approached. He dismounted from his Bedouin mare in front of the tent. He stuck his spear into the ground, tied his Bedouin mare to it, and raised the flap of the tent. He entered and salaamed. Each in turn received his greeting, and then the imperial warrior asked them: "Who is the commander-in-chief of your armies?" They pointed out to him that it was Mujo Hrnjica, as it always had been. To Mujo he gave a well-writ letter. Mujo gave the letter to Halil; Halil broke the seal on the letter and read it aloud. It was from the military commander of the Janissaries. "Respectful greetings to you, my heroes! We have all seen what you have done. Great trouble has come upon me. May God have mercy upon the glorious sultan for having sent the vizier to Buda, for having given that ancient command to that traitor, the Vizier of Buda. He gave a firman into my hands so that I dared do nothing except what the vizier commanded. For fifteen years I have suffered torment. He has caused sorrow throughout the city of Buda. There is no kind of evidence for me to overthrow him before the sultan, but he has done everything which he wished. He has taken captives and cut off heads; he has levied moneys in pack-loads, and he takes half of the aga's and bey's rightful portions of any inheritance money, saying that half of everything belongs to him by order of the glorious sultan. The vizier would not have been able to do this alone, were not the Turkish traitors willing, and half of them agreed. They have done as the vizier wished. Now, my brothers, all imperial heroes! I have awaited this day. All his evil deeds can be repaid with the help of almighty God and with your help, my agas and heroes. As soon as you read this letter of mine, tighten the girths on the breastplates of your horses and your stallions. Press on and divide your armies. (11350) Divide them into four divisions and attack the four citadels. Fire your rifles in a single volley at one time and make your attack upon the citadels. I shall give a command to the divisions, and the divisions will give it to the regiments, and the regiments to the battalions, and the battalions to the captains, and the captains to the sergeants. I shall summon the commander of the artillery and have him order his cannoneers not to hit you, not even to take aim at you, but to send their shots over your heads. Thus shall the cannon do, and no less the rifles, until you arrive with your army beneath the ramparts. I shall then order the cannon to redouble their fire. Whoever among you in the army has a mace in expectancy of single combat, let him strike upon the gates with his mace. When the beating of the maces is heard, and until such time as the traitor is in your midst, I can help you only in secret, but when you have bound the traitor's hands, then you will see what help is! I shall rout the people out of the houses of Buda, and put ten families in one house and billet the army in the other nine. I shall give you all aid. I shall give your command to my army and I shall accomplish your commands. Hasten, brothers, do not delay!"

When they had read the letter, some of the Turks gave thanks, but others said: "Do not let them deceive us!" Then Tale said to them in the fewest possible words: "Whether it is deceit or not, have we not undertaken to attack them?" So there was naught else to do. They tightened the girths on the horses and mounted their ready steeds. They divided the army into four divisions, and the armies crowded onto the plain. They attacked the four citadels. When the cannon on the ramparts boomed, twenty cannon from each bastion, one would say that Buda was falling in ruins and that the houses of Buda were crumbling. But the volley did no harm. The cannon fired far over their heads. (11400) When the Bosnian wedding guests saw that there was no deceit on the part of Buda, they moved nearer, and the cannon increased their fire. Now the rifles of the infantry fired at them, but the shots did them no harm; the guns shot far over their heads. The army saw that God's help was on their side and the help of the heroic commander. They rode their horses to the ramparts and brought them alongside the walls. Whoever had a mace on his horse struck the gates with the mace. The pasha winked at the young soldiers: "Slide back the bolts in the gates, and then flee and keep out of the path of the army. Let the Bosnians rush into Buda, while you hasten to the imperial barracks and close the doors of the barracks. Whatever you hear, pretend you heard it not. Pay no attention to the uproar in Buda. There are the wedding guests, and there is the traitor!" The Janissaries drew back the bolts and the gates

in the ramparts opened. The Bosnian wedding guests, brimming with
bloody woe, crowded into the city. Every street was filled with soldiers.

Who was the first to enter the courts, even the palace of the ruling
judge? The first of all was the new alaybey and with him was Osman
the standard-bearer. They came to confirm the marriage with Fata.
Who was the first to enter the courts, even the courts of the Turkish
traitor? Hrnjica Mujo and Tale of Orašac. Dear God, what was afoot in
Buda? They entered the vizier's chambers and the soldiers of the wedding guests fell upon the executioners. The time and season had come
that the executioner found himself before the executioner; they put
twenty-three of them to the sword, and they bound the hands of the
chief executioner. Mujo went up to the imperial traitor. He carried a
heavy mace in his hand and he struck the traitor between the shoulder
blades, so that his arms were bound together of themselves. Then the
traitor implored Mujo: "Alas, Mujo, imperial hero! What are you doing
to the imperial vizier? I paid you high honor and waited upon you in
my court. (11450) There is no blame in me, your vizier, if the enemy
attacked you. Had I been to blame for the enemy attack, I would have
struck you from the rear." "O traitor, vizier in Buda! Had the pasha of
the Janissaries been willing, you would have attacked from the rear, and
I have attacked you likewise. For the service and the honor you paid us,
O vizier, I shall send you to Stambol with that blood-brother of yours.
I shall gather together those traitors who have helped you in working
evil. They have pulled down the crescent and raised the enemy standard.
Then you may answer to the sultan!"

Then the Turks filled the houses. Whenever they came upon a noble,
they either cut off his head or brought him bound before Talaga. They
pushed them in crowds before the vizier. For three days and three dark
nights they examined and questioned them as to who had done wrong
to them, and they divided the traitors into three groups and made a
reckoning of them in three places, exactly a hundred in each place.
They plucked out the beards of the elders, the judges and the nobles,
with their fingers and with pincers, Those who had been the first men
of the city, all those who had known what the vizier was doing, what he
was doing and had done, they struck between the shoulder blades with
a mace, so that they were neither alive nor dead, and then cast them
bound into the dungeon with the vizier and the general. The Bosnians
gave the order and the Janissaries placed guards over them. They put to
the sword a hundred of those who had been farther away from the seat

of power. The third group, those who had made the decision to give half of the property of the agas and beys to the traitor and had divided it with him, they bound with their hands behind their backs, hung a stone about their necks, and drowned in the muddy Danube. Then afterwards for an entire week, four times every day, they brought the treacherous vizier into the presence of Tale and Sirdar Mujo.(11500)

Then Tale spoke thus to the vizier: "How many bags of gold will you give me, rogue, if I free you?" And the vizier implored Tale to save him. "Give me three bags of ducats then!" The vizier gave his word, but did nothing. Tale did not know whence he would give them, from which of the treasuries that the vizier had. So he sent him back again to the prison and kept him there for three or four hours. Then Tale said these words to the pasha:[220] "The three imperial pashas took from me those three bags of ducats which you gave me, and I had no profit from them. If you have another three bags of ducats, seek them out and redeem your life." The vizier sought his retainer. Again he brought the money to Tale, and again he sent him back to the dungeon, and he stayed there for four hours. Then he brought him back to the council chamber again: "Hrnjica Mujo, the commander-in-chief of the armies, took from me those ducats which you gave me, pasha, and I had no profit from them." Then the vizier implored Tale: "Alas, do not dispose of my life too!" "You know, O vizier—do not be a fool—that I shall not deceive you in what I have promised." Again the vizier sent his retainers, and he gave him three bags of ducats, and Tale sent the vizier back.

When he had let four hours pass, Tale said to the Vizier of Buda: "There is no ransoming for bags of gold, traitor. Whence have you taken this money? Give me the keys to your secret chamber, where the money is which you stole from each estate in Buda during fifteen years. Do you think that we do not know, you rogue, that your treasuries in Buda contain more than our sultan possesses?" Then he led forth the black executioner, who had been his chief executioner. "Either tell us where the money is, traitor, or here is the chief executioner with whom you terrorized the Turks! Listen well, imperial traitor! Had you received this treasure by honorable means, (11550) you would have received good in return. But you got the treasure by the sword, and by the sword you will give it to me. You know, pasha, whoreson that you are, that evil is repaid by evil and good by good. Either give me the treasure, or I shall give the command that we cut off your head like a dog!" When the pasha saw the executioner, he knew that Tale was telling the truth, and he implored him: "Alas, Tale, by your father and mother! Put your hand in my pocket; for my hands are tied. The keys of my treasure chamber are there. I shall go with you to the treasury. Will you give me your word that you will not dispose of me, Tale?" "God is your witness, Vizier of Buda. Do not fear. I shall not cut off your head, nor dispose of you by a death of any sort." Then he drew forth the keys of the treasury.

The vizier went ahead, and Tale followed him, until he had led him to the lowest level. There was a door all of iron. On the outside the door was painted, and where the key was to be inserted in the door was an ornamental covering. The vizier said these words to Tale: "Tale, move aside the hinged cover. Push it with your hand and then insert the key. The door will open of itself." When Tale opened the door, he saw a marvel he had never seen before! There marble blocks with the help of mortar had been used to form a vault which was then coated with bronze. Were thunderbolts to strike it from the heavens, they would scarce have done it any harm; and cannon never until the end of time. Were all Buda to be consumed by fire, the cold stone walls of that treasure chamber would not even be aware of the fire! When Tale looked into the treasury—dear God, praise to thee for all things!—he saw yellow treasure in countless vessels round about the chamber. There was no counting them without a scale. The money almost turned Tale's head. He asked the Vizier of Buda: "What is here is not proportionate, imperial traitor, (11600) to the evil which you have done!" But the traitor swore an oath: "Had I seven or eight heads, and were you to cut them off one after the other, I have not a farthing more elsewhere, to say nothing of Venetian crowns[221] or ducats." Then Tale believed the vizier. "But, you rogue, where are the Hungarian ducats?" "Whatever I received from anyone from either side I divided with the judge. The servants have told me that Mehmed put fear into him and that the judge gave him permission to marry. He has plucked out the judge's beard and taken away the money; he has carried it away to some place according to his own desire and has led away the judge in bonds. There was as much treasure with the judge as with the vizier." Then Tale closed the door. He returned to the treasury the bags of treasure which he had taken and then closed the chamber door and sent the vizier back to the dungeons.

They supped in the vizier's courts, even all the Turkish leaders from Kanidža, and in the courts they passed the night. On the vizier's lordly couches all the men of the Border slept in comfort. Still more at ease were the Janissary brothers, but most at ease were the people of Buda whose sorrows the Turks had avenged. In the morning they arose early, and Tale summoned Sirdar Hrnjica. "Mujo, summon your men of Kladuša to the gate of the court of the Vizier of Buda! Dip a rope in wax and then fashion from it two nooses. Place one upon the neck of the general and one on the neck of the treacherous vizier. Hang one on the other side of the gate and one on this side. Let the one pull upon the other, and let them have no mercy on one another! I would do all this, Mujo, but I gave him my oath that I would not dispose of his life nor cut off his head." And Mujo said: "Tale, are you not really going to send him to Stambol?" (11650) "What, Mujo, are you beside yourself? If I send him before the sultan's council, there are other traitors near the sultan, and they will whisper and lie to him and release our enemy, even both these men who seek our land. And at the very least, if they do not release him, they would question him in council as to what treasure is left, so that the sultan might send out orders for it to be brought, and the imperial traitors might divide it among themselves. As long as Tale lives, there will be no trifling!" Thus Tale decided, and Mujo carried out his order. He hanged Peter and the vizier from the gate in front of the vizier's courts. Then he took the judge and loosed his beard and cut off his head with a saw. Whatever they desired, they had accomplished.

Then they summoned the new alaybey. They had rested well and were ready. They returned the precious Fatima to him and to the courts of Zajimbeg's wife together with the pack-animals and the wedding gifts. In the morning Tale went into council with that Turk, the military commander, all three pashas and all the imperial beys, Hrnjica Mujo, and all the chieftains. The mighty pasha was a good man without an equal. He joined with the Turks, and they discussed how he would prepare a petition accusing the vizier of murder and seeking his life, in whose name it should be drawn up, and to whom it should be sent. The pasha then decided: "This well-writ petition is on behalf of the people of Buda. For fifteen years they have suffered heavily at the hands of the imperial vizier. He presented orders from the sultan, and he took away our possessions to enrich the treasury of Al Otman, so that the treasury might be filled and ready for a great war against the enemy. We all thought that that was true, until he began to take away our men, all chosen heroes, one after the other, under the pretext that the sultan was seeking them. He sent them away, and they did not return. We thought that this was true, but we asked the vizier, your pasha: 'Where are our men from Buda? (11700) Why do they not return here from Stambol?' He said to us: 'The sultan is keeping them there. He has put them all in the service of a pasha.'[222] We thought that that was true. He concealed everything from the military vizier, from your pasha of the Janissaries. But today the time has been fulfilled, and we see now that he was a deceiver; that he had killed our men. Some he had put to the sword, some he had cast alive into the Danube, and some he had sent to Bagdad so that they would never see their homes again. The heroic imperial pasha who governs the army and the troops saw in secret little by little how he was betraying our lands to the enemy. Buda was ready for delivery and Bosnia was not far off. He began to take captives and to send them to Kara Bogdan to give up their Turkish faith for the faith of the infidels. But this is what has happened:

"Your fiery fosterling came hither, even the dear son of Smail the alaybey, that he might take the command from his father and his uncle upon himself in accordance with your order and decree. He met a maiden upon the plain of Muhač whom the imperial guards were escorting away from Buda. It was Fatima, the daughter of Zajimbeg who is now in Bagdad and whom the vizier had exiled. The youth Mehmed is a hero's child, and he scattered the vizier's guards and returned the maiden who had been sent away, whom the vizier had sent to Bogdan as a gift to General Peter. With her he had sent a letter saying: 'My blood-brother, General Peter! Since we became brothers in God, I have not given you a gift. Today I am sending you a maiden, the glorious Fatima, daughter of Alibeg, that she may marry my blood-brother. Then shall you see what a wedding is like! It will be such a one as we have never had before!' Hadji Smail now has this letter, this document from your vizier, in which he promised Peter that that would not be all. (11750) 'I shall send you a better gift, even the two heads of the two alaybeys, Hadji Smail of Kanidža and his brother Hasanaga, and a third will be his one and only son's. If I send these heads to you, Bosnia will straightway fall to you, and Buda will be yours before that. You will soon govern in Buda.'

"We came to know about this, and the military advisers of your commander turned the matter over to the agas of Bosnia. They gathered Bosnia and the Border, one hundred and thirty and two thousand men; apparently they came hither as wedding guests, but in reality it was to see what was happening here. The wedding guests arrived before the city of Buda, and the men of Buda and their infant children received the guests in their lodgings. For an entire week they kept the wedding guests here, and on the seventh day the guests prepared to depart. Then the vizier gave them his decision: 'What will you do, Bosnian heroes? You have visited Buda and the Border. I have prepared lodgings for you. If you will and are willing, stay three days at my expense that you may rest the wedding guests well!' He did not retain them here, O shining empire, because he loved the Turks, but he sent a letter to Bogdan for the general to mobilize his country, the lands of Karavlah and Kara Bogdan, and a mighty host without number. He seized the Klima at Buda and the great drawbridge there. There he stationed his cannon, and he packed his armies together on the plain and waited until the wedding guests departed. The vizier held the wedding guests until the enemy had broken the resistance on the roads. Then the vizier said farewell to the guests and commanded his younger officer[223] —and the younger man had to obey his elder—to fortify the ramparts on Buda and turn the muzzles of the cannon against the Turks. He commanded the younger man to fire the cannon on anyone of the wedding guests who returned.

"The guests passed the first night, (11800) having led the maiden away from Buda. Then in the morning they arose early, and they saw what was before them. They looked behind them, but the vizier had shut the gates of Buda. The Bosnian wedding guests saw what the vizier had done to them. There was now no turning back, nor was it possible to advance forward. They pondered and came to one conclusion. They put their souls in the balance and fell upon Peter's troops. Peter's forces received them with living fire from rifles and cannon. O our sun, that was a sad sight! There the armies mingled. For the first day and the first night both rifles and cannon roared. On the second day there was no rifle fire but only cannon on all sides. On the third day neither cannon nor rifles were to be heard, but they fought only with sabers and sharp swords.[224] The men of the two borders attacked one another. Thrice did the Klima run dry, so great were the armies which crowded into it. They cut off heads, and the living were drowned. The Klima flowed half-filled with blood, half with blood and half with water; on the second day it flowed with blood alone. On the first day the Klima carried Bosnian fur caps, on the second day both fur caps and shakos, and on the third day only shakos. The Turkish forces had overcome theirs.

"At the point where the Danube and the Klima meet, they slaughtered them in their camps. They seized a great host and their leaders and bound them alive. Then, our sun, they brought their army back and made a reckoning of the dead and inspected all that were alive. Half of their army was martyred, either dead or wounded, and less than half had survived safely. Fire had scorched the living; bullets had torn away the manes of horses, their manes and their tails, as well as the clothes and plumes of the heroes. They brought the wounded back to the plain and buried their dead. (11850) They did not bury them each in a single grave, but forty in one burial-ditch. For seven days and seven nights Fatima stayed with the drivers of the pack-animals in the midst of the plain alone. The Turks furled their standards, silenced their trumpets and drums, and each man placed his comrade in the grave. Hasanaga did not place the new alaybey in a grave; for he knew not where he had perished. The Turks mourned for him and were in great travail, when the new alaybey appeared leading General Peter, their high commander. Then the Turks rejoiced; they fired cannon in honor of the bey, they unfurled their standards and came with rejoicing to their tents. In the morning they decided that all the Turks would come to Buda to ask your vizier: " 'Why have you done this to us? Are you striving to overturn the empire?' The vizier ordered me to fire the cannon from the ramparts and leave not one of them alive. I did not obey that order. Our sun, I fired over their heads, and the Turks took the ramparts. The vizier, with those men of Buda who had always aided him, attacked the wedding guests. This he did, but I surrendered. I saw clearly that it was contrary to the faith. That battle destroyed the power of the vizier, and he lost his life as well as those who had aided him. Then they returned Fatima, Zajim's daughter, and Mehmed to her mother that they might rest for several days, and the wedding guests stayed in Buda to rest, and that we might write this petition. We are sending it to your shining empire. Your long arms are outstretched over us. You may do as you wish. You may send your inspectors to see the Turks in Bagdad. (11900) If you find any alive there, you can question them on your lofty throne. I may say, that as long as there is a Bosnia, you shall rule and hold empire."

Then they folded the well-writ petition, and all the leaders put their seals upon it, swearing that the case was thus and not otherwise. The pasha took forty captains of the guard and sent them with the bloody petition to the sultan, to the lofty and magnificent Sulejman, while the Turks made merry in Buda. The petition traveled to Stambol, to the golden hands of Sulejman. The glorious sultan read the petition and the missive of the pasha of the Janissaries. The sultan was fiercely angered. With his two hands he struck his knees and thus he spoke to his concillors: "My councillors and my viziers! Cursed[225] be your pay and your sustenance. During this whole long time, during these fifteen years, since I sent that traitor, the three foxtail vizier, to Buda, there is not one of you who requested permission of me to go to the city of Buda to see what the vizier was doing. He impoverished[226] the property of the orphans in Buda and said that it was the imperial command. He demanded aid in increasing the treasury and made paupers of the men of Buda. Besides that he seized some of them and cast them alive into the Danube, and others he turned over to the executioners. And my pasha, the commander of the Janissaries, was under the order of the vizier. What the traitor was doing in Buda, whatever he was doing, he hid it all from him. An elder can conceal things from a younger man, and even if he knows, he dares not ask. The vizier would have destroyed Buda, had it not been for God and for Bosnia and for my pasha of the Janissaries. The vizier was ready to surrender Buda, that Kara Bogdan might rule in it; (11950) Buda was ready and Bosnia nearly so; he would have overthrown[227] my entire empire. The vizier was meditating on these evils. See what the petition says of what he has done, and how it all was."

When his councillors had read the petition, they folded their arms before the sultan and swore upon the precepts of Islam: "Our shining sun, Sulejman! We did not know what was happening there. There is your sword, and here are our heads!" Then the sultan strictly commanded them: "My councillors, prepare a firman post haste—and seek a Tartar as a messenger—to my pasha in Buda, and to all the Bosnian heroes. Sincere greetings to them; tell them that I kiss their eyes! And tell them all in the firman that they have my approval and may they be merry! Let them stay there and be merry. The deeds which they have done have benefited both them and me. I shall ask them no further questions about it, nor shall I send them any stranger, but they may have whomever they choose to take the vizier's place. They have preserved my empire, and may God preserve their honor to the end of time! Even as he has preserved me in combat, may he preserve them when they appear before him! May Bosnia endure as long as the bright world lasts, and may its fame be proud! May whoever maintains Bosnia be subject to your questioning[228] even as I am now and my successors

after me. Let them stay there and be merry! And give them greeting in
the firman. Let them appoint as vizier in Buda whomever they wish and
agree upon. I shall confirm their choice in a firman. Let their vizier seek
all from me and I shall return them the good which they have done for
me today!"

His councillors immediately obeyed him; they prepared a firman
and sought out a Tartar. The imperial firman departed from Stambol,
the firman departed, and the cannon boomed. Sulejman the Magnificent
made celebration. In those days and times Bosnia had defended the
empire and broken the power of the imperial traitors. (12000)

Then the sultan gave another command. "Now seek out stewards[229]
to travel to Bagdad under my urgent decree. Let them seek the beys
in Bagdad who were exiled there long ago, to see whether, if God grant
—and good fortune is from God—we can find any one of them alive.
Most happy would I be to find Zajimbeg, even Alibeg the imperial noble,
that I might send him to his lady, for she has been left widowed in her
youth. Let her have her husband beside her, and a good son-in-law at
the side of her daughter! Let her rejoice on two counts!" Whatever the
sultan commands is beyond dispute. Immediately they obeyed the imperial order. They sent a well-writ firman to Bagdad and with it forty
stewards. Day and night the firman traveled.

When the firman arrived in Buda to the hands of the illustrious
pasha of the Janissaries, all the leaders of Bosnia and the lands beyond
the Una, even the agas of the whole Border, the pasha received the firman and bowed low over its seal, twice for the sultan and once for the
firman itself. Then he broke the seal, and he read aloud of the satisfaction of the glorious sultan. Tears came to their eyes and bedewed their
white faces. Then he spoke to the commander, and they brought in four
scholars and four hundred pupils from the school. All the wedding
guests and all the Janissaries, the pupils and the children of Buda, said:
"Amen," and a scholar read the prayers. They prayed for the glorious
empire, that it might shine in Stambol for years to come. Then the cannon in Buda boomed, and they celebrated anew at the reading of the
imperial decree that gave all the reins of government to Bosnia. Whatever they desired they could accomplish by themselves. Each could
marry whence he wished and extend the land whither he wished, and
they could appoint their own pashas. The sultan would not send them
anyone except the one whom they desired. (12050) Then they held
festival in Buda for a whole month and a week besides. They reached

agreement and chose Jahja Efendi of Buda as the new vizier, even the brother's son of Zajim Alibeg. The young man was only twenty years old, but there was no Turk like him in all Bosnia. Then there gathered together the children of Buda, the whole army and proud Bosnia, and all the learned men of the city of Buda. They read the prayers for the new vizier in Buda, that he might rule with his whole heart according to the faith, and according to justice and the precepts of Islam; that he would apply his thoughts to naught but the empire and the imperial heroes and the defense of his fatherland against the enemy. Such was the document which was dispatched to the sultan.

Now others had gone to Bagdad, far across the white world, sometimes by sea and sometimes by land, day after day for an entire month. When the stewards arrived in Bagdad the time was past the middle of the night. They spent the night in a brightly decorated inn, and in the morning they arose early and betook themselves to the palace of the imperial governor,[230] carrying with them the firman from the sultan. When the noble governor[231] received the firman he did honor to his sultan, to his sultan and to the imperial firman. Then he broke the seal upon it, and when he saw what was written therein he struck both his hands on his knees. "Why does he seek fifty exiles, when I have only twenty; not so many have come nor do I know of them." Now the minister called his courtiers: "Quickly summon hither the imperial jailers! Let them open the doors of the prison and bring to me the men of Buda who have been in the prison for a long time!" The nobles obeyed the governor.[232] They opened the doors of the prison, and the turnkeys summoned the men of Buda: "The pasha is seeking in audience whoever is here from imperial Buda." When the sad prisoners heard, they leaped up and went to the pasha. (12100) They had fallen into a sorry state. Their beards were so long that they had girded themselves with them; their ruddy hair fell to their sashes; and their nails were like ploughshares. Languishing in jail and captivity is no trifling matter even for thirteen days, to say nothing of thirteen years. The governor was a good man; he had no equal. He sent them to the shops of the barbers and paid the account from his own pocket. They cut their hair and beards. Then again the pasha summoned his steward: "Bring me the keys of the wardrobe and give each man clothes such as are worn by the imperial Janissaries, and give them their expenses for the trip to Stambol." The stewards waited for the beys. They led forth the men of imperial Buda from Bagdad across the white world, day after day, week after week,[233] until they brought the Turks to Stambol and announced them to the sultan.

The sultan summoned them to his residence,[234] and the unfortunate men of Buda entered. They were the best of beys from noble houses, all gentlemen from goodly families, and they had not become accustomed to the hard days of imprisonment. Their prison house had weakened them. Each one flew to the imperial hand; they kissed the imperial hands and the prayer rug of holy Ali. Then they stepped back and stood at attention to serve him. Now the sultan looked at the beys, and he saw that they were all of noble houses. He asked the men of Buda: "Men of Buda, Turkish heroes! Who sent you to Bagdad, unfortunate ones?" "O sultan, the Vizier of Buda sent us to Bagdad, to protect Buda, to fortify Buda against the enemy, whom we had kept at bay with our swords. When the vizier ruled in Buda, (12150) it was thus, O sultan, that he protected us: from some he took all their property, from some only half. He told us that the sultan required it, and we did not begrudge it to you. After that not much time passed before he summoned the choicest nobility in audience before him, and they did not return to their homes. We did not know what had happened to them until we had lost a hundred noble men who had fought for you. We fifty closed our courts and thus made dungeons for ourselves voluntarily. But there was no peace for us even there. At night he gathered us from our courts. A hundred of the pasha's men were waiting for us, and they said: 'The sultan now seeks you in Stambol!' He drove us away on a moonless night, and the vizier ordered that they place us in dungeons during the day and drive us across the country at night. They brought us to the Black Sea and embarked us all into a steamboat. They drove us onward for many days, and wherever we spent the night the next day at dawn two or three of us were missing; this happened every day after our night's lodging. We did not know what had become of them. Twenty of us arrived in Bagdad, and they gave us a well-writ document telling us that we were captives as long as we lived. O sultan, our shining sun! Such were our misfortunes."

Tears fell from the sultan's eyes, and he said: "Who was that who was speaking, who gave the sultan such a wise answer?" "That was the hero Zajim Alibeg." Now the sultan said to them: "Men of Buda, my children! When you were free in Buda, before the vizier began to rule, whose house was the eldest in Buda, my children?" "O sultan, the house of the man who spoke to you was the eldest and most noble. He

was the head of Buda, O sultan, even Zajim Alibeg." The sultan summoned him to his chambers, (12200) and then embraced Zajimbeg.
"Alas, my hero, for what you and all these heroes have suffered! You
have fallen on evil days without my knowledge. God be praised that
you are alive, and Allah be merciful to those who are dead! May He give
you health; I shall restore you to your place. You will receive your reward now for what you have suffered. If you wish, Zajim Alibeg, I shall
place you at my right hand and appoint you Master of the Privy Seal,
that you may put my seal on my decrees and oversee what is written in
them and see how I shall help Bosnia, even level Bosnia and crooked[235]
Buda. If you wish, you may return to Buda. Yesterday the news came
to me that they have appointed as vizier your brother's son Jahja Efendi,
one of the best Turks of the Faith. Go there, my son, if you long for
Buda, for your lordly courts, and for your true love. God has granted—
and your daughter Fatima is responsible—that the empire has survived."
Then he lifted his silken prayer rug and gave him the petition from
Buda. The bey knelt on his right knee. He saw all that was written in
the petition; he read it all and wept. Then he flew to the sultan's hand
and in rejoicing he kissed his hand and the cushion on which it rested.
Then he spoke humbly[236] to the sultan: "O sultan, sun of the world![237]
My happiness is now complete![238] For I have lived to see the day when
I have appeared in audience before you and am free to choose what I
wish. I implore you to send me to Buda, in the name of God and of your
long life! Thus will you reward me well. I may be vizier in my own
courts, with the help of God and of your illustrious empire. There I may
attain full happiness, even as you have given it to these men now."
"Alibeg, I shall not hinder you. Your brother's son is of few years, but
he is as goodly and mighty as there is in the world. Watch over him, and
may he rule with justice (12250) over all of you and all Bosnia. And do
not feel ashamed that you have sought from me the lesser part."

The beys kissed the hem of the sultan's robe. Then the glorious
sultan gave the command and the twenty were given all new raiment,
and he presented them with stallions and swords upon their thighs and
plumes upon their heads. He gave a firman to Zajim Alibeg; he tore the
firman in half, and the sultan kept half of it for himself. Then thus he
spoke to Alibeg: "Hearken to me! When this half of the firman comes
to your hands, then will you know that the command is from the sultan. Obey nothing else!" Day and night the beys longed for their home
in Buda, and each at last arrived at his own house.

The main market-place in Bijelo Polje on market day in 1935. The hotel where Parry recorded is on the left.

When the wedding guests departed from Buda, taking with them Fatima, the daughter of Zajim, they left Buda with rejoicing. They met the bey and embraced one another, and they congratulated Alibeg on his freedom and on the new Vizier of Buda, Jahja Efendi. "May he rule long in Buda, he, and you, and all of us with you!" "So be it, my brothers! And May Fata be happy with you and you with her! Fata is a good maiden from a good house, and she has married a good hero, even Mehmed the new alaybey, the good son of a good father." The bey returned to his own house in Buda, and the wedding guests led Fata to the Border. Now let there be two new weddings accomplished, that of Mehmed with Fata, and of Alibeg with his lady.

Mighty[239] Bosnia in its prime found a wife for its new alaybey and brought the maiden to his courts. His father lived to see all the rejoicing over his own son. "My son, may you find happiness with your true love for many summers and for many years! May you breed falcons with her, my son, and may one generation take its roots from another."[240] They celebrated the wedding for a whole month. There was a horse race with many horses; there was a horse race, and then the guests departed, and the mountain spirit[241] remained with her falcon.(12300)

These deeds were accomplished in the days of Sulejman the Magnificent. Goodly was Bosnia, and goodly were the times, and the sultan aided them well. From me you have had brief entertainment, but from God may it be both long and full! O slender fir tree, raise your branches to protect the lives of all these lords! O green pine, may God be our help! It shall be, O God, if God wills. And now is it time for us to be merry, to be merry and to sing songs!

Notes to "The Wedding of Meho"

The following dictionaries are cited frequently in the notes:

Abdulah Škaljić, *Turcizmi u srpskohrvatskom jeziku* (Turkicisms in the Serbo-Croatian Language), Sarajevo, 1966. In Serbo-Croatian.

Türkce-ingilizce büyük lŭgat (Comprehensive Turkish-English Dictionary), compiled by Tarhan Kitabevi, Ankara, 1959.

H. C. Hony, *A Turkish-English Dictionary*, London, Oxford University Press, 1947, reprinted 1950.

Vuk Stefanović Karadžić, *Srpski rječnik*, Fourth State edition, Beograd, 1935.

---

1. Avdo's introductory song (*pripjev*, foresong) is here divided into two parts. The first paragraph is the proverbial section of the introduction, and the second leads into the song itself, giving some historical setting. In conversation (Text No. 12445, lines 1ff.) Nikola tried to find out what Avdo called this introductory part of the song, but it was quite clear that Avdo had no term for it at all; in fact, he did not recognize the word *pripjev* and at the beginning did not know what Nikola was talking about. Here's the way the conversation went, with Nikola first asking Avdo from whom he learned his *pripjev*. "*Avdo:* What? *N:* The *pripjev* that you sing, from whom did you learn it? *A:* What *pripjev*? *N:* That which is in front of the song, the *pripjev*. What do you call it? *A:* The song? *N:* The *pripjev*, man, *začinka, pričinka* [other words for *pripjev*] which you sing before the song. How is that? What do you call it? *A:* Oh, that:

> The first word is, "God, help us,"
> And the second . . .

N: Yes, yes, that's it. *A:* Oh, so. Well, from everyone little by little. *N:* But what do you call it? *A:* This is how I call it. In one song, when there are bold and fine young men, in order that people might laugh a little beforehand, I have one song, and this is what I like to sing beforehand:

> It is hard for a fire of hazelwood,
> And for a son-in-law living on his mother-in-law's food.
> It is hard for a mother-in-law at her son-in-law's fire log,
> And for a maiden . . . .
> It is hard for a village through which an army passes,
> And for a maiden who arrives alone.
> Then when she fights with her father-in-law and mother-in-law
> (*Hasna ljutu*), thus they cry out to their daughter-in-law:
> 'If you were any good, you would not have arrived alone,
> But your mother [grandmother?] would have married you off.'
> It is hard for a thorn bush which has no honey,
> And for a maiden who marries an old man [grandfather].
> Up to midnight she is chasing fleas,
> After midnight she is pushing the old man.

Then after that we begin to recount the song of the olden times. *N:* But what do you call that? *A:* I call that, so that first of all in the beginning my audience (*društvo*) may be merry. *N:* From whom did you learn that? *A:* I learned that from a man who came here year before last. They pointed out the notices on his chest, and the order of the White Lion. I've forgotten his name. They affixed those notices here, saying that he was the greatest (*najviši*) guslar, and that that was confirmed in Germany. And he had been there in Czechoslovakia. In our country he was counted as great. Began will tell you about it. I was there as one of the poor, as you know me. I spent a night at that same coffeehouse keeper's, except that he had a coffeehouse there at the end of the street, above those fountains; he hired it. They said that admission to hear that man was five dinars. I entered and put down nine dinars, and it did not seem to me that he was a good singer. *N:* They why did you learn a pripjev from him if he was not a good singer? *A:* I learned the pripjev because it was good for a laugh. You know why he wasn't good? He sang three songs in three hours minus a quarter (*frtalj*). *N:* Was he a Serb? *A:* A Serb. From Montenegro; Began will tell you his name but I've forgotten it.

    "*N:* Do you have any other pripjev? *A:* Well, there's the one that is among us, that I learned from my father and heard from all these singers. [Here he gives a version of the one with which "Smailagić Meho" begins. I quote the Serbo-Croatian text:]

> Prva riječ, Bože, nam pomozi.
> Evo druga, hoće ako Bog da.
> Samo da ga pominjemo često,

> Da se š njime ne kunemo krivo,
> Pa će Bog svuj pomagat',
> I od svake muke zaklanjati,
> Svake muke i ruke dušmanjske,
> I svakoga hala i belaja,
> I bijede gore od belaja,
> Što je gora od sedam belaja,
> Od zlog druga, pa nevjernog duga.
> Biće kiša, rodiće godina.
> Dužan će se duga odužiti,
> A zlog druga nikad do vijeka.

N: Is that the whole pripjev? A: One version (*od jedne ruke*), yes. N: Is there another? A: There's some more!

> It is hard for a wolf when the birds feed him,
> And for a husband when the women defend him.
> With difficulty do the birds satisfy the wolf's hunger (*nahranile*),
> And the women cannot successfully defend the husband [man].

N: Is there any more? A: That's one. N: From whom did you learn that? A: From Sade, from Latif. They have *pripevak*'s [he seems to have a term after all] of several words, some longer, some shorter. Then there are some who don't have a single one.

> Aj! The first word is, O God, be Thou our help!
> Here's the second, it will be if God grants.
> Now we say we shall recount a song.

That's a fine beginning.

"N: Did the old Moslems make a pripjev like that? A: Those that I remember they say that they heard from them. N: Is there any longer? A: I don't have any longer; perhaps. N: When you sing in the coffeehouse, do you sing some pripjev like that before the song? A: I do. N: Let's say, the first night, or every night that you sing? A: The first night, and the second, and perhaps the tenth. Some nights I begin the song right away."

2. Provinces: *valiluka, vilayets, pashaliks*. A pashalik was formed from a group of *sandžaks*. The pashalik of Kaniža was formed in 1600. The first pashalik in European Turkey was that of Rumeli, centered at Adrianople, founded between 1371 and 1385. This pashalik was extended by the conquests of the Turks, and by the beginning of Sulejman's reign (1521) it included twenty-seven sandžaks, and, when the second pashalik was founded in 1541 in Buda, the Rumeliski pashalik had over thirty sandžaks. The third pashalik to be formed was that of Bosnia in 1580, which included six sandžaks in addition to that of Bosnia: *hercegovački, kliški, pakrački*, and *krčki* were taken from the *rumeliski pašaluk*, and *zvornički* and *požeški sandžaci* from the pashalik of Buda. Towards the end of the sixteenth

century a new sandžak was formed in the Bosnian Krajina (Border), that of Bihać, and that became part of the Bosnian pashalik. In 1600 the sandžak of Požega became part of the new pashalik of Kaniža. According to the article in the *Enciklopedija Jugoslavije* on "Bosna i Hercegovina," the Bosnian pashalik in military matters seems to have been subordinated to the pashalik of Buda. Our song reflects that subordination.

3. Kanidža. Kaniža in southern Hungary. Avdo has inherited this place-name from the songbook, whose singer does not mention Bosnia. To the songbook singer, Kanidža is not placed geographically in Bosnia or anywhere else, but the men of Kanidža call to their aid the heroes of the Krajina, Mujo, Halil, Mustajbeg, Tale, who are associated with Bosnia. (The 1925 songbook spells the name "Kaniža," but the Krauss edition of Šemić's text spells it "Kanidža." Except when referring specifically to the Hungarian city, I have normalized the spelling to "Kanidža.") Avdo had no idea where Kaniža was; it was a name from the songbook. But he assumed it was in Bosnia. Kaniža was taken by the Turks in 1600 and was the center of a new pashalik formed that same year, the pashalik of Kaniža. It was never part of the Bosnian pashalik or of any other. In its formation it absorbed the sandžak of Požega, which had previously been part of the pashalik of Bosnia from its formation in 1580. In short, there was no pashalik of Kaniža in the days of Sulejman the Magnificent; in fact, Kaniža was not Turkish at that time.

4. This is the first of numerous lists of titles. One of the most difficult problems in translating has been to find some proper equivalents for such titles. Parry began to use terms like "lord," "duke," "baron," and so forth, but I have felt that the flavor imparted by these English titles smacks of England and Western Europe, and this is a very Balkan-Turkish poem. The English Middle Ages do not fit. Often there are no real equivalents, and it would have been better to keep the Turkish titles. Some of them are well known, anyway, and have English forms, such as "vizier," "aga," "bey," "pasha," and even "sirdar." In the list at this point the English terms stand for the following: "chief men," *glavni*; "men of war," *delije* "elder," *ajan*; "fortress commander," *dizdar*; "captains," *buljukbaše*; "standard-bearers," *bajraktari*; "peer," *akran*. A few lines later we find "warriors," *deli*, the Turkish root of *delija*, often coupled with a name, e.g., deli Hasan and deli Husein. Of the above, *dizdar, bajraktar*, and *akran* are pretty straightforward, but it might be noted the *akran* means peer in either age or honor and rank, corresponding, indeed, to our usage, of "peer' both for age group and for equals in general. *Delija, ajan*, and *buljukbaša* are somewhat more difficult to translate. *Delija* is the Serbo-Croatian substantival form for Turkish *deli*, which is both noun and adjective. In modern Turkish it means "mad," "insane," "eccentric" (Tarhan Kitabevi). Škaljić gives three sets of meanings for *delija*, as follows: (1) a hero (*junak*), a great hero (*junačina*), a mighty man (*silovit čovek*), or better, a violent man, a man of violence, a man given to fighting and quarreling (*nabodica*), (*zanesenjak u junaštvu*) an "enthusiast" in heroism, one who is transported in fighting and heroism; a man who leads life without any concern and spends time senselessly (*čovek koji provodi život*

bezbrižno i koji troši vreme uludo). (2) In the Turkish Empire the *delije* were a special kind of cavalry. They appear at the end of the fifteenth and the beginning of the sixteenth century. A part of this cavalry was recruited from the Balkan Slavs. Because of their heroism and violence (*silovitosti*) they were called *delije*. (3) *Delije* were also a type of security guard for a vizier (*vrsta straže sigurnosti kod vezira, valija, i paša*), a vali, or a pasha. Either meaning 2 or 3 fits here, especially 3, since we see the pasha surrounded by his *delije*.

Ajan, *ayan* in Turkish, is listed in the Turkish dictionary as a nominative plural meaning "senators," or, figuratively, "notables." Hony lists it in the singular, also meaning "a village headman." Škaljić gives us two meanings, or sets of meanings, in Serbo-Croatian usage: (1) a distinguished person (*prvak, odličnik*), a respectable and respected person (*ugledan čovek*); the distinguished representative of a class or of the most distinguished levels of the city population. (2) At one period of the Turkish rule in Bosnia, ajans were functionaries of the local administration. Where there were no captains (as administrators of a *kapetanija*), there were ajans, and they were ordinarily men of the most distinguished families of beys. Clearly the second meaning is helpful here.

Finally, a *buljukbaša* is, according to Škaljić: (1) in the Janissaries the commander of a *buljuk*, and officer of the rank of *juzbaša*, a captain, and (2) the leader or commander of a *buljuk* in general. A *buljuk* is (1) an army company; in the Janissaries it numbered ordinarily a hundred men; (2) a section, part, division; (3) a gathering, or group in general. *Juzbaša* is a captain, literally the head (*baša*) of a hundred (*juz*).

5. Hasan Pasha Tiro. I have not been able to identify this pasha or any of the other individuals mentioned here in Kanidža—Cifrić Hasanaga, Smail, or Mehmed himself.

6. Breeches of finest make: *eždegske čakšire*. In conversation (Text No. 12445, lines 99ff.) Avdo said the trousers are thus called because they were made by a master-tailor named Eždeg. In reality *eždegski* seems to be a corruption of German *Jaeger* plus the Slavic adjectival suffix-*ski*. These are, therefore, a kind of hunting trousers, culottes.

7. Thick forest. *Gora čajna* means literally "a forest in the mist," or "a misty, or mist-obscured or -covered, forest." The original image may have been of trees protruding above the mist in a mountain forest, a sight common enough in the early morning in the mountains. This may also be a distortion of *gora čarna*, "black forest."

8. Alaybey. It is not easy to translate this title adequately. An alaybey was military commander of a sandžak. Until the formation of the Bosnian pashalik in 1580 there were only sandžaks in Bosnia, which were subject to the pasha of Rumelia or, after 1541, to the pasha of Buda (see n. 2, above). The military leader of a sandžak, if it were placed on the frontier, was an important figure, for not only was the defense of the sandžak in his hands, but also the obligation of further conquest, of "broadening the Border" as the songs say, was on his shoulders.

9. Rosary: *tespih*, from Arabic, according to Škaljić, with a basic meaning "to praise God by the recitation of sacred words." A full rosary had 99 beads; a small one had 33.

10. Avdo seemed to have no explanation of why the devil was said to have such fine, close-set teeth. See conversation, Text No. 12445, lines 2116ff., where Avdo was asked about this characteristic in the description of Halil. See also line 8650.

11. Good-luck charm: *hamajlija*, a talisman, often a saying from the Koran put into a locket and affixed to the arm or hung about the neck.

12. Vila: a white female spirit, dwelling in mountain lakes. They have wings and fly. They are sometimes helpful to mortals, even becoming sisters-in-blood with, or marrying, mortal men. Sometimes they may be malicious, especially if their lakes are violated.

13. Oke: Turkish weight of 400 drams, 2.83 lb., 1.285 kg.

14. Kara Bogdan: Moldavia, a part of Rumania.

15. General Peter. My favorite candidate for this identification is Peter IV Rares (1527–1538 and 1541–1546), the last really independent prince of Moldavia. See my article, "History and Tradition in Balkan Oral Epic and Ballad," in *Western Folklore*, 31 (1972), 53–60.

16. The reference to Smail is a slip on the part of the singer.

17. All the seven kingdoms: the tradition thus designates the Christian "coalition." The seven vary, but usually include Austria, Hungary, Germany, France, England, Italy, and Russia, or, as it is ordinarily called, "Muscovy."

18. Hypocrite: *hiljav*. This word, of Turkish origin, means squint-eyed, sly, contrary, deceptive.

19. Karavlah: Wallachia. Rumania was formed by the union of Wallachia and Moldavia.

20. Unđurovina: see below, n. 133.

21. According to Škaljić, *Mehdija* is not connected with Mehmed or Meho. Mehdija is the name of the Moslem Messiah, who will appear before judgment day and renew the faith of Islam and inaugurate a rule of justice. Turkish *Mehdi* comes from Arabic *Mähdiyy.* a name meaning "he who is directed on the right path, leader." *Mehmed*, on the other hand, is given as a Turkish form of Arabic Muhammäd, which means "glorious."

22. Imam: the Moslem clergyman who leads the services of the men in the mosque five times a day. At the time of prayer he stands in front of the congregation (Škaljić).

23. The covering and seclusion of horses as described here is still practiced in Asiatic Turkestan, and perhaps elsewhere. Turkish tradition concerning magic horses who fly is exemplified in the stories of Kurroglou and his horse. Avdo does not know why horses were kept secluded, although in conversation he admitted that he believed that in the old days they were secluded like this. He also said in the same breath, and without being asked, that the horse could fly (Text No. 12445, lines

156ff., esp. lines 179ff.). Nikola said, speaking of the horse, that he was sure that he could not live shut up like that for so long. Avdo replied: "I am sure that he lived, and what is more, that he could fly." A look at the Kurroglou and other stories shows the connection between the confinement and the wings. According to tradition, a horse thus hidden from the sun grows wings, but if the light strikes him the wings will not grow. See *Specimens of the Popular Poetry of Persia as found in the adventures and improvisations of Kurroglou, the bandit-minstrel of northern Persia, and in the songs of the people inhabiting the shores of the Caspian Sea,* orally collected and translated, with philological and historical notes, by Alexander Chodzko (London, 1842), pp. 3–4. I do not understand lines 830 and 832 and have, therefore, had to omit them from the translation, which obviously suffers accordingly.

24. Damascus the noble: *Šam-i šerif*. The expression is pure Turkish. *Šam* is Damascus, and *šerif* is a postpositive adjective meaning "noble" or "sacred." Avdo was not exactly sure where it was. In conversation (No. 12445, lines 186ff.) he said it was under France, not a city, but a little state (*državica*) near "Halep."

25. Ali Otman: the dynasty of Osman's descendants. *Al*, Arabic, means "family." Osman I, the founder of the dynasty, son of Ertoghrul, whose place as leader of a large group of Turks he took in 1288, ruled until 1326, when he was succeeded by his son Orkhan.

26. Lit. "my brain has fallen in my gorge," *Mozak mi je pao po grkljanu*, line 970. At line 6450 Miško wrote in the margin of the typed text: *znak da je već postao matuh od starosti,* "a sign that he has already become senile."

27. Vizier with three horsetail plumes: a very high rank. Horsetails on the standard were a way of showing rank: the higher the number, the greater the rank. Cf. five-star generals.

28. Leader of a thousand: *bimbaša* means literally that. Škaljić gives: "a major, leader of a battalion of the Turkish army, which ordinarily numbered a thousand soldiers."

29. Guards: *sejmeni*, in the Turkish dictionary *seğmen*, listed as obsolete, "keeper of the hounds." Škaljić gives (1) a member of a type of Janissary infantry, (2) a guard (*stražar, pandur*).

30. With imperial pay by firman and order:

> Pod fermanom i ulefom, sine,
> I beratom sjajnog Sulejmana.   1304

Ulefa in Škaljić is given as "pay, ordinarily military pay?," from Turkish *ulüfe*, obsolete, "pay of troops," which comes from Arabic *ulufä*, "fodder for horses."

31. Commanded: i.e., he has been "alaybey."

32. See n. 4, above. A buljukbaša ordinarily commands an army company of one hundred men, but Škaljić noted that in the folk poetry companies of as many as twelve thousand men are mentioned.

33. Ali Otman: see above, n. 25.

34. Imperial pay and the golden marten: for "imperial pay" see n. 30, above. The golden marten is clearly part of the insignia of an alaybey.

35. Gold-adorned hamper: *varakli sepet*. Avdo's explanation of this phrase is worthy of note. "Woven of wire, of silver, then afterwards adorned (*isarat*) with gold. That gold was not Venetian but *varacko*, that gold was mined from Varazdin." This is not true, but one might remark that Avdo did not know that *varakli* in Turkish meant gilded. *Varak* means "gold leaf."

36. Bundle: *bosca*. In Škaljić "a covering for the head, kerchief; table cloth; a piece of cloth of rectangular shape in which something is wrapped." For a *bosca* as gift for wedding principals, see below, n. 110.

37. The likeness of Sulejman the Magnificent, etc. In conversation (Text No. 12445, lines 313ff.) Avdo said that they had pictures of all thirty-three Otmanović sultans in a reader (*čitanka*) or a songbook. There you will find the pictures, he said, of Sultans Selim, Sulejman, the two Murats, Mehmed Fatih, Aziz, Medžid, Mahmut, Hamid, Rešad, Mehrihudin, and all of them in uniform. Also the picture of Mehmed Soko pasha Sokolović. They are all dressed as dervishes, with dervishes' turbans and long coats to the ground. Avdo offered to show the book which one of his nephews had, but in actuality it could not be found. I believe that Avdo was referring to a book published by the bookstore of Mihail Milanović in Sarajevo entitled *Povjest Turske carevine od najstarijeg do najnovijeg vremena*, napisao E. ef. S. Skopljak (The History of the Turkish Empire from the oldest to the newest times, written by E. ef. S. Skopljak).

38. In this sentence we come upon two other titles not previously encountered, *musir* and *ridžal*. The first means "field marshal," Turkish *müşür* (Hony); the second, a distinguished man, a man of dignity, in modern Turkish, *rical*, n. pl. of *recül*, "man," meaning "men; men of importance, high officials" (Hony). Tarhan Kitabevi adds "statesmen." Here is a case, like "ajan" (see n. 4), in which a Turkish plural is treated as a Serbo-Croatian singular, developing a Slavic plural. *Begler* is another such, because it is the Turkish plural of *beg*, but it is treated as a singular in Serbo-Croatian.

39. Coffee hearth: *kahve odžak*, the hearth or room in which coffee is prepared. Here it was in the outside building which was one of the guardhouses in Smail's dwelling.

40. Green: the national color of the Turks.

41. Orlovac: a plateau region in southeastern Bosnia.

42. Osman's story of himself is reminiscent of the stories told by characters in Homeric epic, especially of Eumaeus or of Eurykleia. It is the story of the loyal retainer, who has given up all to serve his lord.

43. Both Bajrams. What Avdo calls the Day of the Pilgrims is the Qurban Bairam or "Sacrifice Bairam," that falls on the tenth, and two or three following days, of the last month of the lunar calendar, when pilgrims sacrifice animals, such as a ram, a he-goat, a cow, or camel in the valley of Mina in commemoration of the

ransom of Ishmael with a ram. The Bajram of Ramazan, or *Küçük Bairam* (Lesser Bairam), follows immediately the ninth or fasting month, Ramadan, thus forming the first three days of the tenth month.

44. Squire: *kavaz*, Turkish *kavas*, is translated in Tarhan Kitabevi as "kavass; chasseur, footman (of Embassies)," and in Hony as "guard of an embassy or consulate; attendant at a court, doorkeeper of a big establishment." Škaljić gives "guard (*stražar, pandur*), bailiff in the court (*sudski pozivar*), bodyguard of a dignitary, especially for foreign diplomatic representatives in the Turkish Empire." He adds the interesting note: "Kavazi were at first servants of a noble who carried their master's bow."

45. Steward: *kavadar*, Turkish, *kafadar*, friend, companion. Not in Škaljić. It clearly does not mean "friend" here, however, and I have translated it according to context.

46. Perfumed soap: *rakli sapun*, meaning soap from Iraq. In Škaljić *irakli safun* is a kind of fragrant soap which during the Turkish rule was imported from the East. Avdo in conversation (Text No. 12445, lines 351ff.) describes the washing and grooming of the horse and knows the soap is fragrant, but has no idea of the meaning of the word *rakli*; "perhaps it got its name from the factory, or maybe it was mixed with *raćija*," he said. "I couldn't tell you."

47. Cover. *Haša* is a cloth that covers, according to Avdo himself (Text No. 12445, lines 376ff.), the saddle holsters and the saddle, or, according to Škaljić, the saddle and the rump of the horse.

48. Buda has just been taken from the Magyars into the hands of the sultan. Buda was first taken by Sulejman I in 1526 and retaken from Ferdinand in 1541. Both these dates, interestingly enough, coincide with the two periods when Peter IV Rares was ruling in Moldavia. See n. 15, above.

49. Sharp sword: *mač grebenica.* The Serbian dictionaries give under *grebeštak* "a kind of old sword or saber," but they do not elaborate (*Matica srpska* and *Srpska akademija* dictionaires). Avdo fell back on the explanation that it was "the best kind of sword," "called after the smith who forged it!" (Text No. 12445, lines 405ff.). Vuk's dictionary, often most helpful in such cases, refers to *grebeško gvožđe*, which he notes as "*starinsko*" (archaic), and which the Serbian Academy dictionary defines as "steel used in making swords." The root word here is *greben*, "rake," with its sharp points, referring also to the sharp blade.

50. Heath rows: *sokak čalije*, literally, alley or lane of heath or bush. This seems to refer to the lanes, especially on the outskirts of town, that become overgrown with heath and bushes.

51. Vukašiće. In the songbook the name of the first village at which the heroes stop is Jasika. Avdo has made up the name Vukašiće from Vukašin, the name of the householder given in the songbook.

52. Village elder: *knez*. An entire page in Vuk St. Karadžić's dictionary is devoted to this word. It is largely concerned with the *knez* who was head of a *kne-*

žina. Vuk's article on *knežina* says that each *nahija* was divided into several *knežine*, and each *knežina* into several *srezovi*, over which was a *kapetan* or buljukbaša. The head of a *knežina* was a *knez* or in some parts at some time a *voyvoda*. Vuk says that when Miloš Obrenović began to rule, the *knežine* were about the same as they had been during Turkish times, but that gradually they came to be called *srezovi*, and so the name *knežina* practically disappeared. Vuk differentiates between the knez who was head of a knežina and the knez who was head of a village. As far as Vukašin is concerned, I think Avdo considered him as a village elder, and so I have translated it. See below, n. 160.

53. Bulgarian cloak: the heavy, shaggy wool cloak or cape characteristic of Balkan shepherds in general, not peculiar to Bulgaria.

54. Note that it is Vukašin who first warns him of the treacherous vizier, but only in general terms.

55. Vujadinovići. As in the case of Vukašinoviće, this place name comes from the name of the knez, Vujadin. In the songbook the place is Veselica and the knez is Toroman Vuk.

56. The similarity in tone between these scenes of hospitality on the journey and those of Telemachus in the Odyssey is striking. Cf. Lord, "Composition by Theme in Greek and Southslavic Epos," *Transactions of the American Philological Association*, 82 (1951), 71–80.

57. Violet-hued: *meneviš*. This is the meaning from the dictionary (Škaljić). Avdo in conversation (Text No. 12445, lines 477ff.) said it was silk without gold, used in women's vests.

58. Saddle roll. *Terkija* means the equipment that is rolled up and fastened behind the saddle. The roll contained such things as a prayer rug, blanket, cloak, and so forth.

59. Lady Vukašin: *Vukašinovica*. Elsewhere I have been able to translate this as "Vukašin's wife," but this is difficult in direct address, and "Mrs. Vukašin" would be ludicrous, as would be "Ma'am," "Madame," or even "m'lady!"

60. While there are many similarities between the two scenes of hospitality, there are pleasing variations as well. In the first, the heroes are served by Vukašin and his wife, twin girls prepare their couches for them, and Vukašin and his wife watch over them all night. In the second case, the guests are sighted by the two boys, sons of Vujadin, and they are ordered to go to the courtyard to meet Meho and Osman and to serve them all night. In their room the guests are served by Vujadin's two daughters-in-law. The households are different in each case. The furnishings are different, too, and the conversations of Meho and Osman with their hosts. In a number of ways Avdo has varied the internal elements of the same theme in a manner not un-Homeric. See my article, "An Example of Homeric Qualities of Repetition in Međedović's 'Smailagić Meho'," *Serta Slavica* (Gedenkschrift für Alois Schmaus), Munich, 1971, pp. 458–464.

61. Klima. The name of the river in the songbook is *Glina*, and it is this that

Avdo has corrupted. Krauss notes that there is no river of that name between Kaniža and Buda, but that there was a river Glina in the former Croatian military march (remember he was writing in 1886). The river at Buda is, of course, the Danube. The description of mud and quicksand which follows is suitable enough for the marshes and swamps of the Danube as it crosses the Hungarian plain.

62. The songbook speaks of *čekme ćuprija*, a "drawbridge," and from this Avdo has given the bridge a name (the line seems clearly to indicate this as a name, for it begins *to se zove*, "It is called," *Čekmedže*). *Čekmedže*, Turkish *cekmece*, means a chest of drawers or a box with drawers. Reference may be to the famous and huge suspension bridge at Buda.

63. Muhač. At the battle of Mohács in 1526 the Turks defeated the Hungarians and took Budapest, and at the battle in 1687 the Turks lost it on the same plain.

64. Actually fourteen horses listed in seven pairs. Twelve were drawing the coach, and two were reserves.

65. Cf. the following description of the Janissary's uniform and dress. "The janissary's uniform was of dark blue cloth, plainly cut and comparatively free from ornamentation. Its simplicity was compensated for by the elaborate magnificence of their headdress. This consisted of a white felt hat shaped after the fashion affected by Marlborough's Grenadiers, richly embroidered round the base and resolving itself behind into the sleeve-like appendage which commemorated their religious initiation; to the front was attached a gilt sheath encrusted with bastard stones and into this was stuck—if the wearer was a veteran soldier—a prodigious Bird-of-Paradise plume which fell in a magnificent curve down his back and reached nearly to the level of his knees. When stationed at Constantinople the janissaries carried silver-tipped batons some six feet long with which they performed summary execution on anyone found breaking the laws. A feature which distinguished them from the bearded Turks was their shaven chins. This was supposed to impart a fierceness of expression unattainable by the wearer of a beard, and the effect was further enhanced by the cultivation of long and ferocious moustaches" (G. E. Hubbard, *The Day of the Crescent: Glimpses of Old Turkey* [Cambridge, Cambridge University Press, 1920], pp. 43–44).

66. Captain: *delibaša*. See n. 4 for comment on *delija* and *delibaša*. According to Hubbard (see above, n. 65), p. 48, one of the irregular troops in the Turkish army was made up of "Mad-caps." "Another and very extraordinary corps were the volunteers known as the *delis* (anglicé, 'Mad-caps'), who, under the influence of religious fanaticism, used to offer themselves for any particularly desperate enterprise, and of whom it was said that not a single one had ever shown his back to the enemy, whatever the odds. The dress worn by these 'Mad-caps' was of an outrageous design, intended, like the masks of the old Chinese warriors, to strike fear into the heart of the enemy. It consisted of a dolman and breeches made of a lion or bear skin with the hair turned outwards, and a bonnet of leopard's skin with a pair of eagle's wings sewn on in such a way as to stand upright on either side. Another pair of wings

projected from their shields, so that the whole effect was that of a moving mass of fur and feathers—even their horses being cóvered with the skins of various wild animals. Their usual weapons were a scimitar, a club and a long pike." This description better fits parts of Tale of Orašac's appearance to the world than that of Avdo's everyday *delija*, but the *delibaša*, the leader of the troop that was taking Fatima away to Kara Bogdan, seems to share some of the fierceness of countenance here depicted.

67. Gray: literally *zelen*, "green."

68. Vila. See n. 12, above.

69. Troublemakers: *čarkadžije*. This is the meaning given by Avdo himself in Text No. 12445, line 533.

70. Alibeg. This is a name rather than a title, or rather, it is a name, *Ali*, plus the title *beg*. It is to be distinguished from *alaybey* or *alaybeg*, which is a military rank, the *bey* of an *alay*. In modern Turkish *alay* means "troop; crowd; procession; regiment; great quantity of anything." (It has a secondary meaning of "joke, derision," which is not applicable here, of course.) In Serbo-Croatian Škaljić gives three meanings: (1) a crowd of people (*skupina, gomila, masa (svijeta), svjetina, mnoštvo*), (2) a parade or procession (*parada, pompa, svečana povorka, svečanost*), and (3) the regiment in the army whose commander is a colonel (*miralaj; mir* means chief or commander [Hony]). I believe that it would be absurd to translate *alaybey* as "colonel." I have preferred to keep the term *alaybey* in a kind of Anglicized form, or to translate it "commander." It is of interest to note that *alay* in Turkish is said (Škaljić) to have come from Greek *elegion*, a military rank, military service.

71. This passage, in which Fatima thinks that Meho and Osman are from Buda, is not in Šemić's text as published by F. S. Krauss, but it is to be found in the songbook text of 1925 (see Introduction). Clearly Avdo was not following the unadulterated Šemić text, but was influenced, at least, by another.

72. Fifteen years. Avdo's view of the timing in this song is notable. The action takes place, in his mind, not long after Buda has been taken by the Turks (see n. 47 above), yet he also says here that fifteen years ago the sultan had sent a vizier to Buda to help Fatima's father, Zajim Alibeg. Fifteen is here most probably simply a traditional number, but it is a fact that fifteen years elapsed between the capture of Buda at the battle of Mohács in August 1526 and the recapture of the city in August 1541. No matter what the numbers and dates involved, it is, I believe, significant that the history of the city of Budapest, Buda in particular, is one of establishment by the Turks of someone as administrator, who runs into trouble of one kind or another, and the necessity of reestablishing someone else on the seat of authority. The reestablishment of power in or after 1541, a period in which Peter was ruling in Moldavia, would seem to form a good historical background for our song. (See n. 74, below, for more on the sending of a vizier to Buda.) In the songbook version the time between the arrival of the vizier and the moment of the

action of the song is not stated, but the implication is that it was not long. Fatima's being sent away is viewed as an immediate consequence of the exile of her father, which came about the time of her coming of age for marriage.

73. Three horsetail plumes: *uštugli*. In conversation (Text No. 12445, lines 585ff.) Avdo was asked what *uštugli* meant. He replied that it meant that the vizier was permanently in one place and was responsible to none but to God and the sultan. Nikola then asked him if it had anything to do with three horsetails; Nikola said that others had told him that was what it meant. Avdo denied that there was any connection, and insisted that *uštugli* meant a "fourth of the empire" (*četvrtina carstva*).

74. The sending of a vizier to a region in order to honor it and/or bring it stability is itself a repeated pattern or theme in the poetry. The most famous example is the song of the "Arrival of the Vizier in Travnik," which was published in Hörmann's collection and which is part of Avdo's own repertory. For the history see above, n. 72, and the Introduction.

75. Fata: a short form of Fatima.

76. School: that is, the Moslem elementary school, *mejtef*, Turkish *mekteb*, Arabic *mätäb*.

77. Seminary: *medresa*, Moslem theological school, high school (Hony). Škaljić says it is the school to which pupils go from the *mejtef*, or elementary school, or from the *ruždija*, which is an elementary school for adults. The teacher in a *medresa* is a *muderiz*, and a pupil in it a *softa*. These are the words I have translated "teacher" and "pupil."

78. Sealed and stamped petition: *mahzar kakav/Pod pulima i pod muhurima*. The question is, what does *pod pulima* mean? *Pula* means (Škaljić) "button," "postage stamp," "sequin," "scale on a fish," "the head of a nail." Clearly "postage stamp" fits here. The line means, therefore, literally, "under stamps and under seals."

79. That stays at home and will not venture forth: or, "let them stay at home and not venture forth." It is unclear whether Avdo did not finish his sentence or was unusually elliptical. Either is possible, but I have decided on the first. The end of the vizier's order seems very abrupt.

80. There is, of course, an inconsistency here. Previously Fatima told Meho that when she was eight years old her father had taken her from the *mejtef* and put her in the women's quarters. Here she says that her father was exiled when she was four and that her mother brought her up and taught her in hiding. In one context he stresses that she was brought up out of touch with the world of men's conversation, and the picture is the more or less usual one. In the second context he stresses the teaching and life in hiding from the vizier.

81. Revenues: *andaluci*. Avdo (Text No. 12445, lines 705ff.) says this means *prihod*, "income." I do not find the word in any dictionary.

82. Vizier's Plain: *Vezir Polje.*

83. The imperial alaybey. Here Avdo uses the title for Alibeg. There may be confusion in Avdo's mind.

84. A troublesome passage. "od mene ti uzimanja nema, Za mene to pominjanja nema" ("There is no taking of me, There is no mentioning [or thinking] of me").

85. Tale of Orašac: an unusual hero of the Border, who will be met with later and described in great detail. He acts as judge for the men of the Border, and they hand over important enemies to him for judgment.

86. A good two stories high: *dva boja muška.* In conversation (Text No. 12445, lines 743ff.) Avdo explains this means the height of two men, one on top of the other!

87. Blue or yellow. The two words involved are *mavi* and *plavi.* The first, *mavi,* is of Turkish origin, from Arabic *ma'* meaning "water" plus an Arabic adjectival suffix. Its basic meaning is, therefore, "blue as water." *Plavi* is from Latin *flavus* or its German cognate *blau* and means light blue, sky blue, blond, yellow. Avdo might have used *žuti* in this line, but the internal rhyme of *mavi-plavi* was decisive. A few lines later when he speaks of "yellow copper" the sounds of *tumačinom žutom* make a harmonious noun-epithet combination.

88. In conversation (Text No. 12445, lines 750ff.) Avdo explains that steel doors were constructed in fortresses as a protection and that they were whitewashed on the outside so that the enemy could not tell where the door was and find range for the cannon. When asked where he had heard of such doors, Avdo said that in one of his songs the Turkish forces cannot find the gates of Ćirka of Đirit, and Halil is told by Kalauz Rizvan that he must climb the wall up to a small door, pull himself through it, and jump down into the courtyard. Inside on the left he would find a steel door. On the outside it was whitewashed so that one would not know where it was. That was in Đirit. Nikola then asked where Avdo had heard of Zajim Alibeg's doors in Buda, and he said that he had heard of them from the songbook. As a matter of fact, the songbook (both Šemić and 1925) says "our doors are not of wood; the two panels are like a hero's shoulders, and the bars are maiden's hands" (Šemić, lines 544–546; 1925, lines 488–490).

89. I do not know where Avdo learned of this fabulous device. The songbook describes Fatima's house, and it had wondrous accouterments, but not this particular mechanism. For the details of the songbook see the Introduction and the summary of the songbook version.

90. Minaret rod with star and crescent. *Alem* is given in Hony as "sign, mark; flag; proper name; high mountain; peak of a minaret; the crescent and star on the top of a mosque." Škaljić reads, "the crescent (*polumjesec*—half-moon) with three or four balls beneath it, which is found on top of a minaret as an ornament. The 'alem' is made of copper and then tinned or gilded. Instead of a half-moon there is frequently an ornament of pear shape inside which is the name of God in Arabic,

'Allah.' " The songbook described a somewhat similar ornament, even more elaborate, indeed, but this is not unusual in the Moslem poetry.

91. Vlahs: *Vlasi* are the Wallachians. Wallachia, together with Moldavia, formed Rumania.

92. Gypsy's sword. Gypsies were often used as executioners.

93. See the textual notes in vol. IV for comment on this name.

94. Palanquins: Turkish *tahtiravan* from Persian. The line is a bit strange in linking violins and palanquins. Škaljić remarks that until about sixty years ago rich Moslem maidens were carried in these litters, borne by either horses or four men, with the wedding guests to the bridegroom's house.

95. I have translated the second half of this sentence as indirect discourse, but actually the text shifts abruptly in the middle of Meho's speech to direct address: "Will you take me and be my wife, not because things have happened as they did, but just as if you were free and prosperous, as when your father was here?"

96. The same phenomenon is found here as in the previous note. There is an abrupt change to direct address within indirect address for two lines: "I shall take you to your mother and ask for her consent."

97. Literally, "our mirror."

98. Osmanli: i.e., in spite of the fact that the vizier was a traitor, he had the manners and politeness of a true Osmanli Turk.

99. Falcon-children: *Sokolovi*. Falcons are symbols of heroes.

100. Religious statutes: *Šerijat*, "the divine laws of Islam" (Hony), Turkish *şeriat*.

101. Guardian of the law: *Hafiz efendi*, Turkish *hafiz*, "keeper; (obs) guardian, protector, God; (rel) a person knowing the text of the Koran by heart" (Hony).

102. Aman: "Mercy."

103. Cape. This cape (*ćurak*) is fur-lined and can be either long or short. It seems to be a ceremonial garment given to a visitor for an audience with a high official. See Hubbard, *Day of the Crescent*, pp. 57–58. Hubbard gives a description (chap. IV, pp. 50ff.) of the audience with the sultan of the Venetian ambassador in 1682, taken from the memoirs of Antonio Benetti, who was a dragoman in the ambassador's household. His memoirs, *Viaggi a Constantinopoli*, were published in Venice in 1688. The garment described in the memoirs is called a "kaftan," but it, like the *ćurak*, was fur-lined, or of fur.

104. The idea being, of course, that the daughters will marry and have left the house before the sons marry and bring their brides to live together in their husbands' house or compound. This is a commonplace of the poetry.

105. Amin: "amen; so be it." Not the same as "aman" (see n. 102).

106. This scene of hospitality should be compared with the two previous examples at the overnight stops on the journey to Buda by Meho and Osman. The theme is the same in all cases, but it is skillfully adapted to circumstances each time it is used.

107. Shining light of our house: literally, "my shining countenance." *Obraz* is frequently used in the sense of honor; hence, "my shining honor."

108. Groom's attendants, *đeverovi*; they not only attend to the groom, but one, at least, is assigned to accompany the bride. Bride's maids, *jenđikade*; maidens from the side of the groom who go to help prepare the bride; they go before her or after her in a bridal procession. There are from one to thirty of them, says Avdo in conversation (Text No. 12445, lines 1118–1122). Škaljić says "a woman or girl who goes for the bride among the wedding guests and accompanies her so that she may not be alone among the men."

109. Large metal, often copper, trays, sometimes ornamental or used for tables and beautifully etched; sometimes the smaller ones are used for cooking *pita*, a kind of pie.

110. Gifts, *boščaluk*. Škaljić says: "a gift which consists of clothing wrapped in a piece of cloth, a *bošča* [see n. 36, above, for Škaljić's definition]. In the old days it contained pants, shirt, a square kerchief (*čevra*) and a long rectangular one (*jagluk*), or a belt of embroidered silk. A present-day man's gift ordinarily contains shirt, pants, tie and socks; and a woman's gift, a set of women's lingerie, including a nightgown. A bride gives a 'boščaluk' to the bridegroom and his family and to the wedding guests; the owner of a newly built house gives one to the master-workers; a child carries a 'boščaluk' to the hodža when he has finished his reading of the Koran."

111. Blue silk: *meneviš svila*, blue silk, or violet-colored (Škaljić). In conversation (Text No. 12445, line 1125), Avdo says that it is silk that is not embroidered with gold. Hony gives "wavy appearance of shot silk" among other meanings for *meneviš*, and "watered (silk)" or "blued (steel)" under the adjective *menevišli*.

112. Younger. *Mlađi* is used to mean both younger in years and of lesser rank, as Avdo explains in conversation (Text No. 12445, lines 1127–1133), "That one [Smail] is the alaybey, and this one [Meho] is the alaybegović, and he is their standard-bearer."

113. Light cakes: *lake brašnjenike*. *Brašnjenik* or *brašnjenica* is the cake or bread carried for food on a trip. Vuk gives the Latin "viaticum." The "sweet cakes" in the same line are *gurabije*, which Škaljić calls "a hard round cake (*kolač*) made of flour, sugar and butter. If honey is used instead of sugar it is called 'honeyed gurabija' (*medena gurabija*)."

114. Imam: see above, n. 21.

115. Wretched: *domuski*. In conversation (Text No. 12445, lines 1239–1242) Avdo did not recognize that he had used this word and denied any knowledge of it: "I must have said something else." But he did say that *domuzin* meant "swine" (*svinja*). Turkish *domuz* has that meaning. I could not find an adequate translation; "wretched" is a weak substitute. Actually the play between *domuski* and *Otman*, the forbidden food and animal on one side, and the house of Al Otman on the other, is effective between two opposites.

116. The sirdar: Mujo Hrnjica. He too is famous for his moustaches, his flashing eyes, and his broad brow.

117. To Bagdad, to the third empire. In conversation (Text No. 12445, lines 1269ff.) Avdo explains that Bagdad was the third shah after Stambol. The second was Arabia, "as it is even today" (1935). At this point Nikola asked Avdo if Bagdad was then in the sultan's hands. Avdo said that it had been taken by "Selim, that is to say, Sulejman." "*Nikola:* Then it was surely after that war when Đerđelez and Fatima took Bagdad? *Avdo:* No. Đerđelez was earlier. From Đerđelez's time to ours is four hundred and some odd years, and from the Hrnjicas two hundred sixty-five or six. *N:* Then Mustajbeg was not alive in Đerđelez's time? *A:* Probably not even born. *N:* So? A singer sang for me that Mustajbeg was in that war on Bagdad with Đerđelez. *A:* If I had been like that singer who sang for you, I would have sung it for the gentleman [Parry] in the coffeehouse that day [referring to the day when we first met Avdo and he was asked questions about the songs he knew]. But I cannot sing when I know that Đerđelez lived nearly two hundred years, one hundred and seventy, and then the men of the Border began. *N:* Was Ćuprilić Vizier alive when Đerđelez was? *A:* Ćuprilić Vizier lived according to our reckoning three hundred and sixty years. *N:* And Đerđelez? *A:* Đerđelez lived only a short time. He was born and brought up in Gazi Hrustembeg's court. He was an orphan. He used to clean the stables . . . . *N:* Do you know where he died? *A:* There's nothing about it in my songs . . . . *N:* But you see the trouble is that when Ćuprilić was alive so was Mustajbeg. *A:* But I tell you. Ćuprilić was with Murat on Kosovo five hundred and sixty years ago; he was young. And he was with Sulejman the Magnificent and took Temišvar, and he was at Vienna, when Sokolović went there. Then he was very old, but he was alive. Think of how many years there are from Murat to Sulejman.

"*N:* Do you know where Bagdad is? *A:* The hadžije have told me that it is far away as you go to Mecca . . . . *N:* Is it in Asia? *A:* Yes in Great Asia but not in Little Asia [Asia Minor]. In Arabistan; there are Arabs there. *N:* Then, when the vizier exiled them from Buda, they went via Istambul. *A:* Well, it may be that they did not go by way of Istambul, so that nobody could see them and report it, but that they had gone around; Romunija was under the sultan, and Ozija was in the middle of the Turkish Empire. *N:* It seems to me that there was no other way than via Istambul. *A:* It's possible they went by Istambul, because he had two cousins there, the Master of the Privy Seal (*muhur sahibija*) and the High Pontiff of Islam (*šeh ul islam*). They conspired with him. *N:* How was it that the sultan had not heard of the oppression of that vizier, when he exiled them? *A:* For twelve years it had been going on, and he knew nothing about it. Those who were at his side hid it from him . . . . The Šeh ul islam, who was the sultan's hodža and most trusted person. He was head of the whole faith and the Koran and was God's vicar. When he commits a crime, one believes in it; for a long time one cannot believe that he is a traitor."

118. Black mourner: i.e., dressed in black.

119. Do not worry about us here: i.e., Do not think about what we may say.

Literally, "do not turn your head in this direction" (*Amo nemoj okretati glavu*; line 6050).

120. Brotherly alliance: *Bratimstvo*, blood-brotherhood.

121. Girl's protector. See n. 108.

122. The following line, 6170, I cannot understand. It reads: "što ne visiš mlados od staroga."

123. Steward: *kavadar*, a word not in Škaljić's excellent dictionary, strangely enough. In Hony and the Tarhan Kitabevi dictionary under *kafadar*, the meaning of "companion, intimate friend," is given. See above, n. 45.

124. Fortress gate. The line (6213) originally read, "sad iziđi na grad na Udbinu," but the mention of Udbina was clearly a mistake. In Text No. 12445, lines 1345ff., Nikola asked Avdo about this. Avdo admitted the error and changed the line himself to "sad iziđi na grad na kapiju."

125. Captains and commanders of a thousand: *baše i bimbaše*. See n. 28, above.

126. Guns: *kumbara*, bomb, grenade, and even the guns that fire them (Škaljić, Hony, Tarhan). The line reads "neđe topom, neđe kumbarama," and I have tried to keep the parallelism.

127. This sentence is the best I can do for the two aphoristic lines:

> Hajanje je dobro vojevanje,   6255
> I na svakoj strani prodiranje.

128. See above, n. 26.

129. Here begins the catalogue of forces.

130. Crooked. *Egri* means just that in Turkish, and in Text No. 1244, lines 1383–1386, Avdo confirmed this meaning.

131. Lit. colleague, *kolega*.

132. See n. 133, below

133. Unđurovina. In Text No. 12445, lines 1404ff., Avdo says that Unđurovina is across the Una, which flows on the edge of (*naskrajm*) Bosnia, the other side of Osijek; it flows to Hungarian Šabac. It was received (by the Turks) later. It's beyond Bosnia. Osijek is not in Bosnia but in Slavonija. "*N:* Is the Una in Brčko? *A:* No, Brčko is this side of the Sava. That's Bosnia, the Posavina. *N:* Is Brčko in the Unđurovina? *A:* No, in Bosnia. *N:* Have you been in Brčko? *A:* I have. *N:* Did you sing of Brčko before you were in Brčko? *A:* I did. *N:* Who was the aga that you sang of from there? *A:* Alibeg. *N:* Where did you hear of Maglaj, Doboj, Zenica, and those other cities in the songs? *A:* All from the men of the Border (*Krajišnici*), from those who are guslars. *N:* Those places aren't in the songbook, I would say. *A:* I haven't noticed them in the songbook. *N:* Then you added them to the song, is that it? *A:* No, but I got them from that singer, Maglaj and Zenica; they are not in the songbooks .... *N:* Who were these borderers? *A:* Men like Sado Hadžović, Latif Zeković, Avdaga Šahavić, Reša Alihadžić, Hasan Radoglavac, Bajraktar Tale-

vić, Hasan Nišić, Hamid Nišić, and my father. *N:* Are those all borderers? *A:* That's what I call them. Up to now we called them Krajišnici, but now they call those who sing songs guslars."

(Same conversation, beginning line 1446) "*N:* Avdo, when you gather an army in a song, are there any heroes, or agas, or places, whose names you make up? For example, when you sing that there was a Tarić Omer [or Fatić Omer] in Visoko [line 6854]. Did you put that in yourself, or did you hear that from a singer? *A:* I heard it from a singer. *N:* From whom? *A:* From several. *N:* Did you hear from them of all those places that you dictated to me? *A:* Yes. I haven't been to any of them; if I hadn't heard of them how would I know them?"

"*N:* Has there been any other singer who has been able to gather an army the way you do? *A:* In my generation, since I took up the gusle, not one. *N:* But when you took up the gusle, for example, old Zeković, Kaljić, and Šahović were still alive. How about one of them? *A:* I said in my rank (*boj*); I heard it from them. *N:* So they gathered an army the way you do? *A:* They did. *N:* Much like all this? *A:* Much like it. From where would I know these buljukašas and standard-bearers, and agas and elders (*ajan*) if I had not learned from them, heard them from them, and taken them into my mind?"

Nikola went on to ask Avdo if he had ever seen a map. He said that he had seen one in the railroad station in Doboj, for example. He could not read it, but a cashier had shown him it. He had a nephew in Doboj and he (Avdo) had gone to visit his sister's son in Posavina, in Brčko. He had seen the map in the station in Doboj, and he had seen ours. But he had not understood any of it.

Avdo had spent two nights at that nephew's house. "He [the cashier] was the husband of his wife's sister (*pašenog*); two sisters married two brothers; one married my nephew, and one married the cashier. I was free there, and they were saying that I should go from Doboj to Gračanica, and then by way of Majevica either on foot or by auto. But my nephew and the cashier wanted to pay for my ticket to go by way of Derventa to Bosna Brod, and then Slavonski Brod, Vinkovci, and then to Osijek and back again to Brčko. *N:* Did you look for those places on the map in Doboj? *A:* No. They showed me the way. They didn't point out the places, except that the cashier showed how they wanted to send me by way of Slavonski Brod and Bosanski Brod, so that I would not have to go across on foot, all alone. *N:* Were you in Maglaj? *A:* I know only the station, when I returned from Doboj, they told me, but I was not in Maglaj. *N:* Were you in Zenica? *A:* I went through Zenica on the train. *N:* I thought that you had not sung of those places until you had gone through them. *A:* I did. Ask these people, one of the older ones, whether Avdo sang of those agas and ajans and those places and buljukbašas only from 1928, or before then . . . . *N:* How long is it since you were on that trip? *A:* In twenty-eight. *N:* Seven years, then."

134. In Text No. 12445, lines 1942ff., Avdo says that Fildiš and Filduš were not brothers, but captains (*kapetani*). "*N:* Were they comrades (*jarani*), coevals

(*akrani*), colleagues (*kolege*)? *A:* They were under imperial charter of the same rank, Fildiš and Filduš. *N:* Did they live together? *A:* No. There were two Janjas, two Bijeljinas, an upper and a lower. It was far; there was a difference; those were two separate towns."

135. See note 133.

136. See note 133.

137. In Text No. 12445, lines 1512ff.: *"N:* I have heard, and it is true, that there was a certain Šala in Mostar; but you sing of some Ćemalbeg. *A:* Šala is not in my songs, only Bey Ćemalbegović. *N:* What more do you know of Ćemalbegović except in that song? *A:* In every song in which there is the gathering of a large army, I know that they summoned him. *N:* Is there any particular heroic deed that he did himself? *A:* Only that he was an army leader, and then afterwards they summoned him whenever there was an army. He gathered Mostar and the region around Mostar."

138. See below, note 175.

139. Avdo (Text No. 12445, lines 1523ff.) says that Vrelo Cetina is in the Krajina, on this side, in the Lika, in the west, from Croatia, the upper part of the Lika. A spring wells up there and there is a town there. It forms a river. (See the article in the *Enciklopedija Jugoslavije* for more on this place.)

140. (Text No. 12445, lines 1568ff.) *"N:* Now tell me what you know about Grdan Omeraga of Orlujac other than what is in the song. *A:* Well, he was "grdan," and wherever he went the army was left "grdna" because of him. That was Grdan Omeraga. That much I know, that he was a might man (*sila*), and that wherever the army was, everything remained "grdno" because of him, because of what happened before him. *N:* So he was a good hero? Was anybody ever in single combat with him? *A:* In my songs I don't know of any single combat. Only when there were groups of the army. He attacked with his company and accomplished "grdno" deeds there in the army." Clearly Avdo knows nothing more of this figure than he tells us in the song itself. Note that in Avdo's "Smailagić Meho" the hero is not Grdan Omeraga but Grdan or Grda Osmanaga. Nikola used the name that is in the songbook, and Avdo did not notice the difference, although at one point his tongue slipped and he said "Omen . . . Omeraga"; the "n" may have come from a stifled Osman. The adjective "grdan" has several meanings. It means, "big, huge, enormous, many in number" (*golem, velik, ogroman, mnogobrojan*); also "ugly, nasty, disgusting" (*ružan, gadan*); "evil, bad" (*zao, rđav, loš*); "unfortunate, luckless, sad, sorrowful, wretched, miserable" (*nesrećan, jadan*). Osmanaga or Omeraga is pictured, I believe, as some combination of the first and of the last of these meanings: he is big and mighty, and he causes suffering and woe and loss both to his opponents and to his own army.

141. The word is *ćehaja* and it means, according to Škaljić, "the assistant, or representative, of a vizier, pasha, keeper of the books, or any other high official in the Turkish Empire" (*pomoćnik, zastupnik, vezira, paše, defterdara ili kojeg drugog*

velikodostojnika u Turskoj Carevini). It comes from the vulgar form (*kehaya*) of Turkish literary *kahya*, meaning "steward, housekeeper," from Persian *ked* ("house") and Persian *huda* ("master, owner"). The name Ćejvan also comes to Turkish from Persian, but, according to Škaljić, not from the same words as *ćehaja*. Ćejvan is Turkish *Keyvan* and comes from Persian *keywan*, meaning "one who guards and oversees a high position," from *key* meaning "high position" and the suffix *-wan*. Ćejvanaga, and more particularly his son Mehmed mentioned here, Ćejvanović Meho, are well-known heroes of the Moslem epic.

142. Orlić Mustafaga came from Udbina. Text No. 12445, lines 1593–1594.

143. In Text No. 12445, lines 1595ff., Avdo discusses this name and similar ones. He was from Čekrk, and the proper form of his name, according to Avdo, is Alem Kadunić, not Alemkadunić. Kadunić means "mother's son" and was a family name stemming from the name of the mother rather than that of the father. The same holds for other family names such as Fatić, from Fata, Fatima; Hatić from Hata. Avdo did not know why these names came about. He also cited the name of one of Mustajbeg's standard-bearers, Mejrić Ibrahim, whose family name, Mejrić, comes from Mejra. Nikola said he had never heard of him, but he is in Avdo's catalogues.

144. Vlahinjić Alija's mother kept the sheep for the *dizdar* (fortress commander), presumably of Udbina, and it was there that Alija was born. What happened to his father Avdo did not know, but his mother was a Serb (i.e. Orthodox Christian) and Avdo did not know how or why she became a Moslem. Nikola suggested that it was the other way around, that she was a Moslem and that Alija's father was a Serb. Avdo countered that then the name would be Vlahović, and that this was the way he had always heard it (Text No. 12445, lines 1614–1633).

145. Šarac Mahmutaga was from Otoka, which was between Bihać and the Lika (Text No. 12445, lines 1633–1635).

146. Kunić Hasanaga was also from Otoka, but in this case, the district rather than the town itself. The name Otoka, said Avdo, covered a whole area (Text No. 12445, lines 1636ff.).

147. *Belaj* means "woe."

148. The elder wedding guest (*stari svat*) was the chief of the wedding guests, the one most honored and whose gift was of considerable value. Tale complains that he was never invited in that prestigious and profitable capacity, but only as the chief herald (*Čauš*), whose duty it was to announce the order of events, especially when the time came for the wedding guests to begin their journey, either to the bride's house or from it. The "drum" (*talambas*) of which he speaks in the next line or so is the drum of the herald.

149. Mad Aziza. Note the strange characters by whom Tale is surrounded—a mad sister, a standard-bearer whose name is woe, and a scolding wife with naked and hungry children, to say nothing of the hodža Šuvajlija!

150. Lit. "dog's excrement" (*govno pasje*).

151. Lit. "excrement for Tale" (*govno Tali*).

152. See n. 150.

153. *Krpatina* is an augmentative of *krpa*, meaning "big rag," "big patchwork." In Text No. 12445, lines 1666ff., Avdo explains that Krpatina was the name of Tale's sword. It was patched with pieces of metal, somebody's horseshoes, in place of rings.

154. Tahiraga. Tale is a short form for Tahir, which comes from the Arabic word *tahir*, meaning "pure."

155. Lit. "May a dog copulate with" (*pas mu jeb 'o*).

156. *Karantani*, small copper coins.

157. *Madžarije*, Turkish gold coins.

158. Lit. "May the dogs copulate with his mother" (*psi mu drli majku*).

159. I won't even exchange a greeting with (say *merhaba* to) Mehmed. *Merhaba* means "good day," and is the ordinary Moslem greeting. According to Škaljić it is a shortened form of an Arabic expression meaning "you have come to a large place (i.e., among friends)."

160. Village elders. The Serbian is *knez*, and in Turkish times this indicated either the head of a village who gathered taxes, or the head of a larger unit called a *knežina*. The latter later became *vojvode*. Here, however, I believe the reference is to village heads (*seoski knezovi*). The article on *knez* in Vuk Karadžić's dictionary is very informative. See above, n. 52.

161. Easily. Turkish *kolay* is here used by Avdo. This is an excellent example of Avdo's intimate knowledge of Turkish and his use of it in the songs. I have never seen this before, and, without concordances, it seems to me that this is as much of a *hapax legomenon* as one can find. There is no reason why Avdo could not have used the ordinary Serbo-Croatian word *lako*.

162. I am not sure of this translation, but I believe the idea is correct.

163. *Kavadari*; see n. 123.

164. I am not sure what verb *zaplišila* comes from, but the general sense is followed in "filled."

165. Ljevak means a left-handed person.

166. In Text No. 12445, Avdo locates both Lenger and Silitor in Hungary (lines 1932–1934).

167. Heroic kolos: *viteška kola* rather than *junačka kola*. It may be that the choice of *viteška* (from *vitez*, meaning "knight") was dictated by alliteration with the preceding line. Note the alliterative and other sound patterns in the vicinity of the line in question (8011);

> Sad se zlatne čaše povedoše.
> Sohbet zlatan ode među njima,
> A vojske se s vojskom smiješaše.   8010
> Viteška se kola pofataše.
> Alajli se razviše bajraci.
> Zapevaše u kolo Bošnjaci,

168. Thick forest (see above, n. 7).

169. Splendid fighters. *Dankrlačlije* was glossed in the margin by Nikola as *dobri*, "good," and it is from that gloss that I have taken the translation. In conversation Text No. 12445, lines 1937–1940, Avdo interprets the word as meaning "the large number of horsemen that go along beside a bey and protect him from attack in the close vicinity," which Nikola then shortened to "bodyguard" or "personal guard" (*lična garda*). The closest I have found to this word in the Turkish dictionary is *dağ-kirlangici*, meaning "a sand-martin." I have also noted the *dağ* which means "mountain," and that there is a word *kirlağan* (obs.) meaning "plague," (fig.) "evil men, host of calamities, bandits." This suggests something like "mountain bandits" as a possibility, but that is pure conjecture. Avdo does not seem to have been clear about its meaning, because he gave us two choices.

170. Inspired. *Džinovit* means "like a jinni." The jinn (pl.), according to Škaljić, were "invisible spiritual beings, spirits, demons, either good or bad." Note in the following line (8051) *vilovit*, "like a vila," referring to the "magic" swiftness of the horses. The army, too, had supernatural qualities.

171. Here and in some other places *beyler* is translated in the singular, because the plural form is used in the verse for metrical reasons.

172. David E. Bynum has given a translation in the margin of the typed text, "May the contentment of God be upon you." *Alahrazijala* was interpreted in conversation Text No. 12445, lines 2160–2161, as "that's the way it is and thank you, thanks" (*to je reći, to je tako i fala ti, zafala*). *Raziluk* in the following line of the text (8172) is given in Škaljić as meaning "satisfaction" (*zadovoljstvo*).

173. Avdo places Konjic somewhere in Hercegovina beyond Sarajevo (see Text No. 12445, lines 1955–1956).

174. Right hand: lit. "wings."

175. Shortly before dictating "Smailagić Meho" Avdo had been present at a conversation with an old Moslem inhabitant of Bijelo Polje, Began Ljuca Nikšić, in which Began had said that Bey Ljubović was superior to other beys. Nikola, in conversation Text No. 12445, lines 1957ff., asked Avdo if he had put this passage into his song, telling how Bey Ljubović was superior to the seventy beys in the room, after he had heard this from Began. Avdo was insensed at the idea. He said that Began had said Ljubović was better than three hundred beys and he, Avdo, had said only seventy beys of Unđurovina (*unđurskije*). He said that he sang of Ljubović in Kandija, at Osjek, and he had heard also that Ljubović was in the song of Bagdad. In answer to the question whether he had ever before sung that there was no bey superior to Ljubović, Avdo said that he had in the song when Gazi Hrustembeg had gone to Stambol with Šahin pasha's wedding guests. He (Gazi Hrustembeg) had recognized and admitted that his array (*saltanet*) was as nothing compared to that of Ljubović. Then the vizier of Adrianople, when they were resting overnight, had recognized that there was more richness and silk with Ljubović, much more, than with Gazi Hrustembeg. Avdo swore that he had sung of this long before he had heard it from Began.

176. In conversation Text No. 12445, lines 2012ff., Nikola engaged Avdo in conversation about Mujo and Halil. Avdo said that Mujo had won two sirdar ranks (*serdarstva*) when he had avenged Ograšić and killed Diklić. He was commander in every war and was head wedding guest (*svaski starešina*). When he killed Diklić he was given the twelve plumes of two sirdars. Had Mujo not been there, there might have been two sirdars in Bosnia.

Asked if Halil was always an unmarried youth (*momak*) in every song, Avdo said that in his songs there is nothing about Halil's getting really married. Everywhere when he is married, in the last analysis there is no mention of marriage bed, nor of his ever having had children. Halil had some great friends of his own age, and whatever girl he took for himself, then he said to his friend, "Here, brother, she is for you, I won't marry." Avdo said that he had no indication of Halil's death, or of his grave, or of his marrying. "*N:* But didn't they give him one of the thirty girls they captured in the Coastland? *A:* Of course, they gave him one. *N:* And what did he do with her? *A:* Afterwards he came back to the Border and gave her to someone for marriage. He accepted each one for himself; he gained one at the horse race in Vienna; and he wooed and took Fatima in Buda; and with Huremagić Ibro he fought in single combat in Buda for Fata, daughter of Mahmut Zajim; and in France (*Francija*) when he rescued his uncle, he took a French queen for himself; and in many other places. But I don't notice any real marrying. *N:* I think he married. *A:* Possibly . . . . I have heard that he took girls, but in the end I have not heard of any offspring. There are Ajkunići [of the family of Ajkuna, Mujo and Halil's sister], and Mujo had a wife and two children, Omer and Ahmet. But for Halil there is no mention of marriage bed, although he married.

"*N:* In so many songs Halil was in so many wars, in that amount of time he must have become old. He could not have remained young always. *A:* But that's the way it was. Mujo died when he was sixty-seven. *N:* But Halil never had any moustaches? And you always describe him in your songs as prettier than any girl. *A:* The late Husein [he means Ćor Huso], may Allah rest his soul (*Alahrahmetile*), used to say that Halil's mother had one Halil first of all and then he died. Then a second was born, and she loved him so much that she gave him the same name. Nine Hrnjičići there were and all short-lived, and she gave each the name of Halil, one after another. *N:* Oh, so there were several Halils, you say? *A:* That's what Husein said. In some places I have heard that there were nine Hrnjičići sons born; the ninth was Mujo, and there were eight Halils. The first Halil was the most outstanding; Mujo was the first, the oldest. *N:* It's hard for me to believe that there was more than one Halil. *A:* Well, there you are. I don't say there was; but that's the way people have inquired and interpreted it."

177. Demonic spirit: *šajitan*, Satan, means "demon" or "devil."

178. This description of Mujo with his monstrous moustaches is very reminiscent of that of Kurroglou in the Turkish tales. Cf. Alexander Chodzko, *Specimens of the Popular Poetry of Persia* (London, 1842).

179. Cf. the following from Chodzko (see n. 178), page 32: "The reports that circulate here about thee are so dreadful, that if a child cries and the mother desires to silence it, she tells it, Be quiet, for the wolf is come and is sure to devour thee if thou shouldest shriek any longer; the child cries on. The leopard is come; the child continues to cry. But no sooner is it told, Kurroglou is come to fetch it to Chamly-bill, than the child leaves off crying immediately, and being frightened, hides its face in the pillow and falls asleep."

180. Protector: the *đever*, or groom's attendant, assigned to protect the bride and accompany her to the bridegroom's house. See above, n. 108.

181. Conversation Text No. 12445, lines 2086ff.: Nikola reminded Avdo that he had said that he had worn a pigtail when he was young. All the young in the village at that time wore them, he said, but not all of those in the town; some did and some did not. He had had a pigtail until he went into the army, where they cut their hair. When he had come out of the army he had married and his youth had gone. He left that for the younger. *"N:* You didn't wear it to look, for example, like one of the old heroes? *A:* No, brother, that was another time . . . . That heroism did not belong to us. The old heroes were worthy men, and hajduks, they say; but we are not. Our people have come under discipline. Heroism has passed; a few hold out for wisdom, and they say that whoever behaves wisely is a better hero; and the younger say that whoever has more schooling. Heroic children go barefooted in the street."

182. Parchment: *Knjiga*, "book, letter (in the songs), paper."

183. The same characteristic was attributed to Meho himself earlier. See above, n. 10.

184. Venomous handjar. A handjar is a long single-edged knife, and swords and knives in the songs are often spoken of as being "of poison," as here (*od zehera*), or "of strong poison" (*od zehera ljuta*).

185. Sabers. *Palampuše* was not recognized by Avdo when asked what it meant.

186. Pikes. Avdo explained the word in conversation No. 12445, lines 2144ff., as "bayonets."

187. See n. 172.

188. Beylerbey: i.e., Mustajbeg of the Lika. *Beyler* is plural of *bey*; hence *beylerbey* means "bey of beys." Beylerbey was a term for the leader of a vilayet or pašaluk, but Mustajbeg does not seem to have been that.

189. Many saints, mighty powers.

> Da su s Talom mnogi ćirameti,
> A s vojskom su krupni adaleti.

Nikola glossed in the margin after *ćirameti* "*sveci*," "saints." In conversation No. 12445, lines 2163–2164, Avdo said that *adalet* meant "a help (*pomoć*), a great force (*velika snaga*)." For *ćiramet* Škaljić gives us "kerámet, ćerámet (Ar.) supernatural quality or phenomenon; miracle (it is believed to be a quality belonging only to good, pious men)." The next entry in Škaljić is: "kerámet-sahibija (Ar.) a good, very pious person who is believed to possess supernatural qualities—keramet." Hony gives for *keramet* "Kindness, generosity; miracle; a word or deed so opportune that it appears to be divinely inspired." Avdo's meaning is closer to *keramet-sahibija* than to *keramet* itself, but he has elevated the godly man to a saint. For more on *ćiramet* see n. 201 below. In the case of *adalet* I believe that Avdo may have confused two words that sound very much alike. *Adálet* means justice, and the corresponding adjective is *adaletli*, just. But *adalé* means muscle, and *adaleli*, muscular, strong, having muscular strength. Avdo has confused, it seems to me, these two words, and raised *adaleli*, after changing it to a noun, from the purely physical to the level of perhaps mystical powers.

190. Imperial: possibly just an epithet to fill out the line, but when challenged in conversation (No. 12445, lines 2164–2168) Avdo said he used it because "our sultan was Muhamed" (*Car nam je bio Muhamed*).

191. Jacket. *Jandžik* means a bag suspended on a string over the shoulder, but in the present context I believe "jacket" is meant, and that is confirmed by Avdo in the conversation (No. 12445, lines 2170–2172) when he said that Tale's *jandžik* was worn (*oblačeno*) on his back (*pleći*).

192. Eždeg. Avdo believed that *eždegski* and *eždegliski* came from the name of the tailor who made the cloth from which trousers and caps were fashioned. In reality, the word is a corruption of German *Jaeger* and referred to hunting breeches and hunting cap. That meaning was lost and Avdo constructed a new one. See n. 6 above.

193. Jackets. I have not been able to find the word *tarlagan* anywhere, but it clearly means something worn on the back. In conversation (No. 12445, lines 2178–2180) Avdo said that they were woven of wool and were made specially for Tale's company, but he did not describe them further.

194. See n. 189 above.

195. In conversation (No. 12445, lines 2184ff.) Avdo adds no real information about this character, except that his name was Šaćir.

196. See n. 123 above. The translation "comrade" does not fit here, so I have adopted "steward" as more suitable.

197. It is because of the pashas that Tale is sent to stay with the wife of Smail.

198. Poverty-stricken: *goluguza* means "bare-assed"!

199. In celebration.

200. Kozara. The name is either masculine Kozar or feminine Kozara, according to the demands of the syllabic line. I have normalized it to Kozara.

201. The signs. *Bešareti*, Avdo said (Text No. 12450, lines 51–53), means a sign (*znak*). According to Hony it means "good news." Later in the same conversation Avdo said "Tale was 'ćiramet' [see n. 189 above]; we call 'ćiramet' a pious

(*boži*) man. He had such indications (*dokaze*), and the hodža foretold it to him and those 'amajlije'." For the latter see the following note.

202. The holy book. The line is a little strange: *Hodža gleda čitab hamajliju* (9463). The combining of *čitab* (book) and *hamajlija* (talisman) is unusual. Avdo said that the hodža was also *ćiramet* and that he made himself ugly just as Tale did. For *hamajlija* see above, n. 11.

203. See n. 130 above.

204. Lost its color: lit. he "disguised his face" (*tevdilijo lice*), but in conversation Avdo interpreted it the way I have translated it (No. 12450, lines 411ff.).

205. In his preoccupation with a long rhetorical passage Avdo has omitted saying "is there any who" between the two series of rhetorical figures, *rad* and *da* (*ne*), and I have supplied it. He dictated as follows:

> Sprema toga, izrad boga svoga,
> Rad imana celog muslimana,
> Rad vatana ludog sibijana,
> Radi šana našega sultana,
> Da ne žali danas poginuti
> Da ne misli što su đeca luda,
> Što su sama na kuće ostala,
> Da učini fedah svoju dušu,
> Da od sebe oturi oružje, itd.

206. Allah. In conversation (No. 12450, lines 462ff.) Avdo insisted that he said "Allah" and not "Alah." We have, therefore, kept the spelling of the manuscript.

207. In short, his linen will be his shroud.

208. The three lines which this sentence translates are:

> Nema ljeta bez Đurđeva danka,
> A ni brata dok ne rodi majka,
> Ni jabanu srce zaboljeti.

As David Bynum noted in the margin of the first typescript, the first two of these lines are used in song introductions (*pripjevi*). Those lines are also used in references to the Hrnjičić brothers, Mujo and Halil. The general purport of these three proverbial and to some extent enigmatic lines is, I believe, that the person who will save one in a desperate situation is the one nearest in one's own family or intimate group. Cifrić Hasanaga is, of course, Smail's brother and Meho's uncle and, by this time in the song, the former alaybey. The fact that he is the first to volunteer was not an invention of Avdo, but is in Šemić's text; yet one can appreciate the interest with which Avdo tells it, because of his oft-repeated references to the older and the younger generations and his general contention that the older generation is the better.

The first of the three lines means that there must always be a beginning; St. George's day is the first day of spring. The second illustrates that idea on the human plane. Both spring and summer on the one hand and a brother on the other are beneficial things, blessings in life, that come to help when all hope is lost. These lines celebrate the action of Cifrić Hasanaga.

There is another use of these lines adapted to another circumstance in lines 10861–10864:

> Nema ljeta bez Đurđeva danka,
> Ni junaka dok ne rodi majka.
> Nema žara bez hrastovog panja,
> Nema boja bez njihova soja.

In line 2 above *junaka* (hero) has taken the place of *brata* (brother). The other two lines mean "there is no flame without an oak log, and no battle without their house," referring to the Hrnjičić family.

The third line carries on logically from the word "brother" (*brata*) in the preceding line, but the grammatical parallelism is broken. The meaning, however, is clear, namely, that the responsibility and the action at this critical moment are taken by the family of Smail and his brother; if Cifrić Hasanaga is killed, it will not be a stranger who mourns but the members of the family most involved.

209. Kin. The text reads *zasež*, which we have not been able to find anywhere, and I think David Bynum is correct in considering it a nonce word. Its meaning is clear from the context. In conversation (No. 12450, line 445) Avdo interpreted "zatež" (sic) as *snaga*, strength, body.

210. In conversation (No. 12450, lines 456ff.) Avdo says that *alahrahmetile* means "may God help him," "may God forgive him."

211. Cursed. This has approximately the same force as our colloquial "they and their damned horses." The epithet is also a filler.

212. Wherever seemed best. *Podesna* means either what I have said in the translation, or possibly "a bit to the right."

213. In conversation No. 12450, lines 533ff., Nikola tried to find out from Avdo whether he had learned about the volunteers from any other song than from "Smailagić Meho." Avdo maintained that he learned of them from the songbook, and that he did not know any other song in which there were a large number of volunteers as there are in it. He did cite two songs in which a single person volunteered for an impossible task. One is a song in which Ljubović carries a petition from Šestokrilović through three hundred thousand of the enemy to the vizier in Buda. For three days and three nights the heralds had cried in Osek without success, and the bey wept at dawn before the mosque. Then Ljubović arrived from Stambol. No one saw or heard him arrive, but suddenly he was there in the street with his chestnut horse. The bey rubbed his eyes three times at the sight of this wondrous hero. A second song with a volunteer is the one that tells of Pinjo Trog-

lavar's demanding Osek from the sultan and besieging Stambol. Mahmut Paša Tiro volunteered to go from Stambol through the enemy lines to Bosnia, and Bosnia came to the relief of Stambol. I find it difficult to identify the first of those two songs with any in Avdo's repertory, but the second is clearly his No. 28.

214. The greater bey: *Znaš li što goj za bega višega? Višega* (higher) may be only a filler for the line, but it is noticeable that the bey from Banja Luka is frequently listed in the higher ranks in Avdo's other catalogues. The seat of the Bosnian sandžak was moved from Sarajevo to Banja Luka somewhere between 1554 and 1563, and that sandžak was the central core of the Bosnian pashalik formed in 1580. The Bosnian sandžak was formed before the sandžak of Krk or that of the Lika. Thus the bey from Banja Luka, even before the founding of the pashalik, was older in dignity than his neighbors. (See Hazim Šabanović, *Bosanski pašaluk, postanak i upravna podjela* [The Bosnian Pashalik, Its Origin and Administrative Divisions] [Sarajevo, 1959]. This is vol. XIV, of *Djela* of the Naučno društvo NR Bosne i Hercegovine, and vol. 10 of its Odjelenje istorisko-filoloških nauka. The pertinent pages are 70 and 81.)

215. See note 208.

216. The cadi, the judge. I have tried to reproduce the redundancy in the line itself, which reads "I kadija, hakim efendija." *Kadija* is a judge, a cadi, but *hakim* also means judge, and in the Turkish dictionary under *kadi* it reads "(formerly) judge, a cadi . . . see 'hakim'." The use of both words makes it possible to say "judge" in one full line. *Hakim* appears as *haćim* in line 11242.

217. Spahi. A spahi (in English it is also spelled *spahee*) possessed a *spahiluk*, a grant of land that he received from the sultan and for which he paid no tax or tribute, but he was obligated to go as a cavalryman with one or more horses into the army in time of war (See Škaljić). There is an excellent article on spahis in Vuk Karadžić's dictionary.

218. Priest. *Muderis*, according to Tarhan Kitabevi, is now obsolete; it meant professor, formerly a professor of theology.

219. For this line see note 216.

220. The pasha. In the text the vizier is called *vezir, paša,* and *vezir paša*, as here. That is to say, the vizier was a pasha, and both titles are appropriate for him.

221. Venetian crowns. *Rušpe* in Vuk Karadžić's dictionary is given as "Venetian ducat," but since *dukat* is used in the same line I have differentiated between them in this way.

222. In the service of a pasha. This is the meaning given in Škaljić for *pašalija*, "a pasha's man, in the service of a pasha."

223. Younger officer: in the text simply "younger" (*mlađega*), referring, of course, to the Pasha of the Janissaries, the military commander.

224. Sharp swords. I do not know exactly what a *greben mač* is. *Mač* is "sword" or "knife". See above, n. 49.

225. Cursed. "Haram vama i plata i hrana!" *Haram* is the key word here, of

course. Škaljić gives three meanings: (1) everything that is prohibited by Moslem faith; (2) that which is sinful, not allowed, not just or correct; (3) accursed (*prokleto*). The third is clearly applicable here.

226. Impoverished. The idiom used is *on opasa likom* ("he girded [something] with bast"). The same idiom is used a few lines later: *Te Budimce likom opasao* ("And he girded the men of Buda with bast"). Vuk Karadžić gives *opasati koga u liko, arm machen*, and the recent dictionary of the Matica srpska and Matica hrvatska gives "vezivati (krpiti) liku za oputu (opasivati se likom), bedno životariti."

227. Overthrown: *cmar'o i obar'o*. I have translated both verbs as one.

228. Questioning. I find this line difficult and am by no means sure of this translation.

229. Stewards. *Čohadar* means the individual who cares for the cloth, *čoha*, in a noble or official's house. Tarhan Kirabevi gives under "çuhadar, (çukadar) (obsolete) (formerly) lackey; foot equerry."

230. The palace of the imperial governor (*U sadatu carskome valiji*). I have not found the word *sadat* anywhere, and Turkish *sadet* (*saded*), "subject or point of a discussion, topic, matter in hand" (Tarhan Kitabevi), does not seem to help, although one can force a kind of meaning, "In the morning they arose early and went on the imperial business to the vali (governor)." I have taken *sadat* to mean from its context "seat" or "residence," hence "palace," possibly "place of business," "office," (?). *Valija* is the governor of a vilayet.

231. The word *lala* is difficult to translate, and I have repeated "governor," because it is to the governor that it refers, but added "noble." It originally was a "tutor or man-servant having the care of a child-prince" (Tarhan Kitabevi). In Škaljić this meaning is treated as secondary, or at least is listed second, and the first meaning is a "court noble, imperial official, imperial favorite." It is common in the songs, especially in the phrase *lale i veziri* in the second half of the line, which could be translated "viziers and nobles."

232. *Vali paša*, or *valipaša*, is a combination similar to *vezir paša* in n. 220, above. The *vali*, or governor, was also a pasha.

233. Week after week. I have freely translated by this *vreme za vremenom* in the line *dan za danom, vreme za vremenom*, day after day, time after time."

234. Residence: Turkish *mekan*, "place, locality, site, space, (fig) home, abode, residence" (Tarhan Kitabevi). Since this word is not in Škaljić, I believe this is an instance of Avdo's use of a Turkish word that is not in regular usage in his Serbo-Croatian dialect.

235. See note 130 above.

236. Humbly. *Aman učiniti*, "to make 'aman'," is to say "aman," "have mercy," "forgive me."

237. Sun of the world: *dunjalučko sunce*. *Dunjaluk* means "this world" or "the human beings on the planet earth" (Škaljić).

238. My happiness is now complete: lit. "On me are all dukedoms (marshal-doms, or what not) one after another." *Mušir* is a military rank, sometimes given as marshal, sometimes as *voyvoda*, "duke."

239. Mighty: *Bosna kleta*. *Klet*, of course, means accursed, damned, but it really does not mean that here nor in a number of other places in the songs. No dictionary seems to take this common idiomatic usage into consideration. It is a filler, like our "damned" and other less signified eipthets in very colloquial usages.

240. Lit. "Let good family (*odžak*) be founded from good family."

241. Mountain spirit: *Vila* and *sokol*, the traditional images of beautiful girl and bride, the *kore* and the hero.

Appendices

BY ALBERT B. LORD

A. Other Versions and Variants of "Smailagić Meho"

Outside of the Milman Parry Collection I know of only four texts of "Smailagić Meho," three published and one unpublished. The earliest was written down in 1885 from the singer Ahmed Isakov Šemić of Rotimije by Friedrich S. Krauss and published in Dubrovnik in 1886 under the title *Smailagić Meho, pjesan naših Muhamedovaca*. Krauss provided his text with an introduction and copious notes. A popular paper-cover edition of this text, with a change of dialect from *ikavski* to *jekavski* and sometimes of the wording of lines as well as some additions and deletions, appeared in Mostar in 1925 as the first volume in a series, *Muslimanske narodne junačke pjesme*, published by Prva muslimanska nakladna knjižara (M. B. Kalajdžić). This popular edition was without any introduction or notes, without any reference to the Krauss edition or mention of the redactor. There appears also to have been another popular edition of this song published by the firm of Mihajl Milanović in Sarajevo; I have not had available a copy of this book, but it is listed among "Naša najnovija izdanja" (our newest publications) on the back of two other popular songbooks in my possession dated 1927. I do not know what this text is, but I believe that it is safe to assume that it is some form of the Šemić text, possibly even the same as the 1925 Mostar redaction. I have, however, counted it as a separate text, making three published texts, that is to say Šemić plus two redactions of Šemić, one published in Mostar in 1925 and the other in Sarajevo in or before 1927. The popular editions are the most interesting for us, because it was through them that Šemić's "Smailagić Meho" became widespread among singers.

Outside the Parry Collection there is an unpublished text with the

title "Krvava ženidba malog Mehmedage Gazi-Smailagina" (The Bloody
Wedding of Little Mehmedaga, Son of Smailaga), written down from
Mehmed Malkoč of Mujdžić near Jajce, April 29, 1916, by Muharem
Kurtagić. Kurtagić's collection was acquired by the Matica hrvatska in
1943 and bears the number 197. Malkoč was eighty-one at the time of
dictating. In spite of the title, his song is not the same as Šemić's tradition, although there are some elements of similarity between the two.

We can already discern, therefore, outside the Parry Collection
two distinct traditions of the "Wedding of Smailagić Meho," that of
Šemić, or, better, that to which Šemić belonged, and that represented
by Malkoč's text, which I shall term simply non-Šemić.

Finally, there are several texts in the Parry Collection which, although the Šemić tradition is somewhere in the background, have been
influenced by it only slightly or very generally. Moreover, other story
elements, some akin to those in the Malkoč tradition, have joined with
the Šemić tradition, or been joined by it, as the case may be. These
might be termed "mixed" versions, and I have included a summary of
two of these to illustrate the process.

In what follows, I shall first concern myself with the Šemić tradition and then with the non-Šemić and mixed versions.

THE ŠEMIĆ TRADITION

The majority of texts of "Smailagić Meho" that we have stem from
the Šemić text through the redactions. Since the Mostar text of 1925 is
the only one of the two available to me, I shall use it to represent the
Šemić tradition, because, as explained above, the redactions, rather than
the Šemić text of 1885, were the texts known to singers. The following
account of the 1925 text includes, usually as footnotes, comments on
the differences between it and Šemić's original.

THE 1925 TEXT

Thirty-four agas of Kanidža were drinking wine. At their head was
Cifra Hasanaga, next to him his brother's son, young Mehmedaga, next
to Mehmed, Nožinagić Ibro, and next to him Pločić Orućaga. All the
court of Hasan Pasha was there with the captain of the pasha's guard at
their head.[1] They were all boasting of themselves or of their horses, of

1. Šemić lists only the agas of Kanidža, thirty in number, and the forty *ićage*
of Hasan Pasha Tiro, Cifra Hasanaga, and Mehmedaga. He says nothing of either
Nožinagić Ibro or Pločić Orućaga, or the pasha's *delibaša*.

whither they had ridden and brought back booty, where they had cut
off Hungarian heads and carried away Latin girls on their horses. Only
Meho was silent, and his uncle asked him why he was sad, and why he
did not praise himself or his chestnut horse or some comrade at his side.
Meho told him that he had nothing of which to boast. He had not gone
on raids, nor seen what heroes do, how they died at each other's hands
or for one another, how blood flows from heroes.[2] He had not been
able to go courting, because the girls had made up a song about him.
They said that he was now twenty-two years old, but they would not
give themselves to him, were they never to marry.[3] Meho swore to his
uncle that he would revolt and go to Karabogdan to the seat of General
Peter, from whom he would seek mercenaries with whom he could
ravage the Border, cutting down the young men and carrying off the
maidens.

Meho's uncle told him that their house had never been treasonous,
but they had always been leaders. Smailaga, Meho's father, was buljukbaša for twenty-seven years, and when he had grown old he had given
the writ to him, Hasanaga, and he had been buljukbaša now for twenty-
two years. But he too had grown old, and he suggested that they give
him a petition to take to Buda to the vizier, asking him to give Meho a
writ as buljukbaša. Meho agreed to this, and the old man put on his
cloak and slippers and with his long pipe went into the market place to
the shop of Hodža Šuvalija. He brought him to the stone bower. The
hodža wrote a petition, and the agas put their seals upon it.[4]

2. Šemić stresses the fact that Smail does not allow young Meho to go raiding.
In the 1925 text Meho simply says he has not been raiding, but does not say why.
In Šemić, on the other hand, Meho says that his father does not allow him to go
raiding—he is now twenty-one—for his father cannot get over the idea that he has
only one son. Meho says he wishes his father did not have even that one, since he
will not let Meho go raiding. All his friends and peers do.

3. In Šemić the girls in their song say it would be better if he had been born a
girl, and then he could be married to a hero who would bring him honor.

4. In Šemić Meho says that he is going to seek some master who will send him
raiding. He will seek him in the sultan's empire, but if he cannot find him there, he
will look to the "ćesarevina," the other empire. He has heard of General Peter in
Karabogdan and his blood-brother Mate Kapetan. Whichever door he knocks on
will not be dishonored. The uncle counters: Your father has been our leader for
forty years, and he is old. If all the rest are in agreement, Meho, I'll get the hodža
and we'll send a petition to Buda to make you buljukbaša. The vizier is a friend of
ours, and he will agree. The people assembled agree, and the aga fetches Hodža

Meho and the standard-bearer Osman went to Smailaga's house. Smail asked his son why he was so early; had he quarreled with the agas or had the drink gone to his head? Meho told him that neither was true, but that the agas had given him a petition (100) to take to the vizier in Buda to obtain a writ as buljukbaša. When Smail had ascertained that the agas were in agreement with this, that they had signed the petition, and that Hasan Pasha Tiro agreed, and that Meho's uncle not only agreed but had actually started the conversation and brought the hodža from the marketplace, and sent him, Meho, to his father to ask his permission and blessing, then the old man consented. He sent his son to dress and then to appear before his father.

Meho went to his room, put on his clothes, and came before his father in full regalia. The old man looked and smiled at his son. He said he was handsome enough to be vizier of all Bosnia, to say nothing of being a buljukbaša! Then the old man lifted the rug on which he was sitting, and from under it he took coins and gave them to his son, telling him not to spare them and bring shame on his father's honor.[5] He bade Meho farewell. The boy kissed his hand, and his father kissed Meho's forehead. At this point Osman came and kissed Smail's hand and was himself kissed on the forehead.

The two went down to the courtyard where their horses were ready, and they mounted. Then came Meho's mother, bringing their rifles. She gave them her blessing: may their enemies be beneath their

---

Šuverija. He prepares a petition, which is read aloud. It is signed and then handed to Pločić Orućaga to sign, and then to Pandžić Husein, and then to Ložinagić Meho to sign and to hand on until it comes to Cifra Hasanaga, and finally to Mehmedaga himself. Hasanaga then tells him to go home and prepare himself and his horse and Osman. When he arrives home he calls Osman and tells him to prepare the horses for a journey to Buda.

5. In Šemić, when Meho returns to his father "in full reglia," Smail asks for the petition (no comment on how fine the boy looks) in order to put his own seal upon it. Meho gives it to him, Smail reads it, puts his seal on it, and then reminds his son that the vizier is a friend of theirs. The sultan sent him to Buda nine years ago, and the vizier has granted whatever Smail has asked. "You, Mehmed, will be successful also."

In short, in Šemić, the role of Smail is significant at this juncture in the story. He is protective about Meho, and the Šemić version is clear about that. He is also sure of the friendship of the vizier in Buda; the Šemić version is clear about that, also.

feet like the nails and shoes on a horse's hoofs; may good fortune go
before them as the daystar goes before the sun; may he return safe and
sound to his father and mother. Meho said farewell, and Osman called
out from his horse, saying that he feared neither wolf nor hajduk; the
wolves were old friends of his, and the hajduks avoid the hand which
cuts down heroes with the sword and the good horse beneath a hero.
He declared he would not return without Mehmed. Then the two riders
departed.

That day they went far, to the village of Jasika, to Knez Vukašin.
There they spent the night and were well entertained; Knez Vukašin
stood holding a candle, and all night he poured rakija for them. At dawn
they drank wine and then made preparations. Vukašin's wife brought
their rifles, while Vukašin led their horses to the mounting block. Meho
came out, and the lady held the stirrup for him and gave him his rifle.
She opened the gate, and Meho gave her a gold piece. She wished them
well and invited them to stop again on their way back.

They drove on, and the second day they spent the night in the
small village of Veselica at the house of Toroman Vuk. There they were
well entertained (200) and served, and in the morning they arose early.

And so they pressed on along the border and came to the river
Glina and to the drawbridge, over which they passed, riding out onto
the plain of Muhač, from the midpoint of which one can see Buda.
When they came to the middle they saw a wondrous sight. The gate of
Buda opened, and the drawbridge came down over the cold Danube. A
mist arose from Buda, stretched to the gate, and reached to the clouds.
From out of the mist emerged a band of a hundred warriors of the
Pasha of Buda. Behind them came a coach covered to the ground with
silk cloth and ornamented with precious stones. In it someone was
wailing and cursing Buda and vizier. "May Buda be consumed by fire,
and may the sultan hang the vizier, who is sending me into infidel
hands!" Mehmed wondered aloud to Osman who might be wailing in
the coach, and said he would ride up to it on his chestnut horse and
open the coach and see who was in trouble. They quickly caught up to
the warriors, and Mehmed gave greeting. The greeting was returned, and
the warriors rode past. Then came the coach, drawn by two white Bedouin mares. Meho raised the curtain on the coach, and within was a girl
all alone, all dressed in black. She had torn out some of her red hair and
scratched her face so that the blood was flowing. And ever she wailed.

Meho asked her what was wrong. At first she thought that he was one of the warriors from Buda, and she bade him to leave her alone. She wished that all of his ilk in Buda had never been born. Better had they been born girls, and then their mothers might have married them to heroes who guard the border and the marches. "May they be as dishonored on the day of judgment as they are today on the battlefield. They are giving one of the true faith into the hands of the infidels." She said that she would bring complaint against them to God on the day of judgment. Her bloodstained hands would hang about their necks in the other world. But Mehmed assured her he was not from Buda but a stranger, and she agreed to tell her sorrows.[6] Her father was Zajim Alibeg of Buda. She told how when the vizier had come to them from the sultan, the agas of Buda had welcomed him with great honor. (300) With much ceremony the hodžas and hadjis welcomed him, together with the small children from the school, and led him to his place. The morning after the first night a council was held. Then it turned out that the vizier was a traitor. He executed a hundred agas of Buda and sent five hundred into exile; at their head was her father, Zajim Alibeg. She and her mother were left alone. Her father was very rich, and therefore suitors came to woo her. In a year five hundred rings came, all from

6. There is only one change of any length from Šemić to 1925 in the text from line 213 (1925) or line 299 (Šemić) to line 445 (1925) or line 507 (Šemić). In Šemić Fata's first speech to Meho (lines 349–353) represents her as saying that if he were to hear her troubles, he would forget all his own; to which he answers that she should go ahead and tell him. In the 1925 text her first speech is much longer (lines 268–293, including a reply to it by Meho and the beginning of a second speech). In it she does not say what she did in Šemić, but, thinking that Meho is one of the men from Buda, she inveighs against all Buda's males. Had they been born girls they might have been married to heroes who guard the borders. As it is they should be ashamed for giving the faithful into the hands of the infidel. In vain are the calls to prayer given, in vain do the imams go to the mosque, in vain do the children go to the mosque schools. At the last judgment she says she will be witness against him before God; her blood-stained hands will be about his neck in the other world. He replies that he is not from Buda but a stranger. "Since you are a stranger," says she, "I will tell you my woes;" At this point the two texts continue together. The confusion here of Meho with a man of Buda is a characteristic of the 1925 text but not of Šemić.

In addition there is a five-line passage of description in 1925 that is not in Šemić in this section. It consists of lines 257–261 (1925) (and 479–483 [1925], the latter of which are repeated again 518–522 [1925]) and contains a further description of Fata in the coach, when she is discovered by Meho. She was dressed in black and had plucked out her hair and torn her face, which was running with blood.

their chief men, from agas and standard-bearers. Three viziers courted her, but she did not accept them and her mother did not give her away. One morning while they were wailing like cuckoo birds in their house, the courtyard gate opened and the delibaša of the vizier brought a bundle containing a thousand ducats and four golden apples and seven golden rings. He asked the girl's mother to give her to the vizier. The girl was not willing, and her mother did not give her. The delibaša returned in anger with this news to the vizier. The traitor could not stand the sight of the girl in Buda, and so he was sending her to Karabogdan to General Peter. But, she said, their faith cannot condone marriage with an infidel, and she asked Meho not to allow that to happen, if perchance he thinks he will ever die and have to answer to God.

When Meho heard that, he told Osman that he, Osman, might go back to Kanidža, if he was afraid of dying; for his part, said Meho, he would rather die seventeen times a day than fear dying for his honor. Osman replied that when he had left his own land and his mother and gone to serve Meho's father, Smail had given him the standard and great reward, and Osman's mother had given him over to "wolf and hajduk." He was not afraid to die. Meho then told the girl that she would never go to the infidel as long as he was alive and asked her blessing for him and for Osman. He advised Osman to attack from the left while he attacked from the right. This they did. Fate brought Mehmed against Ibro the leader. In the four-hour battle that followed between the two heroes, the enemy Ibro was killed.

As Fata was praying God to help Meho, he came up to her and lifted her onto his horse. She began to weep, and, when questioned, said it was because he would die for her sake at the hands of the traitorous vizier, who would also drown her. Meho reassured her that he would be willing to answer to the Master of the Privy Seal, to say nothing of the vizier.

When they enetered Buda, Meho spurred his horse. The horse champed on the bit and the foam at its mouth was bloody. The streets resounded. The girls and widows flew to watch Meho and the horse; they cast bouquets of flowers before them, but Meho paid no attention. Instead, he asked Fata where her house was, since he was unacquainted with Buda. Fatima then gave a lengthy description of her father's house in Buda (lines 471–509).[7]

7. The same description is found also in Šemić, but it is five lines longer in the 1925 text, lines 479–483 having been added. These lines describe the golden apple on the roof of the house which is decorated with precious stones and "with

The three entered Fatima's courtyard and heard Fatima's mother wailing at the loss of her husband and her daughter. Mehmed called to her to descend to the courtyard, and when she arrived below he asked her what was wrong. She told him, and he inquired what she would give for news of Fata; would she give her to him? Fatima's mother agreed, and Meho then helped Fatima down from the horse. The mother objected that if the vizier were to hear of Fatima's being betrothed to Meho he would kill him, cast both women into the water,[8] and seize their property. Meho said that he was not afraid but would go and get a marriage license, and leave Fatima at home with her mother while he went and returned with wedding guests.

He and Osman then went to the judge's court. Meho left his horse with Osman and himself went to the judge. He was well received, given a place at the judge's side, and regaled with coffee and tobacco. After the first cup the judge asked why he had come to him, and when told it was for a marriage license, he inquired who Meho was and who the girl. At the name of Fatima, the judge cast aside his pipe, knocked his cup on the floor, and told Meho that the girl had been sent to Karabogdan. If the vizier were to hear that he had given a marriage license for her and Meho, the vizier would have his right hand cut off and he would be exiled on a donkey to Vranduk. "See if you can find another judge to give you the license." When Meho heard that he tossed aside his pipe, knocked his cup on the floor, leaned to the right, his hand flying to the hilt of his sword. He drew it out halfway.[9] When the judge saw that Meho was in earnest, he took pen and made the license. Meho paid him scornfully, tossing coins at the cashier's window.[10]

After receiving the license, Meho, together with Osman, proceeded

---

imperial coins. Whenever the wind blows strongly along the Danube the silver vane (*filandra*) revolves, the precious stones flash, and the imperial coins tinkle." The added lines are in quotation marks. This same description with the same added lines is repeated in the description of the action (lines 511–524) which follows Fatima's directions.

8. This line is omitted in Šemić.

9. At this point three lines of obscene curse are omitted from Šemić (725–727) and the following three lines are added instead (674–676) in 1925: "Either prepare the license for me, or I shall drench your beard in the blood of your white face!"

10. Šemić said it was one hundred ducats (line 739, Šemić), but the 1925 omits the sum. Šemić also includes another obscene curse (line 741, Šemić), but 1925 omits this line.

to the vizier's dwelling, and, again leaving Osman outside with the horses, he entered the vizier's chamber. The vizier was sitting by the window watching the girls promenading along the Danube. Meho, fully armed, strode across the velvet straight to the vizier and placed the petition from Kanidža in his lap. The vizier read it, then told Meho that he confirmed him as buljukbaša and in his inheritance. He advised him to be fair to all the members of his družina and to give his, the vizier's, respects to Meho's father and uncle and Hasan Pasha when he returned. He then gave Meho the certificate that he had had his scribes draw up. Meho returned to Osman, who asked how the interview had gone. Meho replied that the vizier caused no trouble, but that if he had, Meho would have cut off his head. The two then returned to Alibeg's house.

Fatima's mother asked Meho and Osman to stay the night, but Meho refused, saying that he would return in fifteen days with wedding guests, including Hasan Pasha Tiro, Mustajbeg of the Lika, and Hrnjica of Kladuša with his men. Meho gave the lady five hundred ducats to help with entertaining the guests. Fatima's mother returned into the house, and afterwards the captive slave Kumrija appeared, on her head a golden platter with sixty bundles, each containing a hundred "rušpe" (coins). She then recited for Meho the rich properties of the lady of the Alibeg.[11] After this, Fatima and her mother appeared at a window, and the latter gave Meho her blessing for the return trip to Kanidža. Meho and Osman departed, and arrived at their house in Kanidža.

Smail and his brother Hasan from the window saw them coming. After exchange of greetings, the old man asked his son if they had a friend in the vizier. Meho told him not to praise the vizier, for he was no Turk but a traitor. His father warned him not to talk like that, because his words might come to the ears of the vizier and cause trouble for all. Meho then told of his encounter with the warriors and the coach, of Fatima's story. Smail asked why Meho did not fight with the warriors, and Meho said he was afraid of his father's censure for so doing. Smail took his sword from the peg and was about to kill Meho for letting the girl go to the infidels. Meho took refuge behind Osman, who told Smail that Meho had not told the whole story. They did fight with the warriors and took the girl back to Buda where she and Meho were betrothed. They had fifteen days in which to gather wedding guests. Smail was pleased and began to summon the guests.

11. This passage of description covers lines 821–846 of 1925, 876–901 of Šemić. See lines 5315–5347 of Avdo for a comparison of details.

We now come to a part of the song that is most enlarged by Avdo: the summoning of wedding guests, their arrival and entertainment at Kanidža, and their journey to Buda. The 1925 catalogue has additions to the Šemić one covering 33 lines (1005–1037). Both present the list in the frame of Smail's instructions to his servant Husein concerning to whom and to what places he should go with the summons. On the way back from delivering the other letters Huso stops at Tale's house. (For details of Tale see the notes to Avdo's song at this point, and later when Tale appears at Kanidža.) In addition to the list just mentioned, the 1925 text expands three other parts of this section of the song, that is, the gathering of the army. First, lines 1206–1230 of 1925 are added: when Huso returns from delivering all the messages, including the one to Tale, he is amazed at what he sees. In first place in this text, but not in Šemić, is a description of the tents of the cooks and butchers, the kettles, the sheep and rams, the horseloads of rakija and wine, of barley and hay. Huso dismounts and goes to the top of the house and reports to Smail; Smail tells him that when this rejoicing is over, he will wed Huso with one of his captive slave girls and build him a house next to his, even better than his. Both texts then turn to a brief description of Hasan Pasha's tent, since he will be the leader of the wedding guests, and to a general description in 10 lines of the arrival and disposition of the men of Bosnia. Rifles are fired, the men shout, the horses whinny, the black earth trembles; servants receive the wedding guests, the horses are put in the meadow, and the guests are seated at ready tables. At this point comes the second addition to Šemić by the 1925 text. It consists of 48 lines and is thus the longest addition (lines 1249–1296). This addition moves from the general to the particular, telling of the arrival of Bešire of Stina, Mustajbeg with Vrcić the standard-bearer, and seven others, Hrnjica Mujo, Tanković Osman, and Mujagin Halil.

For a while then the two texts again go forward together, returning for a few lines to a general description of arrival. Finally Hasan Pasha inquires of Mustajbeg if all are assembled, and Mujo Hrnjica answers that only Tale is missing. Hasan Pasha Tiro suggests that they proceed without him, for they do not have much time, but Mujo says they cannot go until Tale arrives. At this point Tale appears, and there is a description of him and of his horse.[12] Mujo greets him and gives him a leather bottle of wine, which he drinks without wetting his moustaches

12. Again an obscene element is eliminated from Šemić's text by the omission of lines 1287–1288.

and throws empty at Mujo's feet. Tale asks whether they have taken counsel as to who will be the various officers of the wedding party. He then decrees who they shall be: Hasan Pasha will be leader (*starešina*), and Mustajbeg will be chief of the groom's attendants (*djeverbaša*); Mujo will be *selamaga*,[13] and Tale himself will be herald (*čauš*); the two groom's attendants (*djeverovi*) will be Halil and Nukić Ibrahim. Tale ends by saying that whoever will not obey him will not journey with them. They finally all agree to obey him, although some had demurred. Šemić now tells how Hasan Pasha gives orders to the heralds to give the call to horse, and this they do. In the 1925 text there is found the third addition (lines 1390–1399), a speech by Tale, to the accompaniment of the drums as he calls them to horse, saying they have not gathered to eat and drink this aga and his tenant farmers (*kmets*) out of house and home, but to go to Buda where they can eat in abundance.

As the wedding guests leave they are numbered by Tale and Ramo and the report given to Hasan Pasha: there are fifteen thousand horsemen and twelve thousand on foot. Thus ends the gathering. It covers 336 lines (1025–1360) in Šemić, or 16 percent of the poem; 447 lines (968–1414) in the 1925 text, or 21 percent of the poem. In Avdo's song the gathering covers 3,056 lines (6430–9486), or 25 percent of the song. Avdo's "additions" are similar in kind to those in the 1925 text, namely, additions in the particular list of summoned and of arrivals.

The army set forth in full parade. The first night they camped at Jasika, the second at Veselica, and on the third day they camped at the river Glina. There Tale stopped the army and asked for someone to guard the bridge.[14] All the Turks replied that they should leave Grdan

13. The *selamaga* is the wedding guest who, in the name of the others, gives and receives greetings: official greeter.

14. In Šemić, they were halted by the pasha, who inquired whom they would leave to guard the drawbridge, because this was the border between the lands of the Turks and those of Peter, and he was afraid that Peter or his blood-brother Captain Mate and his cousin Šeremetović might attack. We may detect here and in some earlier passages as well the tendency of Šemić to show Hasan Pasha as leader of the army, with Mustajbeg as his second in command, whereas the 1925 text tends to place Tale above Hasan Pasha. Indeed, both texts indicate some rivalry between Hasan Pasha and Tale, from the very moment when Hasan suggests they proceed before Tale arrives and Mujo forces them to wait. Note also the strange passage in which Tale challenges those who do not want to obey him to remain behind. It looks as if Šemić favors Hasan Pasha, and the 1925 text favors Tale.

Omeraga.[15] Grdan accepted the commission, and the army proceeded onward then toward Buda.

As the army approached Buda the hosts came forth to greet their guests. Hasan Pasha was lodged with the vizier, Selamaga Mujo with the Dizdar, Mustajbeg with the Alibegovica, and Tale and the heralds (*čauši*) in the tavern, because Tale does not know when a joke has been carried on long enough and so no one wished to receive him in his house. As they entered Buda, the vizier had three cannon fired and sent a letter to Peter telling him to gather his armies and intercept the Turks at the bridge.

Tale was the only one who thought that the vizier might be tricking them. He warned that the firing of the cannon was not in rejoicing for the arrival of the wedding guests but that it was a signal to General Peter to go to Muhač and to block the bridge. Mujo refused to believe Tale. That night all were comfortable in their lodgings, and the next morning Tale called for the wedding guests to depart. Just then the vizier's messenger told them that it was the custom in Buda for guests to spend three days resting before departure. So they stayed two more nights.[16] The following morning Tale aroused the wedding guests, and they were given gifts. There was cloth for the chief of the groom's attendants (*djeverbaša*, Mustajbeg),[17] and for the chief herald (*čaušbaša*, Tale) a bundle of clothes and a hundred ducats. Tale trod the clothes underfoot, but put the ducats into his pocket and began to load the gifts. It took sixty horses to carry them, and Tale complained about the effort in loading them and about the poor pay he had for his pains. After the wedding guests had left Buda and the gate had been closed, the vizier issued orders that anyone who opened the gate again for a week would be executed.[18]

15. In Šemić Mustajbeg suggests that Grdan Omeraga and his twelve thousand footmen remain behind to guard the bridge.

16. Šemić at this point has Tale on the third morning start to call forth the wedding guests again for departure, asking them why they are obeying the treacherous vizier who is tricking them. Once again the vizier's messenger intervenes, telling them not to move for two days. They therefore spend that night and a third (*sic*).

17. In Šemić, a good stallion for the leader of the wedding guests Hasan Pasha (*stari svat*).

18. These two actions are unaccountably reversed in the 1925 text. I have, exceptionally, here followed Šemić.

When the wedding guests were halfway across the plain of Muhač they saw that a mist covered the river Glina on both sides and that ravens were croaking in the mist. The pasha wondered if the mist was from the clouds or from rifles; most said the former, but Tale alone said it was from rifles and that all was not well with Grdan Omeraga. As they were speaking a young footsoldier came from the drawbridge. He was blackened, and his clothes had been carried off, and the pole of the standard in his hands was empty. This was Omeraga's standard-bearer. (The 1925 text gives him the name of Hajduk Ibrahim.) Hasan Pasha asked him what was happening at the drawbridge.

There now follows the recital by the standard-bearer of the events at the bridge, a tale within a tale, covering over a hundred lines in each text.[19] The youth related that the firing of the cannon was not for rejoicing but was trickery, and that a letter had been sent to General Peter telling him that the wedding guests had arrived at Buda. "They attacked the bridge at seven o'clock at night [i.e. seven hours after sunset], but Omeraga had foreseen the treachery and we were ready for them. We met the first twelve thousand, and then at dawn Peter arrived with artillery and dug in. In the fourth hour of the next night Šeremetović attacked with twelve thousand. After the last call to prayer the following day [one hour after sunset], Mate Kapetan arrived with four thousand men and the three forces were joined. The next morning we expected you to come from Buda, and when you did not appear we thought that you must have perished. Instead, you were staying there and feasting! In the morning they attacked us on three sides. We defended ourselves against odds until seven o'clock [seven hours after sunrise], when we ran out of powder and lead. Then Grdan Omeraga gathered us all together in one place, we said farewell to one another, and attacked. I took the standard in my left hand and my sword in my right and first attacked the bridge. By the time I had crossed it I had no more clothing nor standard nor comrades. I do not know what has happened to them."

The pasha of Kanidža listened and wept. He asked what they should do, petition the vizier for aid and return to Buda, or attack? Kozlić Huremaga and Ćejvanaga the Elder advised returning to Buda and asking the vizier for help, but Tale cursed them, pointing out that the vizier was a traitor. He suggested that the pasha offer a good sum to

19. Šemić, lines 1573–1679; 1925 text, lines 1606–1712.

volunteers who would strip to their linen and, with standard in hand, lead the attack. Hasan Pasha offered a purse of five hundred ducats and bewailed the fact that he was too old to volunteer. The first to come forward was Cifra Hasanaga, and then in turn came Smailagić Meho, in spite of his father's prayers not to leave his bride a widow, and Hrnjica Mujo came next with blessings and encouragement from Mujo.[20]

Then hero after hero volunteered. Each broke his scabbard and took his sword in his right hand and his rifle in his left. The pasha counted them, and there were one hundred and thirty-four. Tale advised Hasanaga that when the volunteers were crossing the plain the enemy would see them and open fire with the cannon. "There is no cover on the plain, no trees or bushes, so they will have to hide behind one another until the cannon fire ceases." Tale then told the hodža to offer a prayer for them. Then Hasan Pasha advised Hasanaga, when the cannon fire ceased, to run forward until the rapid-fire guns open up. They should fall to the ground until that fire ceases. They should then fire their pistols and throw their empty pistols aside and take naked steel and jump over the trenches, to see if they can reach the cannon and take them, thus making a path for the cavalry. He, then, Hasan Pasha, would attack with all the horses. Thus they spoke and then said farewell to one another.

Hasanaga followed the advice given. At the cannon fire not a single Turk was lost; from the rapid-fire guns only four were killed. They fired their pistols and then seized naked steel and attacked the cannon.[21]

Cifra Hasanaga was the first to attack the cannon. He killed four men and stuck the banner in the ground. As he did so, he caught sight of a hero on the other side of the river with naked sword in hand. He recognized Grdan Omeraga. They ran and met him in the middle of the bridge. Hasanaga asked Omeraga if he had any comrades left alive, and Omeraga said that scarce five hundred of his men were left, and that five hundred had perished.[22]

Now Tale led the attack and the main battle was under way. In it they drove to the River Glina and crossed over on the material that blocked its flow, namely the capes and caps of the fallen and the corpses

20. This last is not in Šemić.

21. In Šemić the volunteers threw their empty pistols on the green grass, but in the 1925 text they put them back in their belts.

22. In the Šemić text Grdan Omeraga said that all had perished except himself.

of horses and heroes.[23] That crossing was on the fourth day of the battle. After it the army of wedding guests began to assemble. The following were missing: Mustajbeg, Mujo of Kladuša, Tale, Smailagić Meho, and five hundred young men.

At the beginning of the battle Mustajbeg with thirty buljukbašas had gone to Buda because of the vizier. They had entered the vizier's palace, cut off his head, and made Mustajbeg the new vizier. They named Mujo Master of the Arms (*siliftar*) and Tale Chancellor of the Exchequer (*haznadar*). They had then returned from Buda to Hasan Pasha Tiro, to whom they announced the new appointments. Next they buried their dead, in a way befitting those who had died blessed in battle; their legs were visible to the knee, their arms to the shoulder, and their faces to the eyes.

Smailagić Meho was still missing, and Smail wept for him. Tale told the old man not to weep. Meho was a hero, and he died. His bride will not be left unwed as long as Tale is himself unmarried; he has been her suitor before, he claims, and at least she will be married to a hero. At this moment a cloud was seen on the plain and from it emerged a rider. All his clothes had been burnt from him in battle and his horse's mane was gone also. Tale saw him and recognized Meho and saw that he was leading General Peter, whom he had taken alive and was bringing to the Pasha of Kanidža. The Turks received Meho with rejoicing, but he was embarrassed because of his nakedness. He leaned over from his horse and plucked the grass from the field and covered himself. The Pasha of Kanidža received Meho and congratulated him, and Meho delivered the general to him to send to the sultan in Stambol. Tale asked Meho to give him General Peter and, when he did, Tale jumped on his back, took the whip from his boot and beat General Peter, saying with a laugh that he would rear him for dueling, because he was fiercer than his mouse-gray horse.[24]

Now there was general rejoicing, and Tale ran to General Peter's cannon and filled all twelve with powder, without measuring it. When they were fired they all burst, and Tale almost perished from his own joke. Booty was then divided equally, the sons of the dead receiving their portion. They spent one more night there, and the next morning they assembled again as wedding guests with the girl; the drums rolled,

23. This last detail is missing in Šemić.

24. This bit of "horse-play" (pardon the pun) is an addition by the 1925 text and is not in Šemić.

the groom's attendants brought forth the bride, Tale drove the pack-loads, and thus singing and firing off their rifles they returned to Kanid-ža. Meho was married and begat two daughters and four sons.[25]

THE ŠEMIĆ TRADITION IN THE PARRY COLLECTION

There are nine Parry Collection texts that clearly stem from the Šemić text through the redactions mentioned at the beginning of this appendix. In order of date of collecting they are:

1. No. 865 from Džemal Zilić, in Stolac, dictated Dec. 14, 1934
2, 3. Nos. 901, sung, 905, dictated, from Hajdar Habul, in Gacko, Dec. 1934, Jan. 1935
4. No. 6840 from Avdo Međedović, in Bijelo Polje, dictated June 1935
5. No. L.8 from Ramo Babić, in Novi Pazar, sung, May 16 and 19, 1950
6. No. L.35 from Avdo Međedović, in Bijelo Polje, May 24, 25, and 26, 1950
7. From Ramo Babić, in Novi Pazar, sung 1962
8. From Bejito Smakić, in Karajukići Bunari, sung 1963
9. From Avdo Kevelj, in Nevesinje, sung 1965

Only 77 lines of Zilić's text were written down, because he had memorized the text from the Mostar 1925 songbook almost word for word, with a few omissions of lines and a handful of minor line variations. The dictating was discontinued.

The case of Hajdar Habul is much more complicated. He was a very competent singer of traditional tales before the songbook version of "Smailagić Meho" came to him, in whatever way that may have been. He learned the song from the book, probably by someone else's reading it to him, and a certain number of lines in runs, usually quite short and sporadic, testify to this. But he did not memorize it. He follows the events in the song in the way in which Šemić reveals them. Hajdar was not very retentive of proper names. He never names the river, Glina or otherwise, and his catalogue is different from Šemić's and even more scanty. Yet the story remains very much the same; the only possibly significant variation, in this case addition, is in the treatment and execution of General Peter. When Meho appears with General Peter after

---

25. To this the Šemić text adds a postlude (*začinka*) in a 4/4 meter, but this is not germane to our purposes (lines 2130–2160).

the battle, he gives the general over to the pasha, who summons Tale to his tent and delivers General Peter to him. Tale puts a bridle on Peter and a club and beats him, remarking that he prances better than his mouse-gray horse. Then he takes a paraffin shirt, puts it on Peter, and sets fire to it, telling him to stand guard against the Turks. While the riding of Peter is characteristic of the 1925 text, the execution of Peter is not mentioned in either Šemić or the 1925 text.

We know that Avdo Međedović was influenced by the songbook, because he told us of how it was read to him, but there was no attempt on his part to memorize any lines. He retold the story in his own way and his own verses.

Ramo Babić was a traditional singer before the songbook reached him, even as was Hajdar Habul, but Ramo, unlike Hajdar, memorized to a larger extent than our other singers the lines of the printed text, which he follows in story as well. For the study of memorized, or partially memorized, texts those of Hajdar Habul of Gacko and Ramo Babić of Novi Pazar are extremely instructive and useful.

The same is true of the two other Parry Collection texts of "Smailagić Meho" in the Šemić tradition from the sixties recorded on tape, as were the Babić texts, by David E. Bynum and myself. The first of these was from Bejito Smakić of Osmanbegovo Selo, Korito, recorded at Karajukići Bunari on the plateau of Pešter in 1963. Bejito was sixty-five years old and had been singing since he was about twenty. He had learned this song, he said, from his uncle (*stric*) Arslan Smakić a long time ago. Bejito was an excellent singer, and he probably did hear his uncle sing this song at some time, but the Šemić tradition is strong in Bejito's text, especially at the beginning, where the verbal correspondence is very noticeable. But like all good singers Bejito found the fixed text confining, and he very soon began to move away from it, to reshuffle it, in short, to sing his own text, establishing contact with the text of 1925 from time to time, just often enough so that one may with difficulty follow the text from his singing. The story remains close to the songbook version.

What all these texts have in common is that they have all been influenced directly by the Šemić redactions, and in all cases except that of Avdo that influence is apparent in the undoubted verbal correspondence between the texts and in their general closeness to the story of the earlier version.

B. Avdo's "Smailagić Meho" of 1950

In June 1950 Avdo gave us another text of "Smailagić Meho," the first 998 lines of which were dictated and the remainder recited for the microphone and recorded on magnetic wire; it contains a total of 8,488 lines. Avdo was then about eighty years old, and he said that he had not sung the song since 1935, because there was no one with a deep enough interest (*meraklija*) to listen. He said that he had not added anything to the song as he had sung it in 1935 nor left anything out, except perhaps in the listings of the agas and beys. He had not wanted this text to be as good, he said, as the old one, which had been translated into English. It is not as good as the earlier text, especially, indeed, as Avdo said, in the catalogues. He clearly had not put a catalogue together for a long time; the really amazing thing is that he could actually reconstruct as much of it as he did. In spite of what he said, there are a number of interesting changes in the narrative, some shift of emphasis, and several fine passages. It is still a superb song, as I hope the following account will demonstrate.

The opening of the later text is somewhat subdued compared with the earlier one, and it lacks the leisureliness and expansiveness of telling; but with the speech of Meho in the assembly and his uncle's reply it is clear that Avdo has once again become *engagé* in his song. Perhaps the best way to show this growing involvement is to quote the first scene of the song in its entirety.

The council was gathered in the tavern in Kanidža. Hasan pasha Tiro with his fifty men was there, and also the twelve beys of Kanidža and the twenty-four agas, and three imperial elders who

Avdo Međedović and Albert Lord in the yard of Avdo's house at
Obrov in the summer of 1951.

raise an army on their own authority. Cifrić Hasanaga was beside them. He was eighty years old, and his white beard encompassed him. There were also thirty captains, who lead a thousand men, and twenty-five standard-bearers, who carry gilded banners. Everyone was sitting in order, the imperial pasha and his men were between the windows. (25)

Each was boasting of something; they had drunk their fill of wine and brandy. They thought not of lunch or supper, but of good things, as was fitting. The imperial treasury was at their command, imperial help in their hands. The men of the border began to boast: who had built the better tower, or gained the better wife, or sired the better family, daughter or son. One boasted of his daughter, another of his sister, and another of his brother's daughter. One boasted of his house, another of his belt and arms. They boasted of who had broadened the imperial border, who had won more duels, or married off a youth. Their beards began to wave. They put their golden caps on the tables, hung their cloaks from the shining pegs, and placed their sharp swords across their laps. All were merry in the tavern. (50)

But one young man was sorrowful. There was none like him in all the company. He was not yet twenty; he had neither beard nor moustache. His black eyes were like a falcon's. His forehead was broad, his countenance fair. Such nobility not even the mountain *vile* had. His clothes were golden. On his head was an imperial fur cap, surrounded by a sash in which were placed seven plumes from the sultan. On the one between his eyes was written his name in gold: he was the son of Hadji Smail, Mehmed by name. Four standard-bearers served him, as the pashas serve the sultan, leaning upon their supple sabers. But the youth was sorrowful. (75)

No one asked him what was wrong, until Cifrić Hasan's heart was touched; he was sitting beside him. This was his brothers' child. He spoke to Mehmed: "Why are you sad, my son? There is no one here like you. None is handsomer or better accoutered, or of better family. You are the son of Hadji Smail, than whom none is richer. Even the sultan knows of your father. The alaybeyship is in your house. For twenty-seven years your father Smail ruled, with his thirty imperial captains, each with a thousand men on a thousand spirited horses. He waged war on all sides with the Hungarians and the Italians (100), and frequently with the czar in

Vienna. He broadened our land. But your father's limbs grew old. He could not ride or endure duels, nor could his aged body withstand the enemy's sabers. A decree came and took the alaybeyship from him and gave it to me. It is now twenty-two years that your uncle Hasan has had command. And I have grown old, my son. You are too young to know the extent of Smail's possessions. He has so much money that you couldn't count it or weigh it without heavy scales. He has five hundred landholders from old, with seed and oxen. His palace has eight stories and sixty rooms (125), each covered with silk. Let me tell you his other properties. He has inns and stores. Everything in them is yours. Why should you be sad? You will inherit all that we two old men have.

"When you were born, my son, imperial pashas came from the sultan to congratulate your father; and all Bosnia and the Border came, too. Your father had married seven times before he took your mother. By none of his wives had he any offspring, either boy or girl. We have waited, but now we shall marry you off, and then all will be well, my son."

When old Hasan had finished talking, Mehmed leaped up. From his teeth living fire flashed and his eyes were clouded as if overflowing with blood. (150) "Listen, Uncle Hasan, to what Mehmed will say. You have been listening to what my young friends say. As for your possessions and legacies,—may the floods carry them off! My comrades of my own age boast of taking Hungarian prisoners, German heads, and land from the Emperor. By your and my father's undoing, I have seen no raids or warring. I have not known where the border is, nor what it means to cut off a head, nor take a prisoner, nor marry off a comrade. Besides the pasha and his men and, by Allah and my faith, besides you and my father, there are a hundred and thirty youths here! (175) Till now I have served you both, but from now on I shall serve neither. Tonight will be the last. When the council breaks up and each goes home, I shall wait upon you both as I have been accustomed to do. When I leave to go to my mother in the harem, I shall not enter there, but go on to the dark stable and prepare my well-fed chestnut horse. I myself am already wearing my finest. I shall leap over the iron gateway and flee across the plain of Kanidža. I shall ride to the land of the enemy. Nor shall I stop at any border, but ride on to the land of Bogdan. People have told me of a certain General Peter, who is a

ruthless blood-letter without equal. He has harrassed our lands
(200) and drunk his fill of our blood and captured our people.
When I come to this bandit, he will know from my golden raiment,
from the plume above my forehead, the plume sent me from the
sultan on which my name is written, that I am the son of Hadji
Smail. Peter of Bogdan will recognize me and wonder how it is that
Mehmed is in his land. He will send out his guards for me and I
shall enter his palace and approach his hand. Then he will be
amazed and leap to his feet and say: " 'What is wrong, Mehmed.
Your father is fiercer than anyone else, than even me or any
king!' " And I shall say to Peter: " 'Listen, General Peter. In spite
of my father and uncle, I have come to you in Bogdan, (225)
neither submissively nor without thought of service. Give me an
army and cannon, that I may guide your army. First—I swear that
I am not lying—I shall set fire to Kanidža and then I shall cut off
the heads of my father and uncle and all the agas and beys. I shall
take their people captive and leave everything around Kanidža,
even all of Bosnia, in ruins. I shall marry all the Bosnian girls to
youths of Bogdan, and cause great havoc and woe.' When General
Peter hears that, he will embrace me and kiss my black eyes. You'll
see who it was you sired!"

When Cifrić Hasan heard that, he leaped to his feet and tears
welled up in his eyes. Tears raced down his cheeks and over his
white beard as pearls over white silk. (250) "Have mercy upon us,
Hasan pasha and your men and your other hundred and thirty agas!
Listen to what our dear son has done to our empire! Oh Mehmed,
we are both old. For over forty years we have been counting the
days to the time when we shall bequeath the command to you.
Then could we die without regret. But we have been waiting for
your youth to ripen. It is not easy, Mehmed, to command thirty
captains. The Border is rugged. Now, my son, because of your
anger at me and your father, we shall immediately prepare an imperial mandate (275) that the command pass from us two old men
to you. At this meeting here in the tavern are the principal figures
among us. Each will sign the mandate and Hasan pasha will confirm it. We shall send you, my son, to Buda tomorrow. The imperial vizier is there who rules [commands] a quarter of the empire. We have a good friend in him and he will immediately confirm

you in the command. May it be fortunate for you and long lasting, and honorable as with your father and uncle!"

Cifrić Hasanaga leaped up and had tables placed in the midst of the council. Four scribes were brought, and all the agas of Kanidža in order placed their seals on the mandate (300), agreeing with it. When the agas had signed it, Hasan pasha and his fifty men approved it.

When the hadji's son saw the mandate prepared for him for his departure to Buda the next day, he called out to the tavern maid: "Bring four kegs of wine and an equal number of brandy! Let us drink and be without care!" Then the Turks were merry until evening came and the council dispersed.

With the scene that follows at home between Smail and Uncle Hasan and Meho's mother and with the introduction of Osman the narration proceeds at a moderate pace. There are some changes.

Meho and his uncle returned home and Meho waited upon his father and Uncle Hasan. Smail noted that his son's countenance had changed and asked if he were ill. Hasanaga replied for Meho and told Smail briefly what Meho had said in the tavern and what the chief men had done, namely given Meho a petition to take the next day to Buda. Smail told Meho that he was perhaps undertaking more than he was yet capable of, but that since he had raised such a storm he must, of course, go to Buda. He told Meho then to go to his mother and described briefly the horse and clothes that had been sent for him from the sultan. Meho's mother rejoiced at the news that her son was going to Buda, dressed him (the description is very brief), and gave him parting advice to be sure not to let his father send him to Buda without Osman the standard-bearer.

Smail was delighted at the appearance of his son and advised him to do nothing on the journey without asking the advice of Osman. He told his son also to take good care of his horse. The passage is worth quoting:

> Then his mother sent him to his father and uncle. When he came thus arrayed before them, he approached their hands and then stepped back to serve them as he had always done. When his father saw him he leaped up and embraced him, saying: "Now I see, my dear moon [*meseče*, a playing on Meho], that you will be somewhat like your father (550) and your uncle. May your journey to

Buda be fortunate! Blessed may you be for all time! Now here is serious advice, son. Do not delay in Buda. You will take Osman the standard-bearer with you. From the time you leave until you return do as Osman says. I am a hundred. Not even now would I do anything without first asking him. I expect that your business with the Vizier of Buda will go quickly, because he is our good friend. Take good care of the chestnut steed in the stable, Mehmed. (575) It was sent you from Stambol full twelve years ago. There are four grooms with it. The chestnut has never yet seen the sun. He has fed on oats and rice and been groomed three times a day. He is not like other horses, not even Arabian stallions or Bedouin mares. Until he grew his wings he was groomed three times a day and once at night with lukewarm water and soap from Iraq. Like the clothes you are now wearing, you have never seen the horse before. Osman will prepare him for you. But I think that I shall see you on the horse. My palace has eight stories and the wall around the courtyard two. I shall not open the gate for you. The chestnut steed will leap over it. Let me see my son on the chestnut. The courtyard wall is twenty feet [elbows] high. You are my son; I love you more than all the world. If you are in any way like your father, you will not fall from the horse as he leaps over the wall. Then shall I know and be convinced that you will be like your father. If you fall, I shall not be angry with you, but it will be as if I had another son."

Then Smail opened the window and called to Osman to prepare his horse and himself for the journey to Buda with Meho. When Osman appeared all prepared and arrayed in the courtyard, Smail tossed him a purse of ducats from the window and gave him lengthy instructions about the journey. "You will spend the night in my villages. The first night from Kanidža is exactly twenty hours away. (700) You will cover it in one day by evening. In the village the Vukašinovići will receive you." And Smail went on to describe their house and the family, which included two daughters and twin sons, and he advised Osman not to stay more than one night. Twenty hours away from that, said Smail, was the village of Vujadinovići, and he described it and the family, which included two brothers and two twin sons, but the village was otherwise very much like Vukašinovići. From there after one night they were to go on to the river Klima [Knin?] and to the drawbridge over it. "The Klima is very wide, and wide is the bridge over it. On it there are twenty-four towers. Beside the bridge are forty coffeehouses and among them the imperial customs houses; for it is a link from the whole of Europe. Choose the best coffeehouse and spend the night." The next day they were to proceed quickly to Buda, arriving as early as possible. After spending the night they should see the vizier, who would not keep them long, and then they should return quickly to Kanidža.

When the young men had received the injunction, they straight-way mounted their horses. The retainers closed the gates so that they both might leap the wall and test the mettle of the chestnut. Both youths loosened the reins to leap. The horses knew what they wanted and lifted their hoofs into the air. They flew as on wings, (800) cleared the gate and the rampart, and alighted on the heath outside the walls. The old man was watching to see whether his son would fall or be frightened, but he saw that the boy showed no sign, but was flying over the plain of Kanidža with Osman at his side, like two dragons in a golden cloud. The old man rejoiced. Now he saw that he had a son who would be a little like his father.

The description of the overnight stays with Vukašin and Vujadin is lengthy, particularly the first of the two, and elaborate. It is of the same kind as in the earlier text. The heroes then went on to the river and the drawbridge, and, since this stop is not in the 1935 text, I shall present it here; it is not without a certain charm.

Osman dismounted and said to Mehmed: "We must pass the night here. Your father gave us excellent advice; to choose the best coffeehouse where there is splendor and a garden and cool shade." Mehmed obeyed. He had sworn to his father that he would do nothing but what Osman ordered. There the youths spent the night. The coffeehouse attendants came and took their spirited horses. They cared well for them. They sponged them down, for they had traveled hard all day and the dust was heavy. They loosened the girths and gave them barley and hay. They led the two youths into the comforts of the coffeehouse (1625) where there was a park and lights, where all was splendor and cool. The youths stayed there until nightfall, when they had a lordly supper. They ate and drank wine and brandy as they wished. All kinds of delicacies were brought them. When nightfall came, they dined and had a great plenty. When time came for them to go to bed, they lay on soft mattresses that they were scarcely aware of, they were so comfortable. Mehmed said to Osman: "Osman, my dear brother, you are old enough to have sired me two or three or more times. I am very inexperienced here. The luxury here is like the sultan's. There is nothing similar at my father's house." "Mehmed, (1650) level Budapest is no laughing matter; great is its luxury. Do not be amazed."

The next day, soon after they had entered the plain of Muhač, they saw a coach coming from Buda. Meho wondered at it, the sound of screaming coming from it, and the appearance of the leader of the guard with it. Osman gave him permission to question the guard, who at first refused to answer his greeting or even to look at him, but finally said: "O boy in the golden clothes. A good house reared you in vain, because you are mad. I can see you are inexperienced or that drink has gone to your head in the coffeehouse at the drawbridge. Listen, boy! Don't say anything about all this. Get your horse away from here and pull your cloak about you. Don't prattle on about trifles. I'll strike you with my sword and cut you in two. Your mother will wail and also your father, if you have one." Meho was very angry, but did not know what to do. He went back to ask Osman, who told Meho he should return and speak sternly to the guard and ask again. This Meho did, and the guard started to attack him, but Meho again did not know what to do and returned to Osman. Then Osman decided that Meho should deal with the leader of the guard while he fought with the forty guardsmen. This is what they did; Meho dispatched the leader, Osman killed half of the guardsmen, and the other half fled, leaving the coach.

Meho now approached the coach, drew his Persian saber, and cut the cords which held the curtain. The girl he found inside was lovely, but she had scratched her face and plucked out some of her hair, and she was screaming and lamenting. She complained that no hero had been found in Buda for twenty years, ever since the treacherous vizier had arrived. She described his reception and then his subsequent actions, including the fate of her father, Zajim Alibeg, who had been exiled to Bagdad. She had been born after her father's exile and kept hidden; but the vizier had found out about her and three or four times a year had demanded her in marriage, but she had refused. Meho spoke to her then and asked why they had not let someone know of the vizier's oppression; the Turks of Buda were not to be blamed. The girl said: "Leave me alone, useless man of Buda! Do not mock me!" Meho asked her name, and when she told him she was Zajimova Fata, he told her he was not from Buda but from far-away Bosnia. "O Fatima, by your Moslem faith, have you any wine or brandy, that you might wash your black eyes and remove the blood from your cheeks, that I may see how you have been disfigured? . . ." When Fata understood, she said: "We have wine and brandy." Then she washed her face. (2050) Her appearance and clothes are then briefly described, and Meho asked her where the vizier was sending her. "To Bogdan, to General Peter," she said. Meho reacted to this immediately with: "O Fatima, would you take me; would you be my wife? Let me take you to Kanidža and marry you." She agreed gladly, saying that her mother had brought her up with the hope of marrying her to Mehmed, and she implored him not to take her back to Buda, because the vizier would kill him, and on his and his family's life the future of the empire depended. They disagreed much on this point, and Meho went to ask the opinion of Osman. Meho explained the situation to Osman, and the latter suggested that Meho take the girl on his horse, covering her with his cloak, and return her to Buda. Osman himself would come along later with the coach and inquire for the Alibegovica's house. Fatima would be able to direct Mehmed. After more difficulty with Fatima, Meho finally persuaded her and he returned her as instructed to Buda.

In this text it is clear that both Osman and Mehmed's horse play a larger role than in the earlier text. The following passage about the horse in Meho's advice to Fatima as they are about to depart is noteworthy:

> Then he said to Fatima: "Put your lovely arms about my waist, because the chestnut horse has no equal in speed. He has nine sets of wings underneath and the tenth set by the pommel. Clouds of smoke and dust will hit you, Fatima, and the great winds that blow across Muhač. Your black eyes will be blurred. But you can protect yourself behind my back. My queue will defend you from the great smoke of the horse. Hold on; don't fall! (2275) for the chestnut is without equal in his strength. I cannot hold him back."

Fatima immediately obeyed Mehmed, though not without a wail, because the girl was afraid of the vizier. She clasped her arms about Mehmed like iron bonds and hid her white face behind his back. When he saw that she was ready, Mehmed released the horse, urged him but a little with the stirrups, and the chestnut steed spewed flame from his nostrils like living fire and gnashed the bit. Mehmed raised the horse's hoofs with their heavy shoes and nails to the clouds. There was a great roar and a great cloud of smoke and dust across the plain of Muhač. When it was just two hours to sunset, the horse was clattering along the square in level Buda.

In Buda Meho asked Fatima for directions to her house, and she described it as well as her father's riches. When they reached the house it was as described, and when they went into the courtyard Meho was amazed at the glories there to be seen. At that moment he heard Fatima's mother lamenting and he saw that she was about to leap from the window. Meho shouted to her and lifted the cloak, revealing Fatima. She asked who he was and Mehmed told her, and the lady rejoiced for, as she said, she had reared Fatima with the hope of betrothing her to Meho. Meho told her that he would first go to the vizier and receive the command and then return to the Alibegovica to ask for her daughter's hand. The lady was fearful of the vizier, and when the sound of the coach and horses was heard as Osman brought them back into Buda, Fatima's mother thought that the soldiers had come to take Meho away to the vizier. After Osman's arrival, at long last, Fatima dismounted and was greeted by her mother, and they in turn greeted Meho and Osman with due ceremony.

Fatima went into the house and with her mother's help dressed in her finest. Meho and Osman were then summoned to the upper chambers, but, over protests, they decided first to take a walk in the gardens and along the balconies, and then repaired to the upper chambers where they supped and slept.

The next morning after breakfast Osman and Meho mounted and went to the vizier's house. "That courtyard was so large one could have held a horse race in it, and the horses would have tired themselves in the run. In it stood executioners. In one place there was a black executioner with white teeth, holding a sharp sword in his hands. There were stairs for each story, and on each an executioner with a sharp sword ready. This was because of the great terror in Buda from their traitor." Osman and Meho dismounted, and Osman sent Meho alone to see the vizier. Mehmed went unchallenged past all the guards straight into the audience room to the vizier, who was sitting in an alcove surrounded by his councillors. The pasha received him with open arms, and after he had learned the purpose of Meho's visit he ordered his scribes to prepare a decree for Mehmed. When this was done the pasha himself performed the investiture:

On Meho's head he put a golden cap surrounded by a golden sash in which was the feather of the alaybey and golden plumes. When the cap had been placed on the youth's head, one would say and swear that the bright sun was shining from him. Great was the richness—without equal. Here was youth! Here was beauty! On him the magnificence of the raiment was enhanced (3050), most of all the imperial cap itself and the feather of the alaybey which shone as the bright sun.

After taking his leave of the vizier, Meho returned to Osman, told him how he had been received, and they departed. On the way back Meho asked Osman if he thought that it would be unseemly of him to stop at the mufti's and judge's residence to obtain a marriage permit. Osman laughed and said he should go right ahead, but advised him that the vizier's quarters would seem poor compared to those of the judge (*cadi*), who was a very dangerous person; he had destroyed some five hundred families in Buda and cast fifteen hundred youths into the river or hanged them from the ramparts. Osman warned Meho to keep his eyes open for trouble. The encounter that follows is presented by Avdo in striking contrast to that between Mehmed and the vizier:

> When the youth went up the stairs, the cadi's retainers met him, spears in hand, waiting for the sign to kill, the sign indicating who could be expended and who could not. Mehmed entered the court and passed through the antechambers until he came to the cadi's door. The door was covered with fine cloth, and on it were three strips of gold, on one of which was a finely written imperial order forbidding entrance to anyone who had not given prior notice of his coming. On another was written that the cadi should be carefully obeyed. Mehmed read this. There were four retainers nearby with imperial spears in their hands, and when Mehmed came to the chamber, he said to the retainers: (3200) "May I enter to see the cadi? I am a stranger from afar. May I enter and accomplish my urgent business? It cannot wait." The retainers frowned and said to the youth: "Go away! Are you drunk or crazy? Talking about entering like that! There are people here who have been waiting days and even a month! There is no waiting line to enter or to see the cadi himself or his scribes or our mufti." Mehmed's hand went to the hilt of his sword, and his sword flew from its scabbard and

rang against the floor. The cadi's residence trembled, and all the retainers rushed to the scene from the cadi's gate. Then the door opened before him (3225) and Mehmed surged angrily into the room.

The cadi was looking out the window and paid no attention to Meho's greeting. Meho moved two paces closer and then angrily addressed the cadi, asking why he did not return his greeting. The judge turned around then, saw the feather of the alaybey, and was all apologies. Mehmed berated him for all the crimes he had committed in Buda and said that Tale would take care of him when the wedding guests came. Then he asked for a marriage permit, to which the judge agreed, but when he found out who the girl was he told Meho that she was no longer in Buda. Meho explained that she was, and the marriage permit was granted, and quickly. Mehmed rejoined Osman, and they went back to the house of the Alibegovica.

Mehmed and Osman were received joyfully by the ladies, and after refreshment they were taken by the maid Rukija to the roof of the house to look out and be shown the extent of Alibeg's possessions. Meho was duly impressed by what he was shown and told Rukija that he was to marry Fatima, but that first he must go to the Border so that his father might gather wedding guests. The maid lamented and wailed, saying that he should not leave Fatima in Buda, because the vizier would destroy them all in his absence. But Mehmed replied that he could see that Buda would be filled with corpses and wounded, and that the river would run troubled to the Danube, from what the Border would do against the vizier. Then they returned downstairs, and in tears Rukija told her mistress and Fatima what Mehmed had said about returning to Kanidža. The women tried to persuade Meho to take Fatima with him, but he insisted that his father would object, since it would be dishonorable to avoid the traitor from fear, and he would even kill his son for besmirching the honor of the house. Osman confirmed that what Mehmed said was true. When Fatima heard this she fainted and they had difficulty reviving her.

Mehmed and Osman remained in Buda at Fatima's house that night and the following, but on the second day Osman announced to the Alibegovica that they could stay no longer, that they had, indeed, already disobeyed the orders of Mehmed's father in delaying as long as they had. Gifts were then brought forth for Meho to take back with him to Kanidža. There were forty-three gifts, including special ones for

Smail and his wife and for Cifrić Hasan and Mehmed. Meho felt embarrassed and asked Osman what he might do, since they had spent half of the ducats that Smail had given them for the journey. Osman suggested that he had a ring and in his pocket a golden apple. He might give them these gifts now and tell the lady that he would bring others when the wedding guests came for Fatima. Mehmed agreed because his father had told him to follow whatever advice Osman might give him. When the Alibegovica heard of his embarrassment, she assured him that he should not worry, because they were rich enough anyway, but she graciously accepted the ring and the golden apple.

Then the heroes mounted and with the ladies' blessing departed for Kanidža. They traveled much faster on the return journey than on the journey to Buda. They did not stop at the village by the bridge but came to Vujadinovići by nightfall; at dawn they went on to Vukašinovići, where they explained about the treacherous vizier and the coming wedding, and the following morning they departed thence, arriving at Kanidža by noon. When Smail learned of their coming, he ordered the cannon to be fired and criers to be dispatched announcing the return of Mehmed and Osman. They were met and brought to Smail, and after exchange of greetings, Mehmed related to his father the incident with the coach. Meho told what had happened up to the time that he returned with Fatima to Buda, to be followed by Osman with the coach. After relating to Smail the various evil deeds of the vizier and his fellow conspirators in Buda, Meho said that he would have killed them had it not been for his father's friendship with the vizier. At this Smail leaped to his feet and took his sword from its peg, shouting "What good was it for you to receive the command as alaybey, thus to shame us? Why did you not take Fata?" Meho then spoke up and assured his father that that was what he had indeed done. He showed Smail the vizier's letter to Peter of Bogdan and told how he was well received by the vizier and how he was granted a marriage license by the authorities.

Smail greatly approved of his son's actions in not bringing Fatima back with him from Buda. The old man had been keeping his inheritance from his father and grandfather for this wedding, and he was pleased that Meho had chosen to fight for the girl; had Meho done otherwise, his father would have killed him. Then father and son embraced, and Smail went to his rooms and Mehmed went to see his mother. He told her of what had happened, and his lady mother rejoiced.

Meho slept like a lamb all that night, but his mother did not sleep, praising God until dawn. The next day the cannon announced the return of the new alaybey from Buda, and the leaders of Kanidža were summoned for forty and seven days to come to congratulate him on the command. Smail asked Meho what arrangements he had made with Fatima's mother concerning the wedding, and in the presence of the forty chiefs of Kanidža and his father and uncle Meho answered. He gave greetings from Fatima's mother and reported that she was sure that there would be a great battle and therefore there should be many wedding guests. They should be accompanied either by Smail or by his brother, and Mehmed himself should come with the wedding guests, because Peter might challenge him to a duel. Meho said that the lady had told Smail not to spend money except for the journey to Buda; the rest would be paid for by Fatima's mother. She had also said to tell Smail that if fate allowed and they should find Fatima's father, Zajim Alibeg, alive in Bagdad and return him to Buda, he would see what a father-in-law and mother-in-law his son had gained. At these words Smail rejoiced, saying, however, that he had money enough from his own inheritances for all the expenses of the wedding guests. He said that he would gather Bosnia, but that he could not himself go, but his brother Hasan would be the leader of the bride's protectors (*djeverbaša*) in his place. Smail then told Meho to go to his mother's chambers and rest while his father gathered the scribes and sent letters to the leaders.

For ten days the forty scribes wrote (the letters are not given separately, nor is a detailed catalogue of the leaders), and then Smail summoned forty messengers to deliver the letters. Now comes the catalogue. As Smail gave the letters to the messengers he told them to whom they should be delivered. This catalogue section extends from line 4535 to line 4893.

After the last of the messengers had departed, Smail summoned his two chief overseers and consulted with them concerning food for the wedding guests when they should arrive at Kanidža. When they had gone, he and the chiefs of Kanidža discussed the preparations to receive the guests. At this point Avdo comments on the greatness of the battle which is to come from the gathering of these hosts, namely, the battle on the plain of Muhač by Buda. "Even today it is sung of in songs, it is sung and it is true. Much blood has been shed in our Balkans, but most of all around Buda, when the Danube was turbulent with the blood of heroes. That was the main battleground between the great king of the Magyars and Selim the Turkish sultan. . . . Even now on the plain of

Muhač the grass does not grow on the earth; it was burned out by the blood of heroes and of good horses. That is true and is no lie" (lines 4990–5008).

The men arrived to prepare the plain of Kanidža for the wedding guests. For forty days the preparations continued. Tents were set up, ditches were dug for the fires, and contributions came pouring in, cows and oxen, stallions and mares, serge cloth and velvet, and gold coins. A thousand youths were sent to the plain to receive the wedding guests and take them to their lodgings. For fourteen days then, day and night, the mountain echoed as the armies assembled.

The army began to arrive. First came Mustajbeg and then others until all had come except Tale. Unlike other gathering passages in Avdo's poems this is very short, less than a hundred lines, and the difference in length between the 1935 and 1950 texts of Avdo is largely attributable, as he himself said, to the shortness of the catalogues in the later text. When all had come except Tale, the pashas of Travnik and of Banja Luka together with the other chiefs told Smail that the time had come for them to set out for Buda, but Smail impored them to wait for Tale, for without him and his three hundred men of Orašac they could not depart. Finally Tale arrived, and he and his men are described in the usual way. Those wedding guests who came from afar wondered at Smail for his concern about Tale, because they felt that Tale would only bring disgrace upon them. But Smail went throughout the host, speaking to each of the leaders in turn in appropriate wise imploring them not to insult Tale, for they could not go without him. When Tale arrived he scolded Smail for having gathered such a large army at such great expense, and he said that he had himself three times sought the hand of Fatima in Buda, but she had not been willing even to see him. He was a bit angry, therefore, at Smail for winning Fata for his son. Smail asked his wife to go and meet Tale and give him a purse of ducats (madžarije) and to take him and his companions to her quarters and give them wine and brandy and money. The Smailaginica obeyed her lord. Tale repeated the story to her of his wooing of Fatima in vain, but he and his companions went with her and his men of Orašac remained outside.

Tale wanted the army to move off the next day, but Smail asked for time for all to rest for three or four days, and Tale agreed to allow them two days. Then the cry to depart was raised, and Tale told Hodža Šuvajlija, his comrade, to go with him to the heights of Kozara and there form a gate with Tale on one side and the hodža on the other, to foretell the number that would be killed and that would survive. When the first of the army reached the heights the last contingent, that of Cifrić Hasanaga, was still on the plain of Kanidža. For two days and a night Tale counted the army on Kozara. He counted a hundred and forty thousand horsemen, without taking into consideration the infantry or the artillery or the supply trains. Then for twelve days they traveled until they reached the river Knin and the drawbridge over it. Avdo listed some of the stops on the way. On the first night after leaving Kozara they stayed on Mount Brešljen; the second on Mount Ogorelica, after crossing Krblja; on the third day they came to Mount Konija and then over Ornanija and through the dark and deep valley until they spent the fourth night on Mount Havridžan below Dinara; the fifth night on Romanija; and thus in time they came to the Knin.

There Tale advised them to leave Mustajbeg with an army of twelve thousand and twelve cannon from the Lika. As commanders under Mustajbeg they left Grdić Husein and Grdan Osman. They were to guard the bridge lest Bogdan take it and cut off their return from Buda. That night the wedding guests stayed on the plain of Muhač and early the next day arrived at Buda. The Alibegovica received them very well in Buda. Tale and Mujo, the two viziers, and twenty beys and forty agas of the Krajina stayed with the Alibegovica herself, while Halil and the forty protectors of the bride went to Fata's quarters.

Mujo then asked Tale how he thought they would fare in Buda. Tale replied: "You will yawn and drink and fill your belly, Mujo, but we must return to the Border, and when you leave Buda and proceed across Muhač you will meet Bogdan and his cannon. Here you will drink your fill of brandy, but there you will drink blood. You will remember this wedding!" Mujo hung his head and was displeased with this. After the first night in Buda the gardens were filled with maidens and the dancing began. The festivities went on for a whole week and then the wedding guests thought to leave. But the treacherous vizier wrote a letter to General Peter of Bogdan telling him to attack the men of the Border when they left and destroy Bosnia. Peter replied that he needed a week in which to gather his army. So the vizier summoned the leaders of Bosnia and invited them to stay on for another week in Buda at his expense. Tale advised Mujo against this, repeating what he had said earlier to him about drinking brandy in Buda and later drinking blood on Muhač. Yet it pleased Mujo to stay on at the invitation of the vizier, and they agreed that half of the wedding guests should stay at the vizier's expense. If trouble came they would hang the vizier from the ramparts and call his wife to tell them where the vizier's treasure was and that of the imperial agas of Buda. Finally Tale spoke to all the army and said that they should not touch the vizier until the wedding guests had departed and were on the plain of Muhač. If the vizier were deceiving them he would send a note to Peter to block their path. If there were a battle, the wedding guests could return to Buda and implore the commanders on the walls in the name of good Turks to give up Buda.

And so half the guests went to the vizier's and half to the cadi's. The festivities continued for another week, until the vizier received a letter from Peter, saying that his army had occupied the bank of the river from Varadin to the drawbridge and that their cannon were in place and especially strong at the bridge. Then the vizier said it was time for the guests to depart. With all their beasts of burden laden with gifts they left Buda.

When the wedding guests reached the first stopping place on the plain of Muhač, the trumpets in Buda were blown and the orders given to close the four gates of the city and to turn the guns on the ramparts in the direction of the departed guests so that none of them could return into the city alive. The soldiers and their commanders did not like the orders and some of them wept, but they had to obey. The following morning Tale looked back at the walls of Buda and saw that the gates were closed. He pointed this out to Mujo. At the next night's stop on the plain, before nightfall, they looked in the direction of the Knin, and from Varadin to the drawbridge the banks of the river were covered by a dark mist. Mujo was puzzled. He had been to Buda three times before, once in the summer and twice in the winter, and had not seen such a sight before. He sought out the oldest man in the army, Cifrić Hasanaga, and asked him if he knew what it could be. Hasan told Mujo that that was not a mist, but that the vizier had tricked them. He had brought the armies of Bogdan to the Knin and they were in position along the river from Varadin to the drawbridge.

Now Fatima's party dismounted and gathered together for the night. In the morning they held a council, and it was decided to send a herald throughout the camp to ask for volunteers to attack the forces at the river and the bridge. For four hours the herald made the announcement, and a standard was set around which volunteers might gather, but nobody appeared. In the fifth hour a rider appeared, an old man with a white beard, to volunteer. If was Cifrić Hasanaga, Meho's uncle! He was soon joined by the seven Atlagići and the seventeen beys from across the Una, and in the course of an hour a thousand had volunteered.

The volunteers attacked, and of the thousand only three hundred survivied. The forces of Grdan Osman and Grdić Husein had all perished. Then the main body of the wedding guests attacked, and for three days and four nights the battle raged. The river became filled with corpses, and riders and infantry crossed over them. Finally Tale prayed that the smoke clear, and when it did, the desolation was apparent. At the foot of one of the turrets of the bridge he saw a naked hero, and when he approached he saw that it was Grdan Osman, or rather Husein, his brother. He reported that he was the sole survivor of the twelve thousand who had been left with him.

Then Tale looked with his spyglass out onto the plain of Muhač and there he saw a group of seventeen, but neither he nor Husein could make out who they were; they too were naked. When he looked again he saw Fatima and the three hundred men who had been left with her, the forty protectors of the bride, and the twenty burdens of gifts. Tale and Husein rejoiced that Fatima had survived the battle. Then again Tale took his spyglass and looked at the place where he had seen Fatima. Now there were more people with her, and Tale and Husein joined them. Many of their comrades had perished, but General Peter's army had been routed.

After many of them had gathered together and pitched their tents again, it was discovered that Cifrić Hasan and the Pasha of Kanidža and Pasha Ibrahim of Travnik and their armies of Janissaries were missing. The men first waded into the river and dragged forth the bodies of the dead and buried them on the plain. Then they attended to the wounded.

On the eighth day a mist rose along the Knin river, and with a rumbling the army with Cifrić Hasanaga appeared at its head. He had been the first to volunteer to attack the bridge and the strong positions of General Peter. Tale had one or two cannon fired to inform Fata that Meho's uncle had been found. After Hasan had been greeted he mourned that Meho was still missing. At that moment there was thundering on the plain of Muhač, and Meho appeared, driving General Peter before him. When Hasan saw them he asked Tale to have the cannon fired and suggested that, when they had returned to Buda, they send a letter to the sultan to tell him what had happened in Buda for so many years to the present.

They waited four more days, and during that period the blood-stained heroes appeared, until Tale told Hasanaga that it seemed to him more than half of their wedding guests were present. For two more days they buried the dead, and then for four days they placed the wounded on the riderless horses and sent them back to Bosnia. And now there came together Hasan Pasha Tiro of Kanidža, Pasha Ibrahim (of Travnik), the Bey of the Lika and the Border (Mustajbeg), the two beys of Cetina (Zenković and Babahmetović), the Bey of Pločnik (Gavrić Alibeg), the Alaybey of Klis, Fetibegović of Banja Luka; of the seventeen beys from the Una only nine were alive, the rest had perished. (I have given the details of this list for those who wish to compare them with the catalogues in Avdo's 1935 text.)

Now they took counsel as to how they could get at the vizier in Buda. The city was fortified with a three-story-high wall pierced by only four gates manned by the pasha's men. Tale suggested that they prepare a letter to them asking that they not turn their guns against their brother Turks as the treacherous vizier had done, but that they open the gates for them to enter Buda. They wrote such a letter and sent Vilić Husein of Grbava and Ćejvanović Meho with it under a white flag. As this embassy was approaching, the pasha's leaders on the ramparts noticed that Bosnia had destroyed the forces of General Peter and they decided not to fight with Bosnia. Later the sultan might have found out about their having fought with the Bosnian Turks and their lives would be forfeited. So they decided to fire twice into the air and not to fire the third time. Then the letter came from the wedding guests, and when the pasha's leaders read it they wept. Then the vizier's order came to fire from the walls and destroy the remainder of the wedding guests, including Zajimova Fata, but the leaders refused to obey the orders. Four times they fired into the air with no harm to the Bosnians. The fifth time their fire reached to the mountains on the other side of the plain of Muhač, where the River Knin was.

Then Tale gave Mujo the order to attack Buda. They took Fatima and the beasts of burden loaded with gifts and set out for Buda. The pasha's leaders opened the gates for them without permission from the vizier. Fatima returned thus with her retinue to her mother. Tale decided to go with his men to the cadi to demand an accounting of what had happened for many years in Buda, what had been done with Turkish land, how many people had been killed, how much money had been collected, so that they might report to the sultan, and that they might punish the evil-working traitors.

Now they sent Mustajbeg, the Bey of Klis, and the two beys of

Cetina with forty thousand men to the vizier. The vizier ordered his men to fire on them, but none would. Instead they allowed the Bosnians into the residence. After greeting the vizier, the Bosnians asked if he thought that he was ruler of the Turkish Empire and reminded him that Allah was mightier than anyone. The pasha shrugged his shoulders. Tale, who had been to the cadi's and then come on to the vizier's residence (here Avdo took a break), struck the vizier on the turban, from which fell crosses, for he had been faithful to the Latins.

The Bosnians bound the vizier and suspended him from the door of the room. The vizier's wife was in great distress and, in order to save her husband (Tale promised that he would not harm the vizier), delivered to Tale the keys to the treasury. For four days they carried out the gold and piled it in the vizier's room. Even more treasure was found under the floor of the harem. All the sultan's possessions in Buda had fallen into the hands of the vizier.

Avdo now returns to tell what had happened between Tale and the cadi. Tale and his people together with Grdan Husein had gone to the *haćim efendi* and the mufti and forced them to tell where their treasure was, and for twelve days and nights they had extracted fourteen loads of ducats. After this the Bosnians executed the vizier, the cadi, the *haćim efendi*, and mufti. They impaled the vizier on the door of his residence.

(Here Avdo rested for a while.) For a whole month now the city opened its doors to the Bosnians. Finally Tale declared that the time had come for the marriage of Mehmed with Fatima. For a whole week there were festivities, dancing in the gardens and singing. Then they took Mehmed to Fatima's marriage chamber, and before the door of the chamber they beheaded General Peter and put his head on the walls of the city.

When Mehmed's wedding was over, Tale suggested that they write a report to the sultan of what had happened in Buda. For four days they wrote, and the imperial pashas confirmed the letter. When the sultan received it, he gathered together his councillors and, weeping, told them of events in Buda. He asked them why they had not told him, but all, including the Sheh ul Islam, averred that they had not known anything of what was going on in Buda. The sultan vowed to give all the help and support he could to the widows and children of his subjects who had suffered in Buda. He then sent a firman to the Shah of Bagdad asking whether there were any exiles from Buda in his city and explained what the situation had been in that city. He requested the shah to send any such exiles he could find to the sultan in Stambol. The shah received the firman and wept. For fourteen days he sought out the exiles. Of the five hundred exiled, he found only three hundred, and they were ill. He sent them at his own expense to Stambol. When the sultan saw them he wept and had them lodged in his guest house, where they were fed well and where they slept on silken featherbeds. He gave them clothes and money. In due time he put them on a steamboat for Buda, and then sent a firman to Buda confirming grants of money to their women and children as well and to the orphans. When they arrived in Buda, all rejoiced as families were reunited.

Then the Bosnians and people of Buda desired to send a delegation to the sultan. They asked in a letter whom they should send, and the sultan replied that he would be glad to receive anyone, even the poorest. There follows now a catalogue of those who went to Stambol:

> Mustajbeg
> Pasha Ibrahim
> Cifrić Hasan
> The eight beys of the Una
> Twelve Kurtagići
> Ćejvan, Mustajbeg's uncle
> Ramo of Glamoč
> Mujo Hrnjica and Halil
> The bey's standards
>> Vrcić
>> Mejrić
>> Two Ibričići
>> Deli Kurtagić
> Alibeg of Pločnik
> Alaybey of Klis
> Čavić Alibeg, Brčkovo
> Mujo buljukbaša of Teslić and Doboj
> Pecigović of Banja Luka

These emissaries were well received by the sultan, who granted them the right to choose a vizier for themselves in Buda. Moreover, he said that he would send Mehmed Bošnjak (Solkolović) to Bosnia, who would grant gifts of money, clothes, land, and honors to the men of Bosnia. And so the emissaries of Bosnia returned to Buda, where the cannon boomed in greeting.

Finally, after four months, a letter came from Smailaga of Kanidža congratulating Meho and praising his daughter-in-law. The agas and beys took counsel now as to whom they should choose for the new vizier in Buda. Tale's choice fell on Umer Efendi, whom, as vizier, they called Jahja Pasha Tiro. The wedding guests and Fatima at last prepared to return to Kanidža. Zajim Alibeg had been brought back from Bagdad and had renewed his own marriage bed with Fata's mother. He very much approved of the marriage of his daughter with Mehmed. The Ali-begovica told him how much she had spent for the wedding and advised him that she had promised that much to Meho. Zajim Alibeg agreed, and the money was loaded to go with Fatima to Kanidža. Thus the wedding guests departed from Buda and came to Bosnia and the Border.

(At this point, the end of spool 22, there is a lack of continuity in the text. Something was lost at the beginning of spool 23. As the text resumes Smailaga is about to speak to Meho and the leading men of Kanidža. The arrival and reception by Smail have been lost.)

Smail told the men of Kanidža that up to now the wedding guests had been involved in bloodshed and fighting. From now on there would be rejoicing. He did not see his son's wedding in Buda, and he would, therefore, now hold a wedding celebration for his son. The cannon boomed, and the agas of Kanidža gathered together. In the course of his speech to them Smail asked his wife how Fatima was as a daughter-in-law. The lady said that never in her whole life had she seen a finer girl. She rejoiced at their good fortune. Smail told her that Fatima's mother had sent them the money spent thus far for the wedding, and they agreed that there was nothing better on which they could spend their own wealth than on Meho's wedding.

Smail went with his brother Hasanaga to their home and sat down to write letters to gather Bosnia again. He was planning also to have a horse race and a foot race, and he began to think of prizes. He summoned his two head farmers, Matija and Matoš, and asked them once again to prepare to entertain Bosnia. He told them of the money Fatima's mother had sent. Smail then summoned forty retainers to go to Mounts Roša and Peruša and Brešljen for cattle. Then he sent off the letters to the agas or to their widows. He invited the latter to forget their husbands and to come with their children to the wedding of his son. He sent letters from the top of the Lika to Unđurovina, from the bottom of Bosnia to the green Sava, and from the Sava to Osjek, from Osjek to Klis, and from there to Herceg (ovina?).

For forty-eight days the guests assembled for the feast. "As many

from the Border who had gone to Buda, just so many more youths now
gathered, their sons and grandsons and their daughters' sons. Each one
had a stallion or a mare with wings under its girths. For Bosnia was no
laughing matter; Bosnia was a quarter of the sultanate, and it held the
empire together. Ever since we lost Bosnia the empire has been eroded.
Such was the case, and that is the truth" (lines 8180–8192). The wedding lasted a whole month. "Smail lodged the gentry in his dwellings
and the other wedding guests on the green plain. The stallions and the
Bedouin mares neighed and the other steeds whinnied. A great mist
arose from the breath of horses and heroes as it came from their nostrils,
as from a great rain or from a snow storm" (lines 8201–8209). At the
end of a month criers announced the horse race. Tale measured off the
place on the level plain and determined how many stallions and Bedouin
mares might enter; of other horses there was no count. They stretched a
golden cord as starting line. It was a long race, four hours, from the
middle of the plain of Kanidža to the dwellings of Smailaga. There were
two hundred stallions and three hundred Bedouin mares and countless
other horses. Two cannon were fired, and the race started. The first to
arrive was the chestnut-red steed of Hadji Smail; and then among the
first were the Bedouin mare of Cifrić Hasan, the dark steed of the Pasha
of Travnik, the white horse of Sirdar Mujo Hrnjica, the chestnut of
Vlahinjić Alija, the brown Bedouin mare of Bosić the standard-bearer
with its nine wings, the mouse-gray of Mrša Husein from Projorje, that
great plain, the light-gray (*zekan*) of Zuka of Stijena, the chestnut of
Kraga Šabanaga and that of his blood-brother Topal Mustafaga, and the
two brown Bedouin mares of the two young Hamdijići from Prodorje
and Upper Sijena, the sorrel of Ivičević (Ibričić?) Alija and the chestnut
of Mumin the standard-bearer. To those who came in first they gave
bags of gold. To those who came in second bolts of cloth were given,
both serge and velvet, sent by the sultan, of the kind worn in the court.
To those who came in third were given golden bundles of clothing
worth a city or a province. The cannon boomed and trumpets blared in
celebration. There followed music and dancing throughout Kanidža.

After the horse race Tale ordained a foot race of youths. Two
hundred young men like golden dragons took part in the race. To those
who would come in first Smail would give gold; to the second unridden
horses, stallions and Bedouin mares in golden trappings, good gifts for
good heroes. The first to come in were the two Prženići from below
Bihać, the two Šejtanovići from beside (?) Bihać, Balević's son from

below Bihać, Ibrahim by name, and Hamajlić's son from Čekrk, Vlahinjić Alija from Otoka, Orlanović Mujo, two agas from Banja Luka, and Filduš's two sons from Bosnia, two brothers and both heroes, who held captaincies. "More prizes were given than for the stallions and Bedouin mares, because a man has a heart in his breast and is ready to sacrifice his life; thus he would do tomorrow in battle, surviving with his life but not showing his wounds."

Another twenty-four days of festivities followed and then Mehmed Pasha arrived from Stambol. Before him rode an imperial tatar, and behind him a hundred warriors and twenty imperial courtiers. Mehmed Pasha rode a white horse, a gift to the sultan from Egypt. A thousand young men and a thousand maidens went out to meet him and to spread serge cloth upon the plain for him. After the pasha had rested, he congratulated them all on the wedding and on the new alaybeyship and on the son of Hadji Smail, who would leave a name for himself to be remembered forever. The pasha stayed for twenty days and made lists of how many men had been lost, how many children were left, how many widows, how many unmarried sisters, how many would marry, and how many were married again. He made grants to all; to some he gave monthly pay, to some spahiluks, to some military pay, to others, farms, so that they might be civil servants in perpetuity in the sultan's employ and never be without work. When he had finished these things, the pasha told Smail that he was now returning to the sultan to fill the sultan's heart with his report. The men of Kanidža from this day forth would always be welcome at the sultan's palace. "Without you," the pasha said, "the sultan cannot rule." Then Mehmed Pasha Sokol, his courtiers, and his horsemen departed. When the sultan heard the pasha's report, he rejoiced.

The agas of Kanidža continued their celebration with merriment, wishing the newlyweds many children, first daughters and then sons, that the daughters-in-law should not overtake the daughters in the house. Long life to Meho's father and his uncle and to the whole Border!

The song closes with the usual formulas: "From me you have had a bit of entertainment; you will have more and for longer from God. So shall it be, if God wills. Let us be merry in good health, all of us brothers who are here, all of us here and any other who may come."

It will be noticed that Avdo has elaborated the portion of the song after the battle more than in the 1935 version, and that he has also changed some of the details. The wife of the vizier, for example, and not the vizier himself, discloses the whereabouts of the treasure. There is added the marriage chamber in Buda and festivities there at the house of Zajim Alibeg, and this addition makes it necessary for Smail to have a second wedding feast in Kanidža. Perhaps the most striking element in that feast is the race, first of horses and then of youths. All this is topped off by the visit of Mehmed Pasha Sokolović to the feast, an incident which brings the song back to the theme with which it began, the greatness of Bosnia in those days and its importance in the empire.

Avdo had great difficulty constructing good ten-syllable lines as he spoke this song for the wire-recorder, but except for that it is not an inferior song. As I said at the beginning, he cut short the catalogues, especially in the arriving of the wedding guests at Kanidža. But there would be those who would argue that in this way the catalogues in the 1950 text are in more suitable proportion to the rest of the song than those in the version of 1935. The races give the song a Homeric touch; the catalogue of horses is reminiscent of medieval French epic as well.

Yet all in all the astonishing fact is that Avdo Međedović of the village of Obrov near Bijelo Polje in eastern Montenegro by the age of eighty, after a life that included service in the Turkish army in the Balkan Wars and the experiences of two world wars, had left to those who can hear and read two superb songs of the "Wedding of Meho, Son of Smail," composed fifteen years apart, in themselves worthy monuments to oral epic song in the Balkans.

Glossary

(References are to Notes to "The Wedding of Meho")

Aga (agha), lord, master.

Ajan, elder. See note 4.

Akran, peer. See note 4.

Alaybey, military commander of a sandžak. See notes 8, 70.

Aman, mercy.

Amin, amen; so be it.

Bajraktar, standard-bearer.

Bajram, a Moslem religious festival. See note 43.

-beg, titular suffix used with proper names, meaning the same as *bey*, q.v.

Bey (*beg* in Serbo-Croatian), governor of a district; a title of courtesy inferior to pasha and superior to aga.

Beylerbey, bey of beys, governor of a province. Not always used accurately in the poem. See notes 38, 188.

Buljukbaša, captain. See notes 4, 32.

Delija (Deli), warrior, man of war. See notes 4, 66

Dizdar, fortress commander.

Firman, an imperial decree.

Hadji, a Moslem who has made the pilgrimage to Mecca.

Hajduk, a brigand, a rebel against the Turks.

Han, a wayside inn; karavanserae.

Hodža, a Moslem priest.

Imam, the Moslem clergyman who leads the services of the men in the mosque five times a day. See note 22.

Janissaries, a body of Turkish elite soldiers. For a description of their dress, see note 65.

(Kara)Bogdan, Moldavia, a part of Rumania.

Karavlah, Wallachia. See note 19.

Knez, village elder. See note 52.

Knjeginja, wife of knez, village elder.

Kolo, a ring dance.

Muhač, Serbo-Croatian form of the Hungarian place-name Mohács.

Oke, Turkish weight of 400 drams (2.83 pounds or 1.285 kilograms).

Pasha, the highest title of Turkish civil and military officials in the old days.

Rakija, brandy.

Sandžak, an administrative district of a province (vilayet). See note 2.

Shabracque, a cavalry saddle cloth or housing.

Sirdar, commander or chief. See note 116.

Stambol, Serbo-Croatian form of the Turkish place-name Istanbul.

Unđurovina, a district across the river Una, which flows on the edge of Bosnia. See note 133.

Vila, a white female spirit, dwelling in mountain lakes. See note 12.

Vizier, a minister or councillor of state in the former Turkish Empire. Vizier with three horsetail plumes, see notes 27, 73.

Vlahs, the Wallachians. Wallachia, together with Moldavia, formed Rumania.

CITERIOR
Regni a

A.

B.

PEST.

Danubius fl.

A. Propugnaculum nouum. B. Arx et Palatium Regium. C. Templ
F. Genus Hominum apud Turcas Barbarum, ac temerarium, ad
plumis in ipsa capitis carne insertis quo truculentiores appareai
Communicauit Georgius